Health Technology Assessment and Diffusion of Health Technology

Peter Bo Poulsen

Health Technology Assessment
and
Diffusion of Health Technology

Odense University Press 1999

The printing of this monographs is generously supported by

The Faculty of Social Sciences
and
The Faculty of Health Sciences
at
University of Southern Denmark - Odense University

© Peter Bo Poulsen and Odense University Press 1999
Printed by Special-Trykkeriet Viborg a-s
Cover design by Uni Sats
ISBN 87-7838-481-8

Cover illustration:
Anatomy lesson of Dr. Tulp by Rembrandt
Photograph C Mauritshuis, The Hauge, cat.nr. 146

Odense University Press
Campusvej 55
DK-5230 Odense M

Phone: +45 66 15 79 99 Fax: +45 66 15 81 26
E-mail: press@forlag.sdu.dk
Internet bookstore: www.sdu.dk/press

Costumers in the United States and Canada please direct orders to:

International Specialized Book Services
5804 NE Hassalo St
Portland, OR 97213
Phone: 1-800-944-6190

Tables of content

Foreword .... *vi-vii*

Dansk resumé (Danish summary) .... *viii-xiv*

Chapter 1:
A Reader's Guide *1-7*

Chapter 2:
An International Comparative Study of Health Technology Assessment *9-74*

Chapter 3:
Models of Innovation *75-118*

Chapter 4:
Models of Diffusion in Economics and Sociology *119-137*

Chapter 5:
Diffusion of Laparoscopic Technologies in Denmark *139-163*

Chapter 6:
Timing of Adoption of Laparoscopic Cholecystectomy in Denmark
and in the Netherlands. A comparative study *165-181*

Chapter 7:
Economic Evaluation and the Diffusion of Health Technology
- objectives and methodological issues *183-220*

Chapter 8:
Systems for Early Warning of Emerging Health Technology *221-250*

Chapter 9:
Concluding Remarks
- policy recommendations and future research *251-261*

Literature (alphabetic order) *263-285*

Supplement: article (in Danish):
Poulsen PB, Hørder M. Medicinsk teknologivurdering i praksis. Ugeskrift for Læger 1998;160(35):5041-5044. [The practice of health technology assessment (English abstract)].

Foreword

This book - *Health Technology Assessment and Diffusion of Health Technology* - is written as a Ph.D. thesis. It represents work carried out in the period December 1994 to September 1998, while I was enrolled as a Ph.D. student in the Health Economic Research Unit at Institute of Public Health (IPE), University of Southern Denmark, Odense (IPE was previously called Centre for Health and Social Policy (CHS)). The thesis was made possible by a grant shared by the Danish Ministry of Health and the Danish Research Academy. Furthermore, the Faculty of Health Sciences at University of Southern Denmark, Odense, financed six months of the thesis period.

The thesis was defended on March 22, 1999 at the Faculty of Social Sciences, University of Southern Denmark, Odense. The Scientific Assessment Committee reviewing the Ph.D. thesis consisted of Director Ph.D. Finn Kamper Jørgensen[a], Associate Professor, Ph.D. Per Carlsson[b], and Associate Professor, Ph.D. Ivar Sønbø Kristiansen[c] (chairman). The Scientific Assessment Committee concluded that *the thesis represents an important milestone of health technology assessment* and that *anyone wishing to know more about health technology assessment is urged to read this book*. On behalf of the thesis and the defence, *the Degree of Ph.D. in Health Economics* was awarded March 22, 1999 in the recognition of academic achievements in the area.

The publication of the thesis as a book from Odense University Press is made possible by financial support from the Faculty of Social Sciences and the Faculty of Health Sciences, University of Southern Denmark, Odense, as well as the willingness of Odense University Press to publish the book. I thank both faculties and the University Press for their interest and support.

In writing the thesis I would first of all like to thank Professor Terkel Christiansen, IPE, University of Southern Denmark, Odense, Consultant Torben Jørgensen, Odense University Hospital (previously at DSI - Institute for Health Services Research, Copenhagen), and Professor Mogens Hørder, Faculty of Health Sciences, University of Southern Denmark, Odense, my *"troika"* of supervisors, for their constructive support, ideas and critical comments during the four year period.

In 1997 I visited The Free University of Amsterdam for a longer period. A stay which both provided me with a lot of inspiration and new ideas for my research as well as made new friendships. I am grateful to the Department of Biostatistics and Epidemiology, The Free University of Amsterdam, and in particular Ph.D. Hindrik Vondeling, for having me as a guest. I am especially indebted to Hindrik for our cooperation and for introducing me to the idea of writing articles. Today I can see the benefit of this learning process. Furthermore, I thank Karla and Hindrik for making my stay in Amsterdam a pleasant one.

I am also grateful to several other people for their cooperation with me in writing this thesis. I thank MD Sven Adamsen, Hillerød Hospital for a good and constructive cooperation in two projects and three Dutch colleagues; Ph.D. Carmen Dirksen, University Hospital Maastricht, MD Peter Go, St. Antonius Hospital, Nieuwegein, and André Ament, Maastricht University for their interest in cooperating with me in a study of our two countries. Likewise I thank all individuals and institutions involved in my empirical research.

At the Institute of Public Health, University of Southern Denmark, Odense, I thank both present and former colleagues for their interest in my work in general and especially their support in periods in which things didn't go the way I wanted. You all supported me and kept me on the track. Special thanks go to my former colleague, Ph.D. Lars K. Langkilde (now at AstraZeneca, Gøteborg, Sweden), who always encouraged me and gave me input for my projects. For all of you, I just hope that I did something in return.

The invaluable help and assistance from the secretaries at IPE, and previously CHS, are also acknowledged. Inger Pedersen and later Mette Tornbjerg for their practical help and for being my *"ministers of finance"*, and Kirsten Gauthier and Helle Møller Jensen for correcting my English. I hope you saw *improvements?* At least you should know a lot more about health technology assessment by now!

Finally, I thank my family and friends for supporting me and for being patient with me in this long period of four years. Writing this thesis used part of my resources and time, which probably could have been used otherwise. Especially I thank my friends Kenwyn, Marianne and Thomas for showing interest in my thesis work, but also to let me know that there is more to life than just writing a thesis.

Institute of Public Health, July 1999

Peter Bo Poulsen

---

[a] Director of The Danish Institute for Clinical Epidemiology (DICE) and Chairman of Institute Advisory Board in the Danish Institute for Health Technology Assessment, Copenhagen, Denmark.

[b] Associate Professor at The Centre for Medical Technology Assessment, Linköping University and Project Director at The Swedish Council on Technology Assessment in Health Care, Stockholm, Sweden

[c] Associate Professor at Health Economics, Institute of Public Health, University of Southern Denmark, Odense University, Odense, Denmark

Dansk resumé (Danish summary)

Medicinsk teknologivurdering (MTV) blev introduceret i USA i 1975 med etableringen af et program for medicinsk teknologivurdering i Office for Technology Assessment (OTA) [1]. OTA definerede teknologivurdering som *en alsidig form for "policy" forskning der undersøger kort- og langsigtede samfundsmæssige konsekvenser (eks. samfundsmæssige, økonomiske, etiske, lovgivningsmæssige) af applikationen eller anvendelsen af teknologi* [1]. Indenfor sundhedssektoren er fokus for teknologivurdering på medicinske teknologier defineret som *lægemidler, medicinsk udstyr og apparatur, og medicinske procedurer, såvel som den omkringliggende organisation*. MTV tager det brede sigte på medicinsk teknologi og teknologisk forandring, og udfører analyser ud fra en række perspektiver, inklusive studier af diffusion, og af omkostninger og konsekvenser [2]. Siden midten af 1970'erne har MTV-begrebet og dets anvendelse spredt sig hastigt. I 1995 blev 103 organisationer i 24 lande identificeret som værende involveret i en eller anden form for MTV aktivitet [3]. Dette antal forventes at være endnu højere i dag.

Danmark var ret tidligt involveret i MTV i 1980 [4,5]. Siden har MTV været på dagsordenen i Danmark med skiftende intensitet og omfang. En øget teknologisk forandring og diffusion af nye teknologier, opmærksomhed på evidens-baseret medicin, og knappe ressourcer har fornyet interessen blandt professionelle, beslutningstagere og politikere for et instrument til at kontrollere udviklingen i sundhedssektoren og sikre evidens af benyttede teknologier. MTV er derfor blevet et *hot* emne igen i 1990'erne. Specielt er interessen skærpet de sidste 4 år med nedsættelsen af Sundhedsstyrelsens Udvalg for Medicinsk Teknologivurdering i 1994 og senere Folketingets finanslovsbevilling med henblik på etablering af Statens Institut for Medicinsk Teknologivurdering i Sundhedsstyrelsens regi i 1997.

Denne bog - *Medicinsk Teknologivurdering og Diffusion af Medicinske Teknologier* - der er skrevet som en Ph.D.-afhandling, har nydt godt af den øgede interesse for MTV i Danmark. Bogen falder i to hoveddele. Den første del, specielt kapitel 2, fokuserer overordnet på begrebet medicinsk teknologivurdering, dets definition og praktiske anvendelse. Definition og indhold af MTV, til trods for at det er mere end 20 år gammelt, bliver stadig bragt op til diskussion [6-8]. Formålet med denne første del er at undersøge hvorvidt det *normative* begreb MTV og dets definition præsenteret af OTA svarer til det der udføres i praksis under betegnelsen MTV. Arbejdshypotesen der er blevet undersøgt er at trods den brede og alsidige definition af MTV, så har begrebet mere partielle former, når det benyttes i praksis. Denne del af bogen er hovedsageligt karakteriseret ved en deduktiv forskningsmetode, hvori specifikke forventninger til hypoteser udvikles på basis af generelle principper [9].

Bogens anden del, kapitlerne 3-8, er primært helliget forskning i de tidlige stadier af en medicinsk teknologi's livscyklus. Det generelle formål med denne del har været at undersøge innovations- og diffusionsprocesserne for medicinsk teknologi. Centrale spørgsmål til undersøgelse er: hvordan fænomenerne *innovation* og *diffusion* skal forstås ved medicinsk teknologi? Hvilke faktorer bestemmer udviklingen i de to processer? I de tidlige stadier af livscyklusen har ideen om at være i stand til at varsle tidligt om fremkomne medicinske teknologier opnået speciel interesse i form af *systemer til tidlig varsling*. Specielt for beslutningstageren synes disse systemer attraktive for planlægning og med hensyn til at være forberedt. Viden om innovations- og diffusionsprocesserne er her nyttig. Et andet vigtigt aspekt i den tidlige livscyklus er beslutningstagernes behov for tidlig information fra MTV med henblik på at træffe beslutninger om adoption og anvendelse af nye teknologier. Teknologivurderinger i den tidlige livscyklus repræsenterer fremadskuende vurderinger (proaktive) snarere end bagudrettede vurderinger (reaktive). Ved yderligere diffusion, hvor erfaringen med teknologien øges, bliver den reaktive vurdering relevant.

Denne del af bogen repræsenterer en interaktiv forskningsprocess hvori både induktive og deduktive forskningstilgange har været anvendt. I den induktive tilgang udvikles generelle principper fra specifikke observationer, hvilket har været tilfældet med de empiriske studier der er udført med en eksplorativ baggrund [9]. Men samtidig har en deduktiv tilgang også været anvendt, fordi teori anvendes initielt til at opstille forventninger og til at analysere fænomenet i relation til.

De *laparoskopiske teknologier* i det kirurgiske speciale, specielt *laparoskopisk kolecystektomi*, benyttes i det meste af bogen som en gennemgående case. Laparoskopisk kolecystektomi repræsenterer en kontroversiel case af en tilsyneladende lovende teknologi med en hurtig diffusion internationalt, hvor den har erstattet traditionel åben kirurgi. Dette til trods for en manglende afgørende dokumentation for teknologiens effektivitet, sikkerhed og cost-effectiveness. Aktualiteten af casen er understreget af konsensus konferencen om kikkertkirurgi i bughulen afholdt i Danmark i 1997 [10].

De originale bidrag i bogen ligger først og fremmest i udførelse af nye empiriske studier, både på helt nye områder og overført til en dansk kontekst. Samtidig er der i bogen appliceret teorier til området for medicinsk teknologi, såvel som at der er foretaget litteratur gennemgange af henholdsvis teori og metode.

Kapitlerne 2-8 i bogen kan læses uafhængigt af hinanden og i den rækkefølge man ønsker, idet de fleste kapitler repræsenterer selvstændige tidsskriftsartikler, arbejdsnotater, konferencepapirer eller officielle myndighedsrapporter. Læseren af bogen bedes bære over med en smule repetition af centrale emner/begreber. I næste afsnit præsenteres en oversigt over indholdet af bogens enkelte kapitler, herunder deres formål, metode og resultater.

Oversigt over bogens kapitler

Kapitel 2 introducerer læseren til begrebet *medicinsk teknologivurdering* (MTV). Den historiske udvikling af MTV, vurderede parametre og anvendte MTV-metoder, såvel som MTVs praktiske anvendelse internationalt er undersøgt. Den brede og alsidige definition på MTV udstukket af OTA i USA i 1975 [1] er taget i brug i de fleste lande. I Danmark støtter Sundhedsstyrelsen og Statens Institut for Medicinsk Teknologivurdering den brede definition og fokuserer desuden på fire hovedelementer for vurdering i en MTV; *teknologien, økonomien, patienten* og *organisationen* [11]. Formålet med det internationale komparative studie i kapitel 2 er at undersøge om der er overensstemmelse mellem den brede og alsidige definition eller det der reelt udføres i praksis. I en litteraturgennemgang er 124 MTV-projekter fra nationale MTV-institutioner i Sverige, Holland, England, Canada og Australien gennemgået for kriterier som anvendt metode og vurderede parametre. Resultatet viser, at kun 17 af 124 MTV-projekter kan karakteriseres som brede og alsidige teknologivurderinger med information fra alle fire hovedelementer. Halvdelen af MTV-projekterne har kun medtaget information fra to hovedelementer, typisk *teknologien* og *økonomien*. Blandt de fem institutioner var de svenske MTV-projekter kendetegnet ved at være de mest alsidige. Begrundet i den udenlandske praksis kunne læren af dette studie derfor være, at man ud over at definere MTV som en bred og alsidig vurdering også inkluderer mere partielle fortolkninger under MTV-begrebet afhængigt af den beslutning, der skal træffes. Under policy anbefalinger i kapitel 9 fremsættes et forslag til en modificeret definition på MTV.

Studiet er, med forfatterens viden, det første detaljerede studie udført internationalt med formålet at sammenligne MTV fra nationale MTV-institutioner i relation til metode og definition af MTV. Resultaterne af studiet er ligeledes publiceret i *Poulsen PB, Hørder M. Medicinsk teknologivurdering i praksis. Ugeskrift for Læger 1998;160(35):5041-5044.* Denne artikel er gengivet bagerst i bogen.

Efter en generel introduktion til MTV og en diskussion af anvendelsen af MTV i praksis, skifter fokus i den resterende del af bogen (kapitel 3-8) til de tidlige stadier i livscyklusen for en medicinsk teknologi.

Kapitel 3 - *Modeller for Innovation* - betragter de tidligste stadier for udvikling og innovation - innovationsprocessen. Med en hastig teknologisk forandring i sundhedssektoren er det vigtigt for MTV og tidlig varsling at have viden om den medicinske innovationsproces såvel som de faktorer der bestemmer og styrer denne komplekse proces. Innovationsprocessen beskrives og analyseres ved at benytte tre modeller, primært baseret på økonomisk teori; *the science-push model, the demand-pull model* og *the chain-linked model*. Forventningen i den lineære *science-push model* er, at det er videnskaben og de tekniske muligheder der *driver* innovationer frem. Omvendt forventes det i den anden lineære model - *demand-pull modellen* - at det er efterspørgslen der *trækker* de innovationer frem man har behov for og som derfor skal udvikles. Begge modeller er forsimplinger af virkeligheden, som vil være en iterativ proces præget af feedback fra læring. Læring kan opdeles i; *learning in the R&D process, learning by doing* og *learning by using*. *Chain-linked model* opererer både med push og pull effekter, såvel som læring i innovationsprocessen i en iterativ model. I den anden del af kapitlet overføres modellerne til området for medicinske teknologier ved at benytte elementer fra modellerne i en kvalitativ case studie tilgang til at analysere to cases; *lægemidler med forsinket udløsning* og *de laparoskopiske teknologier*, herunder *laparoskopisk kolecystektomi*.

Stadiet der efterfølger innovationsprocessen er diffusionsprocessen, hvor teknologien spredes i sundhedssektoren med henblik på adoption og anvendelse. Kapitel 4-7 beskæftiger sig med teori og empiriske resultater relateret til diffusionsprocessen, såvel som formål og form for MTV i forbindelse med diffusion af den medicinske teknologi.

Med speciel fokus på medicinsk teknologi, præsenterer kapitel 4 *Modeller for diffusion i økonomi og sociologi*. Kapitlet er et review af diffusionsmodeller baseret på henholdsvis økonomisk- og sociologisk teori. De to videnskabsområder er valgt på baggrund af deres mange bidrag til studiet af teknologi-diffusion. Formålet har været at beskrive og diskutere ensartethed og forskelle mellem modeller, der benytter de to grupper af teorier til at beskrive fænomenet diffusion. I de økonomiske modeller betragtes diffusion som et fænomen, der er styret af udbud og efterspørgsel i markedet med fokus på økonomiske faktorer i forklaringen af diffusion, f.eks. profit-muligheden. I de sociologiske modeller synes kommunikations-kanaler og karakteristika ved det enkelte individ, der tager teknologien i brug, f.eks. social status, at være centrale i forklaringen af diffusion. Generelt er mange empiriske studier af diffusion dog ikke udført for at "*teste en specifik teori*", men har langt oftere haft eksplorative formål.

Kapitel 5 og kapitel 6 er begge empiriske studier af diffusion med den gennemgående case - *den laparoskopiske teknologi*. Kapitel 5 - *Diffusionen af laparoskopiske teknologier i Danmark* - er en eksplorativ undersøgelse af spredningen af laparoskopisk kirurgi i Danmark. Formålet med undersøgelsen var at identificere de faktorer (stimulerende versus bremsende effekt) der forklarer adoptionen og diffusionen af den laparoskopiske teknologi på det kirurgiske område i Danmark. Fem specifikke kirurgiske anvendelser af den laparoskopiske teknologi blev udvalgt; *laparoskopisk kolecystektomi, laparoskopisk appendektomi, laparoskopisk operation for colon cancer, laparoskopisk operation for lyskebrok, og laparoskopisk operation for spiserørskatar*. Studiet fokuserer på en spørgeskemaundersøgelse udført i samarbejde med den Laparoskopiske Komite i Dansk Kirurgisk Selskab i 1997. Spørgeskemaer vedrørende tidspunkt for adoption og 17 faktorer for diffusionen blev sendt til 59 danske hospitaler med kirurgiske afdelinger.

Responsraten var 85%. Studiet viser overordnet, at 98% af de danske hospitaler har taget den laparoskopiske teknologi i brug ved kolecystektomi i perioden 1991 til 1995. For de fire andre laparoskopiske anvendelser har der ikke været samme hurtige og ukontrollerede diffusion, idet de kun er adopteret af 7-65% af hospitalerne afhængigt af metode. Større og specialiserede hospitaler viser sig generelt som tidligere adoptører. Faktorer som *teknologiens art* (minimal invasiv versus konventionel teknik), *træning* (tilgængelighed af kurser), *konkurrence* (mellem specialer og mellem hospitaler) og *medie opmærksomhed* har stimuleret kirurgens beslutning om at adoptere den laparoskopiske teknologi ved alle fem anvendelser. Tre budget-faktorer (investering, drift og offentlig regulering) har i nogle tilfælde haft en bremsende effekt på diffusionen. De stimulerende faktorer der fremkommer for alle laparoskopiske teknologier indikerer at nogen styring med adoption og anvendelse af teknologien vil være ønskelig. For Danmark er nogle af de foreslåede instrumenter hertil etablering af et tidligt varslingssystem og en kontrolleret introduktion via kliniske studieprogrammer af teknologier med samme potentiale som laparoskopisk kolecystektomi.

Både med hensyn til omfang af analysen og de statistiske metoder anvendt, er det empiriske studie i kapitel 6 en naturlig udvidelse af studiet præsenteret i kapitel 5. Med et multinationalt udgangspunkt undersøger studiet i kapitel 6 *timingen af adoptionen af laparoskopisk kolecystektomi i Danmark og i Holland*. Påvirkningen af tre karakteristika ved hospitalet (*størrelse, undervisningsstatus og beliggenhed*) på beslutningen om at adoptere teknologien i de to lande analyseres. Inkluderet i studiet var 59 danske og 109 hollandske hospitaler. En anden udvidelse af studiet er anvendelsen af multivariate statistiske metoder til at analysere og forklare fænomenet diffusion, idet *proportional hazard regressions modeller* nu benyttes.

Laparoskopisk kolecystektomi blev taget i brug i Holland i 1990 og benyttes i dag på alle hospitaler. I Danmark var ibrugtagelsestidspunktet 1991 og 98% af hospitalerne har taget teknologien i brug i dag. Spredningsmønstret for begge lande synes identisk med en hastig og ukontrolleret diffusion. Dog med et tids-lag i Danmark på 11 måneder. Med brug af proportional hazard regressions modellerne viser det sig, at det kun er i Danmark at størrelsen af hospitalet påvirker tidspunktet for adoptionen. I et lignende studie i USA fandt man, at træningsfacilitet forklarede en tidligere adoptionen [12]. Studiet viser endvidere, at proportional hazard regresions synes at være brugbar i studier af diffusion.

Vurdering af virkningsfuldhed før diffusion i sundhedssektoren er kun påkrævet for lægemidler. Medicinsk udstyr og procedurer er oftest introduceret tidligt uden denne dokumentation. For alle typer af medicinsk teknologi i Danmark er der ikke noget krav om påvisning af cost-effectiveness. Men usikkerheden ved ny teknologi og et stigende antal teknologier udviklet med et behov for prioritering, involverer i beslutningstagning en risiko for at foretage beslutningsfejl så som at anbefale en ikke-favorabel teknologi eller at afvise en favorabel teknologi. Ydermere er dilemmaet i beslutningstagning og timingen af vurdering i livscyklusen ofte, at *det altid er for tidligt at evaluere, indtil, desværre, det pludselig er for sent* [13]. For at tage højde for disse problemer har der været advokeret for en iterativ og kontinuerlig vurderingsprocess der følger livscyklusen og diffusionen af den medicinske teknologi [14,15]. Fokuseret på vurdering af økonomiske parametre var formålet med kapitel 7 at beskrive og diskutere forskellige roller for økonomisk evaluering i en diffusionsprocess for medicinsk teknologi. Fokus er på anvendelse i samfundsmæssig beslutningstagen i sundhedssektoren.

De tidlige fase I og II i det kliniske udviklingsprogram for lægemidler er kendetegnet ved få og ikke-kontrollede kliniske studier. I dette tidlige stadie er to roller for tidlig økonomisk evaluering identificeret. For det første at informere beslutningstageren om efficiensen af yderligere forskning eller MTV og for det andet at informere beslutningstageren om efficiensen af en tidlig ibrugtagelse af ny teknologi. Senere i fase III, før omfattende diffusion af teknologien, vil den økonomiske evaluering ofte kunne baseres på mere sikker klinisk information fra randomiserede kontrollerede kliniske studier. I en iterativ tilgang vil den økonomiske evaluering i fase III også være informeret af økonomiske analyser udført i tidligere stadier. En vigtig rolle for den økonomiske analyse i fase III består i beslutningstagen vedrørende støtte af lægemidler, som det sker i Australien. Reguleringsmyndighederne er interessenter i denne fase. Endelig har den økonomiske evaluering en vigtig rolle ved revurderinger i den sene fase af livscyklusen (fase IV), hvor teknologien anvendes i rutine praksis og ikke længere i kontrolleret anvendelse. Interessenter er specielt system- og hospitalsledelser. Generelt varierer behovet for vurdering over tid afhængigt af teknologiens stadie i livscyklusen såvel som målgruppen, der efterspørger information i de forskellige faser af diffusion.

I kapitel 8 vendes fokuset mod instrumenter for beslutningstageren til forbedring af den tidlige information om medicinske teknologier før deres potentielle introduktion i sundhedssektoren. For at tilvejebringe en bedre planlægning og prioritering i sundhedssektoren har *systemer til tidlig varsling af nye medicinske teknologier* været foreslået som et instrument til at forbedre denne information. Hovedopgaverne for et system til tidlig varsling er tidlig identifikation, tidlig vurdering samt udbredelse af information om de nye potentielle medicinske teknologier med en betydning for sundhedssektoren. I kapitlet præsenteres ideen bag systemer til tidlig varsling. I dag eksisterer der systemer i lande som Sverige, Holland, England og Canada. Deres systemers organisering, tidshorisont og erfaring med tidlig varsling beskrives i kapitlet. Endelig præsenteres to mulige modeller for tidlig varsling i Danmark, *et uafhængigt system til tidlig varsling,* og *en tidlig varsling aktivitet som del af et teknologivurderingsprogram.* Der advokeres i kapitlet for den sidste model, der tænkes integreret som en del af identifikationsfasen i et prospektiv MTV-program med en tidshorisont på 0-2 år før markedsintroduktion, idet reliabiliteten er informationen her forventes at være højest.

I sidste kapitel (kapitel 9) opsummeres konklusionerne fra bogens kapitler såvel som at anbefalinger for beslutningstagen fremsættes på baggrund af forskningsresultaterne. Endelig berøres videre forskning indenfor området.

Referencer

1. US Congress, Office of Technology Assessment. Development of Medical Technology: Opportunities for Assessment. Washington, DC: US Government Printing Office, 1976.

2. Banta HD. Introduction to the EUR-ASSESS Report. International Journal of Technology Assessment in Health Care 1997;13(2):133-143.

3. Perry S, Gardner E, Thamer M. The Status of Health Technology Assessment Worlwide: Results of an International Survey. The International Journal of Technology Assessment in Health Care 1997;13(1):81-98.

4. Buch Andreasen P. Medicinsk Teknologivurdering. Nyttiggørelse af lægevidenskabelige forskningsresultater i sundhedsvæsenet. Rapport til Folketingets udvalg angående videnskabelig forskning. København, 1980.

5. Jørgensen T. Teknologivurdering. Dansk Sygehus Institut. DSI-Specialrapport 80.07. København, 1980.

6. Jørgensen T, Børlum Kristensen F. Medicinsk teknologivurdering i Europa. Ugeskrift for Læger 1998;160(16):2367-2371.

7. Andersen M. En fællesnævner for lægen og økonomen. Ugeskrift for Læger 1998;160(29):4338-4340..

8. Andersen M. Sund fornuft på skemaform. Journal for Sundhedsvæsen 1998;10(2):7-8.

9. Babbie E. The Practice of Social Research. Seventh Edition. Wadsworth Publishing Company, Belmont, California, 1995.

10. Danneskiold-Samsøe B (ed). Abdominal Laparoscopic Surgery. Report from a medical consensus conference 3-5 March 1997. Copenhagen: Danish Medical Research Council and and Danish Institute for Health Services Research and Development. Consensus Report, 1997.

11. The Danish National Board of Health, the Health Technology Assessment Committee. National Strategy for Health Technology Assessment. Copenhagen, 1996.

12. Fendrick M, Escarce JJ, McLane C, Shea JA, Schwartz JS. Hospital adoption of laparoscopic cholecystectomy. Medical Care 1994;32(10):1058-1063.

13. Buxton M. Economic evaluation early in the life cycle of a medical technology. Abstract. European Workshop: Scanning the Horizon for Emerging Health Technologies. Copenhagen, September 12-13, 1997.

14. Banta HD, Vondeling H. Strategies for successful evaluation and policy-making toward health care technology on the move: the case of medical lasers. Social Science & Medicine 1994;38(12):1663-1674.

15. Bloom BS, Fendrick AM. Timing and Timeliness in Medical Care Evaluation. PharmacoEconomics 1996;9(3):183-187.

Chapter 1

A reader's guide

Introduction

Health technology assessment (HTA) was first introduced in the United States with the establishment of a programme for health technology assessment within the Office of Technology Assessment (OTA) in 1975 [1]. OTA defined *technology assessment* as *a comprehensive form of policy research that examines the short- and long-term social consequences (e.g. societal, economic, ethical, legal) of the application or use of technology* [1]. In health care the focus of technology assessment is upon health technologies defined as the drugs, devices, equipment, clinical- and surgical procedures used in the health care sector as well as the organisation surrounding it. HTA takes a broad view of technology and of technological change and carries out analyses of such issues from a number of perspectives including studies of diffusion and the costs and consequences of the use of health technology [2]. Since the mid-seventies the idea of HTA has diffused worldwide with 103 organisations in 24 countries identified as being involved in some kind of HTA activity in 1995 [3].[1] This number is likely to be even higher today.

Denmark was involved quite early in HTA with two reports on the subject published in 1980 [4,5]. Since then, HTA has been on the agenda in Denmark with varying emphasis. However, increasing technological change and diffusion of new technologies, rising awareness of *evidence-based medicine*[2], and the scarcity of resources have renewed interest among professionals, decision-makers and politicians for policies to control the innovation and diffusion of technology in the health care sector. HTA has therefore become a hot topic again in the 1990s. Especially in the last four years interest has increased with the establishment of The Health Technology Assessment Committee of the Danish National Board of Health early in 1994. Further stimulation occurred with the Finance Act of 1997, in which parliament decided to allocate resources to the area of HTA, at least for a five-year period, and to create the Danish Institute for Health Technology Assessment (DIHTA).

This book - *Health Technology Assessment and Diffusion of Health Technology* - written as a Ph.D.-thesis, has benefited from this strong interest in the field of HTA in Denmark during the period. As indicated by the title, the book has two major purposes. The first

---

[1] Universities doing research in HTA or elements of HTA were not included.

[2] The conscientious, explicit and judicious use of current best evidence in making decisions about the care of individual patients. In practice it means integrating individual expertise with the best available external clinical evidence from systematic research [6].

part of the book, chapter 2, focuses, on the concept of health technology assessment, its definition and its practical uses. The definition and content of HTA, although more than twenty years old, are nevertheless frequently brought up for discussion [7-9]. The purposes of this part of the book is to investigate whether the normative HTA concept and its definition presented by OTA correspond with the assessments actually carried out in practice under the heading HTA. The working hypothesis to be investigated is that, despite the broad and comprehensive definition of HTA, the concept has a more partial form when used in practice. This part of the book is therefore mainly characterized by a deductive research approach, in which specific expectations of hypotheses are developed on the basis of general principles [10].

The second part of the book, chapters 3-8, is primarily devoted to research in the early stages in the life cycle of health technology. The general aim of this part is to study the process of innovation and the process of diffusion of health technology. Central questions to be investigated are: how are the phenomena of innovation and diffusion to be understood in the case of health technology? What factors determines each of the two processes? In these early stages of the life cycle the idea of being able to warn about the impending arrival of new technologies an early point in time has attained central interest in the form of systems for early warning. Decision-makers especially find early warning attractive to improve planning and to be better prepared in a fast-changing sector. To be able to warn early, knowledge about the process of innovation and diffusion of health technology is therefore valuable. Another important aspect in the early life cycle is the decision-makers' need for early information from technology assessment in order to decide upon the adoption and use of new and emerging technologies. In the early life cycle the technology assessments carried out regarding emerging technologies represent forward-looking (proactive[3]) assessments rather than backward-looking (reactive[4]) assessments. During diffusion, when experience with the technology increases, the reactive assessment becomes relevant. To provide a full picture of the specific technologies studied or the assessment methods considered, these later stages of diffusion are also included in the book.

This part of the book represents an interactive research process in which both inductive and deductive research approaches have been used. The general principles are developed from specific observations using the inductive approach, as evidence in the empirical studies reported in this book [10]. The inductive process begins with the observation of a phenomenon, e.g. the diffusion of a technology; we try to find a pattern for the phenomenon observed which should finally result in some tentative conclusions concerning the phenomenon, e.g. that specific factors explain the diffusion of technology. However, at the same time it can be argued that deductive elements are also involved due to the fact that theory is used initially to formulate hypotheses as well as to analyse the empirical findings.

---

[3] Or prospective assessment.

[4] Or retrospective assessment.

Laparoscopic technologies in the field of surgery, especially *laparoscopic cholecystectomy*, are used in the book for much of the analysis. Laparoscopic cholecystectomy represents a controversial case of a promising technology with a rapid diffusion internationally. It has been replacing the traditional open procedure despite the absence of evidence regarding its effectiveness, safety and cost-effectiveness. The interest in this area was highlighted by the Danish Consensus Conference on Abdominal Laparoscopic Surgery in 1997 [11].

In the next section *a reader's guide* is presented with respect to the specific content and research topics in each of the remaining eight chapters of the book.

An overview of the chapters in the book

As noted above, chapter 2 in the book introduces the reader to the concept of health technology assessment. The historical evolution of health technology assessment, the parameters assessed, and the methods used to perform technology assessment are investigated. Furthermore, the international application of technological assessment in practice is studied. The broad and comprehensive definition of HTA, given by OTA in the United States in 1975 [1], is adopted in most countries. In Denmark, the National Board of Health and the Danish Institute for Health Technology Assessment support this broad definition officially, by focusing upon four main elements to be assessed in HTA: clinical[5], economic, patient-related and organisational elements [12]. However, the hypothesis put forward in this book is that less comprehensive and more partial approaches to HTA have been applied in practice, when the concept of HTA is used. To investigate this further, chapter 2 contains an *International Comparative Study of Health Technology Assessment*. The parameters assessed in 124 HTA-projects at national HTA-institutions in Sweden, the Netherlands, the United Kingdom, Canada and Australia were compared and analysed. This revealed whether HTA was considered as a broad and comprehensive assessment in practice or whether less comprehensive approaches to HTA were used instead. The study found some interesting, although not surprising, results, which may lead to a reconsideration of the definition of HTA and its use, at least in a Danish context. This study is, to the knowledge of the author, the first detailed study carried out internationally with the purpose of comparing health technology assessments from national HTA-institutions in relation to the definition of HTA.[6] The

---

[5] In the Danish context, the clinical element is called *the technology element* (teknologien). However, as the technology is the object for assessment, the concept *the clinical element* is chosen in this book to avoid any confusion. This typology is furthermore consistent with the one used internationally.

[6] When the International Comparative Study was carried out in 1996-1997, a German study was published [13]. As a part of this German study, a brief investigation and descriptive reporting of the parameters assessed in 280 HTAs around the world were presented. However, the study did not focus only upon national HTA-institutions and no comparison of the parameters assessed was made in relation to the definition of HTA.

results of the International Comparative Study have furthermore been published in *Poulsen PB, Hørder M. Medicinsk teknologivurdering i praksis. Ugeskrift for Læger 1998;160(35):5041-5044*, which is included in the end of the present book.

After the general introduction to health technology assessment and discussion of the use of the HTA-concept in practice, the remaining part of the book (chapters 3-8) focuses upon the earlier stages in the life cycle of health technology. These chapters deal with theory, methodology and empirical findings related to the process of innovation and the process of diffusion of health technology as well as the identification and assessment of health technology.

Chapter 3 - *Models of Innovation* - considers the earliest stages of development and innovation of health technology: the process of innovation. With rapid technological change in the health care sector, it is important for HTA and early warning activities to be used upon knowledge about the development and innovation of health technology as well as the factors which determine and guide this complex process. The chapter describes and analyses the process of innovation by the use of three models of innovation mainly based upon economic theory: *the science-push model, the demand-pull model* and *the chain-linked model*. By different means these models explain the process of innovation for technologies in general. In the second part of the chapter the models are transferred to the field of health technology. This is done by using elements of the models in a qualitative case study approach to analyse two cases - *sustained release drugs* and *laparoscopic technology* with special reference to laparoscopic cholecystectomy.

The stage following the process of innovation is the process of diffusion, in which the technology spreads into the health care sector for adoption and use. Chapters 4-7 are devoted to theory and empirical findings related to the process of diffusion as well as to the objectives and forms of technology assessment used during the diffusion of health technology.

With special attention to health technology, chapter 4 - *Models of Diffusion in Economics and Sociology* - presents a brief review of models of diffusion based upon economic- and sociological theories respectively. The two fields of social science are chosen for their many contributions to the study of technology diffusion, both theoretical and empirical. The aim is to describe and discuss similarities and differences in using economic- and sociological theories.

Chapters 5-6 are both empirical studies of diffusion and focus upon the general case of laparoscopic technologies.

Chapter 5 presents an empirical survey study carried out in 1997 in cooperation with the Laparoscopic Committee of the Danish Surgical Society. The purpose of this study was to identify the factors which have explained the adoption and diffusion of laparoscopic technology in the field of surgery in Denmark. Five specific uses in surgery of laparoscopic technology were selected: laparoscopic cholecystectomy, laparoscopic appendectomy, laparoscopic surgery for colon cancer, laparoscopic surgery for inguinal hernia and laparoscopic fundoplication. Questionnaires concerning the time of adoption and seventeen factors of diffusion were designed and sent to fifty-nine Danish hospitals with surgical departments. The responses achieved were analysed using univariate and bivariate statistical methods (parametric and non-parametric tests) as well as multivariate statistical methods (factor analysis). This is the first detailed empirical study carried out with respect to laparoscopic technology diffusion in Denmark.

With respect both to the scope of the analysis and the statistical methods used, the empirical study in chapter 6 is a natural extension of the study presented in chapter 5. At a multinational level, the study in chapter 6 investigates the timing of the adoption of laparoscopic cholecystectomy in Denmark and in the Netherlands. The influences of three hospital characteristics (*size, teaching status* and *location of the hospital*) on the decision to adopt laparoscopic cholecystectomy in the two countries are analysed. Fifty-nine Danish and 109 Dutch hospitals with surgical departments were included in the study. The other extension of the study is the use of multivariate methods to analyse and explain the phenomenon of diffusion. Proportional hazard regression models are presented and analysed, and their usefulness in diffusion research is discussed. This study was made in cooperation between Danish and Dutch researchers in the period autumn 1997 to summer 1998. No other studies using multivariate methods to analyse diffusion of laparoscopic cholecystectomy have previously been performed at the multinational level.

At present, assessment of efficacy prior to widespread diffusion in the health care sector is only required for pharmaceuticals. Medical devices and procedures are often introduced early without such requirement. For all types of health technology in Denmark no requirement to demonstrate cost-effectiveness is needed. Due to uncertainty about new technology and an increasing number of technologies introduced and used, leaving a need for priority-setting, decision making involves a risk of making errors such as to recommend unfavourable technologies or to reject favourable technologies. Furthermore, a dilemma regarding decision-making and the timing of assessment is that *"it's always too early to evaluate until, unfortunately, it's suddenly too late"* [14]. To handle these problems continuous assessment in phase with the life cycle and diffusion of a particular health technology has been suggested [15,16]. Focusing on the assessment of economic parameters, the aim of chapter 7 is to describe and discuss the different objectives of economic evaluation during diffusion of health technology. The focus is on the use of economic evaluation in societal decision-making in the health care sector, e.g. reimbursement decisions. The assessment needs vary over time depending on the life cycle of the health technology as well as on the target group requesting the information at different phases of diffusion. Methodological issues relevant for the economic evaluation at different stages of the diffusion process of health technology are also addressed in chapter 7.

In chapter 8 the focus is on policy instruments to improve early information about a health technology prior to its introduction into the health care sector. To provide a basis for better planning and priority-setting in the health care sector, *systems for early warning of emerging health technology* have been suggested as policies to improve this early information. The major functions of a system for early warning are early identification, early assessment and early dissemination of information about the emerging health technology with an impact for the health care sector. In chapter 8 the ideas underlying systems for early warning are presented. Today, systems exist in countries such as Sweden, the Netherlands and the United Kingdom. Their organisation, time horizon and experiences with early warning are described in the chapter. Finally, two different models of systems for early warning in Denmark - *an independent system for early warning* and *early warning activity as part of a technology assessment programme* - are presented, and their expected success discussed.

In the final chapter - chapter 9 - the main issues and conclusions from the studies presented in the book are summarized. A central part of this chapter is devoted to recommendations for policy and future research. It is the view of the author that research findings and research experiences, when relevant, ought to influence policy. This is not least the case when decision makers have financed or sponsored research, as with the present book which the Ministry of Health in Denmark has partly financed. Furthermore, policy recommendations based on research in the field of health technology assessment are relevant, as this field in general can be characterized as consisting of applied research. The recommendations for research outlines some potential future research topics as a spin-off from the research presented in the book that can be studied further.

This book represents an integral framework for description, analysis and discussion of complex issues of health technology assessment. Chapters 2- 8 can be read independently and in any order preferred due to the fact that most of the chapters represent either journal articles, working papers, conference papers, or official government reports. With this structure some repetition on core issues may, however, be entailed. The reader is asked to bear over with this inconvenience.

References

1. US Congress, Office of Technology Assessment . Development of Medical Technology: Opportunities for Assessment. Washington, DC: US Government Printing Office, 1976.

2. Banta HD. Introduction to the EUR-ASSESS Report. International Journal of Technology Assessment in Health Care 1997;13(2):133.143.

3. Perry S, Gardner E, Thamer M. The Status of Health Technology Assessment Worlwide: Results of an International Survey. The International Journal of Technology Assessment in Health Care 1997;13(1):81-98.

4. Buch Andreasen P. Medicinsk Teknologivurdering. Nyttiggørelse af lægevidenskabelige forskningsresultater i sundhedsvæsenet. Rapport til Folketingets udvalg angående videnskabelig forskning. København, 1980.

5. Jørgensen T. Teknologivurdering. Dansk Sygehus Institut. DSI-Specialrapport 80.07. København, 1980.

6. Sackett DL, Rosenberg WMC, Gray JAM, Haynes RB, Richardson WS. Evidence-Based Medicine: What it is and what it isn't. British Medical Journal 1996;312:71-72.

7. Jørgensen T, Børlum Kristensen F. Medicinsk teknologivurdering i Europa. Ugeskrift for Læger 1998;160(16):2367-2371.

8. Andersen M. En fællesnævner for lægen og økonomen. Ugeskrift for Læger 1998;160(29):4338-4340..

9. Andersen M. Sund fornuft på skemaform. Journal for Sundhedsvæsen 1998;10(2):7-8.

10. Babbie E. The Practice of Social Research. Seventh Edition. Wadsworth Publishing Company, Belmont, California, 1995.

11. Danneskiold-Samsøe B (ed). Abdominal Laparoscopic Surgery. Report from a medical consensus conference 3-5 March 1997. Copenhagen: Danish Medical Research Council and and Danish Institute for Health Services Research and Development. Consensus Report, 1997.

12. The Danish National Board of Health, the Health Technology Assessment Committee. National Strategy for Health Technology Assessment. Copenhagen, 1996.

13. Petermann Th, Sauter A. TA-Monitoring. "Stand der Technikfolgen-Abschätzung im Bereich der Medizintechnik". TAB Arbeitsbericht Nr. 39. TAB Büro für Technikfolgen-Abschätzung beim Deutschen Bundestag. April 1996.

14. Buxton M. Economic evaluation early in the life cycle of a medical technology. Abstract. European Workshop: Scanning the Horizon for Emerging Health Technologies. Copenhagen, September 12-13, 1997.

15. Banta HD, Vondeling H. Strategies for successful evaluation and policy-making toward health care technology on the move: the case of medical lasers. Social Science & Medicine 1994;38(12):1663-1674.

16. Bloom BS, Fendrick AM. Timing and Timeliness in Medical Care Evaluation. PharmacoEconomics 1996;9(3):183-187.

Chapter 2

An International Comparison of Health Technology Assessment[7]

---

[7] The study was presented at *the 13th International Conference in the International Society of Technology Assessment in Health Care* in Barcelona May 27 1997. The results of the study are furthermore published in Poulsen PB, Hørder M. Medicinsk teknologivurdering i praksis. Ugeskrift for Læger 1998;160(35):5041-5044. [The practice of health technology assessment (English abstract)]. This article is included in the end of the present book.

Table of contents

Abstract 11

1.0 Introduction 12

2.0 Health Technology Assessment and Its Definitions 13

3.0 Health Technology Assessment in Denmark 19

4.0 National Institutions for Health Technology Assessment 21

5.0 The International Comparative Study of Health Technology Assessment 24
    5.1 The Purpose of the Study 24
    5.2 Method 24
        5.2.1 Selection Criteria 25
        5.2.2 Obtaining the Data 25
        5.2.3 Review Process 26
        5.2.4 Parameters Assessed 28
    5.3 Results 30
        5.3.1 Descriptive Part 30
            5.3.1.1. The study Sample 31
            5.3.1.2 Technologies Assessed 32
            5.3.1.3 Methods Used 33
            5.3.1.4 Parameters Assessed 34
            5.3.1.5 HTA Score 37
        5.3.2 Qualitative Analysis 38
            5.3.2.1 Comprehensive Broad HTA 39
            5.3.2.2 Semi-Comprehensive HTA 41
            5.3.2.3 Semi-Partial HTA 42
            5.3.2.4 Partial HTA 42
            5.3.2.5 Conclusion 43
    5.4 Discussion 44
        5.4.1 Bias in the study 44
            5.4.1.1 Bias in the Data Sample 45
            5.4.1.2 Bias in the Method Used 46
        5.4.2 The Results of the Study 47
        5.4.3 The Implications of the Study for HTA in Denmark 50
        5.4.4 A Future Perspective of the Comparative Study 51

References 52

APPENDIX 2.1: Used Abbreviations. 58

APPENDIX 2.2: The Institutions in the Study 59
        SBU, Sweden 59
        The Health Council, the Netherlands 59
        AHTAC, Australia 61
        CCOHTA, Canada 62
        SGHT/NCCHTA, England 63

APPENDIX 2.3: HTA-Reports/Projects Reviewed 65

APPENDIX 2.4: Parameters Assessed by the Institutions. 74

Abstract

With the establishment of a national institute for health technology assessment (HTA) the interest in HTA is increasing in Denmark. The National Board of Health defines HTA as *a comprehensive systematic evaluation of the assumptions for, and consequences of, the application of health technology*. The focus is on four elements: *clinical, economical, patient-related* and *organisational elements*. However, is this broad and comprehensive definition in agreement with the practical use of HTA? In the present chapter the concept of HTA is discussed and the historical evolution of HTA in Denmark is described. In an international comparison of 124 HTA projects made by five national HTA-institutions the international practice of HTA was revealed. The result of this comparison shows that only seventeen HTA projects can be characterized as broad and comprehensive, focusing on all four elements. The rest is more partial in their form. The future implication for Danish HTA initiatives might then be to include some partial interpretations in the HTA-definition, besides the broad and comprehensive one used today.

1.0 Introduction

The information obtained from health technology assessment (HTA) should be seen as an aid in policy making regarding the priorities and use of emerging, new and existing health technologies.[8] As a *bridge* between the two conflicting paradigms - *the pure scientific paradigm* and *the policy paradigm* [1].

The outcome of technology assessment is information. This information could be regarded as a free available public good. An answer to an optimal supply of HTA information from a societal point of view has been the creation of national HTA institutions or agencies as showed by the trend in other countries. In general the tasks for these agencies are to identify technologies for assessment, coordinate the HTA activity and information, produce HTA information and to disseminate this information to its potential users. In 1997, a national HTA institution have been established in Denmark as well. The content of the HTA information may differ between institutions in different countries, though.

Internationally, the evolution of technology assessment in the field of health care has developed from the clinical sphere to the economic sphere. The first HTAs performed in the United States back in the seventies focused upon the efficacy and safety of the assessed technologies, whereas the investment and operational costs and the relation between benefits and social costs are important topics too in the HTAs published today. In Denmark, HTA is understood broadly as *a comprehensive systematic evaluation of the assumptions for, and consequences of the application of health technology* [2] and four elements - *clinical*[9], *patient-related, organisational* and *economic elements* - are considered. One may ask, however, whether HTA should always have a broad focus on all elements, or more partial interpretations should be included? A difference in opinion, which Banta (1996) explains by its use in different decision making contexts [3].

The purpose of the present chapter is to describe and discuss the interpretation of the concept of HTA. With an exploratory approach the chapter answers *how* the HTA concept is perceived and used internationally. How the HTA definitions are used and what the content of the information is in technology assessments already carried out at established national HTA agencies will be examined in a comparative study. The intention of this empirical study is to examine, which *weights* are given to each of a number of parameters and hence also to the four elements in the assessment of health technologies by the national agencies. This will reveal whether a broad focus on HTA is in fact used in practice and whether a consensus exists with respect to health technology assessments internationally.

---

[8] Health technologies are understood broadly as drugs, devices, equipment, clinical- and surgical procedures used in the health care sector as well as the organisation surrounding it.

[9] In Denmark referred to as *the technology element* (teknologien).

The study sample consists of 124 HTA reports or HTA project notes from five national agencies, which have been chosen for the present study. The agencies are *the Australian Health Technology Assessment Committee* (Australia), *the Canadian Coordinating Office for Health Technology Assessment* (Canada), *the Standing Group on Health Technology/National Co-ordinating Centre for Technology Assessment* (England), *the Health Council* (the Netherlands) and *the Swedish Council on Technology Assessment in Health Care* (Sweden).

In relation to the newly establishment of a Danish HTA institute the present study could be seen as a contribution to the interpretation of technology assessment in Denmark of the value of HTA information and a contribution to the international discussion about HTA.

The structure in the chapter is as follows. Section 2 presents and discusses the definition of HTA as it is perceived in the literature and explains the likely reasons for the different interpretations of the concept of HTA. In section 3 the evolution of HTA in Denmark is described. Section 4 deals with the theoretical and practical arguments for the establishment of nationally funded HTA institutions or agencies. In section 5 - *the International Comparative Study of Health Technology Assessment* - the problem of interest, method used and the results found in the international comparative study is presented. Finally, the results of the study are discussed with respect to their validity and reliability, and the implications of the study in relation to HTA in Denmark.

2.0 Health Technology Assessment and Its Definitions

In 1975, the Office of Technology Assessment (OTA)[10] defined technology assessment as *a comprehensive form of policy research that examines the short- and long-term social consequences of the application or use of technology* [4]. These social consequences were understood broadly as the societal, economic, ethical and legal implications. These *comprehensive impact or assessment studies are a class of holistic studies, which attempt in some sense to embrace everything that is important with regard to technology* [5]. By the establishment of a health technology assessment programme by OTA in 1975 technology assessment was for the first time transferred to the field of health care. Technology assessment in the field of health care thus became the comprehensive and systematic assessment of the social consequences of using health technologies with a broad focus upon societal, economic, ethical and legal implications. However, OTA saw HTA in a narrower sense as well, as the evaluation or testing of safety and efficacy of a technology [6].

The broader perspective in the comprehensive HTA was further pointed out by Fuchs et al. (1990) [7] with the introduction of the concept of *the new technology assessment*. Besides the biomedical perspective with evaluation of efficacy and safety, they proposed

---

[10] Established by the United States Congress in 1972 and closed down in 1995 due to budget cuts.

that a technology assessment should encompass the measurement on effectiveness, considerations of quality of life and patients' preferences, and especially the evaluation of costs and benefits [7]. This assessment focuses on the final outcomes of interest - the clinical, economic and social end points, because Fuchs et al. (1990), and OTA (1976), saw HTA as a decision aid to policy-makers in general. The social end point in the definition of HTA has been further divided, whereby a comprehensive and multidisciplinary HTA could be divided in four main elements - clinical, patient-related, organisational and economic elements, as illustrated below in Figure 2.1 showing the HTA process.

Figure 2.1 : The proces of health technology assessment

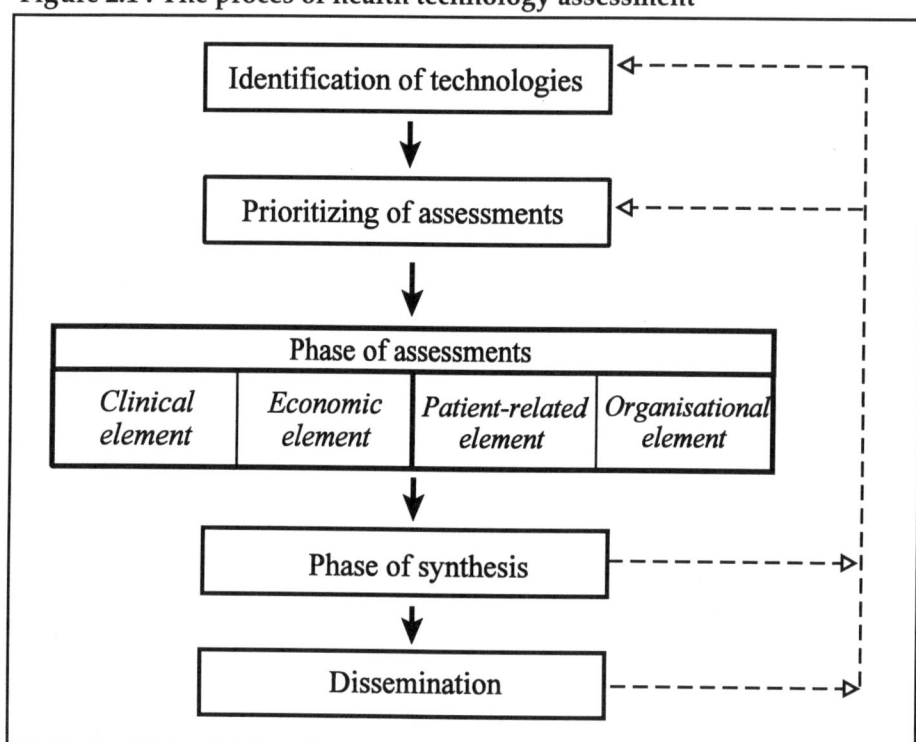

(Jørgensen et al. (1986) [8])

Since the start at OTA the number of HTAs published internationally has exploded as HTA has become an important policy tool. A reference search in the HealthSTAR© database at the National Library of Medicine in the United States, containing documents[11] from the period 1975 to 1997, revealed 2,276 references under the Medical

---

[11] The types of documents referenced in HealthSTAR are journal articles, technical and governmental reports, meeting papers and abstracts, books and book chapters.

Subject Heading (MeSH) *Technology-assessment, biomedical*.[12] However, one consequence of this apparent success with respect to HTAs published might have been that the definition and interpretation of what are actually called HTA differs a great deal. Goodman pushes it to the extremes by proclaiming that "the term health technology assessment is used loosely to refer to any form of evaluation of a health care intervention" [9].

The broad definition of HTA presented by OTA (1976) [4] and by Fuchs et al. (1990) [7], as a comprehensive, systematic and multidisciplinary assessment, is in principle supported by the national HTA institutions, the International Society of Technology Assessment in Health Care[13] (ISTAHC) and in a number of articles and books, as for example Goodman (1992) [9], Banta et al. (1993) [10] and Menon et al. (1996) [11].

Other actors have included more partial and narrower approaches in the concept of HTA, although recognizing its comprehensive approach. The Institute of Medicine in the United States argues that "most assessments stop with a partial effort and we include these when we speak of technology assessment" [12]. Banta (1982) points at "the immediate potential for technology assessment and policy making seems to lie in the evaluation of efficacy and safety and the evaluation of cost-effectiveness" [13]. This focus upon the clinical and economic elements in the HTA is followed by Jennett (1986) [14]. He describes HTA as a four-stage process, where the first three stages focus upon the clinical element by studying the feasibility[14], testing efficacy and assessing effectiveness of the technology in question. The final stage before adoption considers the costs and consequences of the technology in an economic appraisal. Jennett supports a narrower approach too, by saying that "not all technologies will justify all these levels of assessment" [14]. The partial HTA described in Jennett is still supported and used in the literature, as for example a technology assessment of endoscopic surgery by Neugebauer et al. (1994) [15]. A report by the Dutch Steering Committee on Future Health Scenarios (1987) presents, besides a broader definition, HTA in the narrower sense as *the evaluation or testing of a technology for safety and efficacy* [16]. The partial HTA could also have its focus on the economic element, as e.g. in Garber (1994) [17] or in OTA (1976) [4], who labelled cost-benefit and cost-effectiveness analyses as partial technology assessments.

---

[12] Of course one needs to be very cautious about the conclusions made from this search, because the search was only based upon titles and abstracts in HealthSTAR and because of uncertainty in using the MeSH system for any conclusions about HTA.

[13] ISTAHC's definition on their internet homepage (http://www.istahc.org): *HTA is the evaluation of medical technologies, including procedures, equipment, drugs and health care strategies. An assessment requires an interdisciplinary approach encompassing analyses of safety, effectiveness, efficacy, costs, ethics and quality of life measures.*

[14] The assessment of technical efficacy and safety [14].

Sometimes the cost-effectiveness analysis is even seen as an equivalent to HTA [18].[15] The economic element could also focus upon the assessment of the investment and operational costs associated with the adoption of a technology.

The two other elements in the broad and comprehensive HTA - the organisation and the patient (and the *social end points*) - seem less often to be the focus of a partial HTA approach. They are indeed seldom treated in depth in the broad approach.

There appears to be at least five reasons why HTA is perceived differently in the health care sector with different partial approaches as opposed to the traditional broad and comprehensive definition.

First, one has to remember that the broad concept of technology assessment was transferred to the field of health care from its traditional use in sectors such as energy, environment, industry, space and defence. The purpose of technology assessment in these areas is to contribute with a holistic approach to the development of specific policies, e.g. a country's policy with respect to the production of energy from windmills or an investment policy in the industry. Technology assessment in health care differs, however, from that in most industries [7]. The health care market consists of small and discrete technologies, which do not require large investments by a single investor, as is the case in the energy sector or in the industry [10]. Technology assessment in health care has a more practical approach focusing on a specific technology or treatment and not on a whole sector or part of it. The health care market is traditionally financed, at least in Europe, through taxes or health insurance coverage without any direct payment by the patient to the physician at the hospital, apart from a relative minor co-payment share. This reduces the patients' (*the users*) incentive to perform a technology assessment of, e.g. the cost-effectiveness of a technology in contrast to the private industry. Moreover, the assessment of health technologies is complex.

Secondly, a more partial approach in HTA could also be explained by HTA's point of departure in clinical research and clinical evaluation. Methods for this evaluation, such as the randomized controlled trials (RCT) existed long before technology assessment was transferred to the field of health care.[16] Some of the first HTAs were RCTs evaluating the efficacy and safety. The phases of the HTA process - identification, analysing, synthesizing and disseminating - have their origin in similar phases of clinical

---

[15] However, this focus upon cost-effectiveness is according to Banta (1990) one problem with HTA, because the economic element is overestimated, compared with the other elements regarding the organisation and the patient [18].

[16] Bradford Hill formulated the principles of RCT, and RCT was first put to practical use in the MRC trials of streptomycin reported in 1951 [14].

research of efficacy and safety.[17] Other assessment tools have then been added over time, removing HTA from the clinical research field. Cost-effectiveness and cost-benefit analyses[18] are some of these partial assessments, which were added in the eighties because of an increasing concern about economy in the health care sector.

Thirdly, the synthesis in the HTA procedure could be argued to be the most important stage in a broad, comprehensive approach in contrast to a more partial and narrower approach. In the phase where the synthesis takes place the existing information and results of the tests are collected and interpreted in order to submit judgements or recommendations [10]. The synthesis is the critical analysis and weighing of the single elements, which makes the broad HTA information relevant to policy [21]. The synthesis becomes a process of weighing the impact of the impacts. There are different methods of synthesis available. The relevant choice depends on the scope and the purpose of using the information. Methods like *literature review* - the most frequently used method - and *meta-analysis* could be focused upon a single element initially and would hence result in a partial assessment. *Decision analysis*, another synthesis method, analyses medical decisions and in doing so has the clinical focus. According to OTA (1982) [6], STG (1987) [16], Banta et al. (1993) [10] and SBU (1993) [22] *cost-effectiveness analysis* without the prospective collection of data could also be regarded as a method of synthesizing. The clear implication of using this method would be that the HTA becomes a more partial focus on the economic and clinical elements. The non-quantitative methods of synthesis are the group consensus methods, as for example *the Delphi-Method, Focus Groups* and *Consensus Conferences*. To provide data by means of these methods the previously mentioned quantitative methods could be used. Presenting each element to the group or panel of experts for synthesizing, these methods can capture the broad and comprehensive focus of a technology assessment. An explanation of the question, why HTA is perceived differently, could therefore lie in the choice of synthesis method.

Fourthly, the different partial approaches to technology assessment in health care could be explained by the different types of actors, users and producers, who have entered the field of HTA. As Banta (1996) puts it, *at this stage health care technology assessment means different things to different people, depending on how it is used and by whom* [3]. The use of the assessment and the background of the actors clearly has implications for the choice of assessment approach. The consumers of HTA information are actors participating in

---

[17] This is confirmed by the identical descriptions given in Banta et al. (1981) [19], pp.115-116, of "the process for developing and dissemination efficacy and safety information", and in Banta et al. (1993) [10], pp. 66-67, "the process for developing and disseminating health care technology assessment".

[18] The methods of cost-benefit and cost-effectiveness analyses are well-known as they have been carried out since the start of the present century. Their application in the field of health care was, however, delayed to the mid-sixties. A literature search made by OTA (1980) on numbers of Health Care CEA or CBAs conducted found that the first published CBA's or CEA's in the sector were performed in 1966 with a growth in the number of studies in the mid-seventies [20].

different kinds of policy making who need to base their decision-making on information from HTA, e.g. clinical guidelines in the clinical decision-making. The interest of the patient and his agent - the physician - is primarily concerned with information regarding the efficacy (or effectiveness) and safety of a technology (and ethics) [12]. This would be of interest for the hospital too, but not the sole interest. A case-study by Luce et al. (1995) showed that decision-makers at hospitals in the United States used technology assessment almost exclusively to make purchasing decisions and as a means to control expenditures - cost containment [23]. To do this they need information on capital costs and operation costs in order to make their *financial assessment*.[19] The technical evaluation in terms of efficacy and safety would also be of interest for the regulatory agencies when making the registration decisions about new pharmaceuticals. The third-party payers - public and private - are foremost focusing on the costs, effectiveness and cost-effectiveness of the technology, they are supposed to reimburse.[20] The producer of technology would have the same interest as both the regulatory agency and the third-party payer, because technical information is a necessary requirement for marketing of the product and because information on cost-effectiveness could secure the financing of the product. The diffusion, utilization and decentralization or centralization of a health technology are relevant organisational topics for a government and a ministry of health, besides the clinical and economic elements. The politicians and the public would also have a broader concern on, e.g. the social implications and ethics of a new technology [3]. These different actors in the HTA field illustrate the different kinds of partial information required to make decision on a particular problem.

Finally, the choice of assessment type depends on the type of health technology to be assessed and on the level of development in the life cycle of the technology, which could also be a reason for the different interpretations of technology assessment. As required in the legislation in most of the OECD countries drugs are evaluated for efficacy and safety in randomized controlled trials (RCT).[21] Due to different amounts of data available in the life cycle of health technology, the type of technology assessment performed could also depend on whether the technology is emerging, new or already existing. The information required to perform the HTA would clearly be associated with the evolutionary stage of the technology.

---

[19] The perspective of their information is the hospital and not necessarily the society like in many economic studies.

[20] Although the case-study by Luce et al. (1995) revealed that cost-effectiveness studies tend to have a very limited role in technology assessment requested by third-party payers [23]. However, Luce et al. (1995) explains this result with the pressure from society upon the insurers to base decisions on health benefit issues and to avoid the perception of rationing health care based on costs [23]. The authors recommend cost-effectiveness information in order to make the coverage decisions.

[21] Obligatory FDA-like market approval for pharmaceuticals (FDA - Food and Drug Administration in the United States).

This discussion revealed some disagreement about the perception of HTA. Nevertheless, HTA is still understood as a systematic assessment of the *clinical* (e.g. efficacy, safety, effectiveness), *economic* (e.g. efficiency, cost, cost-effectiveness, cost-benefit), *organisational* (e.g. diffusion, utilization, skills, education) and *patient-related* (e.g. social impact, ethics, psychological relations) consequences of the application of health technology. The question is whether this HTA information need to be comprehensive and thereby to combine information from each of the four main elements (clinical, economic, patient-related and organisational), as is the case with the broad OTA definition transferred from other sectors. However, as stated in the recent project concerning HTA, EUR-ASSESS, *HTA, given the broad context, is not defined by a set of methods, but by its intent* [24]. A teleological definition. Arguing the fact that the content of HTA would depend on the decision which needs to be taken (*the intention*), and hence on the required information, as well as the system in which the HTA is going to be used, seems reasonable, as would be seen in the comparative study in the present chapter.

3.0 Health Technology Assessment in Denmark

With the introduction of the concept of HTA in 1980, HTA has generally had a broad and *OTA-like* meaning in Denmark.[22] Jørgensen et al. (1986) defined HTA as *a technically broad and interest-balanced comprehensive assessment of a health technology, its conditions and consequences* [8]. In a similar way the National Board of Health in Denmark have defined HTA as *a comprehensive systematic evaluation of the assumptions for, and consequences of the application of health technology* [2,27]. The four main elements in this assessment are the clinical, the patient-related, the organisational and finally the economic consequences of using technology.

Since 1980, the role of HTA in decision making and research has varied with the shifting governments. To promote HTA research in health service research a committee was established in 1981 under the Medical Research Council [28]. Today the Medical Research Council arrange *Consensus Development Conferences* in cooperation with the Danish Institute for Health Services Research and Development (DSI).[23] The most important institution in Denmark with respect to HTA has been the DSI, which has been involved in the area since 1980. Several research institutions have furthermore touched the HTA field in their research, especially part of an HTA, e.g. the research in health economics at the Institute of Public Health at the University of Southern Denmark in Odense.[24] However, despite an important effort by DSI and other actors these activities

---

[22] Two simultaneous publications introduced the concept of HTA independently in Denmark in 1980; a report to the national parliament about HTA written by Buch Andreasen (1980) [25] and a report about technology assessment written by Jørgensen (1980) [26].

[23] DSI was previously called the Danish Hospital Institute.

[24] Before 1999 named *the Centre for Health and Social Policy*, Odense University.

have not been coordinated at the overall national level and the resources have been limited to fulfil a national HTA activity in Denmark.

With respect to policy-making the responsibility of HTA has been at the National Board of Health since 1982. This Board created the first national HTA committee in 1983 [29]. The purpose of the committee was to introduce and disseminate HTA and initiate the fulfilments of HTAs. The committee was dissolved in 1987. In 1992, an HTA working group was established under the Committee for Quality Development at the National Board of Health to promote the use of HTA in Denmark. An outcome of this committee's work was the publication of an information pamphlet about HTA in 1994 [27].

In 1994 a report from the Ministry of Health about the economy of the hospitals pointed at the need to strengthen the HTA effort in Denmark both at the national level with a new committee and at the regional (county) level [30]. It resulted in the establishment of a new HTA committee in 1995 at the National Board of Health - *The Health Technology Assessment Committee*. In 1995 this committee produced, as a help in decision making, an HTA report about Beta-interferon, using the broad definition of HTA [31]. The HTA committee launched in 1996 a national strategy for HTA [2]. The elements in this strategy focus upon the use, dissemination, priority-setting and coordination of HTA and research and development of HTA methods.

In Denmark, HTA has acquired neither a central placement nor a placement with daily use in the health care sector, unlike the countries that we compare our self with [21]. Although HTA was introduced early in Denmark, and furthermore was an important topic in the mid-eighties, it has apparently not resulted in a general recognition of the importance of HTA by the clinicians and by the government until *The Health Technology Assessment Committee* was established in 1995 and a national strategy was presented in 1996. Because of scarce resources in the health care sector, public pressure and political will, this national HTA strategy resulted in a debate about the creation of a national HTA institute to secure a continued effort. The tasks for an institute are to identify technologies for assessment (new and existing), coordinate the activities and eventually to establish an early warning system for emerging health technologies as suggested in a recent report [32]. In a broad political consensus this institution, the Danish Institute for Health Technology Assessment - DIHTA (*Statens Institut for Medicinsk Teknologivurdering*), have been established at the National Board of Health in the summer 1997.

The next section deals with the arguments for the establishment of a national institution for health technology assessment.

4.0 National Institutions for Health Technology Assessment

Following the requirements for membership of the *International Network of Agencies for Health Technology Assessment*[25] (INAHTA[26]) a national institution or agency for health technology assessment could be defined as an organisation, which assesses technologies in health care as a non-profit organisation and is funded at least 50 per cent by public sources, and thereby have a programme that relates to a national (or regional) government [33].

Today national HTA institutions exist in the United States (*NCHCT*-1978, *OHTA*-1981, *AHCPR*-1989), Australia (*NHTAP*-1982 and today *AHTAC*-1990), Sweden (*SBU*-1987), Canada (*CCOHTA*-1990), France (*ANDEM*-1990 and now called *ANAES*-1997), Hungary (*HCOHTA*-1993), Spain (*AETS*-1994), Italy (*ASSR*-1994), Finland (*FinOHTA*-1995), Denmark (DIHTA-1997) and Norway (*SMM*-1997). Furthermore, the national health authorities have important HTA activities with national programmes and strategies in countries like the Netherlands (*Health Council*-1985, *Sick Fund Council* - 1983) and in England (*SGHT, NHS R&D*-1992, *NCCHTA*-1996). The Swiss Science Council (1991) has national HTA activities too. Finally, regional HTA programs have also been important - primarily in Canada and Spain and there are some HTA activities too in countries like Scotland and New Zealand. The actual form of these institutions varies widely, as it could be an agency (e.g. SBU), a defined program in a ministry (e.g. the Health Council), a coordinating body (e.g. NCCHTA), or some other type of institution [24].

Looking at this rapid international development of national HTA institutions or agencies, one may ask, what is the explanation of this trend. What would be the justification and possible arguments for the creation of national HTA institutions?

As described in section 1, the immediate outcome of health technology assessment is information or rather dissemination of information. Information is characterized as a public good to be consumed collectively (joint consumption - non-rivalry) and in some cases without any possibility of exclusion, depending on the dissemination and distribution. Pure public goods are usually defined as goods where, for a given output, additional consumption by one person or a group of persons does not imply reduced consumption by other persons or groups in society [34].[27] This is the case with HTA information, as discussed in Feeny et al. (1988) [35]. HTA information is normally published and distributed in reports, newsletters and journals that can in principle be

---

[25] The purpose of INAHTA is to provide a forum for the identification and pursuit of interests common to health technology assessment agencies [11].

[26] The full names of abbreviations are shown in Appendix 2.1.

[27] In contrast to *impure public goods*, where an extra comsumption by an individual reduces the benefit available for others in consuming an amount of a public good (e.g. by borrowing a library book).

used by everyone, depending on the process of dissemination, without reducing the possibilities of others to benefit from the information.[28]

However, public goods are characterized by failures in the markets, meaning that a normal competitive market would not result in an optimal level and distribution of the goods in the society. The costs of producing information are high whereas the costs of distributing it without exclusion rights would be low, making it easy for others to get the information. Because of joint consumption market prices would not reflect the social marginal benefit of the consumption. In this situation the optimal solution for a maximizing actor or authority would be to get all the benefits and have others to bear the cost. This problem of *free riding* is, however, not the optimal solution for the society, because of an inefficient level of goods provided.

Transferred to the HTA field this problem of free riding on information is present in situations with many HTA actors working in an uncoordinated manner and with an arbitrary process of priority setting between HTA projects to be undertaken. *Buyers* - the users of the assessment results - bear only a fraction of the costs, so health care innovators do not have the incentive to carry out technology assessments [7]. This seems to have been the case in Denmark previously. Another example concerns differences between the county councils; one would expect that county councils with university hospitals might be interested to a higher degree in HTA information and would use resources in its production, whereas other county councils might tend to free ride and use this information when it becomes available. The possibility of free riding is of course also present at the international level, because the HTA information produced by one country's national institution is available and usable for other countries as well, at least with respect to information regarding the efficacy (effectiveness) and safety of a technology. The benefit in this last example would, however, be the reduction of the amount of duplication of the same projects internationally (e.g. until now six countries have assessed screening for osteoporosis independently), as mentioned in Menon et al. (1996), who argue for international cooperation, which is the case with the previously mentioned INAHTA network [11].[29]

The response from society to this market failure, which is the result of the public good characteristics of information, would be to make a public intervention in the production and distribution of the public good. In the HTA field this would be an argument for having some kind of overall national funding, coordination and priority setting at the governmental level (national programmes) to secure an efficient level of production and dissemination of the HTA information in society. Especially in countries with public-funded health care sectors, this production of HTA information is an important

---

[28] With public goods like information the individual can vary their use differently, although this is not possible with other public goods such as the use of street lights and national defence.

[29] However, it should be remembered that transferring the result of HTA reports from one country to another is not without costs, as it is unlikely that two countries are totally alike, so the information requested would differ.

regulation tool as well. The institutional solution is to establish a separate national HTA institution responsible for these tasks, which can be seen as a theoretical explanation of the rapid growth of the national HTA institutions. Coordination, priority setting, funding, production and dissemination are the national institution's primary purposes and these responsibilities seem to have been adopted by the existing national HTA institutions in practice. In the EUR-ASSESS project it is recommended that *each country should have at least one organisation (or coordinating body) that can serve as a contact point for technology assessment activities, including priority setting, dissemination and implementation* [24].

The reduction of informational asymmetries between different HTA actors in an uncoordinated approach to HTA information could also be a reason for the creation of an institution with a national strategy for identification, synthesising and dissemination of information. The sellers and manufacturers of technology would usually have a greater knowledge about the new technology compared with the hospitals and the physicians, who on the other hand have the authority to make the decision regarding adoption. Systematic and evidence-based information in a coordinated approach might result in improved information and thereby lead to a more qualified decision making regarding adoption. This rests of course on the assumption that a governmental provision of information guarantees its use by the potential users. Information is not enough to change behaviour within health care, though, it also requires changes in attitudes and political will [36]. To fulfil its purpose the information might have to be combined with different kinds of incentives in decision making. A further advantage of *the development of such 'intermediate' organisations is that they can create effective and formalized new channels of communication and dialogue between the economic assessment research* as well as other areas of research *and decision-makers in the health care system* [37].

Another justification for supporting a national HTA institution is that there is complementarity among the activities involved in technology assessment [35]. The elements of an HTA - identification, selection, synthesising, dissemination - are closely related and if the HTA is going to influence policy, these activities should be performed in an early and timely manner. A national coordinated activity has the mechanisms to secure this much better than could be expected in a segmented and uncoordinated approach.

In Feeny et al. (1988) it is also argued that the success of mission-oriented agencies in multi-disciplinary fields of research in general would add to the faith in a national HTA institution [35]. The success of earlier assessments in a country and the success of assessments performed at existing HTA institutions in other countries, as for example signalized by SBU with their first assessment of preoperative routines [38], is also a factor that contributes to explain this international trend of institutionalisation of HTA at the national level.

5.0 The International Comparative Study of Health Technology Assessment

5.1 The Purpose of the Study

The study presented in this section is an international comparative study of health technology assessment performed at national HTA institutions. As discussed in section 2, the concept of HTA seems to be used in a loose manner. The concept was introduced by OTA as a broad and comprehensive assessment of health technology including all four elements (clinical, economic, patient-related and organisational). However, it can be questioned whether HTA should always have a broad and comprehensive form, because situations will appear where for example only the clinical or economic information is needed.

The purpose of the comparative study was to compare how HTA was perceived and performed in practice at national HTA institutions in other countries. This was done in an exploratory approach. Here it was examined, which parameters that were assessed in the HTAs produced by the institutions with the aim of showing the weights given to each parameter assessed and thereby the four elements in HTA. This analysis would reveal whether the institutions had a broad and comprehensive approach to HTA or whether they perhaps tended to use the concept of HTA in a more partial and narrower manner in practice. In the context of the Danish HTA institute, which uses a broad definition, this result would be interesting.

5.2 Method

The method used in this study is a structured literature review of the health technology assessment reports published. The data included in the study are secondary data. This systematic approach involved the steps shown in Table 2.1.[30]

Table 2.1 : Steps in the Structured Review Process

1. Specify the selection criteria
2. Search for the literature (i.e. reports) on the basis of this selection criteria
3. Exclude literature (i.e. reports) that do not represent the problem of interest
4. Establish a guideline of standard questions used to review the reports
5. Review and interpret the literature/reports in consideration of this guideline
6. Integrate and aggregate the results

In the following the content of steps 1-4 will be elaborated where the chosen study sample is described. Step 5 and 6 are the topics of section 5.3, where the results of the study are presented.

---

[30] Inspired by the recommendations given in SBU (1993) [39].

5.2.1 Selection Criteria

Four criteria were used in the selection of an HTA sample to achieve the relevant information and to limit the sample of the many actors involved in HTA activities.[31]

- It should be countries with a national HTA institution or agency
- They should be perennial actors in the HTA field with some years of experience
- The institution or agency should have produced some HTA reports
- Only HTA reports written in English or a Scandinavian language would be included

From these criteria five countries' national institutions or agencies were chosen for the study sample. These institutions or agencies were *the Swedish Council on Technology Assessment in Health Care* (SBU), *the Australian Health Technology Assessment Committee* (AHTAC), *the Canadian Coordinating Office for Health Technology Assessment* (CCOHTA), *the NHS*[32] *Standing Group on Health Technology* (SGHT) or *the National Co-ordinating Centre for Health Technology Assessment* (NCCHTA) in England and *the Health Council* in the Netherlands.[33] As significant actors all these agencies had several years of experience in the HTA field and had produced a number of HTA reports.[34] One exception was in the case of England where no reports have been finished yet due to the late start of SGHT and NCCHTA. However, an English sample was included, because of their national effort in establishing an HTA programme to secure an evidence-based practice at the hospital level. In future research this comparative study could be extended with other national and regional HTA institutions, and the possibility for an updating of the English sample with the final HTA reports published under the commission of NCCHTA exists. In this context the comparative study presented in the present chapter could be seen as a preliminary study of an extended future comparative study of health technology assessment.

5.2.2 Obtaining the Data

Each of the five agencies was contacted in the summer of 1996 and asked for copies of the HTA reports that they had produced to be included in the sample. Only reports

---

[31] As many as 103 HTA organisations participated in a survey made by Perry et al. (1997) of health technology assessment worldwide [40].

[32] The National Health Services in the United Kingdom.

[33] An enquiry was sent to the Director of the Pharmaceutical Benefit Scheme (PBS), Australia, and to The Sick Fund Council, the Netherlands, to get a complete picture of the national HTA activity in those countries. However, as no answer was received, they were not a part of the sample.

[34] Some of the regional institutes in Canada and Spain are perennial actors too with several years of experience (e.g. CETS in Quebec, Canada). However, due to limitation, and because they failed the selection criteria of not being national HTA institutions, they were not included.

presented as health technology assessments by the national institutions themselves were selected for the sample. The Dutch sample was selected after advice from Dr. ten Velden, the Health Council, because no specific list of HTA reports was available from the council. In England, where no reports were available yet, NHS kindly made abstracts available of the HTA projects funded by the NHS HTA programme. These project notes were used instead of reports for England, as they reflect the national HTA activity. However, this might limit the conclusions made on behalf of this part of the sample and one need to be cautious about any generalisations made from these project-notes as they describe what researchers intend to do and not what they have actually done.

No reports and project notes published later than 1996 were included. Some reports or project notes were excluded from the sample, because they could not be considered as HTAs.[35] Contact persons in the HTA institutions or agencies were asked for advice in case of doubt. In total the sample consisted of 124 HTA reports or HTA projects used as data sources. The distribution of HTA reports or projects among the five agencies is presented in section 5.3.1.1.

5.2.3 Review Process

These reports and project notes were reviewed for information regarding a number of standard questions to provide data for the descriptive statistics and comparative analysis. The questions were divided into two groups. A group of general questions concerning the institute, report or project note, publication year, the commissioning status of the report, the type of technology assessment[36], the type of technology assessed, the possible alternatives compared and the research methods used. Another group of questions considered more specifically the parameters assessed in the HTA reports or intended to be assessed in the HTA projects. These parameters were divided into four main groups - 1. clinical parameters, 2. economic parameters, 3. patient-related parameters and 4. organisational parameters - following the broad definition of HTA. A code number was assigned to each answer category and a statistical package was used for the descriptive and statistical analyses of the data. The questions are shown in Table 2.2 below. A description of each parameter is given after the table.

---

[35] The typical example would be reports or projects describing methodological HTA issues.

[36] A technology assessment could as a *technology-driven* HTA focus on the effects of one or more technologies, it could focus upon a general disease problem as a *problem-driven* HTA, or it could finally be a *project-driven* HTA, if it is an assessment of a technology in a specific organisation (a specific technological deployment).

Table 2.2 : Standard Questions Used in the Review of the HTA Reports

General questions:

A. Which HTA institution or committee?
1. SBU
2. SGHT and NCCHTA
3. The Health Council
4. CCOHTA
5. AHTAC

B. What is the title of the HTA report or project?

C. How is the assessment produced?
1. By the institution or committee itself
2. As a commissioned activity

D. Which year is the report or project published or launced?

E. Is the technology assessment ....
1. Problem-driven
2. Technology-driven
3. Project-driven

F. Which type of health technology is assessed?
1. Pharmaceutical
2. Device or equipment
3. Procedure

G. Are any alternatives presented in the assessment?
1. Pharmaceutical
2. Device or equipment
3. Procedure
4. None

H. Which research methods are used in the HTA?
(more than one method could be used) Secondary data ...
Primary data.........
1. Literature review
2. Meta-analysis
3. Economic evaluation
4. (initiated) Randomized Controlled Trial
5. Survey
6. Modelling or evaluation
7. Other method

Questions regarding the parameters assessed:

I. Clinical parameters assessed?
1. Efficacy (RCT)
2. Safety
3. Effectiveness
4. Outcomes
5. Indications
6. Population affected

J. Economic parameters assessed?
1. Efficiency - cost-minimization
2. Costs
3. Cost-effectiveness
4. Cost-utility
5. Cost-benefit

K. Patient-related parameters assessed?
1. Social and environmental impact
2. Ethics
3. Acceptability
4. Psychological relations
5. Other patient-related parameters

L. Organisational parameters assessed?
1. Diffusion - dissemination
2. Centralization - decentralization
3. Utilization
4. Accessibility - equity
5. Skills - routines
6. Education - training
7. Other organisational parameters

5.2.4 Parameters Assessed

The clinical parameters among the possible parameters assessed in HTA consisted of six variables. *Efficacy* is defined as the problem of benefit to individuals in a defined population from a health technology applied for a given medical problem under ideal conditions of use [41]. This parameter is typically assessed in randomized controlled trials (RCT) why HTA reports in the review that had performed an RCT or refers to RCTs in the HTA was recorded as containing information about efficacy. *Effectiveness* means the benefit of a technology under average conditions of use [12]. As opposed to efficacy, effectiveness of a technology is therefore assessed in a real life situation where external variables, which might be controlled for in a research setting, would influence. By the assessment of *safety* is understood a judgment of the acceptability of a risk with respect to the use of a technology. An HTA could also focus upon the *outcome* of a technology or treatment, where outcomes could be measured as life years saved, quality of life, etc. *Indication* is the question of the criteria for using a technology. Typical questions to be answered in an assessment would be: "what is the indication of the use of the technology?" and "is there consensus about this level of indication among physicians?" [27]. The last parameter among the clinical parameters - *population affected* - was concerned with epidemiological information as the study of the determinants and distribution of diseases (incidence and prevalence) and injuries in human populations [10].

The economic parameters assessed in HTA were divided into five variables. An assessment may consider the *efficiency* of a health technology in a certain clinical setting. Economic efficiency is divided into allocative efficiency and technological efficiency, with the former being concerned with the entire resource allocation in the society and the latter with the relationship between input and output in the production of goods. An evaluation of efficiency comparing two programmes is often called a cost-minimization analysis [42], e.g. an assessment of the minimum cost for each Down's syndrome diagnosed at a given level of detection. The *costs* considered in an assessment could be both the analysis of the direct running costs related to a technological application, e.g. the costs of running a CT-unit, the analysis of the necessary capital costs to invest in a technology and the analysis of the indirect costs related to the use of the technology, e.g. the assessment of the production loss caused by the patients disease. The perspectives of a cost analysis could be both the financial costs related to a hospital or the social cost in the society by including the indirect costs. By *cost-effectiveness* of a given technology is understood the incremental costs of a technology compared with the incremental health effects of that technology, where the health effects are measured in natural units as, e.g. life years saved, days of morbidity avoided. *The cost-utility* of a technology is the comparison of the incremental cost with the incremental health improvement measured in one common outcome measure - quality-adjusted life-years (QALYs) gained. In *the cost-benefit analysis* all costs and all benefits are valued in monetary terms [43].

The third group of parameters assessed - parameters related to the patient - consisted of four variables. By *social and environmental impact* is understood an assessment of the implications of a health technology for social and legal values, institutions and relationships [12]. For instance, which impact does the technology have on values and does the application of the technology lead to changes in a patient's social relationship? The assessment of *ethics* is concerned with societal norms and morals. "Would everything which is technologically possible also be ethically desirable from the individual's and the society's point of view?" This is closely related to the third patient-related parameter - *acceptability*. "Would the patient accept the technology used in his or her treatment?" *Psychological relations* in using a technology could also be described in HTA. This could be the question on how the patient perceives his or her own health condition or the patient's possible apprehension and anxiety with respect to a certain health technology [27].

Six organisational parameters were included as the last group of parameters assessed in HTA. The first four parameters were concerned with the structure of the organisation - the health care system, whereas the last two parameters considered properties of the professionals in relation to the technology. *Diffusion* and *dissemination* as a topic appraise the spread and adoption of a health technology after its development and the consequences upon the organisation and society. "Should the technology be *centralized* at a few hospital units or should it be *decentralized*?" This could be an important question, when an expensive and highly specialized health technology is considered or when only few patients can be treated by a given technology. *Accessibility*, and thereby (geographic) *equity*, is linked to the question of centralization versus decentralization by answering, how many patients have access to the technology. *Utilization* refers to how much the relevant patients have used the actual technology. When adopting a new health technology some *skills* will be required by the professionals handling the technology and some existing *routines* might have to be changed. An assessment of skills and routines provide important information for the adopting organisation. When the professionals do not possess the necessary skills further *education* and *training* will be needed. The HTA might reveal the need for education and training of professionals with respect to a given technology.

Compared with a study of *health technology assessment worldwide* made by Perry et al. (1997) [40] there was some accordance with respect to parameters (or properties) included, although the number of parameters was higher in the study presented here. However, a more detailed description of the patient-related and organisational parameters could largely explain the larger number of parameters included here. It is important to mention, however, that the results of the two studies are not comparable, because of a difference in study perspective (comparison of reports opposed to institutions) and a difference in the questions asked. The results of the study presented in the next section were obtained by asking the question, *how often a parameter (or property) was assessed in specific HTAs?*, whereas the organisations participating in Perry et al.'s study were asked, *which properties (or attributes) of a technology do you in general assess?*, which would not necessarily result in the same frequency as in the specific HTAs produced by the institutions.

5.3 Results

In this section the results of the comparative study of health technology assessment is presented. The results are divided into a descriptive part with the presentation of the descriptive findings in the sample and a more qualitative analysis[37] with a classification of the types of HTAs produced in the sample.

5.3.1 Descriptive Part

Five national institutions on health technology assessment - *the Swedish Council on Technology Assessment in Health Care* (SBU), *the Health Council in the Netherlands*, *the Australian Health Technology Assessment Committee* (AHTAC), *the Canadian Coordinating Office for Health Technology Assessment* (CCOHTA), *the NHS Standing Group on Health Technology* (SGHT) or *the National Co-ordinating Centre for Health Technology Assessment* (NCCHTA[38]) - were selected for this study. In Appendix 2.2 a description of each institution is given. Below in Table 2.3 their definitions of HTA are shown.

Table 2.3 : Definitions on Technology Assessment Used by the National Institutions

Institution	Definition on Health Technology Assessment
SBU (Sweden)	SBU's task is to evaluate methods used within health care and to look critically at their costs, their risks and their benefits. SBU assesses the **medical, ethical, social** and **economic impact** of new and established medical procedures [45].
Health Council (the Netherlands)	The Health Council evaluates **efficacy, safety, effectiveness, efficiency** (CBA, CEA, CUA), **social, ethical,** or **legal implications** and **organisational topics** related to health care technology [46].
AHTAC (Australia)	AHTAC evaluates health technologies and highly specialized services looking at **safety & efficacy, effectiveness & cost,** and **equity, access & social impact** [46].
CCOHTA (Canada)	Health technology assessment is the evaluation of medical technologies and their use. Based on an interdisciplinary approach, an assessment can encompass analyses of **safety, efficacy, effectiveness, quality of life** and **utilization**. Other important factors such as **economic, ethical,** and **social implications** and other effects which may be unintended, indirect or delayed, are also considered [48].
NCCHTA (England)	Health Technology Assessment is the production of high quality research information on **costs, effectiveness** and **broader impact** on health technologies for those who use, manage and work in the NHS [49,50].

---

[37] Inspired by a review of sensitivity analyses made by Briggs et al. (1995) [44].

[38] This abbreviation is used in the rest of the chapter for the English HTA activity.

5.3.1.1. The study Sample

In total the study sample consisted of 124 technology assessment reports or projects published or launched in the period from 1989 to 1996 by the five institutions.[39]

Table 2.4 : Number of Reports or Projects by Institutions in the Sample

1989-1996	SBU	Health Council	AHTAC	CCOHTA	NCCHTA	TOTAL
Number	19	13	12	16	64	124

As can be seen from Table 2.4 more than half of the HTAs were English HTA projects commissioned by SGHT and funded by NHS in 1995-1996 and now subject to control by NCCHTA.[40] Another nineteen HTAs represented the reports published until now by SBU. Sixteen reports were published by the national HTA institute in Canada - CCOHTA - in the period 1991-1996. Thirteen HTA reports (1989-1996) translated into English were selected by the Health Council to represent the Dutch HTA activity. Finally, twelve HTA reports (1992-1996) represented AHTAC, as the national HTA institute in Australia.[41] In Appendix 2.3 the titles of the HTA reports or projects included in this study are listed.

Among the 124 reports or projects 70 HTAs were produced as a commissioned activity outside the national institutions. This can mainly be explained by the English HTA projects, which were all commissioned. Five CCOHTA reports and one SBU-report were commissioned too. The rest of the reports (54) were produced by the institutions themselves typically with the establishment of specific project groups.

Most of the technology assessments performed in the sample (107) could be classified as assessments focusing on a specific technology or group of technologies as *technology-driven* HTAs. In total only ten HTAs focused as *problem-driven* HTAs on a general disease problem, as for example the report on *Back Pain* from SBU in 1991 (S1105). The last seven HTAs were *project-driven* HTAs with the focus upon a specific organisation. A problem-driven HTA seems most likely to have been produced by the institutions in the Netherlands, England or in Sweden. On the other hand, all the HTAs produced by AHTAC and CCOHTA were technology-driven.

---

[39] As previously mentioned, the UK-sample did only consist of projects accepted for funding by the NHS, because no final reports were available at the deadline of data collection in the summer 1996. Each project was classified according to the year it was started.

[40] Among the total number of project-notes and abstracts received from NHS 25 were excluded from the sample, as they were considered as methodological projects and not HTA projects and 9 were excluded for other reasons, such as a project-note without an abstract.

[41] Six of the Australian HTAs were based upon abstracts, because the reports were not published at the deadline of the data collection in 1996.

5.3.1.2 Technologies Assessed

In Table 2.5 the types of health technologies assessed by the institutions are shown.

Table 2.5 : Type of Technologies Assessed by Institutions in the Sample

	SBU	Health Council	AHTAC	CCOHTA	NCCHTA	TOTAL
Pharmaceuticals	1	2	-	7	8	18
Devices	5	2	8	6	11	32
Procedures	13	9	4	3	45	74
Total	19	13	12	16	64	124

Procedures[42] seemed to be the group of technologies most frequently assessed, since it was the case in nearly two-thirds of the HTAs (74). Many screening programmes assessed explained the high number of procedures in the sample (27). In the English sample alone screening programmes were the focus of eighteen HTA projects. Devices[43] had been the focus of thirty-two HTAs, whereas pharmaceuticals[44] had only been assessed in eighteen HTAs. The reason for the few number of pharmaceuticals assessed might be that for a long time there has been a tradition in the OECD countries for the assessment of efficacy and safety concerning the registration decision of pharmaceuticals as well as the number of pharmacoeconomic studies has increased, e.g. cost-effectiveness studies. Therefore, there had not been the same need and pressure to assess the group of pharmaceuticals in technology assessments as might have been the case with the two other groups of health technologies.

Broken down into institutions, nearly the same distribution of the three types of health technology emerged in Sweden, England and the Netherlands. AHTAC in Australia had not included pharmaceuticals at all in any of their reports in the sample. The division of objects between AHTAC and the Pharmaceutical Benefit Scheme (PBS) in Australia could perhaps explain this. In contrast to Australia, CCOHTA in Canada had evaluated pharmaceuticals in seven out of sixteen reports as a consequence of their *Pharmaceutical Assessment Program*. In eighty-eight HTAs the assessed technology was compared with and/or discussed in relation to one or more alternative technologies. This distribution between types of health technologies by alternatives is seen in Table 2.6 below.

---

[42] Defined as clinical, surgical or medical working-procedures (software) in the hospital, often only successful in combination with pharmaceuticals and/or devices (hardware).

[43] Defined as *in vitro and in vivo diagnostic substances; surgical, medical instruments and supplies; orthopaedic, prosthetic and surgical appliances and supplies; X-ray apparatus and tubes and related irradiations apparatus; electro-medical and electro-therapeutic apparatus; and ophthalmic goods* [51].

[44] Defined as containing some chemical entity or substance that affect a person's life in achieving a desired biological effect.

Table 2.6 : Alternatives Presented in the Sample

	Technologies Assessed			
Alternatives Presented	Pharmaceuticals	Devices	Procedures	Total (alternatives)
Pharmaceuticals	11	-	4	15
Devices	-	14	6	20
Procedures	5	7	41	53
None	2	11	23	36
Total	18	32	74	124

5.3.1.3 Methods Used

Sixty-five per cent of the HTA reports or projects in the sample (80) had used literature review as one method (Table 2.7), which illustrates that literature review is the most popular and most frequently used HTA method with the use of secondary data. This corresponds with the primary aim of HTA as being *not to produce scientific evidence, but to make it available to policy-makers in a usable form* [52]. In 40 per cent of the HTAs (49) an economic evaluation was performed and 16 per cent of the HTAs (20) contained a randomized controlled trial (RCT).

Table 2.7 : Assessment Methods Used by the Institutions in the Sample.

	SBU (N=19)	Health Council (N=13)	AHTAC (N=12)	CCOHTA (N=16)	NCCHTA (N=64)	TOTAL (N=124)*
Literature Review	19	13	7	8	33	80 (65%)
Meta-analysis	1	-	-	2	1	4 (3%)
Economic evaluation	15	-	-	8	26	49 (40%)
Randomized Controlled Trial (new)	-	-	-	-	20	20 (16%)
Survey	7	1	-	2	7	17 (14%)
Modelling/evaluation	-	-	-	-	9	9 (7%)
Other method	3	1	3	1	5	13 (10%)

* Percentages refer to the use of one method in proportion to the total sample (N=124). Per cents sum to more than 100, because more than one method was used in some assessments.

In all the Swedish HTA reports literature review was used as the basic method. This corresponds with the policy at SBU to *summarize medical and scientific literature from around the world*. Economic evaluation (15), with a specific focus upon Swedish conditions, and survey (7) were two other frequently used methods by SBU. In the Netherlands, the Health Council did also use literature review as the basic method in all the reports included in the sample. In England about half of the NCCHTA HTA projects (33) had also planned to use literature review as the basic method. Economic evaluation as a method was also the chosen method in twenty-six of the HTA projects. However, the most interesting result from the English project-notes was that twenty, or nearly one-third of the HTAs, were planned as new randomized controlled clinical trials with the prospective collection of data from experimental and control groups. The other institutions had not used this primary research method, illustrating that the focus of technology assessment is on the use of existing secondary data and secondary research methods, e.g. literature review. AHTAC and CCOHTA used literature review in about half the HTA reports as well. Three Australian reports used other methods than those showed in Table 2.7. These reports dealt typically with the establishment of guidelines, e.g. *Guidelines for renal dialysis and transplantation services* (S4402). In producing the Canadian HTAs, an economic evaluation was performed in half the cases.

5.3.1.4 Parameters Assessed

As outlined in section 5.2.3, Table 2.2, the content of the reports or projects in this study was reviewed with respect to their inclusion of the twenty-one parameters. These parameters were divided into four main groups. Clinical parameters (6), economic parameters (5), patient-related parameters (4) and organisational parameters (6). The result of the review of the 124 reports or projects is shown in Table 2.8.

Table 2.8 : Parameters Assessed in the Sample (N=124)

		Frequency	Per cents of the total sample
Clinical Parameters Assessed	Efficacy	55	44%
	Safety	57	46%
	Effectiveness	96	77%
	Outcomes	39	32%
	Indications	37	30%
	Population affected	40	32%
Economic Parameters Assessed	Efficiency	11	9%
	Costs	80	65%
	Cost-effectiveness	62	50%
	Cost-utility	8	7%
	Cost-benefit	7	6%
Patient-related Parameters Assessed	Social Impact	14	11%
	Ethics	10	8%
	Acceptability	14	11%
	Psychological relations	16	13%
	Other patient parameters	15	12%
Organisational Parameters Assessed	Diffusion	26	21%
	Centralization/decentralization	14	11%
	Utilization	14	11%
	Accessibility	6	5%
	Skills - routines	20	16%
	Education - training	21	17%
	Other organisation parameters	4	3%

As for the **clinical evidence** the most frequently parameter assessed was *effectiveness*, which was a chosen topic in 96 of the 124 HTA reports or projects (77 per cent). In 46 per cent of the HTAs the question of the *safety* of a technology was discussed, whereas *efficacy* was included in 44 per cent of the total sample. 32 per cent of the HTAs contained an epidemiological part about the *population affected* by a disease. *Outcomes* were considered in 32 per cent of the HTA sample, and 30 per cent had discussed the *indications* in the use of a technology.

The country-specific distribution of the clinical parameters assessed in the sample is illustrated in Appendix 2.4. It confirmed the importance of *effectiveness* information among the institutions, although *efficacy* information was included, as the most important clinical parameter, in 81 per cent of the HTAs from CCOHTA. Efficacy information was also frequently included in HTAs from the Health Council and NCCHTA. However, *safety* is considered far more often by four institutions (Health Council, SBU, AHTAC and CCOHTA) than on average in the HTA reports. Two-thirds of the SBU-reports included epidemiological information on the burden of disease and the *population affected*.

The **economic parameter assessed** most often in the sample was consideration of *costs*, which was included in 80 out of 124 HTAs (65 per cent). The second most assessed economic parameter was *cost-effectiveness*, as it was a part of 50 per cent of the HTA reports. The question of *cost-utility* and *cost-benefit* were less frequently addressed, as seen in Table 2.8. In overall, socioeconomic evaluation was the topic in 53 per cent of the HTAs in the sample. *Efficiency*, as a parameter, was assessed in 9 per cent of the sample.

Broken down into institutions (Appendix 2.4) *cost-effectiveness* seems first of all to be assessed and included in technology assessments from CCOHTA (75 per cent), SBU (58 per cent) and NCCHTA (53 per cent). In AHTAC's and the Health Council's HTA reports *cost-effectiveness* was only a topic in 25 and 15 per cent of the cases. *Costs* of a technology or disease were considered in 95 per cent of the HTAs from SBU and in 94 per cent of the HTAs from CCOHTA (the average was 65 per cent).

The four **patient-related parameters** were less frequently assessed in the HTAs in the sample. The topic *psychological relations* was included in 13 per cent of the HTAs, whereas *social impact* and *acceptability* both was included in 11 per cent of the HTAs considered. The question of the *ethics* of a technology was only the topic in ten of the HTAs (9 per cent) and in seven of these teen HTAs considering *ethics*, the question of *safety* was also dealt with. Finally, in 12 per cent of the HTAs *other patient-related parameters* were also registered. This was typically HTAs focusing on the specific production of patient information.

However, the picture was more varied between institutions. Three of the institutions (AHTAC, CCOHTA and NCCHTA) had a limited inclusion of the patient-related parameters, whereas the Health Council in the Netherlands had attached great weight to the patient-related parameters and especially the *social impact* of technologies. It corresponds with the conclusions given in a report from the Rathenau Institute, where the data collection by the Health Council was concerned with legal, ethical and social implications [53].

Among the six **organisational parameters** included, *diffusion* was the most frequently assessed parameter, since it occurred in 21 per cent of the HTAs in the sample. This focus on *diffusion* was especially the case with the HTAs from the Health Council (54 per cent), SBU (53 per cent) and AHTAC (33 per cent), Appendix 2.4. As seen in Table 2.8, *education-training* and *skills-routines* were dealt within 17 and 16 per cent of the HTAs, respectively. Among the last three organisational parameters *centralization* and *utilization* were a part of 11 per cent of the sample, whereas information about *accessibility* was only a topic in 5 per cent of the HTAs. In 3 per cent of the HTAs *other organisational parameters* were registered as well.

The overall tendency in Table 2.8 seems to be that the most frequently assessed parameters in an HTA in the sample were related to the clinical element (*effectiveness, safety* and *efficacy*) and to the economic element (*costs* and *cost-effectiveness*). Parameters concerning the patient-related and organisational elements in the HTA were less frequently assessed and thereby a part of an assessment. All institutions supported this tendency (Appendix 2.4), except one institution - the Health Council. Besides a significant interest in the clinical element, the Dutch sample revealed a larger focus upon the patient-related and organisational parameters, in contrast to economic parameters. On the whole, the most important information was the clinical information with the inclusion of one or more clinical parameters in 123 of the 124 HTAs in the sample. Economic information was present in 108 HTAs, whereas information about one or more organisational or patient-related parameters was only included in 53 and 45 HTAs.

5.3.1.5 HTA Score

Assuming equal weight to the parameters assessed in the sample, an estimation of an *HTA score* for each HTA report or project was possible. Each parameter was assigned a value of one if it were included in the HTA and the sum of the included parameters resulted in the HTA score for the report or project considered. With twenty-one parameters, the highest possible score was twenty-one. In the sample, the HTA reports with the highest score turned out to be the report about *The Role of Percutaneous Transluminal Coronary Angioplasty in Coronary Revascularization* from SBU (S1109) and the report about *Radiotherapy in Sweden* from SBU (S1120), both with a score of twelve. In Table 2.9 the mean and median values of the HTA scores for each institution are shown.

Table 2.9 : HTA Scores by Institutions - Mean Values. Median values in brackets.

	SBU N=19	Health Council N=13	AHTAC N=12	CCOHTA N=16	NCCHTA N=64	Total Weighted Mean
Clinical score	4.1 (4)	3.4 (3)	2.9 (3)	3.0 (3)	1.9 (2)	2.6
Economic score	1.5 (2)	0.6 (0)	1 (1)	2.1 (2)	1.3 (1)	1.4
Patient score	0.9 (1)	1.4 (1)	0.1 (0)	0.4 (0)	0.4 (0)	0.6
Organisation sco.	2.2 (2)	1.5 (1)	1.1 (1)	0.8 (0)	0.3 (0)	0.8
Total HTA score	8.7 (8)	6.9 (7)	5.1 (5)	6.2 (6)	3.9 (4)	5.4

* Total Weighted Mean (TWM) is the mean of each institution weighted by their sample size.[45]

---

[45]

$$TWM = \sum \frac{mean\ HTA\text{-}score_{institution} * N_{institution}}{N_{total}}$$

In the total sample (124 HTA reports or projects) the mean HTA score was 5.4 explaining that on average five parameters were assessed and included in HTA in those five countries.[46] The median value was five.

SBU had the highest mean HTA score (mean value of 8.7 and median values of 8.0) followed by the Health Council (mean value of 6.9 and median value of 7.0) implying that on average eight and seven parameters, respectively, were assessed in their technology assessments. The HTAs from CCOHTA (mean value of 6.2) captured six parameters on average, whereas five parameters were assessed in the assessments from AHTAC (mean value of 5.1). NCCHTA's HTAs had the lowest mean score of 3.9 (median value of 4), which explained why nearly four parameters on average would be addressed in the English HTA projects.

The non-parametric Kruskal-Wallis U test[47] was used to test whether the distribution of HTA scores of the reports was identical between the independent institutions in the sample. A statistical significant result with a Chi-square as high as 64.6 means that the hypothesis that there is an identical distribution of HTA scores between institutions (DF=4) could be rejected. Thus, the distribution of HTA score by the institutions was not identical. It supported the impression from Table 2.9, that the HTAs produced by some institutions were broader (includes several elements), than HTAs from other subgroups of institutions in the sample.

Summing up, the average HTAs produced by SBU, the Health Council and CCOHTA seemed broader than the average HTAs in England and Australia. However, knowing that the conclusions to be made from average-figures might be too general and miss important details on the contribution from each of the four main elements in the HTA, a more specific and qualitative analysis of the *comprehensive broad HTA* versus the *partial narrower HTA* is referred to in the next section.

5.3.2 Qualitative Analysis

A qualitative analysis was added to assess the HTAs with respect to HTA score and parameters assessed from the four main elements (clinical, economic, patient-related and organisational). On behalf of this the HTA sample was grouped into four different types of HTA - a *comprehensive broad HTA*, a *semi-comprehensive HTA*, a *semi-partial HTA* and a *partial HTA*. The purpose of this analysis was to investigate whether the individual HTA institution in the sample performed broad comprehensive HTAs or whether the HTAs produced tend to be narrower and more partial.

---

[46] The large number of English HTAs (64) and their relatively low mean value explains this low mean value for the total sample.

[47] The Kruskal-Wallis 1-way Anova test, a nonparametric version of the one-way analysis of variance (Mann-Whitney U Test), is used to test for identical distributions among g independent subpopulations. Calculations are based on the sum of the ranks of the combined groups.

5.3.2.1 Comprehensive Broad HTA

As the most ambitious of the four types of HTA the *comprehensive broad HTA* is generally defined as a technology assessment containing information from each of the four main elements. Three approaches to a comprehensive HTA with different requirements to be fulfilled were used in the analysis of the sample.

The first approach with the largest requirements to a comprehensive broad HTA followed the content of the chapters 7-10 in Banta et al. (1993) [10], which describe *how to assess health care technologies*. Assuming that this is the interpretation of a comprehensive HTA, it would include information about the parameters mentioned in Table 2.10 below.

Table 2.10 : Comprehensive Broad HTA
- Criteria based upon Banta et al. (1993) [10]

Parameters Assessed:
- Efficacy (or effectiveness)
- Safety
- Costs
- Socio-economic evaluation (CEA, CUA or CBA)
- Quality of life (outcomes)
- Social, legal, ethical values (social impact & ethics)

The review of the 124 HTA reports or projects of the sample revealed that none of the HTAs carried out by the five national HTA institutions contained all these nine parameters. Accordingly none of the HTAs in the sample could be classified as comprehensive broad HTAs on the basis of these strict criteria.

Relaxing the requirements, the second approach to a comprehensive broad HTA was defined as HTA that contained information about parameters from each of the four main elements and had an HTA score that was higher than a certain limit. As discussed in section 2 and revealed by the results in the descriptive part, the clinical and economic elements in the HTA seemed to be included in HTAs far more often than the patient-related and organisational elements. Therefore, the criteria for this approach to a comprehensive broad HTA demanded that at least two parameters from each of the clinical and economic elements and at least one parameter from each of the patient-related and organisational elements were contained in the HTA. The total number of the twenty-one parameters assessed had to be at least six (HTA score$\geq$ 6). In Table 2.11 below the criteria are listed.

Table 2.11 : Comprehensive Broad HTA
-weight on the clinical and economic elements

Parameters Assessed:	
- Clinical parameters	≥ 2
- Economic parameters	≥ 2
- Patient-related parameters	≥ 1
- Organisational parameters	≥ 1
- HTA score	≥ 6

Among the reviewed HTA reports or projects only ten HTAs fulfilled these criteria to be interpreted as comprehensive broad HTAs. SBU in Sweden made up the eight of these HTAs.[48] An example was the HTA report *Lithotripsy of Kidney Stones and Gallstones* (S1104), which contained information about four clinical parameters (*effectiveness, safety, indications & population affected*), two economic parameters (*costs & cost-effectiveness*), two patient-related parameters (*acceptability & psychological relations*) and three organisational parameters (*diffusion, centralization & skills-routines*). On average the eight Swedish assessments had assessed nearly ten parameters. The last two HTAs in the sample satisfying these criteria were a Dutch HTA *Heredity: Science and Society* (S3301) describing eleven parameters and an HTA from CCOHTA, Canada, *Magnetic Field Strength Issues in Magnetic Resonance Imaging (MRI)* describing seven parameters.

In the third approach to define a comprehensive HTA, the criteria were further relaxed by putting equal weights on the four main elements. Now HTA would be characterized as a comprehensive broad HTA, if it just contained some information from each of the four elements (at least one parameter assessed in each element). Table 2.12 shows the criteria.

Table 2.12 : Comprehensive Broad HTA
- equal weight to the four elements

Parameters Assessed:	
- Clinical parameters	≥ 1
- Economic parameters	≥ 1
- Patient-related parameters	≥ 1
- Organisational parameters	≥ 1
- HTA score	≥ 4

This resulted in seventeen *comprehensive broad HTAs*, or 14 per cent of the sample, which had included information in the HTA about at least one parameter from every element.

---

[48] S1101, S1104, S1106, S1109, S1112, S1114, S1115 & S1118.

More than half of these seventeen comprehensive HTAs were reports from SBU[49], which is the reason that 53 per cent of the Swedish HTA sample could be characterized as broad and comprehensive, following the criteria in Table 2.12. Among the HTA projects commissioned by NCCHTA three were planned as comprehensive HTAs[50] and two HTAs in the CCOHTA sample fulfilled as well the criteria to become a comprehensive HTA.[51] The last two comprehensive HTAs were from the Health Council in the Netherlands and from AHTAC, Australia, respectively.[52] The mean HTA score was eight, which tells us that on average eight parameters from the four elements were assessed in a comprehensive HTA. This distribution is shown in Table 2.13.

Table 2.13 : Types of Technology Assessments by Institutions in the Sample (N=124)

	Comprehensive HTA	Semi-Comprehensive HTA	Semi-Partial HTA	Partial HTA
SBU Sweden N=19	10 (53%*)	9 (47%*)		
Health Council NHL N=13	1 (8%*)	6 (46%*)	6 (46%*)	
AHTAC Australia N=12	1 (8%*)	3 (25%*)	8 (67%*)	
CCOHTA Canada N=16	2 (12%*)	7 (44%*)	7 (44%*)	
NCCHTA England N=64	3 (5%*)	24 (38%*)	35 (55%*)	2 (3%*)
TOTAL N=124	17 (14%+)	49 (40%+)	56 (45%+)	2 (2%+)
Mean HTA Score (an integer)	8	6	4	3

* per cent of the country-specific sample   +per cent of the total sample

5.3.2.2 Semi-Comprehensive HTA

The second type of HTA was called a *semi-comprehensive HTA* and was defined as an HTA that assessed parameters from three of the four main elements. As shown in Table

---

[49] S1101, S1104, S1106, S1109, S1110, S1111, S1112, S1114, S1115 & S1118.

[50] S2204, S2240 & S2257.

[51] S5507 & S5512.

[52] S3301 & S4405.

2.13, forty-nine in the reviewed HTA sample (40 per cent) meet this criterion with a mean HTA score of six, which was the reason that six parameters would be assessed on average in this semi-comprehensive type of HTA. Approximately half the Swedish, Dutch and Canadian HTA reports could be characterized as semi-comprehensive. The most likely semi-comprehensive HTA in the sample was an HTA that had assessed parameters from the clinical, economic and organisational elements, like in twenty-four of the semi-comprehensive HTAs. In another twenty semi-comprehensive HTAs parameters from the clinical, economic and patient-related elements were assessed. An example of a semi-comprehensive HTA was *Stereotactic Radiotherapy* (S3308) from the Health Council in the Netherlands. This HTA described three clinical parameters (*safety, effectiveness, indications*), one economic parameter (*costs*) and three organisational parameters (*diffusion, centralization, skills-routines*).

5.3.2.3 Semi-Partial HTA

A *semi-partial HTA* was defined as an HTA that only contained information from parameters of two elements, e.g. *efficacy* and *safety* from the clinical element, and *cost-effectiveness* from the economic element. Nearly half the HTA sample (45 per cent) could be described as semi-partial in nature with four parameters assessed on average, see Table 2.13.[53] Among the reports from AHTAC in Australia, it was as much as 67 per cent and for NCCHTA projects it was 55 per cent. On the other hand no HTA reports from SBU were classified as semi-partial. The most frequent semi-partial HTA would have assessed parameters from the clinical and economic elements, like forty-six of the fifty-six semi-partial HTAs. An example of a semi-partial HTA in the sample is the report from CCOHTA on *Chiropractic Treatment of neck and back disorders: A Review of Selected Studies* (S5505), which included information on three clinical parameters (*efficacy, effectiveness, population affected*) and on three economic parameters (*efficiency, costs, cost-effectiveness*).

5.3.2.4 Partial HTA

Finally, a *partial HTA* was a narrower HTA approach, where there was only focus on one element, as for example in a clinical trial. In the sample only two English HTA projects[54] appeared to be partial HTAs, see Table 2.13. The clinical element turned out to be the only focus in these HTAs. An example was the English HTA project *Screening for stroke* (S2207), planning to assess parameters as *efficacy, effectiveness* and *indications*.

---

[53] 56 reports or projects.

[54] S2207 & S2242.

5.3.2.5 Conclusion

Despite the definitions of HTA made by the national institutions this qualitative analysis revealed that in practice the technology assessments produced, at least in the five countries considered, were far from all being of the broad and comprehensive type, although this to a higher degree was the case with HTAs from SBU.[55] The overall picture of the sample, as presented in Table 2.13, is illustrated in Figure 2.2 below.

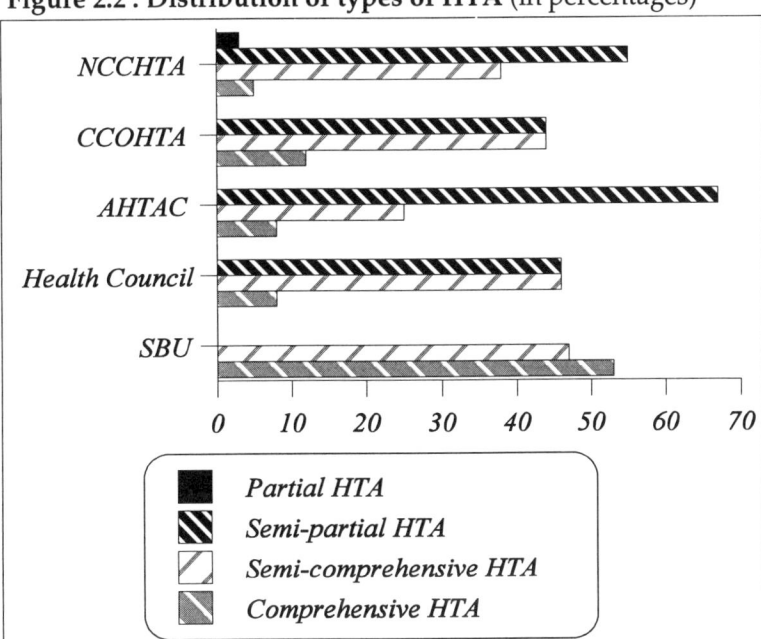

Figure 2.2 : Distribution of types of HTA (in percentages)

The non-parametric Kruskal-Wallis 1-way Anova test was used to test whether the distribution of the variable *type of HTA* was identical among the five institutions in the sample. A statistically significant result with a Chi-square value at 31.6 leads to the rejection on the 5 per cent level.[56] The conclusion was then that the distribution of the four types of HTA by the institutions was different, because they did not come from the same population with the same median. This means that some institutions put a higher effort into broad and comprehensive HTAs or on the other hand partial HTAs compared with other institutions.

---

[55] The specific classification of each HTA report or project with respect to *type of HTA* could be seen in Appendix 2.3.

[56] This is true even on the 1 per cent level.

A Mann-Whitney U test[57] was performed for each paired combination of the five groups of institutions to see whether there was any systematism among the countries with respect to the distribution of types of HTAs.[58] The most interesting results were that the distribution of types of HTAs from SBU was statistically significantly rejected as being identical with the HTA distributions from the other institutions. This statistically significant result corresponded with the impression given in Table 2.13 of the distribution of HTAs from SBU, which both seemed to be more broad and comprehensive compared with the other institutions.[59]

Restricted to the exploratory approach in the present chapter an interesting finding was that the group of Swedish SBU-reports tended to be the broadest and most comprehensive with 53 per cent *comprehensive* HTA reports and the rest of the reports classified as *semi-comprehensive* HTAs. This was consistent with the previously mentioned high mean HTA score for the Swedish HTAs. In percentages CCOHTA and the Health Council seemed to produce the second most comprehensive HTAs, because 56 per cent of the Canadian reports and 54 per cent of the Dutch reports were either *comprehensive* or *semi-comprehensive*.[60] NCCHTA in England was the only institution that has planned to produce HTAs belonging to each of the four types. The reports from SBU were only of the *comprehensive* and *semi-comprehensive* type, whereas the reports from CCOHTA, the Health Council and AHTAC were of the *comprehensive, semi-comprehensive* and *semi-partial* types. The Australian HTAs from AHTAC, together with the English HTAs, seemed, however, to be narrower and more partial in their approach.[61]

5.4 Discussion

5.4.1 Bias in the study

Results from a comparative study have certain limitations due to different kinds of bias that infer upon the validity and reliability. The interpretation of data in a review study is subjective to some degree, although certain criteria for the review are specified. Bias in the study could be divided into bias in the data sample collected and bias in the method used.

---

[57] Test the null hypothesis that two independent samples come from the same populations. As the Kruskal-Wallis test, it is based on the ranks of each sample.

[58] Ten combinations of five institutions resulted in ten Mann-Whitney U tests.

[59] The distribution of HTAs from SBU is right-tailed, as indicated in Figure 2.2.

[60] These conclusions drawn on the behalf of percentages are of course biased by the very different country-specific sample sizes.

[61] 55 per cent of the English HTA projects and 67 per cent of the Australian HTAs showed to be semi-partial projects.

5.4.1.1 Bias in the Data Sample

Some sort of *selection bias* was of course present in the sample, due to the search criteria made for the data collection.[62] First, institutions that are not considered as national institutions were left out of the study, although some regional HTA institutions have been very active in the field for years and have produced many reports, as for example CETS' 21 HTAs [55]. Furthermore, the sample of HTA reports or projects was restricted to reports written in English or Scandinavian languages. The consequence of this criterion was that institutions without any HTA reports written in these languages failed to be a part of the comparative study, as was the case with ANDEM in France. Among the institutions compared, the language criteria limited the Dutch sample too, because some of the most interesting HTA reports from the Health Council turned out not to have been translated into English.[63] Therefore, a selection bias was present in the selection of the Dutch sample used in this study. A selection bias might further have resulted in a lack of completeness in the sample by not including the Sick Fund Council (the Netherlands) and the Pharmaceutical Benefit Scheme (Australia), which both as national institutions produce or request pharmaceutical assessments and on the other hand include reports from a Pharmaceutical Assessment Program at CCOHTA (Canada). This apparent division of labour between institutions in some countries opposed to other countries and the exclusion of some relevant institutions, e.g. the Sick Fund Council in the Netherlands, might have threatened the internal validity of the study. The size of the problem will be revealed in the future, if an extended comparative study is made, where the eventual missing institutions can be included in a larger sample.

The material collected for the sample was very *heterogeneous*. Because a certain *HTA report standard* does not exist but depends upon the institution in question and their working methods, the reports included in the sample were very different in their form, varying from voluminous reports to minor *pamphlet-like* reports. This was the reason that literature review was used as the method instead of a formal meta-analysis. The problem of heterogeneity was further underlined by the inclusion of project abstracts instead of final reports, which was the case with the English sample of project-notes, because no final HTA reports were published at the time of data collection. Furthermore, the country-specific samples turned out to be very different in size. This might limit the degree of comparability of the country-specific samples included.

---

[62] The question of internal validity, which means whether an experiment actually caused what it appeared to cause, or whether there were other factors in the conduct of the experiment which distorted the true experimental purpose [54].

[63] Personal correspondence with Dr. ten Velden, the Health Council. Some of these HTA reports only written in Dutch have considered technologies as transplantation (kidney, heart, liver, pancreas, lung & bone-marrow), vaccination, artificial reproduction, neurosurgery, radiotherapy, diagnostics, cytokines, growth hormone, epo for dialysis anemia, autologous transfusion, breast cancer screening.

However, it is believed that the benefits of the comparison more than outweigh this likely criticism.

A time span of seven years in the sample (1989-1996) could furthermore bias the comparability of the sample. As the HTA field has evolved from the clinical field with a broad comprehensive definition, the implications of a seven-year span in time could be that the content of the assessments performed has shifted over time. Thus the consequences of a time span upon the result in *type of HTA* and *HTA score* was examined in the study. This investigation showed a decreasing tendency in the HTA score over time and a corresponding increase in the more partial-oriented HTAs over time. The findings are consistent with the historical evolution with technology assessment introduced as a holistic and comprehensive assessment discussed in section 2. However, on behalf of this limited analysis of the impact of time it was not possible to make any final conclusions whether the form of the HTAs has shifted over time. A reason for this was the presence of the bias in the English sample with respect to the time span, because the projects were registered according to their start, which biased the time span towards the end of the sample (1995-1996).

5.4.1.2 Bias in the Method Used

When doing a literature review certain review criteria have to be made explicit, why each report in the sample was reviewed with respect to a number of parameters assessed. The parameters assessed were generally defined according to the theoretically defined concepts from the literature. These definitions are the ones that are also used in the HTA reports in practice, which is especially the case with respect to the clinical and economic parameters. Thus the measured data would reflect the theoretical concepts, indicating a high *validity of data* (face validity). This is not the case with the patient-related and organisational parameters due to uncertainty about the theoretical definitions.

With respect to the use of the English project-notes risk appears that the importance of some of the parameters were underestimated, e.g. population affected, because the information from the English HTA projects was only based on short abstracts describing what they intended to assess and not what they actually did assess and include in an HTA report. On the other hand a risk appears too that the two clinical parameters, *efficacy* and *effectiveness*, were overestimated in the sample, because of an apparent confusion of the concepts. The typical example would be the HTA project planning to perform *a randomized controlled trial comparing outcome and resource use in acute stroke patients.... to provide information of the effectiveness of alternative strategies of stroke management* (S2204). This project is registered in the sample as containing both efficacy (information from the RCT) and effectiveness information. However, this problem of overestimation was not only present in the English sample.

An uncertainty about definitions of the patient-related and organisational parameters raises the question, whether the parameters included in the two elements were *exhaustive*. However, the opportunity to group the parameters in a *different* category (*other patient-related parameters* and *other organisational parameters*), when the existing parameters were not suitable, reduced the bias from an eventual insufficient exhaustiveness.

When collecting data the risk of *measurement errors* of the defined variables would always exist when comparing reports in a review, e.g. whether *efficiency* is interpreted and measured in the same way in every report following its operational definition. This is the question of reliability of the data collected and analysed. To secure a high reliability in the study with respect to measurement errors caused by bias in the interpretation, the data matrix was reviewed twice in all directions. Initially a horizontal review following each case (report or project). After the analysis of data was finished, a second review was made vertically across the cases following each variable to limit the likely bias in doing a review. Furthermore, having the same person to review the data did also reduce some of the measurement errors due to differences in interpretation. However, the method used in the study could not eliminate measurement and typing errors in the reports or project notes caused by its authors.

When estimating *HTA scores* and grouping them into four *types of HTA* for each of the reviewed reports and project notes in the sample, an equal weight was assumed for each parameter assessed who formed the HTA score and type of HTA. However, the number of parameters in each element was different. This could lead to the argument that the parameters should have been weighted according to their relative explanation of the elements, so that for example each clinical parameter explained one-sixth of the clinical element, whereas a patient parameter explained one-fourth of the patient element. The implication would be that other results emerge than those presented in the study. The reason behind not weighting them was that there is no evidence given in this study and in the literature that some of the parameters assessed should have higher weights compared with others in HTA.

The results found in the analysis of *types of HTA* depend on the definitions used, which was the reason that the validity of the criteria for the different types of HTA perhaps could be questioned. However, the HTA definition given in section 2 as a broad and comprehensive assessment, including information from each of the four elements, motivated the criteria for a comprehensive HTA. The three other criteria for the less comprehensive HTAs had been defined in similar ways. The explicitly stated criteria will make it possible for people interested to replicate and arrive at the same results and conclusions as those in this study.

5.4.2 The Results of the Study

With a pure exploratory purpose this international comparative study of five national HTA agencies revealed three noteworthy findings. Among the HTA agencies compared there was almost a consensus with respect to the definition used for health technology assessment, as a broad, comprehensive assessment that assesses information about clinical, economic, patient-related and organisational parameters. The definition of HTA in England (SGHT/NCCHTA) could be one exception, as it is limited to *the production of high quality research information on costs, effectiveness and broader impact on health technologies* [50].

Firstly, as the most important finding in the comparative study, the review of the sample of HTA reports revealed that health technology assessment, when it was used for practical purposes as in a report, often had a more partial interpretation. Only 17 of the 124 HTAs reviewed (14 per cent) could be considered as broad and comprehensive HTAs that include at least one parameter from each of the four elements (clinical, economic, patient-related and organisational).[64] In contrast to this as many as 58 of the reviewed HTA report or projects had used a more partial approach, only including information from one or two of the elements. These HTAs would typically focus upon clinical and economic information, such as an HTA presenting information about the *effectiveness, safety, efficacy* and *population affected*, as well as the *costs* and *cost-effectiveness* in the assessment of a health technology or it would simply be an *RCT* or a *cost-effectiveness analysis*, in accordance with the English and Canadian samples.

With respect to the national HTA institutions compared, it could be concluded from the results in the study that the Swedish technology assessments made by SBU were characterized by being the broadest and most comprehensive ones, because all the Swedish reports could be classified as either comprehensive or semi-comprehensive HTAs. Quoting Battista et al. (1995) [1] these broader and value-based HTAs would usually be closer to the policy paradigm in a bridging role between science and policy. Some of the HTAs made by CCOHTA, Canada (56 per cent) and the Health Council, the Netherlands (54 per cent) showed this tendency too. Opposed to this, the HTA projects put forward in England under the control of NCCHTA seemed to have used a more partial (and scientific) approach in their technology assessment programme, because nearly two-thirds of the HTA projects included in the English sample were planned as partial assessments.[65] In the terminology of Battista et al. (1995), the role of these technology assessments would to a higher degree be towards the science end of the science-policy spectrum (*the pure scientific paradigm*) [1].

This result is further confirmed by summing up the parameters assessed in each HTA (the HTA score), where the Swedish reports from SBU turned out to be the broadest HTAs with nearly nine parameters assessed on average. Four parameters were on the other hand planned to be assessed in the HTA projects from NCCHTA suggesting the more partial HTA approach in England.

The second major finding in the comparative study concerned the focus of the information in health technology assessments. The sample of HTA reports and projects

---

[64] Only 10 reports or projects fulfilled the stronger requirements as illustrated in Table 2.11 for a comprehensive broad HTA.

[65] Semi-partial and partial HTAs, as cost-effectiveness analysis and RCTs.

supported the tendency shown in the literature that the primary focus in the HTAs performed is upon the clinical and economic elements. For each institution in the sample the most important parameter assessed at all was *effectiveness*, as a topic chosen in 77 per cent of the HTAs. In general *safety* and *efficacy* were the two second most frequently addressed clinical parameters (46 and 44 per cent respectively), although with some variation. The institution who had put the highest emphasis on the parameters in the clinical element was SBU (especially *effectiveness, indication, safety, & population affected*). Considerations of the economical parameter, *costs*, were overall a part of two-thirds of the HTAs, whereas the question of *cost-effectiveness* was answered in half of the HTAs. Types of evaluation as *cost-utility* and *cost-benefit* were, however, very seldom included in HTA. HTAs from CCOHTA, SBU and NCCHTA did most frequently include the economic element, whereas reports from the Health Council, as the only agency, had a relatively little focus on this element. This result would, however, probably be different in a study setup, where the Sick Fund Council is included in the Dutch sample, because they primarily commission cost-effectiveness analyses.

On the other hand, parameters concerning the patient-related and organisational elements were less frequently part of an assessment. However, this result could not be generalized to the Health Council, because the patient-related and organisational parameters were often addressed in their reports.

The third major finding dealt with the methods used in producing a health technology assessment. The most frequently used method when making an HTA was literature review or systematic review of the literature, which was the case in about two-thirds of the HTAs in the sample. With methods like meta-analysis, this result illustrated that HTA is based upon secondary research with the use and dissemination of existing available scientific information. Sometimes a gathering of new information would be made too, typically by performing an economic evaluation or by using survey methods. However, an interesting detail in the previous mentioned statement that HTA is secondary research was that one-third of the English HTA projects started were designed as (new) randomized controlled trials with the prospective collection of data (primary research).

Overall, the results from the study prove that HTA, when used in practice, often has a more partial interpretation than the one supporting the broad and comprehensive *OTA-like* definition. The result found in this study was consistent with the new recommendation given for an adjusted definition on HTA made in EUR-ASSESS. The European group recommended that HTA should still be defined as a broad and comprehensive assessment, examining short and long-term consequences of the application of a health technology to provide inputs to decision making in policy and practice. However, *given this broad context, HTA is not defined by a set of methods but by its intent* [24]. Therefore a randomized clinical trial (RCT) or a cost-effectiveness analysis, both with the prospective collection of data, done for policy reasons would also be considered as health technology assessment. This is equivalent to the empirical results in the study. However, although prospective research is increasingly being done as part of HTA, the result needs to be viewed in the context of existing knowledge [56].[66]

An explanation for the comprehensiveness of HTA and thereby the chosen content of HTA could be that it depends on the information needed to be able to make a certain decision. This holds true for most of the HTA reports from the Health Council, because they strongly depend on the policy question formulated by the Dutch government, i.e. the Minister of Health. This means that the emphasis in the councils HTAs is on the parameters asked for in the policy question. An example is the report about *Genetic Screening* (S3309), where the policy question formulated by the State Secretary for Welfare, Health and Cultural Affairs dealt with the level of technical development with regard to screening for hereditary disorders, screening methods, risks indicators (S3309). However, a precise explanation for the comprehensiveness of HTA was not investigated further, as it was out of scope for the present study.

5.4.3 The Implications of the Study for HTA in Denmark

This international comparative study showed some noteworthy conclusions that might be generalized to an intensified HTA effort in Denmark in the years to come and would accordingly have implications for the Danish Institute for Health Technology Assessment and other Danish HTA initiatives, in order for the production and use of technology assessment to be effective and efficient.

Although in keeping with a broad and comprehensive definition of HTA at the national institutions, the study shows that HTA carried out in practice by the institutions compared has a more partial and narrower interpretation. Their stated *OTA-like* definition is not used as a stereotype form for the HTAs performed, because the content of the HTAs from each institution varies from report to report.

This seems, however, to have been the case with the first Danish health technology assessment report on Beta-interferon produced by the Health Technology Assessment Committee at the National Board of Health in 1995-96 [31]. In making this report, the broad, comprehensive Danish HTA definition, with its focus upon all four elements (clinical, economic, patient-related and organisational), is used as the model and eleven parameters from those elements are addressed. However, in making a decision regarding the use of Beta-interferon in the treatment of multiple sclerosis, for which problem the hospital authorities requested the report, the only information used to select the patients relevant for treatment seemed to be the clinical and epidemiological information. One could furthermore argue that information on the perspective of the county councils regarding the economic consequences was lacking in the report. This information would, however, be important in the treatment implementation of the

---

[66] This is opposed to clinical research or clinical trials done for the purpose of increasing scientific knowledge and not necessarily influencing decision making [24].

treatment, because the county councils, as the hospital owners, are responsible for a provision of Beta-interferon and thus would have to bear the economic burden of this decision. This might have been the reason that it took the county councils so long time to implement the recommendations given in the HTA.

The implication internationally and for Denmark in particular of the results found in this study, as well as the modified definition of HTA in EUR-ASSESS, would be that the content of HTA should be allowed to vary depending on the information needed for the authorities to be able to decide upon an issue - *the policy reason*. Because HTA is defined by its intent. The focus upon policy is also reflected in the first two steps in the HTA process, *1. identify and define a policy question to be answered and then 2. formulate the assessment question or questions* [56]. The consequence is then that HTA does not always have to be of the broad and comprehensive type, but might also have a more partial form, such as a cost-effectiveness analysis of a health technology, depending on the decision making process for which HTA information is requested. However, the broad and comprehensive type is not rejected, because it would generally be a useful strategy to get some clarification about specific technologies or diseases, e.g. as the HTA report about back pain [57]. An efficient and rational HTA procedure demands that the choice of information to be included have to be made initially at the time of the request for HTA, as with the Dutch HTAs from the Health Council. If this strategy is not realistic, the focus on relevant information is the very important task in the synthesis.

The results and the conclusions made in this international comparative study of health technology assessment would be important for the Danish Institute for Health Technology Assessment and the technology assessments that the institute intends to commission in the future, and other Danish initiatives on Health technology assessment, in order to ensure an effective HTA strategy and an efficient use of scarce resources for technology assessment in Denmark.

5.4.4 A Future Perspective of the Comparative Study

As the discussion has revealed, the study has of course some limitations in the results and conclusions achieved. This was a consequence of the use of project-notes instead of reports for the English sample and the limitation in the number of institutions (and thereby HTA reports) included in the study, because of the selection criteria made, e.g. in language, and limited time resources. However, the comparative study of the health technology assessments presented so far can be regarded as a preliminary study made before an extended study is carried out. In the future, it is therefore a hope that the international comparative study can be extended with additional countries and their national or regional HTA institutions. These HTA institutions could be some of the institutions participating in the international INAHTA network of agencies for health technology assessment, besides those institutions already included. With an exploratory approach an extended review would provide a more thorough picture of the HTA field and the assessments carried out with respect to the definitions and methods used in practice.

References

1. Battista RN, Hodge MJ. The Development of Health Care Technology Assessment. An International Perspective. International Journal of Technology Assessment in Health Care 1995;11(2):287-300.

2. Danish National Board of Health. National Strategy for Health Technology Assessment. The Health Technology Assessment Committee of the Danish National Board of Health. Copenhagen, 1996.

3. Banta D. Putting Healthcare to the Test. The Science of Healthcare Technology Asessment. Odyssey 1996;2(1):18-24.

4. US Congress, Office of Technology Assessment. Development of Medical Technology: Opportunities for Assessment. Washington, DC: US Government Printing Office, 1976.

5. Balaban DJ, Goldfarb NI. Medical Evaluation of Health Care Technologies. Chapter 2 in Culyer AJ, Horisberger B. (ed.). Economic and Medical Evaluation of Health Care Technologies. Symposium April 1982, Wolfsberg, Switzerland. Springer-Verlag. Berlin, 1983.

6. US Congress, Office of Technology Assessment. Strategies for medical technology assessment. Washington, DC: U.S. Government Printing Office, 1982.

7. Fuchs VR, Garber AM. The New Technology Assessment. The New England Journal of Medicine 1990;323(10):673-677.

8. Jørgensen T, Danneskiold-Samsøe B. Medicinsk Teknologivurdering -hvordan? Dansk Sygehus Institut. DSI-Rapport 86.02. København, 1986.

9. Goodman C. It's time to rethink Health Care Technology Assessment. International Journal of Technology Assessment in Health Care 1992;8(2):335-358.

10. Banta HD, Luce BR. Health Care Technology and its Assessment. An International Perspective. Oxford University Press, Oxford, 1993.

11. Menon D, Marshall DM. The Internationalization of Health Technology Assessment. International Journal of Technology Assessment in Health Care 1996;12(1):45-51.

12. Institute of Medicine. Assessing Medical Technologies. National Academy Press. Washington, DC, 1985.

13. Banta HD. Technology Assessment and Policy Making. Chapter 3 in Banta HD. (ed.). Ressources for Health. Technology Assessment and Policy Making. Praeger Special Studies. Praeger Publishers. New York, 1982.

14. Jennett B. High technology medicine. Benefits and burdens. Oxford Medical Publications. Oxford University Press, Oxford, 1986.

15. Neugebauer E, Ure BM, Lefering R, Eypasch EP, Troidl H. Technology Assessment of Endoscopic Surgery. Acta Neurochirogie 1994;suppl.61:13-19.

16. Steering Committee on Future Health Scenarios. Anticipating and Assessing Health Care Technology. Volume 1. General Considerations and Policy Conclusions. Martinus Nijhoff Publishers, 1987.

17. Garber AM. Can Technology Assessment Control Health Spending? Health Affairs 1994;13(3):115-126.

18. Banta HD. Pushing the Limits: Technology Assessment in Health Care. Text of an Inaugural Address Given at the State University Limburg in Maastricht, The Netherlands. Elinkwijk, Utrecht, May 17, 1990.

19. Banta HD, Behney CJ, Sisk Willem J. Toward a Rational Technology in Medicine. Considerations for Health Policy. Springer Publishing Company. New York, 1981.

20. US Congress, Office of Technology Assessment. The Implications of Cost-Effectiveness Analysis of Medical Technology: Methodological Issues and Literature Review. Washington, DC: US Government Printing Office, 1980.

21. Hørder M. Medicinsk teknologivurdering, hvordan - hvorfor? Ugeskrift for Læger 1993;155(4):3622-3624.

22. Swedish Council on Technology Assessment in Health Care. Health Care Technology Assessment Programs. - A review of selected programs in different countries. Stockholm, February 1993.

23. Luce BR, Brown RE. The Use of Technology Assessments by Hospitals, Health Maintenance Organizations, and Third-Party Payers in the United States. International Journal of Technology Assessment in Health Care 1995;11(1):79-92.

24. Banta HD, Werkö L, Cranovsky R, Granados A, Henshall C, Jonsson E, Liberati A, Matillion Y, Sheldon T. Introduction to the EUR-ASSESS Report, pp.133-143. In the Special Section *Report from the EUR-ASSESS Project* in the International Journal of Technology Assessment in Health Care 1997;13(2):133-340.

25. Buch Andreasen P. Medicinsk Teknologivurdering. Nyttiggørelse af lægevidenskabelige forskningsresultater i sundhedsvæsenet. Rapport til Folketingets udvalg angående videnskabelig forskning. København, 1980.

26. Jørgensen T. Teknologivurdering. Dansk Sygehus Institut. DSI-Specialrapport 80.07. København, 1980.

27. Sundhedsstyrelsen. Medicinsk Teknologivurdering - hvad er det? København, 1994.

28. Statens Lægevidenskabelige Forskningsråd. Rapport fra konferencen Helsetjenesteforskning og medicinsk teknologivurdering. Udvalget for helsetjenesteforskning og medicinsk teknologivurdering. København, 31. August 1982.

29. Kamper-Jørgensen F. Medicinsk teknologivurdering. Månedsskrift for praktisk lægegerning 1989;67(12):957-976.

30. Sundhedsministeriet. Rapport fra Udvalget vedrørende Sygehusvæsenets økonomi. København, April 1994.

31. Sundhedsstyrelsen. β-interferon behandling af patienter med dissemineret sklerose. Sundhedsstyrelsens Udvalg for Medicinsk Teknologivurdering. København, 1996.

32. Poulsen PB, Hørder M, Jørgensen T. Fremtidens medicinske metoder - tidlig varsling i international og dansk perspektiv. Sundhedsstyrelsens Udvalg for Medicinsk Teknologivurdering. Sundhedsstyrelsen. København, 1996.

33. INAHTA. INAHTA Newsletter. December 1996.

34. Layard PRG, Walters AA. Micro-Economic Theory. McGraw-Hill. New York, 1978.

35. Feeny D, Stoddart G. Towards Improved Health Technology Policy in Canada: A Proposal for the National Health Technology Assessment Council. Canadian Public Policy 1988;14(3):254-265.

36. Danneskiold-Samsøe B. Technology Assessment Activities in Denmark. Technology Assessment Reports. International Journal of Technology Assessment in Health Care 1991;7(1):76-83.

37. Moatti JP, Chanut C, Benech JM. Researcher-Driven versus Policy-Driven Economic Appraisal of Health Technologies: The Case of France. Social Science and Medicine 1994;38(12):1625-1633.

38. Statens Beredning för Utvärdering av Medicinsk Metodik. Preoperative Rutiner. Statens Beredning för Utvärdering av Medicinsk Metodik. Stockholm, Maj 1989.

39. Swedish Council on Technology Assessment in Health Care. Literature Searching and Evidence Interpretation for Assessing Health Care Practices. Stockholm, 1993.

40. Perry S, Gardner E, Thamer M. The Status of Health Technology Assessment Worlwide: Results of an International Survey. The International Journal of Technology Assessment in Health Care 1997;13(1):81-98.

41. US Congress, Office of Technology Assessment. Assessing the Efficacy and Safety of Medical Technologies. Washington, DC: US Government Printing Office, 1978.

42. Drummond MF, Stoddart GL, Torrance GW. Methods for Economic Evaluation of Health Care Programmes. Oxford Medical Publication. Oxford University Press, Oxford, 1987.

43. US Congress, Office of Technology Assessment. The Implications of Cost-Effectiveness Analysis of Medical Technology. Washington, DC: US Government Printing Office, 1980.

44. Briggs A, Sculpher M. Sensitivity Analysis in Economic Evaluation : A Review of Published Studies. Health Economics 1995;4:355-371.

45. Swedish Council on Technology Assessment in Health Care's homepage on the internet. Http://www.sbu.se/sbu-info.html, 1997.

46. ten Velden GHM. Taxonomy of Health Technology Assessment (TA). The Health Council. The Hague, 20 September 1995.

47. Commonwealth Department of Health and Family Services. Assessing health care technology in Australia. Diagnostics and Technology Branch. Canberra, 1996.

48. Canadian Coordinating Centre for Health Technology Assessment's homepage on the internet. Http://www.ccohta.ca/english/who.htm.

49. Department of Health. Report of the NHS Health Technology Assessment Programme 1995. Research and Development Directorate. Leeds, October 1995.

50. NHS Executive. Report of the NHS Health Technology Assessment Programme 1996. NHS Executive. June 1996.

51. Littell CL. Innovation in Medical Technology: Reading the Indicators: Datawatch. Health Affairs Millwood 1994;13(3):226-235.

52. Sassi F. Health Technology Assessment. An Introduction. Eurohealth 1996;2(4):9-10.

53. Banta HD, Oortwijn WJ, van Beekum WT. The Organization of Health Care Technology Assessment in the Netherlands. TNO Prevention and Health. Report produced on the behalf of the Rathenau Institute, The Hague, 1995.

54. Baker TL. Doing Social Research. International Edition. Sociology Series. McGraw-Hill Book Company, 1988.

55. Jacob R, McGregor M. Assessing the impact of health technology assessment. International Journal of Technology Assessment in Health Care 1997;13:68-80.

56. Liberati A, Sheldon TA, Banta HD (eds.). EUR-ASSESS Project Subgroup on Methodology. Methodological Guidance for the Conduct of Health Technology Assessment. International Journal of Technology Assessment in Health Care 1997;13(2):186-219

57. Sundhedsstyrelsen. Ondt i ryggen. En kortlægning af problemets forekomst og oplæg til dets håndtering i et MTV-perspektiv. Sundhedsstyrelsens Udvalg for Medicinsk Teknologivurdering. København, 1997.

58. Feldt K-O. Värdering av medicinska metoder och sjukvårdens ekonomi. In SBU. Värdering av medicinska metoder och sjukvårdens effektivitet. Rapport från SBU-konferens på Rosenbad den 25 november 1988. January 1989.

59. Jonsson E, Banta HD. Health care technology in Sweden. Health Policy 1994;30:257-294.

60. Bos M. Health care technology in the Netherlands. Health Policy 1994;30:207-255.

61. ten Velden G. Medical technology assessment (TA) and health policy in the Netherlands. Paper presented at the Nordic Conference on *Critical choices in the health care sector - relevant basis for decisions through Medical Technology Assessment*. Copenhagen 26-27th April 1994.

62. Hailey DM. Health care technology in Australia. Health Policy 1994;30:23-72.

63. Hailey DM. The influence of technology assessements by advisory bodies on health policy and practice. Health Policy 1993;25:243-254.

64. Battista RN, Jacob R, Hodge MJ. Health care technology in Canada (with special reference to Quebec). Health Policy 1994;30:73-122.

65. The Alberta Implementation Committee for Health Technology Assessment. Report Of The Alberta Implementation Committee For Health Technology Assessment, 22 October 1993.

66. Canadian Coordinating Office for Health Technology Assessment. Technology Assessment: National and International Perspectives on Research and Practice. Summary of Proceedings. Editors E. Clark & D. Marshall. (Revised Edition). A Satellite Symposium of the Eighth Annual Meeting of ISTAHC. CCOHTA. Ottawa, June 13, 1992.

67. Battista RN, Feeny DH, Hodge MJ. Evaluation of the Canadian Coordinating Office for Health Technology Assessment. International Journal of Technology Assessment in Health Care 1995;11(1):102-116.

68. Spiby J. Health care technology in the United Kingdom. Health Policy 1994;30:295-334.

69. Department of Health. Assessing the Effects of Health Technologies. Paper prepared by the Advisory Group on Health Technology Assessment for the Director of R&D, 1992.

APPENDIX 2.1 : Used Abbreviations (INAHTA institutions - list not exhaustive)

AETS	- Agency for Evaluation of Health Technologies, Spain
AHCPR	- Agency for Health Care Policy and Research, the United States (Federal government)
AHTAC	- Australian Health Technology Advisory Committee, Australia
ANAES	- L'Agence Nationale pour l'Accréditation et l'Evaluation en Santé, France (the new name of ANDEM in 1997)
ANDEM	- L'Agence pour le developpement de l'evaluation medicale, France
ASSR	- Agenzia per i Servizi Sanitari Regionali, Italy
CETS	- Conseil d'Evaluation des Technologies de la Santé, Quebec, Canada
CCOHTA	- Canadian Coordinationg Office for Health Technology Assessment
DIHTA	- Danish Institute for Health Technology Assessment, Denmark
FinOHTA	- Finnish Office for Health Technology Assessment, Finland
HCOHTA	- Hungarian Coordinating Office for Health Technology Assessment
INAHTA	- International Network of Agencies for Health Technology Assessment
OHTA	- Office of Health Technology Assessment, the United States (today a part of AHCPR)
OTA	- Office of Technology Assessment, the United States (closed down in 1995)
NCHCT	- National Center for Health Care Technology, the United States (Congress) (closed down in 1994 - activities overtaken by OHTA)
NHTAP	- National Health Technology Advisory Panel, Australia (closed in 1990 and the activity overtaken by AHTAC, Australia)
NCCHTA	- National Co-ordinating Centre for Health Technology Assessment, UK
SBU	- The Swedish Council on Technology Assessment in Health Care, Sweden
SGHT	- Standing Group on Health Technology, NHS R&D, UK
SMM	- The Norwegian Centre for Health Technology Assessment, Norway

APPENDIX 2.2 : Description of the Institutions Included in the Comparative Study

The Swedish Council on Technology Assessment in Health Care, Sweden

The Swedish health care system, mainly tax-financed, could be characterized as a regionalised system with the county councils responsible for the supply. However, to be able to prioritize and make more rational choices among an increasing number of new technologies emerging and rapidly diffused into the sector, as well as the increased costs, health technology assessment was early seen as an important tool [32].

The Swedish Council on Technology Assessment in Health Care (SBU - Statens beredning för medicinsk utvärdering) was established by the Swedish government in 1987 as a national health technology assessment institute with the purpose to critically assess the methods and technologies used in the health care sector. SBU should provide the government and the county councils with scientific facts about the overall value of health technologies with a special focus on new technologies [58]. By the overall value was understood not only medical information, but also the economic, social and ethical consequences of the diffusion and use of health technologies. SBU's mandate was to coordinate the technology assessment activity at the national level, identify and assess important new and existing health technologies and to disseminate this knowledge to the users. Since 1992, SBU has acted as a permanent and independent body.

As can be seen from Table 2.3 in section 5, SBU defines HTA as the assessment of medical, ethical, social and economic impact of health technologies - a rather broad *OTA-like* definition. Because cost-containment was never the main aim, a narrower and more partial definitions of HTA were not aimed at [59].

Each HTA project started by the SBU Board of Directors involves the formation of a working group to work on the project for about two years, starting with a critical literature review, and ending up with a final synthesis made by SBU. This production process demands considerable resources, which could explain why only 19 reports, which are considered as technology assessments, have been disseminated by SBU between 1989 and 1996. These reports form the Swedish sample of HTAs produced in the comparative study.

The Health Council, the Netherlands

The Dutch health care system is a mix of public and private initiatives, under the umbrella of the central government [60]. Health care is both publicly and privately supplied (non-profit independent hospitals). The financing of health care in the Netherlands through a social security system is pluralistic, with the National Sick Fund Insurance covering about 62 per cent of the population depending on their level of income, 6 per cent are covered as public employees through a public insurance scheme and finally private insurance companies cover 32 per cent. However, on the other hand the central government strongly regulates both the supply and the price setting in this pluralistic health care system through specific legislation provided by the Hospital Provision Act and the Hospital Tariffs Act. One example is article 18 in the Hospital Provision Act that enables the government to restrict certain services to certain hospitals on the advice of the Health Council [61].

The idea of HTA in decision making in the Netherlands developed around 1982 when the Sick Fund Council was confronted with patients who demanded that the costs of heart and liver transplantations that had been performed abroad would be reimbursed by the Sick Fund Council [60]. This resulted in the requirement that all major new health technologies should be assessed for their efficacy and cost-effectiveness to be admitted to the Sick Fund Benefit Package. Thereby HTA was early an important policy tool in the Netherlands. Several policy reports have documented the interest in HTA, e.g. a government White Paper (1984), the 1986 report (*Limits to care*) and the 1992 report (*Choices in Health Care*) from the Health Council. In the 1990s, the government has made the assessment of new health technologies a key component of its policy to promote the appropriate use of health care and to deal with problems of shortage, rationing and waiting lists [60]. A report made on behalf of the Rathenau Institute to describe the organisation of HTA in the Netherlands concluded that *the Netherlands has been a leader in developing technology assessment information* [53]. This is seen by the rapid development of institutions, the many researchers involved and the resources available to support assessments.

Among the many institutions, the two most important agencies involved in HTA as governmental advisory bodies are the Sick Fund Council and the Health Council [53].

The Sick Fund Council (Ziekenfondsraad) advises the government about the health technologies to be reimbursed under the Sick Fund Benefit Package. In doing this the council uses HTA information to answer questions of efficacy, efficiency and cost-effectiveness, which is the reason that the Sick Fund Council commissions and financially supports cost-effectiveness analysis to improve the reimbursement decision making process. Although this interest in the more partial-oriented HTA by the Sick Fund Council is continued in the 1980s and 1990s [61], assessments produced by the Sick Fund Council are not included in the Dutch sample.

The Health Council (Gezondheidsraad) is by law an independent scientific advisory body for the government in health care issues. The council has a long experience with technology assessment, especially with synthesizing evidence [53]. In an HTA framework, the tasks of the council are to identify and prioritize technologies, and when HTA would be useful, to synthesize the existing information (secondary research) and finally to disseminate the knowledge gathered. The HTA would typically be produced by reviewing the relevant literature and bringing together a multidisciplinary group of experts in a specific area on specific topics on the request of the government. To have easily access to expert knowledge, the Health Council has eight advisory boards in specific areas [32].

The definition of HTA used by the Health Council is a broad *OTA-like* one, as seen in Table 2.3. The choice of topics in the HTAs produced by the council and thus the perception of HTA in practice depends to some degree on the composition of each group with respect to experts included. However, in contrast to the Sick Fund Council, where the focus is upon cost-effectiveness information, a special focus is given in the HTAs produced by the Health Council to the collection of data with respect to legal, ethical and social implications of the use of health technologies [53;Table 2].

Many HTA reports have been produced by the Health Council since the beginning of the 1980s. Unfortunately, the best of the HTA reports are only written in Dutch (*Personal correspondence with Dr. ten Velden, the Health Council*). In the comparative study these reports are excluded, which is the reason the Dutch sample only consists of thirteen HTA reports translated into English, selected after the advice by the Health Council.

The Australian Health Technology Advisory Committee, Australia

In the Australian health care system the Commonwealth Government funds programs through taxes and develops broad health policies [62]. The State and Territory governments are on the other hand responsible for the provision of health care services in general. With a universal health insurance all residents are eligible for coverage. In this system HTA was seen as one of several long-term measures to improve the effectiveness in the health care system.

National advisory bodies, established by the governments, have set the major direction over a decade for health care technology assessment in Australia [62]. Back in 1982 a National Health Technology Advisory Panel (NHTAP) was formed to advise the national government on technology assessment issues. In 1990 the activities of NHTAP and of a Superspecialty Services Subcommittee was combined in a new national health technology assessment agency - the Australian Health Technology Advisory Committee (AHTAC), as a permanent subcommittee of the National Health and Medical Research Council.

As the most important technology assessment body in Australia, it is the responsibility of AHTAC to coordinate and prioritize the HTA activities. Besides this coordination, AHTAC identifies and assesses new and emerging health technologies and highly specialised services, including their safety, efficacy, effectiveness, cost, equity, accessibility and social impact in the context of the Australian health care system [62]. Thus AHTAC uses a broad HTA definition with clinical, economic, patient-related and organisational parameters, see Table 2.3.

The dominance of public funding in the health care system means that AHTAC's recommendations can be relatively easily implemented [47]. A survey made by AHTAC about the influence of technology assessments produced by advisory bodies, including AHTAC, on health policy and practice showed that the background information in the reports seemed of rather more immediate help to some policy areas than the information on cost and economic analyses [63]. This follows the broad interpretation of HTA by AHTAC. In contrast the assessments made of drugs to be listed and reimbursed under the Pharmaceutical Benefit Scheme (PBS), which requires the documentation of safety and efficacy, and since 1993 formal evidence of cost-effectiveness as well, focus upon cost-effectiveness.

In the comparative study, the Australian study sample consists of reports published by AHTAC as *Major Technology Assessments* in the period from 1992 to 1996 - twelve reports. Reports produced by the Australian Institute of Health and Welfare (AIHW) under the commission of AHTAC were not included, unless they were on this list of major technology assessments.

The Canadian Coordinating Office for Health Technology Assessment, Canada

Health care in Canada is a provincial responsibility [64]. The governments in the ten provinces and two territories are responsible for the supply of health care services, while the role of the federal government is limited to financing and the overall regulation of technologies. A system of universal health insurance, administrated by the provinces but supported by the federal government through taxes, finances health care in Canada. However, as early as in 1976 an interest in technology assessment in health care appeared with the Canadian Task Force on the Periodic Health Examination. In a regionalised system with universal insurance, global hospital budgets, limitations on physicians' gross revenue [1] and thereby a control of the diffusion of technologies through the fiscal policy at the provincial and federal levels, information from technology assessment was seen as an important decision aid with respect to allocating the constrained health care resources efficiently. This lead in 1988 to the creation of CETS in the province of Quebec, as the first HTA institution in Canada.

However, in 1989 a symposium, proposed by the provincial and territorial ministers of health, showed a consensus in Canada for establishing a national agency to coordinate provincial efforts and to communicate assessment results [65]. This lead to the establishment of the Canadian Coordinating Office for Health Technology Assessment (CCOHTA) in 1989, as the national institution for health technology assessment in Canada, jointly financed by the governments of the provinces and territories, and the federal government.

The general functions of CCOHTA were to coordinate HTA activities in Canada, to produce HTAs, establish links in and outside Canada, and to anticipate the future by monitoring and identifying emerging technology trends [66]. A further responsibility of CCOHTA was added in 1993 with the inclusion of a Pharmaceutical Assessment Programme. The purpose of this programme was to conduct and manage economic assessments of pharmaceutical products to make decisions with respect to reimbursement and utilization.

Generally CCOHTA uses a broad definition of HTA, as the assessment may encompass analyses of safety, efficacy, effectiveness, quality of life, utilization, economic factors, ethics and social implications, see Table 2.3. The Pharmaceutical Assessment Programme would, however, imply more partial assessments focusing on cost-effectiveness and clinical topics.

An evaluation in 1993 of the activities held by CCOHTA showed that CCOHTA primarily disseminates the information from technology assessments through CCOHTA reports [67]. These reports (10) are together with the publications in the Pharmaceutical Assessment Programme (6) - Technology Overview: Pharmaceuticals - the basis for the Canadian sample in the international comparative study, as can be seen in Appendix 2.3.

The Standing Group on Health Technology, England

NHS (National Health Services) are the national tax-financed health care system in England. Although a centralized system, it is divided into 14 Regional Health Authorities (RHA), 189 District Health Authorities (DHA) and 90 Family Health Services Authorities. There has been a long tradition for *evidence-based health care* (Archie Cochrane) and clinical research (RCTs) in England, but technology assessment as a policy-tool had received little attention [1]. The interest in HTA came, however, with the 1991 health care reform that was supposed to improve the effectiveness and competition on the supply-side because of an ineffective system with, e.g. long waiting lists. This reform resulted in the split between *purchasers* (DHA & GP Fundholders) and *providers* (hospitals & NHS Trusts) due to a focus on efficiency in financing and production. To secure the optimal functioning of this internal market, improved information on the effectiveness and costs of health services and equipment was needed, if a better purchasing policy should be obtained. It is this new purchasing role of the districts, based on population needs, which was a major impetus for technology assessment in England [68]. The *Central Research and Development Committee* (CRDC), which was appointed after the 1991-reform, pointed at the importance of tools such as quality assurance and HTA to secure quality and effective health technologies, as a response to the reform's expected price competition [32]. In 1993, CRDC formed a Standing Group on Health Technology (SGHT) in an attempt to make a research-based health care sector. The purpose of the Standing Group was to advise CRDC and NHS R&D about the national prioritizing of HTA and HTA research and thus provide better information for the decentralized levels (RHA & DHA) in their prioritizing among health technologies.

According to Department of Health [49] and NHS Executive [50], HTA is the production of high quality research information on costs, effectiveness and broader impact on health technologies for those who use, manage and work in the NHS, see the earlier shown Table 2.3. Thus to some extent, it seems to be a narrower definition focusing on cost-effectiveness than the broad comprehensive definitions traditionally used. The interpretation of HTA has, however, been broader in earlier reports from NHS, e.g. the report from the NHS Advisory Group on Health technology assessment, where *rigorous assessment of both new and existing technologies is the evaluation of their effectiveness and safety, their cost-effectiveness, and their social, ethical and organisational impacts* [69].

SGHT was not expected to perform assessments themselves, since the HTAs prioritized and funded were expected to be carried out as commissioned activities. By May 1996 ninety-seven projects in sixty-four priority areas were prioritized and commissioned. The newly established national HTA institute at Southampton University in England - the National Coordinating Centre for Health Technology Assessment (NCCHTA) now controls the projects on behalf of NHS R&D. The English sample in the study is selected among these existing 97 projects.

APPENDIX 2.3 : HTA Reports in the Sample - SBU, Sweden		
Study nb.	Title	Type of HTA
S1101	Preoperative Routines. SBU-report. May 1989. ISBN 91-87890-00-3.	Comprehensive
S1102	Gastroscopy in the Diagnosis of Dispepsia. SBU-report. February 1990. ISBN 91-87890-06-2.	Comprehensive
S1103	Vascular Surgery for Arteriosclerosis in the Legs. SBU-report. March 1990. ISBN 91-87890-05-4.	Semi-comprehensive
S1104	Lithotripsy of Kidney Stones and Gallstones. SBU-report. April 1990. ISBN 91-87890-07-0.	Comprehensive
S1105	Back Pain - Causes, Diagnosis, Treatment. SBU-report. January 1991. ISBN 91-87890-10-0.	Semi-comprehensive
S1106	Bone Marrow Transplantation. SBU-report. April 1991. ISBN 91-87890-08-9.	Comprehensive
S1107	Surgery for Epilepsy. SBU-report. Sept. 1991. ISBN 91-87890- 09-7.	Semi-comprehensive
S1108	MRI - Magnetic Resonance Imaging. SBU-report. September 1992. ISBN 92-87890-15-1.	Semi-comprehensive
S1109	The Role of Percutaneous Transluminal Coronary Angioplasty in Coronary Revascularization. SBU-report. September 1992. ISBN 92-87890-16-X.	Comprehensive
S1110	Stroke. SBU-report. November 1992. ISBN 92-87890-21-6.	Comprehensive
S1111	Genetic Diagnosis by PCR. SBU-report. January 1993. ISBN 92-878890-20-8.	Comprehensive
S1112	Diabetic Retinopathy - The Value of Early Detection. SBU-report. August 1993. ISBN 92-87890-17-8.	Comprehensive
S1113	Coronary Artery Bypass Graft and Percutaneous Transluminal Coronary Angioplasty. SBU-report. May 1994. ISBN 91-87890-24-0.	Semi-comprehensive
S1114	The Treatment and Rehabilitation of Traffic Accident Victims. SBU-report. May 1994. ISBN 91-87890-23-2.	Comprehensive
S1115	Moderately Elevated Blood Pressure. SBU-report. June 1994. ISBN 91-87890-26-7.	Comprehensive
S1116	Hysterectomy - Ratings of Appropriateness. SBU-report no.125E. June 1995. ISBN 91-87890-28-3 .	Semi-comprehensive
S1117	Screening for Prostate Cancer. SBU-report no. 126. June 1995. ISBN 91-87890-30-5.	Semi-comprehensive
S1118	Bone Density Measurement. SBU-report no. 127. November 1995. ISBN 91-87890-31-3.	Comprehensive
S1120	Radiotherapy in Sweden. Vol. 1. SBU-report. September 1996. ISBN 91-87890-32-1.	Semi-comprehensive

\multicolumn{3}{l}{APPENDIX 2.3 : HTA Projects in the Sample - NCCHTA, England (1/5)}
Study nb.	Project-title	Type of HTA
S2201	Systematic review of the effectiveness and the CE of the treatment of chronic stable angina and acute myocardial infarction. HERG, Brunel University. Project number 93/01/2. Start 1996.	Semi-partial
S2202	Can the effectiveness of interdisciplinary team care for stroke be improved? Department of Geriatric Medicine, University of Newcastle upon Tyne. Project number 93/03/6. Start 1995.	Semi-partial
S2203	Social-environmental, psycological and physical approaches to stroke rehabilitation. Department of Geriatic Medicine, University of Newcastle upon Tyne. Project number 93/03/11. Start 1995.	Semi-comprehensive
S2204	A controlled comparison of alternative strategies in stroke rehabilitation. Clinical and Health Services Studies Unit, King's College School of Medicine and Dentistry. Project number 93/03/26. Start 1995.	Comprehensive
S2205	Early prediction of rehabilitation needs following acute stroke. Department of Medicine, King's College School of Medicine and Dentistry. Project number 93/03/31. Start 1995.	Semi-comprehensive
S2206	A policy for the drug treatment of high blood pressure. Department of Environmental and Preventive Medicine, The Medical College of St Bartholomew's Hospital. Project number 93/05/1. Start 1995.	Semi-partial
S2207	Screening for stroke. University Department of Public Health, Royal Free Hospital School of Medicine. Project number 93/05/2. Start 1995.	Partial
S2208	Near patient or laboatory testing? An evaluation. Department of Chemical Pathology, Mayday Healthcare NHS Trust. Project number 93/06/4. Start 1995.	Semi-comprehensive
S2209	Near patient testing in diabetic clinics: appraising the costs and outcomes. Department of Public Health Medicine, UMDS. Project number 93/06/22. Start 1995.	Semi-comprehensive
S2210	Effectiveness of counselling, CBT and GP care for depression in general practice. University Department of Psyciatry, Royal Free Hospital School of Medicine. Project number 93/07/66. Start 95.	Semi-comprehensive
S2211	A randomised controlled trial to evaluate the efficacy and cost-effectiveness of counselling with patients with chronic depression and anxiety. School of Social Sciences, University of Greenwich. Project number 93/07/68. Start 1995.	Semi-partial
S2212	Controlled trials of microdiscectomy for lumbar disc herniation. Department of Neurosurgery, Frenchay Healthcare Trust. Project number 93/09/17. Start 1996.	Semi-partial
S2213	A systematic review of the effectiveness and cost-effectiveness of total hip replacement prostheses (THR). Department of Epidemiology and Public Health Medicine, University of Bristol. Project number 93/11/4. Start 1995.	Semi-comprehensive

APPENDIX 2.3 : HTA Projects in the Sample - NCCHTA, England (2/5)		
Study nb.	Project-title	Type of HTA
S2214	Systematic review of factors influencing outcomes and costs of hip replacement surgery. Department of Public Health and Primary Care, University of Oxford. Project number 93/11/8. Start 1995.	Semi-partial
S2215	Assessment of long-term efficacy of early introduction of inhaled steroids in asthma. Department of Thoracic Medicine, Imperial College of Science, Technology and Medicine. Project number 93/14/6. Start 1995.	Semi-partial
S2216	Early asthma phophylaxis, natural history, skeletal development and economy (EASE). Department of Child Health, University of Aberdeen. Project number 93/14/9. Start 1996.	Semi-partial
S2217	A systematic review of studies relating to the efficiency and effectiveness of near patient testing in primary care. Department of General Practice, The University of Birmingham. Project number 93/15/1. Start 1995.	Semi-partial
S2218	Is the outcome for patients with low back pain influenced by GP's referral for plain radiography. Department of General Practice and Primary Care, St George's Hospital Medical School. Project number 93/17/11. Start 1995.	Semi-comprehensive
S2219	A randomised controlled trial to assess the effectiveness, cost-effectiveness and cost-benefit of routine refferal for lumbar spine radiography in patients with LBP. Department of General Practice, The University of Nottingham. Project number 93/17/13. Start 1995.	Semi-partial
S2220	Lumbar spine radiology in primary health care: clinical outcome and cost-effectiveness. University Department of Radiology, University of Newcastle upon Tyne. Project number 93/17/22.	Semi-partial
S2221	Does early imaging influence management and improve outcome in patients with low back pain? Department of Radiology, University of Aberdeen. Project number 93/17/43.	Semi-partial
S2222	A multi-centre RCT assessing the costs and benefits of using structured information and analysis of women's preferences in the management of menorrhagia. Department of Obstetrics and Gynaecology, University of Bristol. Project number 93/18/12. Start 1995.	Semi-partial
S2223	Comparison of medical and surgical treatments of menorrhagia. Department of Obstetrics and Gynaecology, University of Cambridge. Project number 93/18/26. Start 1995.	Semi-comprehensive
S2224	Primary care emergency centres: organisation and impact. National Primary Care Research and Development Centre, University of Manchester. Project number 93/20/1. Start 1995.	Semi-comprehensive
S2225	Systematic review of detection, management and screening for prostatic carcinoma. Department of Epidemiology and Public Health Medicine, University of Bristol. Project number 93/21/2. Start 1995.	Semi-comprehensive

APPENDIX 2.3 : HTA Projects in the Sample - NCCHTA, England (3/5)

Study nb.	Project-title	Type of HTA
S2226	A review of evidence on the cost-effectiveness of different strategies for detecting and managing prostatic carcinoma. Cancer Screening Evaluation Unit, Institute of Cancer Research. Project number 93/21/4. Start 1995.	Semi-partial
S2227	The costs and benefit of paramedic skills in pre-hospital trauma care. Medical Care Research Unit, The University of Sheffield. Project number 93/23/18. Start 1995.	Semi-comprehensive
S2228	An RCT of infusion protocols in adult pre-hospital care. Medical Care Research Unit, The University of Sheffield. Project number 93/23/19. Start 1995.	Semi-partial
S2229	Effectiveness and costs of paramedic pre-hospital management. Personal Social Services Research Unit, University of Kent at Canterbury. Project number 93/23/25. Start 1995.	Semi-comprehensive
S2230	A RCT of different approaches to universal antenatal HIV testing: acceptability, costs and benefits. Department of Obstetrics and Gynaecology, University of Edinburgh. Project number 93/24/11. Start 1995.	Semi-comprehensive
S2231	SURUSS (serum, urine and ultrasound screening study). Department of Environmental and Preventive Medicine, Queen Mary and Westfield College. Project number 93/25/5. Start 1996.	Semi-partial
S2232	Establishing appropriate screening practice for Down's syndrome. Department of Environmental and Preventive Medicine, Wolfson Institute of Preventive Medicine. Project number 93/25/24. Start 1995.	Semi-comprehensive
S2233	The cost-effectiveness of MRI for investigation of the knee joint. HERG, Brunel University. Project number 93/26/16. Start 1996.	Semi-partial
S2234	Cost-effectiveness of MRI in the DGH setting. European Office, MEDTAP International Inc. Project number 93/26/17. Start 1995.	Semi-partial
S2235	Critical review of the role of neonatal screening in the detection of congenital hearing impairments. MRC Institute of Hearing Research. Project number 93/27/1. Start 1995.	Semi-comprehensive
S2236	A systematic review of wound care. Centre for Health Economics, University of York. Project number 93/29/1. Start 1995.	Semi-partial
S2237	Systematic review of outpatient services for chronic pain control. University of Oxford. Project number 93/31/4. Start 1995.	Semi-partial
S2238	Information needs for health planners. Centre for Reproduction, Growth and Development, The University of Leeds. Project number 93/32/3. Start 1996.	Semi-partial
S2239	Screening for haemoglobinopathies in the UK: review and economic analysis. Department of Epidemiology and Biostatistics, Institute of Child Health. Project number 93/33/1. Start 1995.	Semi-comprehensive

APPENDIX 2.3 : HTA Projects in the Sample - NCCHTA, England (4/5)		
Study nb.	Project-title	Type of HTA
S2240	Haemoglobinopathy - a systematic review. Department of Haematology, Central Middlesex Hospital NHS Trust. Project number 93/33/3. Start 1995.	Comprehensive
S2241	Information needed for health planners. Institute of Epidemiology and Health Services Research, The University of Leeds. Project number 93/34/3. Start 1995.	Semi-partial
S2242	An assessment of screening for the fragile X syndrome. Mothercare Clinical Genetics and Fetal Medicine Unit, Institute of Child Health. Project number 93/34/4. Start 1995.	Partial
S2243	Neonatal metabolic screening: cost, yield and effect of outcome. Neonatal Screening Laboratory, Sheffield Children's Hospital NHS Trust. Project number 93/36/1. Start 1995.	Semi-comprehensive
S2244	Systematic review of neonatal screening for inborn errors of metabolism. Department of Clinical Biochemistry & Metabolism, St George's Hospital Medical School. Project number 93/36/3. Start 1995.	Semi-partial
S2245	A systematic review of the risks, benefits and costs of home parenteral nutrition. Department of Medicine, Salford Royal Hospital NHS Trust. Project number 93/38/1. Start 1995.	Semi-partial
S2246	Effectiveness of methods of dialysis therapy for end stage renal disease. Department of Medicine and Therapeutics, University of Aberdeen. Project number 93/40/2. Start 1995.	Semi-comprehensive
S2248	Antimicrobial prophylaxis in colorectal surgery. NHS Centre for Reviews and Dissemination, University of York. Project number 94/03/1. Start 1995.	Semi-partial
S2249	A RCT comparing the efficacy, safety and cost-effectiveness of transurethral resection (TURP), LVAP, TUNA and MTA of the prostate. Department of Urology, The University of Sheffield. Project number 94/04/8.	Semi-partial
S2250	Randomised evaluation of alternative electrosurgical modalities to treat bladder outflow obstruction in men with BPH. Academic Urological Unit, Queen Mary and Westfield College. Project number 94/04/9.	Semi-comprehensive
S2251	A systematic review of preschool vision screening. NHS Centre for Reviews and Dissemination, University of York. Project number 94/05/1. Start 1995.	Semi-partial
S2252	Child health surveillanc: an evaluation of screening for language delay. NHS Centre for Reviews and Dissemination, University of York. Project number 94/05/2.	Semi-partial
S2253	Systematic review of alternative analgesics following day case surgery. Nuffield Department of Anaesthetics, University of Oxford. Project number 94/11/4. Start 1996.	Semi-partial

APPENDIX 2.3 : HTA Projects in the Sample - NCCHTA, England (5/5)			
Study nb.	Project-title	Type of HTA
S2255	A RCT to assess the effectiveness, costs and cost-effectiveness of laparoscopic, vaginal and abdominal hysterectomy. Women's Services, The University of Leeds. Project number 94/16/3. Start 1996.	Semi-comprehensive
S2256	The value of digital imaging in diabetic retinopathy. Department of Biomedical Physics & Bioengineering, University of Aberdeen. Project number 94/18/5. Start 1996.	Semi-partial
S2257	Cost and quality implications of the organisation of vascular services. Department of Surgery, The University of Sheffield. Project number 94/20/1. Start 1996.	Comprehensive
S2258	The costs and benefits of post-natal midwifery support - a randomised controlled trial. Nursing Section - Sheffield Centre for Health and Related Research, The University of Sheffield. Project number 94/22/24. Start 1996.	Semi-comprehensive
S2259	Redesigning postnatal care: a RCT of protocol based, midwifery-led care. Department of Public Health & Epidemiology, The University of Birmingham. Project number 94/22/26. Start 1996.	Semi-comprehensive
S2260	Systematic review of use of laxatives in the elderly. NHS Centre for Reviews and Dissemination, University of York. Project number 94/23/1. Start 1995.	Semi-partial
S2261	Scottish trial of arthroplasty or reduction for subcapital fractures (STARS). Department of Orthopaedics, University of Edinburgh. Project number 94/24/3.	Semi-partial
S2262	Screening for ovarian cancer. NHS Centre for Reviews and Dissemination, University of York. Project number 94/26/1. Start 1996.	Semi-comprehensive
S2263	A systematic literature review of spiral and ultrafast CT. Department of Medical Physics, The University of Leeds. Project number 94/28/1.	Semi-partial
S2264	The effectiveness of health visitor domiciliary visiting: a systematic review of the litterature. Department of Nursing and Midwifery Studies, University of Nottingham. Project number 94/36/4. Start 1996.	Semi-partial
S2265	Systematic review of endoscopic ultrasound and gastrointestinal cancer. Research School of Medicine, The University of Leeds. Project number 94/44/3.	Semi-comprehensive
S2266	A cost-utility analysis of beta interferon for multiple sclerosis. Department of Epidemiology and Public Health, University of Newcastle upon Tyne. Project number 95/01/2. Start 1996.	Semi-partial

APPENDIX 2.3 : HTA Reports in the Sample - Health Council, NHL		
Study nb.	Title	Type of HTA
S3301	Health Council of the Netherlands: Committee on Heredity: Science and Society. On the possibilities and limits of genetic testing and gene therapy. The Hague: Health Council of the Netherlands, 1989; publication no. 89/31.	Comprehensive
S3303	Health Council of the Netherlands: Committee on Vaccination against haemophilus influenza type b. The Hague: Health Council of the Netherlands, 1991; pub.no. 1991/14.	Semi-comprehensive
S3304	Health Council of the Netherlands: Committee on CNSRD. Indoor allergenes, allergy and the development of chronic respiratory diseases. The Hague: Health Council of the Netherlands, 1993; publication no. 1992/01E.	Semi-partial
S3305	Health Council of the Netherlands: Committee on Cardiac Surgery and Interventional Cardiology. Cardiac Arrhythmias. Catheter ablation, arrhythmia surgery and defibrillator implantation. The Hague: Health Council of the Netherlands, 1993; publication - no.1993/06E.	Semi-partial
S3306	Health Council of the Netherlands: Standing Committee on Medicine. Lasers in sight. Laser correction of refractive errors. The Ha-gue: Health Council of the Netherlands, 1993; pub.no.1993/19E.	Semi-comprehensive
S3307	Health Council of the Netherlands: Committee on Heart Surgery and Interventional Cardiology. Heart surgery and interventional cardiology for children. The Hague: Health Council of the Netherlands, 1993; publication no. 1993/20E.	Semi-comprehensive
S3308	Health Council of the Netherlands: Committee on Stereotactic - radiotherapy. Stereotactic radiotherapy. The Hague: Health Council of the Netherlands, 1994; publication no. 1994/18E.	Semi-comprehensive
S3309	Health Council of the Netherlands: Committee on Genetic Screening. Genetic Screening. The Hague: Health Council of the Netherlands, 1994; publication no. 1994/22E.	Semi-comprehensive
S3310	Health Council of the Netherlands: Cardiac Surgery and Interventional Cardiology Committee. Heart Surgery and Interventional Cardiology for Adults. The Hague: Health Council of the Netherlands, 1995; publication no. 1995/01E.	Semi-partial
S3311	Health Council of the Netherlands: Standing Committee on Medical Ethics and Health Law. Sex selection for non-medical reasons. The Hague: Health Council of the Netherlands, 1995; pub.no. 1995/11E.	Semi-partial
S3312	Health Council of the Netherlands: Committee on Pharmacological Interventions in Drug Addiction. The Prescription of Heroin to Heroin Addicts. The Hague: Health Council of the Netherlands, 1995; publication no. 1995/12E.	Semi-partial
S3313	Health Council of the Netherlands: Committee on In vitro fertilization. Assisted fertilization: ICSI. The Hague: Health Council of the Netherlands, 1996; publication no. 1996/06E.	Semi-comprehensive
S3314	Health Council of the Netherlands: Standing Committee on Medicine. Marihuana as medicine. Rijswijk: Health Council of the Netherlands, 1996; publication no. 1996/21E.	Semi-partial

APPENDIX 2.3 : HTA Reports in the Sample - AHTAC, Australia		
Study nb.	Title	Type of HTA
S4401	National Health and Medical Research Council. Australian Health Technology Advisory Committee (1992) *Guidelines for CT Scanning.* Canberra.	Semi-partial
S4402	National Health and Medical Research Council. Australian Health Technology Advisory Committee (1992) *Guidelines for renal dialysis and transplantation services.* Canberra.	Semi-comprehensive
S4403	National Health and Medical Research Council. Australian Health Technology Advisory Committee (1993) *Treatment of obstructive sleep apnea.* Canberra.	Semi-partial
S4404	National Health and Medical Research Council. Australian Health Technology Advisory Committee (1993) *Laser Corneal Sculpting.* Canberra.	Semi-comprehensive
S4405	National Health and Medical Research Council. Australian Health Technology Advisory Committee (1994) *Treatment options for benign prostatic hyperplasia (BPH).* Canberra.	Comprehensive
S4406	National Health and Medical Research Council. Australian Health Technology Advisory Committee (1994) *Low Power Lasers in Medicine.* Canberra.	Semi-partial
S4407	National Health and Medical Research Council. Australian Health Technology Advisory Committee (1996) *Diagnostic Ultrasound.* (abstract).	Semi-partial
S4408	National Health and Medical Research Council. Australian Health Technology Advisory Committee (1996) *Beam and isotope radiotherapy.* (abstract).	Semi-partial
S4409	National Health and Medical Research Council. Australian Health Technology Advisory Committee (1996) *Magnetic Resonance Imaging.* (abstract).	Semi-comprehensive
S4410	National Health and Medical Research Council. Australian Health Technology Advisory Committee (1996) *Minimal Access Surgery.* (abstract).	Semi-partial
S4411	National Health and Medical Research Council. Australian Health Technology Advisory Committee (1996) *Colorectal Cancer Screening.* (abstract).	Semi-partial
S4412	National Health and Medical Research Council. Australian Health Technology Advisory Committee (1996) *Prostate Cancer Screening.* (abstract).	Semi-partial

APPENDIX 2.3 : HTA Reports in the Sample - CCOHTA, Canada		
Study nb.	Project-title	Type of HTA
S5501	Canadian Coordinating Office for Health Technology Assessment: *Gallstone Therapies*. July 1991. Ontario.	Semi-comprehensive
S5503	Canadian Coordinating Office for Health Technology Assessment: *An annotated bibliography of the costs and benefits of Prenatal Screening Programs*. October 1991. Ontario.	Semi-partial
S5504	Canadian Coordinating Office for Health Technology Assessment: *Exosurf Neonatal for Surfactant Replacement Therapy*. December 1991. Ontario.	Semi-comprehensive
S5505	Canadian Coordinating Office for Health Technology Assessment: *Chiropractic Treatment of neck and back disorders: A Review of Selected Studies*. February 1992. Ontario.	Semi-partial
S5506	Canadian Coordinating Office for Health Technology Assessment: *An overview of major Breast Screening Studies and their findings*. April 1992. Ontario.	Semi-comprehensive
S5507	Canadian Coordinating Office for Health Technology Assessment: *Magnetic Field Strenght Issues in MRI*. March 1993. Ontario.	Comprehensive
S5508	Canadian Coordinating Office for Health Technology Assessment: *The Introduction of Laparoscopic Cholecystectomy in Canada and Australia*. May 1994. Ontario.	Semi-comprehensive
S5509	Canadian Coordinating Office for Health Technology Assessment: *Reuse of Disposable Medical Devices*. Fourth CCOHTA Regional Symposium. October 1994. Ontario.	Semi-comprehensive
S5510	Canadian Coordinating Office for Health Technology Assessment: *Transcutaneous Electrical Nerve Stimulation (TENS) and pain management..* April 1995. Ontario.	Semi-comprehensive
S5511	Canadian Coordinating Office for Health Technology Assessment: *Finasteride Therapy for the treatment of Benign Prostata Hyperplasia.*Technology Overview: Pharmaceuticals. Issue 2.0. April 1996. Ontario.	Semi-partial
S5512	Canadian Coordinating Office for Health Technology Assessment: *A comparson of fixed and mobile CT and MRI scanners*. November 1995. Ontario.	Comprehensive
S5513	Canadian Coordinating Office for Health Technology Assessment: *Pulmozine - DNase Use in Cystic Fibrosis*. Technology Overview: Pharmaceuticals. Issue 1.0. February 1996. Ontario.	Semi-partial
S5514	Canadian Coordinating Office for Health Technology Assessment: *Pharmaceutical management of peptic ulcer disease*. Technology Overview: Pharmaceuticals. Issue 3.1. June 1996. Ontario.	Semi-partial
S5515	Canadian Coordinating Office for Health Technology Assessment: *Pharmaceutical management of gastroesophageal reflux disease*. Technology Overview: Pharmaceuticals. Issue 3.2. June 1996. Ontario.	Semi-partial
S5516	Canadian Coordinating Office for Health Technology Assessment: *The use of Nitrates in Chronic Stable Angina*. Technology Overview: Pharmaceuticals. Issue 4.0. December 1996. Ontario.	Semi-comprehensive
S5517	Canadian Coordinating Office for Health Technology Assessment: *Interferon Beta 1-B and multiple sclerosis*. Technology Overview: Pharmaceuticals. Issue 5.0. December 1996. Ontario.	Semi-partial

APPENDIX 2.4 : Parameters Assessed by the Institutions (per cents of institution-specific samples)

Clinical Parameters	Efficacy	Safety	Effectiveness	Outcomes	Indication	Pop. affected
SBU - Sweden (N=19)	37 %	95 %	100 %	32 %	90 %	68 %
Health Council - NHL (N=13)	46 %	92 %	85 %	8 %	54 %	54 %
AHTAC - Australia (N=12)	33 %	67 %	83 %	25%	42 %	42 %
CCOHTA - Canada (N=16)	81 %	63 %	63 %	6 %	31 %	56 %
NCCHTA - England (N=64)	39 %	19 %	72 %	44 %	5 %	9 %
Total N=124 (% of total)	**44 %**	**46 %**	**77 %**	**32 %**	**30 %**	**32 %**

Economic Parameters	Efficiency	Costs	Cost-effectiveness	Cost-utility	Cost-benefit
SBU - Sweden (N=19)	0 %	95 %	58 %	0 %	0 %
Health Council -NHL (N=13)	0 %	31 %	15 %	0 %	15 %
AHTAC - Australia (N=12)	0 %	75 %	25 %	0 %	0 %
CCOHTA - Canada (N=16)	13 %	94 %	75 %	19 %	6 %
NCCHTA - England (N=64)	14 %	53 %	53 %	8 %	6 %
Total N=124 (% of total)	**9 %**	**65 %**	**50 %**	**7 %**	**6 %**

Patient Parameters	Social implication	Ethics	Acceptabil.	Psycological relations	Other
SBU - Sweden (N=19)	26 %	21 %	5 %	37 %	5 %
Health Council -NHL (N=13)	46 %	31 %	31 %	15 %	15 %
AHTAC - Australia (N=12)	0 %	0 %	0 %	0 %	8 %
CCOHTA - Canada (N=16)	6 %	13 %	6 %	13 %	0 %
NCCHTA - England (N=64)	3 %	0 %	13 %	8 %	17 %
Total N=124 (% of total)	**11 %**	**8 %**	**11 %**	**13 %**	**12 %**

Organisational Parameters	Diffusion	Central - decentral	Utilization	Access	Skills	Training	Other
SBU - Sweden (N=19)	53 %	42 %	42 %	0 %	53 %	32 %	0 %
Health Council (N=13)	54 %	31 %	0 %	15 %	31 %	23 %	0 %
AHTAC - Aust. (N=12)	33 %	17 %	0 %	8 %	17 %	33 %	0 %
CCOHTA - Can (N=16)	31 %	0 %	19 %	13 %	0 %	13 %	0 %
NCCHTA - UK (N=64)	0 %	0 %	5 %	2 %	6 %	9 %	6 %
Total N=124 (% total)	**21 %**	**11 %**	**11 %**	**5 %**	**16 %**	**17 %**	**3 %**

Chapter 3

Models of Innovation[67]

---

[67] Chapter 3 was presented as a paper at *The International Health Economics Association Inaugural Conference* (iHEA) in Vancouver, Canada. May 19-23, 1996.

Table of contents

Abstract 77

1.0 Introduction 78

2.0 Case study methodology 79

3.0 Concepts and definitions 80

4.0 Health technology and the institutional structure 84
    4.1 Pharmaceuticals 84
    4.2 Medical devices 85
    4.3 Medical procedures 86

5.0 Linear models of innovation 87
    5.1 The science push model 87
    5.2 The demand pull model 89
    5.3 Demand pull or science push? 92

6.0 Learning and feedback in innovation 93

7.0 The chain-linked model 95

8.0 Case studies 99
    8.1 Sustained release drugs 99
    8.2 Laparoscopic cholecystectomy 104

9.0 Concluding remarks 109

References 113

Abstract

With scarce resources, rising costs and many health technologies being developed, the focus is upon technology assessment and early warning of emerging health technologies. Therefore it is important to improve existing theoretical and empirical knowledge about technological change. This chapter presents different models of innovation based on economic theory. A simple model is the linear innovation model, where change is originating in the present scientific knowledge and flowing forward uni-directionally to the market-introduction (*science-push model*). Alternatively, technological change could be driven by a market demand (*demand-pull model*). However, the development of health technology is a more complex and iterative process with a mix of push and pull effects, and learning effects. All these effects are contained in the *chain-linked model of innovation*. The use of the models on two cases - *sustained release drugs* and *laparoscopic cholecystectomy* - shows that the innovation process typically consists of a mixture of science pushes, demand pulls and learning effects, e.g. as user-producer relations. Finally, knowledge about the process of innovation of emerging health technologies may provide valuable inputs for an early warning system.

1.0 Introduction

To develop national industrial policies to stimulate innovation[68] an understanding of the principal factors that determine the rate and direction of inventive and innovative activity is desirable [1]. The focus has been on how to stimulate technological advances and change. In the economic literature this understanding is sought by presenting different models to describe and explain the process of innovation.

An understanding of the process of innovation and technological change is furthermore important, when a government considers to establish systems to warn early about future emerging innovations in a sector - *an early warning system.*[69] This concern about the future is especially seen with respect to health technology. The growing number of health technologies developed and diffused into the health care sector and the rising costs associated with it explains this concern. This interest in getting value explains the demand for health technology assessment and early warning systems. The aim of an early warning system in the health care sector is to identify potential health technologies expected to diffuse into the sector in the years to come and to perform early technology assessments of the identified health technology [2,3]. The policy-maker should then be in a better position to control and regulate the introduction of new health technologies. A regulation that could either support an innovation by speeding up the time for introduction or delay its introduction and restrain diffusion.

However, as expressed by Paltiel et al. (1993) [4] with respect to the Food and Drug Administrations (FDA) drug approval decision making[70], the policy-maker using the early warning information encounters the challenge of protecting the patients from unsafe and ineffective technologies while at the same time reducing the delay associated with bringing potentially useful technologies to the market. Important elements in this decision making is the costs to society by delaying an introduction, the value of improved information and the consequences of doing nothing. Improved information can be obtained at the early stage when a decision is made to undertake further studies, e.g. clinical trials, or to gain more experience with the innovation (learning effects). The higher the degree of uncertainty, the more desirable it becomes to buy information via a clinical trial [4]. Little uncertainty on the other hand, e.g. about efficacy and safety, makes an immediate decision possible: a recommendation to adopt or reject the emerging health technology.

The purpose of the present chapter is to explore the process of innovation of health technology. Special reference is given to the flow of information and to the uncertainty in innovations. This uncertainty in the process of innovation was illustrated in the

---

[68] E.g. subsidizing research activities or the establishment of new innovative firms.

[69] Early warning systems are discussed further in chapter 8.

[70] Paltiel et al. (1993) are modelling, when to accept less than ideal clinical data for license of a drug to treat AIDS and are estimating the optimal length of a clinical trial [4].

eximer laser coronary angioplasty case, where the technology changed relatively rapidly during its early diffusion [5]. Substantial learning effects in the processes of innovation and technological change could make it difficult at an early stage to make any final conclusions about the efficacy of an innovation, its safety, cost-effectiveness, etc. This poses the risk for a decision-maker who uses early warning information to make a type II error by rejecting a promising technology and thereby restricting the innovative activity [6,7].[71] The opposite risk is to make a type I error by recommending an earlier introduction of an expected promising technology, which later appears to be inefficient or even harmful as the experience increase [6,7].

Knowledge of the innovation process and the uncertainty in innovations is therefore of value for the benefit of early warning and health technology assessment, when the challenge of a trade-off between the risk of too early introduction of harmful technologies and the costs to the society for the delay of potentially effective technologies is accepted.

In the chapter, three different models of innovations are presented and used as a framework for the discussion of the case studies of selected health technologies. These models are primarily based on economic theory.[72] The first two models described and discussed are two linear models of innovation, *the science push model* and *the demand pull model*. Both have an unidirectional innovation flow. However, as these models ignore uncertainty, learning and feedback in the innovation process, a model that incorporates both learning and feedback and hence both effects of the linear models is described afterwards. It is *the chain-linked model* presented by Kline et al. (1986) [9], which will be discussed in relation to health technology.

2.0 Case study methodology

Economic literature regarding the process of innovation and technological change has been criticized for being restricted to macro levels, in which the empirical studies deal with patent data and aggregated national output data, e.g. gross national product. Mowery et al. (1979) [10] have expressed a need for studies at a less aggregated level that considers specific innovative outputs of industries and firms as well as the forces explaining the differences among them.

However, to avoid the macro perspective and because of a lack of empirical data at the micro level, a case study design was chosen. A case study is an empirical inquiry that investigates a contemporary phenomenon within its real-life context [11]. It is especially useful when the boundary between phenomenon (*health care innovation*) and context (*health care innovation process*) is not clearly evident. In an exploratory approach the case

---

[71] Examples of technologies are eximer laser coronary angioplasty and visual laser ablation [5,8].

[72] In sociology, theories of innovation are also present. These are, however, out of the scope of this chapter and will not be dealt with further.

study is best suited for answering questions of the *how* and *why* type. *How* the innovation process for health technology can be characterized and *why* there may be differences among health technologies.

However, when the same study contains more than one single case study, a multiple case design has to be used [11]. The present chapter contains a multiple case design consisting of single cases. These single cases may then be compared with each other. The unit of analysis in the models and the single case is then based on a technological unit, a technology.[73]

With the exploratory aim of the chapter, theory is used as the framework to analyse and compare the empirical case studies. This results in a deduction of theory (elements of the models) in relation to what seems to characterize and explain each specific case. Limited analytic generalizations, as opposed to statistical generalizations, might then afterwards be made on behalf of it.

The data sources used in the case studies are literature (books, articles, informal and formal documents, etc.) and interviews with key-persons in industry and hospitals.

Two case studies of the process of innovation were selected. The first case considers *sustained release drugs*. These types of drugs are in the form of tablets coated with material that delays the release of medication until after they leave the stomach. The second case is *laparoscopic technology*, with special reference to *laparoscopic cholecystectomy*, where the laparoscope, as a device, both has diagnostic and therapeutic purposes.

3.0 Concepts and definitions

In the chapter a number of concepts describing the process of innovation and diffusion are used. Prior to the presentation of the three models of innovation these concepts are defined in this section.

Invention refers to an idea for a new or improved product or process that *require an act of insight going beyond the normal exercise of technical or professional skills* [13]. These acts of insight result in an accumulation of new and valuable knowledge and experience with learning possibilities in the future. However, the use of existing knowledge and skills in a novel way could also result in an invention. Inventions are expected to be linked to technical or scientific basic research. At the time of invention the first patents may be sought. Therefore, invention is often seen as a starting point for any emergence of changing skills, which will lead to innovation and thereby technological change.

---

[73] And not an economic unit - the industry, where focus is upon the output which could be produced by different technologies (production frontier) and not upon any specific technology [12].

Innovation is the process from the point of invention through applied research and development to practical use.[74] The accumulation of knowledge resulting from the idea of invention is in the innovation process transformed into a marketable product (a technology). The innovation process is then understood as the process that includes all the necessary activities for bringing a new product into the market and thereby leading to technological change. Hall (1994) [12] defines technological change as *changes in the knowledge associated with producing goods and services of economic value*. The process of innovation will always imply some sort of technological change. It could then be asked whether there is a causality the other way round implying that technological change always leads to innovation. However, the existence of such a causality would ignore the fact that invention and imitation both lead to some degree of technological change.[75] This distinction between technological change and innovation is made in the present chapter.[76]

Invention, the emergence of an idea, is only one of several necessary requirements that has to be fulfilled before marketing of innovations. Other activities are entrepreneurship, investment and development. These are activities that have the aim of producing the technological good - the innovation. As an economic act, innovation then is a result of a commercialization of the new product when it is sent on the market for the first time.[77] This commercialization illustrates the difference between invention and innovation.

Technical knowledge (or skills) can be divided into three interdependent levels [15]. The first level is a practice level, understood as a certain combination of production factors used in a specific process. At a higher level appears a technique, which is understood as a set of practices that allow a kind of substitution between factors of production by changing practice. Finally, at the highest level is the technology, based on the technical

---

[74] The concepts of invention and innovation and their distinction differs in the literature, treating innovations more or less as the basis for change in knowledge.

[75] At the stage of imitation several competing producers characterize the market, which in their production have adopted the invention and thereby innovation, originally only produced by the innovator. This corresponds to the stage of diffusion that is explained later.

[76] However, if innovation on the other hand is defined as *the whole technological change process representing a shorthand for doing something new* [14] the causality between technological change and innovation holds both ways. Invention and imitation then becomes part of this innovation process.

[77] Of course to use this terminology of an economic act could be problematic with method-based health technology, as the group of health care procedures. The software component accounts for a large amount of these technologies as information or knowledge. Information could be characterized as free goods without any market price. This means goods that are free obtainable in a market or obtainable with a little effort (e.g. getting knowledge through participation in conferences). The extent of free goods depends on the level of capital-intensive hardware technologies (e.g. devices) used in the health care procedure.

knowledge available. Technology then becomes the sum of all known techniques [15]. An example of this definition could be that a hypertension technology, which is used by the doctor to help the patient getting a lower blood pressure and which comprises all methods (techniques) available. These methods might consist of different kinds of anti-hypertensive drug treatments (e.g. Doxazosin or Atenolol) or it might be methods to change the patient's diet. In a production function approach these techniques can then be considered as input factors to produce the final outcome - the technology.

An alternative approach, supported in the present chapter, is to divide technical knowledge into two interdependent levels, almost corresponding in content to the first two levels in the neo-classical approach. A technique could be defined as *a utilized method of production* [16] corresponding to the previous definition of practice. A technology is then defined as *the social pool of knowledge of the industrial art* [16].[78] The consequence is that technology in itself is a body of knowledge of certain classes of events and activities [17]. This is different from the previous mentioned definitions of technique and technology. The last definition is broader, less technical and does not reduce technology to a question of substitution between factors of input in the production process. The choice in this definition with emphasis on knowledge makes it easier to interpret more soft notions such as technical know-how and work of organisations as concrete technologies. A further advantage of this definition is that the concept of technology can be made more specific - to represent a certain product. E.g. in the hypertension example the sum of all methods to treat hypertension was understood as the technology. With the new and more specific definition the different methods correspond to different technologies, e.g. Doxazosin is now a technology.

When a new technology or product is put on the market for the first time at the end of the innovation process then the potential users may respond by adoption and the technology diffuses, if successful. This is known as the diffusion process. It constitutes the last stage in technological change [18]. A study of this process will show the adoption of the new health technology (e.g. magnetic resonance imaging - MRI) and its consequences for the individual user (e.g. the patient), the adopting firm (e.g. the hospital) and the society. Important feedback and other learning aspects from this stage of diffusion may influence the previous phases of invention and innovation. A usual response from competitors in the market at the end of the patent period would be to try to imitate the technology and produce it themselves. For the firms the purpose of this imitation activity is to get a share of the stock of profit resting in the market. Further improvements of the technology by the innovator or by the imitators can be considered

---

[78] Hall (1994) [12] supports the definition made in Mansfield [16]. Another definition is expressed in Stoneman (1995) [14], who defines technology as the ability to carry out productive transformations. Of course the two definitions coincide as the fact that *the ability to carry out productive transformations* in Stoneman's definition could be argued to require *a social pool of knowledge*, which is the basis of Mansfield's definition.

as the beginning of a new process of innovation and a launch of a new technology into the market.[79]

The question can then be raised: what are the circumstances under which an innovation is developed in the innovation process and introduced on a market as a new technology? In other words, what is the requirement for successful technological change in society?

One requirement that has to be fulfilled is that the innovation has to be *feasible* - scientifically and technically. There has to be some kind of inventive activity to generate an idea or a new skill. The feasibility of the new invention and its development in the innovation process is guided by the available and the newly experienced *act of insight*, known as the existing *state of the art* and new insight in technical and scientific basic research. A consequence of this existing knowledge base is that the developed innovation is often characterized as incremental rather than radical in nature, as no big steps are usually made in research knowledge.

In overall this requirement for technological change is known as *science push effects*[80] to symbolize that the accumulation of technical and scientific knowledge *pushes* the development of new technologies in certain directions.

However, we do not expect technologies to exist in a vacuum. They are part of the activities in the society as they are sent on a market and adopted by users to fulfill certain purposes. They fulfill a need. Therefore, another requirement for innovation and technological change is that users in society must demand them. This requirement is known as *demand pull effects*[81], because the demand by potential users in the market *pulls* the development activity in the direction of their need or demands.

A consequence of these two directions of effects on innovation and technological change is that *rather than viewing either the existence of a market demand or the existence of a technological opportunity as each representing a sufficient requirement for innovation to occur, one should consider them each as necessary, but not sufficient, for innovation to result; both must exist simultaneously* [10].[82] Later in the chapter the two effects on innovation - demand pull and science push - are described using linear models. However, in the next section

---

[79] Theories of diffusion are further discussed in the next chapter of the book.

[80] Technology push or discovery push effects.

[81] Need pull effects.

[82] Layton (1977) [19] seems to blur this distinction between necessary and sufficient requirements as he argues that *the recognition of need is a sufficient requirement for technological development, just as technical feasibility is the necessary requirement*. However, need or demand could never alone be taken as a sufficient requirement and off course Layton's mistake diminishes in that he finally states that *both requirements must be met for successful technological development* to be achieved [19].

a short description is given of the broad group of health technology and the institutional setting where innovations emerge.

4.0 Health technology and the institutional structure

Health technology is classified into groups according to its nature. Thus, health technology could be divided into two groups of product technologies; *pharmaceuticals* and *medical devices* and one group of process technologies; *procedures*.

A central characteristic of the development process for health technology is the extremely diverse and complex institutional structure within which decisions regarding developments take place [20]. This institutional structure and the organisation seem to differ between the three types of health technology; pharmaceuticals, devices and procedures, e.g. with respect to different degrees of regulation and public control of the adoption of the technologies. In this section a short description of the institutions and the process of innovations is given for the three types of health technology and specific requirements relevant in Denmark are mentioned.

4.1 Pharmaceuticals

Health technologies belonging to the group of pharmaceuticals could be said to contain some chemical entity or substance that affects a person's health by achieving a desired biological effect. According to Maxwell (1984) [21] there are four different sources for the discovery and development of a new pharmaceutical.[83] Two sources are basic research performed by the industry and academic institutions or the outcome of a screening of chemical compounds (lead[84] discovery [21]). Both could to some degree lead to radical innovations like new chemical entities.[85] Two other sources, which are based on more incremental approaches, are the making of some kind of molecularly modification of an old chemical lead or a known drug, or clinical observations with respect to new applications of existing drugs (lead development [21]). A source could

---

[83] Although Spilker (1989) [22] operates with seven sources, they correspond to Maxwell's four.

[84] By *lead* is understood chemical compounds with biological activities that are constructed as having therapeutic potential [21].

[85] However, the number of pharmaceuticals discovered and developed, where basic research could be argued to be the primary source, is rather limited. In fact among 717 completed applications in 1992 made by the registration authorities in Denmark (Lægemiddelstyrelsen) just 20 were concerned with original preparations (four approved). The other applications concerned synonyms, new dispensing forms, new indications and parallel import, etc. [23]. In total only 13 new chemical entities were introduced in Denmark in 1992. The same evidence is shown with figures from Germany where of 1,698 pharmaceuticals released in 1993 by the registration authorities in Germany (Bundesgesundheitsamt) only 26 consisted of new chemical entities [24].

also be a specific company's license arrangements and joint ventures with external business partners [22].

The pharmaceutical industry consists of large multinational companies with their own research departments and a high rate of resources devoted to research and development of new products.[86] In this science-based industry[87] patents are important in order to protect the developing company in its research and development process (R&D), because pharmaceuticals or chemical substances are easy to copy [20]. This risk is enhanced because of a tendency to longer lead times, a decrease in the number of new chemical entities and a significant increase in the costs of R&D of new drug introductions during the 1980s [26]. Many patents on a portfolio of different chemical compounds are therefore sought early during innovation.

Pharmaceuticals are the heaviest regulated health technology among the three groups listed above. This regulation exists almost worldwide. In Denmark, as in other European countries, the FDA form used in the United States has inspired the regulation. Before the regulatory authority allows diffusion in a market, the new pharmaceutical has to prove its efficacy and safety in clinical studies with three phases and after diffusion post-marketing clinical studies of effectiveness can be made. This documentation adds some extra time to the lead time and implies to some extent that the public authorities control the initial adoption. Some arguments for this regulation are that society fears the consequences of a monopolistic market consisting of multinational firms; that safety of the pharmaceutical is an important parameter, because possible damage on patients could be led directly back to the pharmaceutical and a fear of a high level of profit in the industry and the often opaque relation between a pharmaceutical and the resources used for R&D.

4.2 Medical devices

Medical devices represent a rather heterogeneous group of technologies with more than 50,000 different products, capturing both very capital-intensive technologies, such as computed tomography and magnetic resonance imaging scanners and on the other hand less capital-intensive technologies, such as diagnostic tests and utensils. Medical devices refer to in vitro and in vivo diagnostic substances; surgical, medical instruments and supplies; orthopaedic, prosthetic and surgical appliances and supplies; X-ray apparatus and tubes and related irradiation apparatus; electro-medical and electro-therapeutic apparatus; and ophthalmic goods [27].

The medical device industry consists of many small firms that are important in the phase of innovation, whereas the larger companies in the industry often adopt these

---

[86] The expenditures used by Danish companies on research and development of new pharmaceuticals correspond to 15.8 per cent of the total sale of pharmaceutical in 1993 [23].

[87] According to the taxonomy for firms by Pavitt (1984) [25].

innovative ideas thus having an important role in the phases of development and marketing. Although medical devices are a heterogeneous group, the value of patents is generally smaller than for pharmaceuticals [27]. The reason is that equipment is difficult to imitate, less investments are involved and because most of the medical devices are incremental[88] in nature with a short life-cycle. Current product modifications are often made in close interaction with physicians using the equipment at the hospital. The incremental nature of the medical device innovation makes applied research, findings in other sectors (e.g. the army and space industries) and on-site development important, while it typically is less dependent upon basic research after the first breakthrough. Furthermore, because of the heterogeneity of the medical device technologies the amount of resources spent by the industry differs a lot. Finally, this early research in devices is also financed by public research grants.

By the gradual implementation of European Commission Directives, the public regulation and control of medical devices in Denmark do only focus on safety of equipment [28]. There is no requirement to document efficacy as in the United States (Premarket Approval or Premarket Notification), although health technology assessment has been performed on a few number of high-ticket technologies. The guidelines for the planning of specialties among the Danish hospitals, issued by the National Board of Health, exert an indirect control with respect to some high-ticket and low volume treatments [29]. These guidelines define, after negotiation between the 14 counties and the Copenhagen Hospital Corporation, which specialties that have the character of national or regional specialties and where they should be located as opposed to specialties which can be found at a local level [30].

4.3 Medical procedures

Medical procedures can be characterized as clinical, surgical or medical working-procedures (software) in the hospital, most often only successful in combination with pharmaceuticals and/or medical devices (hardware). These innovations are normally incremental, as they are improvements of existing procedures used in the daily practice at the hospital. The innovator of these kinds of innovations is most often the professional, who is often the user too. The industry is only expected to be involved in the innovation process of procedures to the extent that the specific procedure is a result of either a device or a pharmaceutical. Therefore, the resources for research and development of new procedures are primarily public.

Diffusion of procedures is not expected to take place in the same kind of markets as for pharmaceuticals and devices. Possible sources for this diffusion would be scientific and

---

[88] This tendency to develop incremental device innovations is illustrated with premarket approval and notification 1993-data from FDA in the United States. Only 40 requests for premarket approval of new devices (radical innovations) were received by the regulation authority, whereas 6,288 requests for premarket notifications of new devices (incremental innovations) were received [27].

medical societies, conferences and information from quality assurance activities, guidelines, audits, etc. Consequently, there is wide geographical variation in the procedures used for the same treatment.

In Denmark, as in most other countries, there are no formal public regulation and control of medical procedures, which is also reflected in geographical variations explained by differences in need, visitations and facilities [31]. At a more informal level one could say that regulation and evaluation of procedures are based on the confidence between patient and professional. Firstly, the professional has to act according to his medical oath. Secondly, the medical community is expected to regulate its own behaviour in a professional self-regulation. Thirdly, the National Board of Health has a legal control and monitoring function with respect to the practices used in the hospitals.

5.0 Linear models of innovation

Innovation is complex and involves many different institutions and actors. A simplification of the understanding of the innovation process is therefore a useful starting point, when the aim is to describe and analyse demand and supply effects. The linear models of innovation are such simplified frameworks. These models are attractive, because they operate with two basic elements inherent in the different innovations - either *demand pull* or *science push* effects [32].

5.1 The science push model

The first linear model presented assumes that the process of innovation consists of a linear sequence of events of cause and effect originating from basic research and flowing through the more goal-oriented phases of applied research, development and production, before the innovation as a technology via marketing is introduced into the market. The feasibility resulting from scientific (and technical) knowledge *pushes* the development of the technology in the innovation process. The idea behind the linear *science push* model is illustrated in Figure 3.1 below.

Figure 3.1 : The science push model

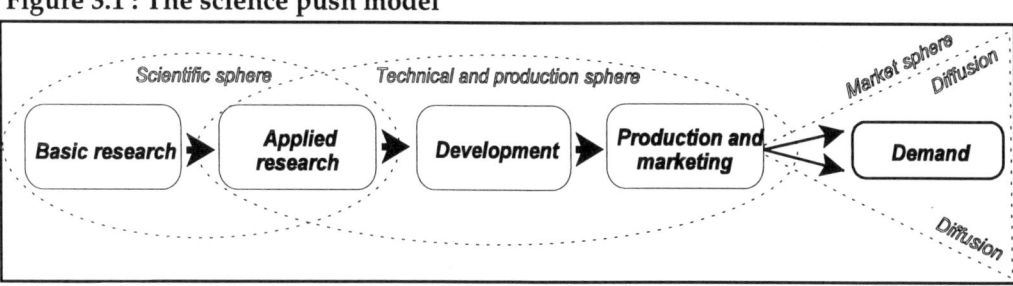

An implication of the model is that scientific (or technical) knowledge decides which innovations that are going to be developed by the industry or hospitals and afterwards diffuse into the society. An innovation reflecting this process is called *supply-induced*. This is because the users are expected to adopt what is supplied on the market as a response to the present scientific knowledge. Need or demand in the market are taken for granted and are expected to be present when the new technology reaches the market. The technology and the technological change are then perceived as autonomous activities separated from the rest of the society. The effects on the market of a supply-induced innovation are illustrated in Figure 3.2.

Figure 3.2 : Supply-induced innovation

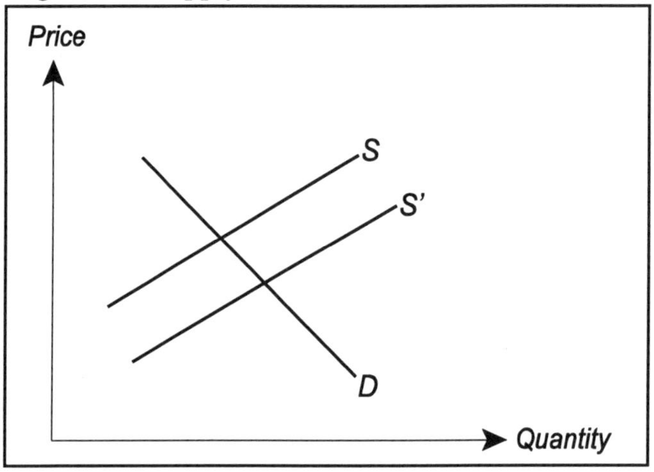

A supply-induced innovation is reflected in a downward shift of the supply curve from S to S' with demand taken for granted [10].[89]

Langrish et al. (1972) [33] present two modifications of the science push model. In the *science discovers and technology applies model* science and scientific discoveries are seen as the first innovative activity in the linear flow of events. In the *technological discovery model* the innovation is based on a technical invention without any use of new scientific knowledge. The first model typically includes the small group of radical innovations, whereas incremental innovations can be described by the last model. Kline et al. (1986) [9] support the last model, stating that the central process of innovations is a result of design and existing and accessible knowledge, rather than new scientific research.

---

[89] However, this diagram provides only part of the explanation. In the short run prices do not necessarily have to decrease as a consequence of the science push effects and the new technological invention. In the long run, prices are expected to decrease with technological change and economic growth.

The dependence on science as the primary input in the innovation process might be positively related to the R&D intensity, the patent activity[90] and therefore the number of radical innovations developed. Development of new drugs by the pharmaceutical companies based upon substantial accumulation of knowledge is the group of health technology that in some degree meets these characteristics.[91] Evidence from earlier studies has supported this [16,25]. Pavitt (1984) expects the relative importance of product innovations[92] in a sector to be positively associated with its R&D and patent intensity [25]. Based on 2,000 innovations in UK since 1945, he shows that product innovations accounts for 78 per cent of the total number of innovations in the pharmaceutical industry (129 observations) compared with a mean of 61 per cent for all sectors. This result supports that this type of (science-based) industry has a high R&D intensity. On the other hand the trend of the medical device innovations is that the methods and techniques applied in these innovations are well-known from other product areas and depend to a lesser extent on new scientific knowledge [34]. The R&D intensity as a measure of science-based innovations is questioned with respect to the medical device industry. However, Andreasen et al. (1990) [35] state that the R&D intensity in the Danish device industry varies according to product groups considered with 2.6 per cent of the total amount of sales spent on R&D in disposables up to 10.3 per cent in electro-medicals - almost as high as in the pharmaceutical industry (1987 figures).

A huge R&D intensity does of course not have to be a conclusive sign of a science-based technology or industry. It might just explain the fact that there in the innovation process has been a need for an extremely high level of information or knowledge to develop a technology and that considerable resources are needed to get this knowledge from inside and outside the organisation.

5.2 The demand pull model

Another reason for innovation to occur could be to respond to a demand expressed by the consumers (the potential adopters) in the market. Economists, considering invention and technological change as exogenous variables controlled by economic variables, have

---

[90] In the medical device industry patents in capital goods (capital equipment) may be a measure of the inventive activity and by that science push effects. On the other hand in the less capital-intensive pharmaceutical industry it is patent in new or improved products and processes. In the study by Walsh (1984) of science push versus demand pull patents in the pharmaceutical industry are treated as a measure of demand, with the output of the sector as the measure of the inventive activity - science push [1].

[91] Biomedical technologies (in the group of drugs) are science-based too. It is especially reflected in the fact that the starting point for biomedical technologies is in the science of genetics and biomedicine and the increasing public R&D funds to these areas.

[92] Which Pavitt (1984) defines as "innovations that are used in different sectors as opposed to process innovations that are used in the same sector as those in which they are produced" [25].

argued that market demand is the prime mover of innovations and that this demand *pulls* the development of technologies and initiates the necessary research and experiments needed. The origin in demand rotates the endpoints in the linear science-based model, which then becomes a demand-based model of innovation.

Dosi (1982, 1984) [32,36] explains the idea of demand pull as a phenomenon following a sequence of events in a functioning market. At a given point in time in any market it is expected that a set of goods exists which satisfies the needs of different purchasers - an equilibrium. The individuals in the market express their preferences regarding special features and characteristics of these goods through their demand functions determined by preferences and budget constraints.[93] If the consumers' preferences change for specific characteristics the patterns of demand change, as it happens in Figure 3.3. With increasing income this leads to an increase in the demand for goods embodying these characteristics. Now the firms and the supplier observe the change in consumer behaviour and reveal the changed preferences. This is the start of the innovation process with the firms trying to respond to the changed demand by developing and bringing the improved goods with the new characteristics on the market. A new equilibrium has arisen in *b*, see Figure 3.3.

Figure 3.3 : Demand-induced innovation

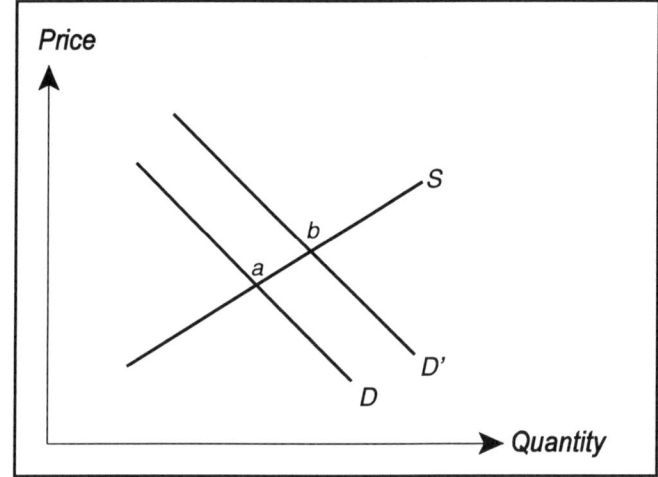

The change in demand seen as an upwards shift in the demand curve from D to D' illustrates this demand-induced innovation. This framework is based on the important assumption that it is possible to achieve this *a priori* information about the direction of the *pulling* by the market of the inventive activity (the upward shift) and that the

---

[93] Maximized utility behavior assumed.

producers get the signals and information through the changed prices and quantities (the new equilibrium).[94]

The change in preferences and thereby the demand of the users (professionals and patients) could be caused by medical circumstances, e.g. a change in a prevalence. Organisational conditions could be another reason for the pulling of the innovation in health technologies. University hospitals are expected to be more innovative and positive regarding new technologies, which is the reason why a large number of these hospitals could explain a high demand for technological changes in a country. Factors related to the patient are other possible demand pull factors, e.g. a demand for certain technological characteristics made by patient organisations.[95] Regulation and control of health technology, and strategic market conditions, in the innovation process are also examples of these demand pull effects. A final group of demand pull effects is guided by economic conditions in the society. A weight on cost containment in society would perhaps result in a demand for cost-effective health technology in the innovation process through a change in demand for some characteristics satisfying an efficiency requirement.

The actions in the linear demand pull model and their sequence are illustrated in Figure 3.4 that flows in the direction right to left.

Figure 3.4 : Demand pull model

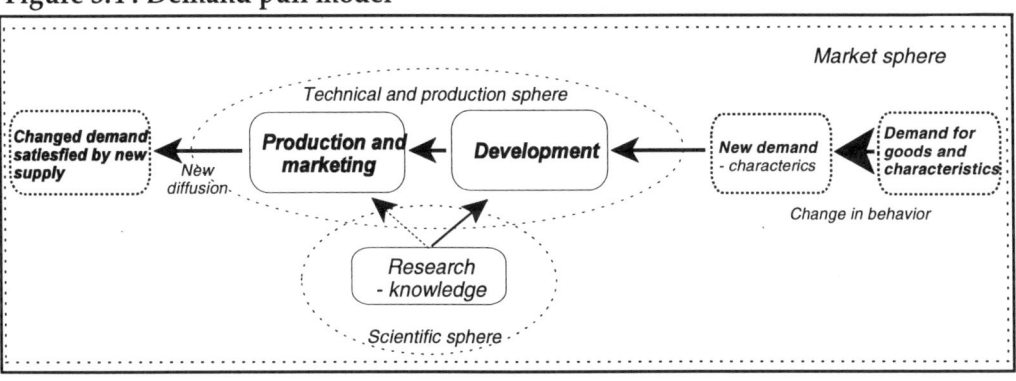

Langrish et al. (1972) [33] distinguish between two demand pull models. A *customer needs model* guided by market demand as shown in Figure 3.4 and a *management by objective model*, where demand arises at the request of management inside the firm/industry and is not directed by market demand.

---

[94] However, this demand curve framework, guided by the combination of prices and quantities to explain demand-induced innovations, may restrict the interpretation of demand because of the difficulties in knowing the demand in the early innovation process and because of the uncertainty in identifying whether a shift in or along the demand curve occurs.

[95] E.g. to develop fewer painful technologies, which was an argument for the development of minimal invasive therapies.

5.3 Demand pull or science push?

Does any of the two presented models explain the process of innovation and development of health technology?

A confirmation of the existence of a demand pull model would be that a market response from the consumers exists at least in the neo-classical approach. This response is reflected in the learning capabilities in the use of innovations, where the *pulling* is seen as a change in the desired characteristics of the innovation resulting from this learning-by-doing activity. There is an increasing interest in the western society in regulation and control of health technology, e.g. reforms regarding cost containment, internal markets (purchaser and provider functions) and the growth in health technology assessment. The aim of these policy reforms, as demand pull factors providing certain stimuli, is to alert the direction of the innovations to a development of cost-saving health technologies in the future [37].

However, some problems are embodied in the demand pull approach when used to explain the process of innovation. A general problem is to be able to distinguish between shifts in demand curves and movements along the same demand curve. It is difficult to conclude whether it is demand or supply that has induced the innovation. How long time after the shift in the demand curve does it make sense to characterize an innovation as demand-induced? Consider the case of AIDS. For a long time now constant (or perhaps slightly increasing) demands for a vaccine to help the infected persons have been present (a shift in the demand curve). Simultaneously, research and development in finding a vaccine have increased enormously. The unanswerable question then is, whether it was the early shift in the demand curve, when AIDS first was found, or it is the later intensified research and development activities by science which as a supply-inducement are reflected in a move along the demand curve that have guided the innovative activity in the AIDS case today? Another problem with the demand pull model is that it cannot explain what happens between the moment when change in demand is recognized by the producer and the moment when the outcome reaches the market [32]. In the demand pull model in Figure 3.4 *the technical sphere* illustrates this black box, with technological opportunities taken as given, and only reacts upon market requests. A demand pull approach is not able to describe radical innovations. The time of origin is difficult to decide, because needs are nearly infinite, when talking about innovations in the health care sector.

It is argued that the increased complexity in the innovation process and the long-run planning of the R&D policy in the industry almost reject the hypothesis of prompt responses from the manufacturer, when demand in the market changes [32]. The level of scientific and technical knowledge available also determines the technological change in any sector at a given time. With a R&D lead time for pharmaceuticals up till ten years or more a quick response by the pharmaceutical industry seems unlikely.

Does this criticism of the demand pull approach then instead support a science push model in the health care sector? In a historical perspective the role of scientific input in the innovation process has been increasing and the importance of information and know-how is significant today. There is a growth in the resources spent on R&D and the previous mentioned studies showed a positive correlation between R&D resources and the number of requested patents, as the output of innovation. Innovations in health care are dependent on interdisciplinary research between individuals with different professional backgrounds or between different medical specialities [37]. As a consequence of this interdisciplinary effect another supply-induced effect arises - the interinstitutional effect on supply. Today innovations in health care are increasingly a result of a process of natural crossing of institutional borders, as interactions between universities and other academic centres with the industry are almost the rule.[96] The regulation of pharmaceuticals and a higher demand for cost-effectiveness explain some of these interactions. A pharmaceutical has to show efficacy and safety according to regulations before it can be sent on the market. For medical producers to illustrate this to the public authorities, cooperation with clinicians in the academic centres is natural. A cooperation that also signals important information on needs to the manufacturers (the *a priori* information in the demand pull approach). Furthermore, the outcome of science is uncertain and full information on technological choices ex ante, as required in the science push model, is impossible to achieve.

This discussion reveals that both models obviously have their drawbacks in explaining the innovation process for health technology. As concluded above with respect to the necessary conditions for technological change, an innovation does not exist in a vacuum and is thereby autonomous neither of the science sphere nor of the market sphere. The linear models may be used to decide whether health technology tend to be more influenced by demand than by science or the reverse. However, the models ignore the uncertainty in innovations by excluding the experience from learning and feedback in the process of innovation. Below a short description of the different types of learning is given.

6.0 Learning and feedback in innovation

The innovation process is a process of knowledge accumulation and every accumulation of knowledge involves learning of different types [39]. These different steps of accumulation of knowledge and learning are aimed at reducing uncertainty embodied in the innovation, e.g. uncertainty about the effectiveness of the innovation.

The R&D process could be regarded as a process of internal learning or a process of learning based on interaction with external sources of knowledge, e.g. universities. An example of this type of learning process is seen by the collection of knowledge of laws of nature in basic research [17].

---

[96] Discussed in Rosenberg (1982) [17] and for medical devices by Gelijns et al. (1995) [37,38].

Learning by doing is the learning generated as a by-product of ordinary production following the R&D process with the focus upon costs and efficiency of production [40]. During production the change in knowledge from this *in-house* learning by doing results in increased working skills, efficient production and may have feedback to the further technological change and development of the technology considered.

An interesting type of learning in the context of demand pull factors, feedback and a more iterative model of innovation, is *learning by using*. As presented in Rosenberg (1982) [17], *learning by using* refers to learning as a function of the utilization of the technology by the final user after a market introduction. It generates embodied knowledge from the early experience and a better understanding of the relationship between characteristics of the technology and its performance. As feedback loops to the development phase appear, this learning experience from actual use will finally lead to improvements in the technology's design. A disembodied knowledge from the learning is the change in use of the technology resulting in a higher productivity of the technology. Again feedback loops with respect to design characteristics of new product developments are signalized backwards to the development phase. For innovations in health care some characteristics related to *learning by using* can be described by a high degree of systemic complexity in the technology, typically high fixed costs of equipment and its operation (devices), huge costs for R&D, long lead time (pharmaceuticals), uncertainty about knowledge and performance to be reduced through use and experience, e.g. the future practice uses of the technology (procedures).

In overall, the expected amount of learning is related to the degree of uncertainty contained in the innovation considered. With respect to pharmaceuticals the highest extent of learning is expected in the complex R&D phase, because of its relatively large amount of radical innovations and the long lead time. *Learning by using* is on the other hand expected to be one of the most important contributors to feedback to the development and design in medical devices and procedures. Frequent product improvements of a device, because of different kinds of user-producer relations, are usual. Feedback from *learning by doing* is expected in all three types of innovations.

The output resulting from activities and feedback in the innovation process can be viewed as iterative information flows. In this process, information flows forward and backwards between the linked activities, e.g. the flow of information gained from use of technology. Activities are not experienced as unidirectionally linked as in the linear models of innovation. The amount of information used, and hence the amount of feedback, is dependent upon the quantity of scientific or technical knowledge available at the time of development. The success of getting this information is dependent upon factors such as characteristics of knowledge, its communication and absorption, incentives and threats throughout the system [12].

In the next section a frame for an iterative feedback model with multidirectional flows of information and learning incorporated presented by Kline et al. (1986) [9] as a *chain-linked model* of innovation is described and analysed for innovations in health care.

7.0 The chain-linked model[97]

As a more realistic alternative in describing and analysing the activities in the innovation process, the *chain-linked model* seeks to capture the multidirectional flows of activities and information without restricting the focus to either demand or science as single explanations. The chain-linked model is a nested model capturing both the flows of the science push model and the flows of the demand pull model. With its multidirectional character on flows of information and the separation of the process of innovation in five interdependent paths, the possible learning and feedback responses are also included. Figure 3.5 illustrates the model.[98]

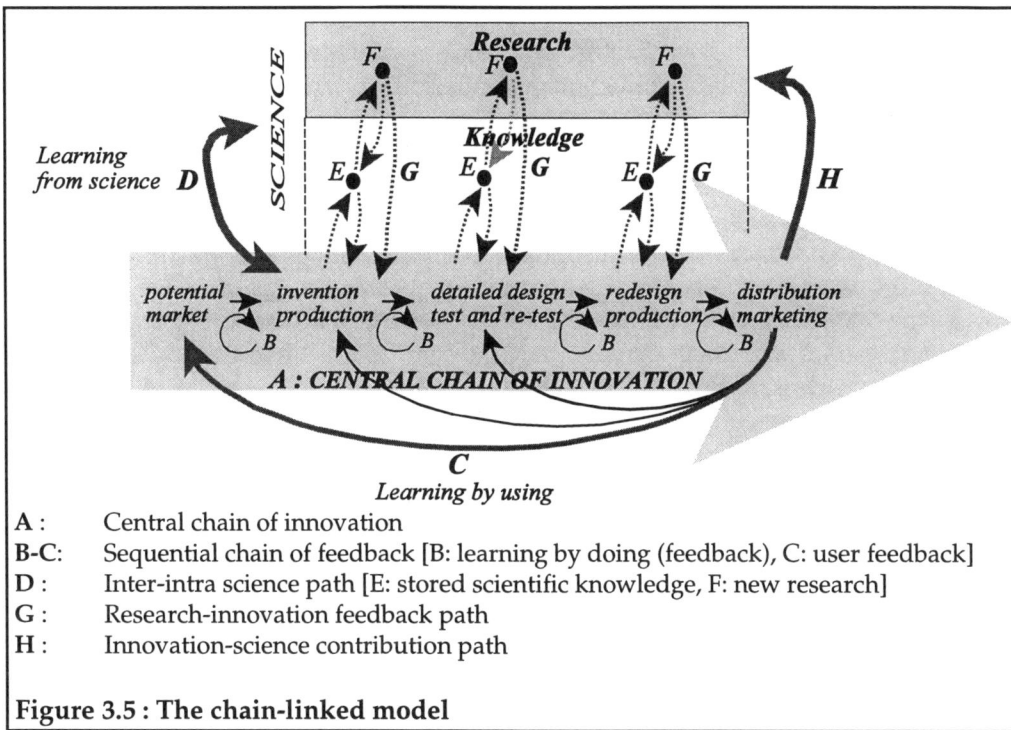

A : Central chain of innovation
B-C: Sequential chain of feedback [B: learning by doing (feedback), C: user feedback]
D : Inter-intra science path [E: stored scientific knowledge, F: new research]
G : Research-innovation feedback path
H : Innovation-science contribution path

Figure 3.5 : The chain-linked model

The **first path** is the *central chain of innovation* running inside the firm after a potential market demand has been discovered. This path, marked with *A* in Figure 3.5, links the activities when an innovation is going to be designed, developed, produced and finally distributed into the market. If the innovation corresponds to the potential market demand, the marketing changes the conditions in the market. This path looks a bit like the invention-innovation-diffusion pattern of technological change in the science-push model, apart from the links to the market in both ends of the process. However, the

---

[97] This model is presented in Kline et al. (1986) [9]. The contribution here to these authors' model of innovation is the application to the field of health technology.

[98] Figure 3.5 is primarily based upon [8], although names of links are added.

single-cause effects of either demand pull or science or technology push must then be rejected, because of the link between the market and the innovation process in the central chain of innovation. Taken as a kind of sequential decision making by the innovator, a fulfilment of a potential market demand would only succeed if the necessary conditions of design, development and production are available. However, these conditions would only be mixed to become an innovation if a market demand exists. The process of innovation described in the central chain rests upon existing knowledge available inside each firm. Therefore innovations resulting from this process are expected to be incremental and based on scale economics, where the amount and novelty of used knowledge are not decisive factors.

The **second path** is a series of feedback links [9]. Here I call them the *sequential feedback paths* as they consist of many iterative steps inside and between activities considered as either demand or technical/production dependent. Two types of feedback exist in the paths. The first type is the internal feedback between the firm departments because of cooperation and learning in the process (*learning by doing*). These are the iterative steps inside the central chain of innovation. In Figure 3.5 the internal feedback is shown with the letter *B*. It could be feedback on design and development units from a production unit, when a new tool or method introduced in production gives opportunity for new and different designs to be developed.[99] It could also be a feedback inside the production unit because of learning by doing. The second type is the feedback from the users (*learning by using*) and their market demand back to the first step of design and development regarding possible changing characteristics and improvements of the innovation.[100] This is an iterative step, marked *C* in Figure 3.5, between the two separate groups of activities belonging to the demand and technical/production side, respectively.

Until now science has not entered the model and accumulated knowledge of science has not been part of any innovation and technological change process. The **third path**, as I call *the inter-intra science path* and marked *D*, in the chain-linked model represents learning from science and scientific knowledge. This path is lying exogenously alongside the central chain of innovation. In this model the idea of science is not necessarily the first step in the development phase (*learning in the R&D process*), as it was in the science-push model. Science is used when needed, which is the reason why it is stretched along the whole process of development.

---

[99] E.g. the introduction of a method to coat tablets with different amounts of sealing-wax made the development of a multi-unit principle in the sustained release drug technology possible.

[100] This could be illustrated by a patient demand in the treatment of kidney stones for methods less painful than open surgery or the Dornier lithotripter available in the beginning of the 1980s. With the availability of the second generation Piezo lithotripters in 1984 in Germany this demand was satisfied because the advantage of the Piezolith was that it was a painless device [41].

However, as realized from Figure 3.5, the use of science occurs in two stages (knowledge and research) both lying alongside the central chain [9]. The reason is that most of the innovations are incremental rather than radical in nature and therefore not necessarily a result of new scientific research. The usual way to learn from and use science along the central chain of innovation is to use the existing and stored scientific knowledge iteratively. A huge accumulation of scientific knowledge is already present and available in books and journals etc. This external knowledge is only needed when the internal knowledge available in the firm's own R&D department is not sufficient. In Figure 3.5 these links to the existing base of scientific knowledge are marked with E. However, from the *knowledge box* to the *central chain* in situations in which the stored scientific knowledge is not sufficient any more one has to gain experience from research. New research will be undertaken at universities and at other research institutions to obtain new scientific knowledge in the area. Research then becomes the other stage of science, as seen in the *research-box* and with the links between scientific knowledge and research E-F in Figure 3.5, where F represents the new research activity undertaken.[101] The type of scientific knowledge or research used at a certain point in time differs. The usefulness of pure basic science is normally restricted to the early phases of development, whereas the later phases demand more specific and goal-oriented knowledge and research. Furthermore, this depends on whether the innovation is incremental or radical in nature.

When research is needed according to the third path, a research outcome F will be transferred to the scientific knowledge base E and afterwards used for invention, design or production purposes in the innovation process. However, the outcome of basic research resulting from research activity can also directly create new ideas and influence the invention and design in the innovation process without passing through an intermediate knowledge base. This will typically characterize the few radical innovations found in science-based industries [12] like the pharmaceutical industry, e.g. the development of genetic technologies. This direct learning link between research and the central chain, *the research-innovation feedback path* - a **fourth path**, are illustrated in Figure 3.5 with the arrow at G.

The **fifth path** in the chain-linked model of innovation, and not included in the linear models, is the feedback from the resulting products of innovation in science and new research, *the innovation-science contribution path*. The application of endoscopes, developed in gastroenterology, gynaecology and orthopaedic surgery, for the treatment of cholecystectomy in general surgery may be an example of this kind of feedback. This is because the new use of the innovation contributes to science and research in a new minimally invasive area - general surgery. Another example of this feedback and contribution to science is the equipment developed and sold to research institutions, e.g. microscopes, computers, etc. The scientific institutions use these technologies for

---

[101] This science-relation most often exists between larger companies and e.g. universities in specified research contracts or license agreements. Small firms less frequently cooperate with universities. It might be a question of resources or academic personnel employed.

research and thereby contribute to the scientific knowledge. This feedback path is marked *H* in Figure 3.5. Of course a contribution to science can also occur internally in a firm's own R&D departments without any research institutions involved.

Besides the pushes and pulls from science and demand in the process of innovation this nested chain-linked model consists of feedback responses from the three types of learning - *learning in the R&D process* (*learning from science*), *learning by doing* and *learning by using*. The feedback and these different learning effects reduce the uncertainty in the innovation process. Learning seems to be an ongoing activity in the model and then feedback can even occur late. This may have implications for an early warning activity, where one does not know with certainty, when a health technology is fully developed. It poses the risk of imperfect advice to the decision-maker in the early identification and signalizing activity.

The separation of scientific knowledge and scientific research in the chain-linked model makes a more realistic picture of reality, when a technology is developed. Scientific methods do not have to be invented each time before a technology is developed. Because scientific knowledge can be stored, innovations are expected to start with a search in existing knowledge, when learning from science is needed. Often the starting point is not in the scientific knowledge base, but perhaps in some technical knowledge or idea, which is the reason why science is treated as an external activity lying alongside the central chain of innovation - only used when needed.

However, the implications of this model do not make demand and supply conditions useless in the exploration of the process of innovation for health technology. Both factors of demand and supply as well as learning are expected to be present in the process of innovation. Analysis of these factors and learning effects is possible in the chain-linked model. With learning and feedback on innovation this exploration of factors of demand and supply could have very important consequences for an early warning system and the information signaled from such a system, as discussed in the introduction to the present chapter and in further detail in chapter 8.

8.0 Case studies

In this section two case studies - *sustained release drugs* and *laparoscopic cholecystectomy* - are presented and discussed in relation to demand and supply conditions and learning feedback.

8.1 Sustained release drugs[102]

In this case study of the sustained release technology applied on different kinds of drugs a short description of the idea of the technology will be given. Afterwards some applications of the technology are presented and the motives for their innovation and development are discussed.

Traditionally, a drug will be quickly released with a total release of its clinical efficacy shortly after entering the patient's stomach and bowels. The clinical efficacy of the active substance of the drug in the serum concentration must be between the toxic effect and the minimum effective level, as shown in Figure 3.6 below. With a short half life[103] $T_{½}$ of a drug and a high minimum effective level several doses of the drug will normally have to be taken each day, as illustrated in Figure 3.6 with the two peaks in serum concentration showing the two times the drug is taken. Sometimes, the quick release technology has disadvantages such as unsatisfactory compliance, not securing a stable level of efficacy and not releasing the efficacy of the drug when needed.

Figure 3.6 : The traditional release of a drug (serum per time unit)

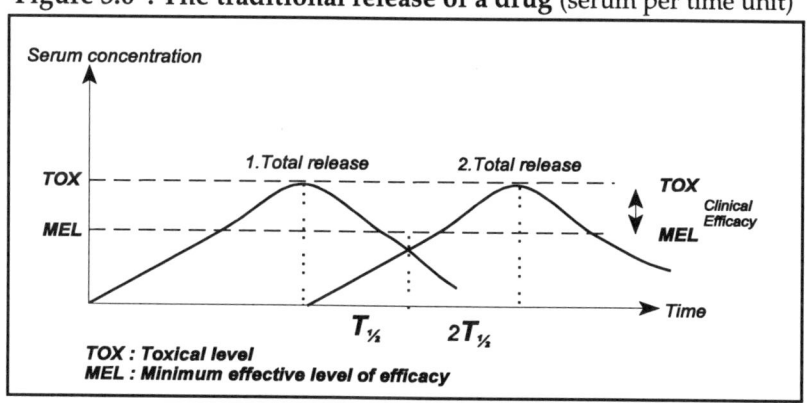

The idea of a *sustained release technology* applied on a drug is to find a constant level of the drug's efficacy in serum per time unit between the toxic effect (TOX) and the

---

[102] Data for the case are based upon interviews (with Medical Chief Poul Erik Branebjerg and International Marketing Chief Jørgen Dich, Nycomed DAK AS), articles, statistics and informal documents.

[103] The time taken for the concentration of a substance in the serum to fall to half its initial value.

minimum effective level (MEL). The purpose is to try to control and guide the release of effects in the serum concentration through a period of time.

However, controlling the release level with respect to effects in the liver and kidneys to get the same release per effect is not possible directly. The relation between the dosage level and the serum concentration could instead manage this control. It will be as a control of the entrance in the human body.[104] This is why the sustained release technology is a dosage form of a drug that acts over a period of time.

There are two different types of sustained release matrices - a single-unit principle and a multi-unit principle. In the single-unit principle the active substance is founded in a small plastic container to be swallowed as a normal pill. The drug is released when the container dissolves in the stomach. This method ensures a sustained release, but not a gradually delayed action. With this technology and depending on the level of acid in the stomach only the time of release can be controlled but not the amount of active substance release at that time, as a total release will occur.[105] The risk of the single-unit principle is that dose-dumping with a rapid release of the drug in the patient takes place. A high level of acid in the stomach, e.g. because of food consumed or a crushed container, increases the risk of dumping.

To avoid dose-dumping, a method that ensures that the release is both sustained and gradual - the multi-unit principle - was developed. In the multi-unit method small pieces of the tablets with the active substance are coated with different depths of sealing-wax. The purpose of this wax method is to avoid a focused release on a small area in the stomach as well as dose-dumping and instead have a gradual release. A plastic container can still be used to make the sustained release. This technology is less sensitive to the acid in the stomach and the food consumed, and the consequences of crushing are limited as well.

If the application of a sustained release technology to a specific drug is to have any medical and economic justification[106] compared with the traditional quick release drug a set of requirements has to be fulfilled when an application of a drug is considered. First, it has to be drugs whose level of serum concentration is important. Secondly, the half life of the drug has to be short. If the time for halving the efficacy of the drug is long, e.g. 24 hours, there will be less reason to delay its release, as the benefit from an

---

[104] This control of efficacy through the level of dosages is, however, not without problems. Human factors impede the control, because the release in serum concentration varies with size.

[105] In an attempt to obtain the gradual release a modified single-unit method was developed. A laser was used to get a small perforation in the plastic container, which resulted in this gradual release of the substance. However, the risk of the method was that a concentrated release occurs at the same place in the stomach. Therefore the modification of the single-unit method is not used anymore.

[106] And thereby increase the likelihood of being a success in the market.

easier administration is limited. Thirdly, the milligram-content of the substance has to be limited due to the size of the container. Fourthly, because this application technology is expensive the elasticity of prices on the market for pharmaceuticals with respect to competing preparations should not be high.[107]

The application of the sustained release technology

The group of patients in which this incremental innovation is used is very heterogeneous with respect to applications of the technology in different drugs. However, a potential group of patients with a given disease has to fulfill the requirements mentioned above, e.g. to have benefits from a gradual release of the morphine in a preventive prophylaxis treatment to reduce pain, or perhaps a need for a sustained release due to working conditions. Some examples of applications of the sustained release technology are shown in Table 3.1.[108]

Table 3.1 : Sustained release drugs (examples)

Chemical substance	ATC-Code[1]	Anatomical group	Therapeutic group	Sustained release drug	Price index[2]
Glyceryl trinitrate	C01 DA 02	Cardiovascular	Cardial therapy	Nitroglycerin	0.8
Diltiazem	C02 DE 04	Cardiovascular	Antihypertensives	Myonil retard	1.3
Furosemide	C03 CA 01	Cardiovascular	Diuretics	Furix retard	1.4
Metoprolol	C07 AB 02	Cardiovascular	Beta Blockers	Selo-Zok	1.5
Morphine	N02 AA 01	Nervous	Analgesics	Contalgin	1.7
Theophyllinge	R03 DA 04	Respiratory	Anti-Asthmatics	Theo-Dur	1.1

1. ATC-code: Anatomical-Therapeutic-Chemical-classification system.
2. Price-index: price per 24 hour doses for SR-drug is compared with the cheapest drug that has the same chemical substance.

Four of the examples of sustained release drugs are from the anatomical group of the cardiovascular system. In the group of antihypertensive drugs based on the chemical substance, diltiazem, one sustained release drug is Myonil Retard, developed and produced by Nycomed DAK AS. This sustained release is an application of the original drug Myonil, which is the cheapest drug in the diltiazem group, showing that Myonil Retard is a more expensive drug (by a factor 1.3 in the price index). Another sustained release drug belonging to the anatomical group of the cardiovascular system is Selo-Zok, developed and produced by Astra Hässle AS. It is also used in the treatment of hypertension and angina pectoris as a beta-blocking agent and is based on the chemical

---

[107] As the subsidy from the regulatory authorities is a fixed subsidy for each drug.

[108] The sources are the Danish Drug Statistic [42] and the database from the Physician Association's Drug Register [43].

substance Metoprolol. An example of a sustained release application belonging to another anatomical group than the cardiovascular system is Contalgin, which is a morphine drug for the nervous system, produced by KABI Pharmacia AS. The price of this sustained release drug is 1.7 higher than the cheapest non-sustained drug in the same group - Morphine (Nycomed DAK).

The motives for innovation and development of sustained release drugs

The most important reason for the development and application of the sustained release technology is that the scientific and technical knowledge and experience with the relationship between dose level, serum concentration and efficacy became available. This relationship, together with a low half life of the efficacy in the serum concentration, are two important medical factors, when a development of a sustained release drug is considered.[109] Furthermore, there could have been some learning by using (or perhaps learning by doing) involved in the innovation process of a multi-unit principle to replace the existing less advanced single-unit principle. At least this might be the case with the negative experience gained from the use of the single-unit principle where a laser perforation in the container enabled a gradual release.

Looking at the examples of sustained release applications in the table above, it seems to be demand pull factors that in general can explain the drive in the process of innovation for the specific drugs. First, a change in demand for a sustained release technology may be explained by medical or patient-specific circumstances. Patients and physicians are expected to demand a drug with a high patient compliance because of a better drug consumption with fewer side-effects. The importance of this is especially significant, when the half life is short, as the number of times a drug has to be consumed each day increases when the half life of the drug decreases. With a SR-drug this will be limited to a few times, because the sustained release of the efficacy in the serum concentration is more gradual. It is the case with a SR-drug as Myonil Retard, where the consumption is reduced from twice to once a day, which may be important, e.g. when the patient still is on the labour market. Other drugs where this is the case are Contalgin (reduced from 3-4 to 2-3 times a day), Nitroglycerin, Theo-Dur and Selo-Zok. In the innovation of Theo-Dur one may argue that another medical demand factor for the development of a sustained release alternative is a new trend on prophylaxis in the treatment of asthma to replace the traditional use of drugs and only to take them when needed.

Other reasons for innovations in the sustained release technology and its applications to different kinds of drugs can be explained by demand pull factors belonging to the

---

[109] At least if medical conditions are to explain the SR-drug as a success in the market. The fulfilment of the medical needs for a sustained release might be present in a SR-drug as Theo-Dur from Astra Draco AS with $T_{1/2}$ equals 20 minutes. On the other hand, medical needs are a problem with SR-drugs in the group of non steroid anti-inflammable drugs, because of a missing serum-efficacy correlation and a high $T_{1/2}$ (twenty-four hours).

market and its environment.[110] Most of the developed sustained release drugs are a kind of relaunch of an existing product.[111] The regulation in the pharmaceutical market could explain this relaunch and modification of an existing drug, where developed innovations are protected against competitors by patent rights. A patent right provides a favourable market position for the firm. Therefore, as a commercial interest there is a demand for the maintenance of these patent rights by the end of the patent period of an existing drug. The development of a modified sustained release formula for this drug will prolong the patent period and change the market demand from the expired patent to the new registered sustained release patent and thereby keep the share of the market. According to Lossius (1991) [44], one example is Astra's development of Selo-Zok, where the quickly release alternative Seloken was removed from the market and replaced by the more expensive sustained release drug - Selo-Zok.[112] A demand for further patent rights can be seen as a strategic move in the market, which makes the development of synonymous drugs by the competitors more expensive and difficult and delay their possible introduction into the market.

Pharmaceutical prices as a demand from the firm generated by economic factors cannot be rejected either as a motive for innovation. The development of a sustained release technology on an existing drug could be explained by the possibility of having a higher price and a profit on the drug. Lossius (1991) [44] criticism may show this, although Astra in the same journal rejects it.

As a conclusion on the drive in the innovation process of the sustained release technology, demand pull are likely to explain the application of a sustained release technology on the drugs in Table 3.1 and their introduction onto the market. Most successful SR-drugs have experienced a demand generated by medical and patient reasons because of the possible improvements in compliance from the sustained release technology. Furthermore there are reasons to suspect that strategic-commercial market interests caused the development of SR-drugs because of a demand for maintenance of patent rights and a less price-sensitive product. A demand pull as a consequence of specific conditions in the market.

---

[110] The rules and regulations in the market.

[111] For example as is the case with Selo-Zok, Myonil Retard, Contalgin and Theo-Dur.

[112] Astra, however, refuses the criticism of Lossius (1991) [44] by stating that the development of a sustained release drug was an improvement and therefore the increase in price is justified.

8.2 Laparoscopic cholecystectomy[113]

Each year in Denmark around 3,800 cholecystectomies are performed for the treatment of gallstones and inflammation in the gallbladder. Traditionally, the responsibility for the treatment of cholecystectomy has belonged to the field of general surgery using an open surgical technique. However, diagnosing of gallstones has to a larger extent been the responsibility of the internal medicine specialities. Open surgery is an effective method for the removal of the gallbladder. However, the disadvantages are that it is painful, fully invasive and results in large scars. Finally, it involves long hospital stay and time for convalescence afterwards.

Like the tendency in other areas of surgery, minimally invasive surgery (minimal access surgery) in the form of the laparoscopic technology was in the early 1980s introduced in general surgery. With its introduction in Germany in 1982, appendectomy was the first surgical area where the laparoscopic technology was used [45]. However, since this early adoption the diffusion of laparoscopic appendectomy has been modest internationally, although its diagnostic capabilities must not be overlooked. The first laparoscopic cholecystectomy conducted internationally seems to have been carried out in Germany in 1986, although the first laparoscopic cholecystectomy reported in the literature was in France in 1987 [46,47]. In Denmark, cholecystectomies were for the first time carried out as a laparoscopic procedure with the adoption at two hospitals in January 1991.[114]

The advantage of the laparoscopic technology is that it is a minimally invasive procedure where only 3-4 punctures[115] in the abdominal cavity are needed instead of an open invasive procedure. Furthermore, the diagnostic and therapeutic phases can be combined by using the laparoscopic technology. The benefits to be expected for the patient are less pain and trauma, shorter hospital stays and a quicker convalescence. A Danish study showed that the median postoperative inpatient stay was two days for patients treated with the laparoscopic technology as opposed to six days for traditional cholecystectomy patients, and the median time for convalescence decreased to eight days from a normal of four to six weeks [50].[116] Besides the possible increase in quality of life for the patient, this technology also made expectations as a potentially cost-saving technology for the society [52]. In around 80 per cent of the cholecystectomies the

---

[113] Data for this case are based on conferences, books, articles and informal documents.

[114] Hillerød Hospital and Aarhus University Hospital [48,49].

[115] One punctation to get the scope through, while the others are used for the different surgical tools, e.g. laser or electrocautery to burn the gallbladder.

[116] Recent evidence suggests, however, that inpatient stay and convalescence period decrease in open cholecystectomies as well, simply because of changing traditions in the surgical field [51].

laparoscopic technology can be used, whereas the last complicated cholecystectomies still warrant the traditional open surgical procedure.

The consequence is that there has been a fast, uncontrolled and wide diffusion of laparoscopic cholecystectomy in the United States, Canada and Europe. This is the case in Denmark as well, where laparoscopic cholecystectomy has experienced a wide and rapid diffusion with a close to 100 per cent adoption of the technology today by the Danish hospitals.[117]

A historical preview[118]

The development of the laparoscopic technology has historically emerged from other invasive fields such as gastroenterology, gynaecology and orthopaedic surgery, where different kinds of endoscopes were invented and developed, especially for internal diagnostic purposes. Back in 1805, about 180 years before the introduction of laparoscopes in general surgery, the first primitive endoscopy in the urethra with a tube and candlelight was attempted by Bozzini [38].

Two characteristics are central in the incremental innovation process of endoscopic tools - *flexibility* and *visualization*. Both were needed if the scope was to be used for diagnostic purposes, which were not only restricted to a constrained area of the natural entrances of the body. With respect to visualization of the diagnostic target, the quality of the light sources and the lenses used for the scope were important parameters. The early innovation process at the end of the last century could then be characterized as guided by a number of *technology pushes*. Examples are Edison's development of the light bulb and Nitzhe's improvements on the optical lens system, which offered some new technological possibilities.

The need for flexibility was another characteristic in scope innovation, especially in *the gastroenterological field* with the development of gastroscopes. With the development of fiber-optics in 1954 in another sector an important technological push was enabled to develop a fully flexible scope that could reach internal organs which was only seen before in open surgery. In 1957 the first prototype of a flexible gastroscope was developed, although the interest from the industry was limited until a presentation appeared in The Lancet in 1961. Then a number of firms in the United States and later in Japan entered the market in close cooperation with the scientists who initially had developed the technology. This is the learning from science relation, which in the chain-linked model was described by the Research-Innovation Feedback Path G, although the initiative came from the medical scientists, as it was the idea in the science-push model.

---

[117] For additional information about the diffusion of laparoscopic technologies in Denmark and internationally see chapter 5 and 6 of this book

[118] The main source for this section has been Gelijns et al. (1995) [38].

The entry of Japanese firms[119] in the market resulted in a demand pull for scopes for other gastrointestinal purposes, because of a higher prevalence of gastric cancer and gastrointestinal diseases in Japan. This factor and the development of the colonoscope, which enabled a combination of diagnostic and therapeutic processes, stimulated the innovation of gastroscopes in the late 1960s.

In *the gynaecological area* there was an increasing interest around 1950 in the development of a scope that could reduce the length of the hospitalization and the patient's considerable pain from intra abdominal procedures. Opposed to the gastroenterological innovation, this research and development process focused more on advances in visualization. Improved illumination with new lens systems and fiber-optics made it possible to compare pictures of patients at different time intervals and thereby increase the diagnostic accuracy. Further improvements came with the idea of using the newly invented television[120] in the transmission of pictures by putting a camera on the tube, so that the picture could be viewed immediately by the whole operating team [38]. These incremental improvements of the gynaecological laparoscope made it more widely adopted at the end of the 1960s and early 1970s, although the techniques, especially the television, still had to be improved. Sharing the experience from the colonoscope, an operation laparoscope was developed in 1972, which made the gynaecological procedures less invasive. Afterwards, in the 1970s, a demand pull was realized, because of the popularity of sterilization as a contraception method, which further stimulated innovation in the field of gynaecological diagnostics and therapy [53].

Both with respect to the gastroscope and the gynaecological laparoscope some very important science pushes (learning effects from science on innovation) were encountered at the end of the 1970s with the invention of a microprocessor chip to replace the fiber optic. The development of the video-guided endoscope with superior images, smaller instruments and cheaper technology had been achieved. Again Japanese companies were the most important producers. With the introduction in the 1980s of the laser and the electrocautery, the consequence of this video-guided instrument was an increased rate of adoption of both video-guided gastroscopes and gynaecological laparoscopes. Because of learning and the fulfilment of certain parameters such as precision, flexibility and visualization, the technology had now become of interest in other areas of medicine (interspecialty relations). The first other field to use scopes for diagnostic and therapeutic purposes was in orthopaedic surgery, which started to perform arthoscopies in treating arthrosis at the end of the 1980s.

---

[119] Japanese firms (e.g. Olympus) entered because of their expertise in producing cameras, although the reason first of all was due to a licence agreement with American firms. An interdisciplinary knowledge (expertise) [38] which could be described as a sequential user feedback from the camera market (path C - learning by using) and learning from science - the inter-intra science path from stored scientific (and technical) knowledge on cameras and visualization (path E).

[120] Another interdisciplinary relation belonging to Inter-Intra Science Path (E-F).

The diffusion to general surgery

Another of the new fields for minimally invasive therapy was in general surgery with the development and introduction of laparoscopic cholecystectomy in 1986-87. There are several reasons for this late interest in the innovation and use of the scope-instruments in general surgery to diagnose and treat for example the gallstone disease. The early laparoscope was of little use for the operating surgeon because of limited visualization [54] and the diagnostic task was, as previously mentioned, not in the hands of the general surgeon. Therefore, a need appeared for development of an improved instrument with respect to visualization, flexibility and precision, if surgeons should adopt the technology. This may signalize a demand pull for these improved characteristics of the technology by the end-users. However, there were other barriers to the introduction. The educational and cultural background of general surgery, where operations outside a patient's body in many ways were anathema to the culture of surgery, might be one of these barriers [38]. This corresponds with the description of surgery by Wickham (1993) [41], in which almost until the mid 1970s *massive surgical procedures were sometimes undertaken with little thought being given to the ultimate welfare or benefit of the patient* - a situation which was followed by a period of more conservative and critical surgery aiming at trauma reductions.

What could then explain the fast adoption of the laparoscopic technology in treating cholecystectomy? One reason was clearly the change in culture and traditions in the surgical field, e.g. orthopaedic surgery, towards less trauma and minimal invasiveness in the early and mid 1980s. Furthermore several authors argue that the patient too demanded a less invasive, less painful and traumatic method, which would make a quick return to normal activity possible - a demand pull effect [54-58]. However, the main reasons for the interest in the laparoscopic technology in general surgery seem to be interspecial competition from other fields in the treatment of gallstones and the exploitation of the improved technological possibilities as a necessary condition in general surgery [38].[121]

Although there has been a delay in the introduction and the existence of a long incremental innovation process in other fields, the specific time of development of laparoscopic cholecystectomy has been short, because the technology was transferred from other fields.[122] One could then argue that the development of the video-guided endoscope with respect to general surgery is an example of an Innovation-Science Contribution Path in the chain-linked model. The reason is the new possibilities of scientific developments and improvements which this technology made available for

---

[121] Before 1980 surgeons had monopoly on gallstone treatment. However, gastroenterologist (gallstone-dissolving drugs) and interventional radiologists (gallstone lithotripsy) challenged this position, although without any success apart from forcing general surgeons to become more innovative [59].

[122] One of the first laparoscopic cholecystectomies was made using a gynaecological laparoscope.

a new area - namely general surgery. Today the use of the laparoscopic technology in cholelithiasis has made it possible for general surgery to undertake both the diagnostic and therapeutic tasks as a combined procedure.

The further process of innovation in laparoscopic cholecystectomy

Opposed to the other endoscopic fields mentioned above the research and development in laparoscopic surgery have from the start been an area for the industry, especially in the United States and Japan. The clinician and the scientist are no longer the initial innovators, as was the case in the early innovations in gastroenterology.

The innovation in the laparoscopic field concentrated on the development of improved scopes, e.g. improvements in the transmission technology to get a better vision. The explosion in demand for laparoscopic cholecystectomy required the innovation and development of a vast new array of equipments for specific surgical purposes to use in combination with the scope [60]. Examples are the development of a less time-consuming device to put on the scope to apply the surgical sutures through the scope. Other examples are the interdisciplinary application of the laser technology from other fields external to the minimally invasive area. To become usable the delivery of the laser energy had to be changed, because CO_2 energy could not be transmitted through endoscopic fiber optics [38]. Instead an argon-laser was developed in 1989 - another Innovation-Science Contribution Path with further possibilities in other scientific areas.

Innovation of instruments is in overall characterized by relying to a high degree on user-producer relations to satisfy the users' demand (learning by using), which seem important in order to become a successful company.

As a perceived cost-saving technology a demand for cost-effectiveness from the users and payers pulls the innovation and diffusion of laparoscopic cholecystectomy, which several studies also have documented.[123] Most of these studies are positive regarding the economic advantages of the technology. However, in the study by Legoretta et al. (1993) of a period from 1989-1992, where a reduction in the health care costs from using this technology was expected too, the opposite result appeared [56]. The overall expenditures for cholecystectomy did rise with 18 per cent in the period, although the total unit cost per cholecystectomy fell with 25 per cent [56]. The reason for this was that the indications for cholecystectomy had changed, leading to a lower rate of admission. The number of gallstone treatments increased because of the introduction of the laparoscopic technology. This effect of the adoption of laparoscopic cholecystectomy has been found in most countries. Furthermore, the few studies that have compared laparoscopic cholecystectomy with the other minimally invasive alternative - mini-laparotomy (small-incision open surgery) found less optimistic cost-effectiveness results

---

[123] Among these studies of cost-effectiveness are Banta (1993) [52], Legoretta et al. (1993) [56], Ure et al. (1995) [61], Vandenbergh et al. (1995) [62] and Wenner et al. (1995) [63].

as well. Therefore, the case illustrates the consequences of a technological progress without any superior control and regulation.

Today the demand on cost-effectiveness and efficiency is pulling the development of application equipment. Now prices and costs are important for the users and payers. One example of this is the competition between a cheap reusable device with cleaning expenditures and a more expensive disposable scope without any cleaning requirements.[124] However, this and other demand pressures have resulted in the development of technology in which the efficacy and to some extent the safety[125] have never been scientifically documented in larger prospective clinical trials. The uncertainty of long term effects of the technology is perhaps one of the reasons why the diffusion has slowed down in England [66]. Scientific evidence to document efficacy, effectiveness and cost-effectiveness as well as additional innovation may be needed.

9.0 Concluding remarks

Besides the pushes and pulls from science and demand which all were described in the linear models of innovation, feedback responses and learning influence the process of innovation as well. Three types of learning were included as feedback in the chain-linked model - *learning from science* (learning in the R&D process), *learning by doing* and *learning by using*. These learning effects reduces the uncertainty in the process of innovation. One example is an innovation which initially seems to be inefficient or ineffective but which with some learning activities[126] later proves to be efficient or effective. An early rejection of the adoption of this favourable technology then results in a Type II decision error [6,7]. The opposite example is a technology supposed to be efficient or effective, but later, when more experience has been gained, turns out to be inefficient or ineffective. An early recommendation of the adoption of this unfavourable technology results in a Type I decision error [6,7]. The risk of making these decision errors due to lack of learning is present in an early warning system for emerging health technology, because of its early perspective. In the end of this section some concluding remarks with respect to learning and early warning systems are given for the case

---

[124] In Ure et al. [61] the cost-effectiveness of both technologies was discussed with the conclusion that the disposable instruments were not cost-effective. As a European study the result was in accordance with the expectations. However, disposable instruments are most popular in the United States.

[125] Studies of safety (Southern Surgeons Club (1991) [64], Adamsen et al. (1995) [50] and Adamsen et al. (1997) [65]) have shown rates of complications between 5-10 per cent due to a lack of user-experience. Consequently, *learning by using* is an important factor in innovation with user-feedback to the producer. With increased training facilities the learning curve would improve and the rate of complication decrease in favour of the laparoscope compared with the traditional alternative.

[126] E.g. a clinical or economic study performed or an improved learning curve.

studies presented above. However, first the important drives in the innovation process of the case studies, whether they were science or demand-driven, are summarized.

To summarize the case of the innovation process of laparoscopic technologies, with special reference to cholecystectomy, the process may be divided in two parts.

The first part, which continues up til 1986-87, when the first laparoscopic cholecystectomies were performed, is primarily characterized by *science pushes* from new technological possibilities and applications of new external technical and scientific knowledge and research. These pushes, because of learning from science and search for new knowledge and possibilities in other areas, may be described by the different paths and feedback in the chain-linked model, e.g. path G (fiber-optics and the microprocessor chip) or path E (light-bulb, lens systems, television and cameras), as shown in Figure 3.7 below. This learning from science was very important in order to fulfill the need for flexibility and visualization. Inter-institutionally interactions with scientists (scientist-producer relations) were an important contributor with respect to learning from science in the early phase of innovation.

Demand pull effects were initially less important in the first part of the innovation process in cholecystectomy. However, effects of demand have emerged today in the second part of the innovation process which could explain the rapid and wide adoption and diffusion of the laparoscopic technologies. Important user-producer relations characterize this second part after the first laparoscopic cholecystectomy were performed and learning by using seems to be one of the main drives in an incremental innovation process of the laparoscopic technologies aimed at fulfilling more specialized purposes. The demand expressed through user-feedback for new equipment as a kind of learning by using and the demand for cost-saving technologies and cost-effectiveness are examples of this. Learning by using has also been important in the improved experience of using the scope (the learning curve). Finally, one should not reject the demand from patients for a less invasive technology, as it is reported in the literature and found in the Danish study of diffusion [67] which is presented in chapter 5. This iteratively formed learning by using (demand-driven) innovation process which reflects an incremental innovation follows the expectations for an innovation belonging to the group of devices, although learning from science (science-driven) was the most important in the first part.

In the case of the sustained release drug it seems to be demand pull factors that were the prime movers in the development and innovation, besides the initial scientific and technical knowledge and possible learning by using experience with respect to the unit-principles.

For some of the drugs shown in Table 3.1, a demand pull based on medical or patient-specific factors could initially explain the application of a sustained release technology. The drives for innovation of a more controlled release of these SR-drugs were the benefit from an improved patient compliance and some new trends for preventive prophylaxis.

This demand pull from physicians and patients is a kind of the user-feedback that is included in the chain-linked model.

Another drive from demand in the innovation process of SR-drugs may be a result of demand pull factors belonging to the market and its environment (regulation). In a market regulated by patents there is, because of commercial interests, be a demand for the maintenance of patent rights by the end of the patent period of an existing drug. An application of the sustained release technology on the existing drug and thereby relaunch of a modified drug could prolong the time horizon of the patent. This strategic move limits the threats to the innovating company in their particular market with the purpose of keeping, or perhaps increasing, the prices in an extended period.

This case shows the opposite result compared with the expectations from the group of drugs belonging to the science-spectra in the innovation process. One explanation of this difference could be that a sustained release technology is an "application" technology in which the prime movers for the application of a sustained release technology seem to be strategic market considerations.

The models presented in the present chapter have shown that R&D policy, and thereby the process of innovation, can be stimulated by different means and incentives. R&D policy involves more than direct subsidization of R&D to universities, research laboratories and firms. An alternative to a *push* strategy of direct funding R&D is a *pull* strategy which involves incentives for R&D by subsidizing demand for a particular type of technology or intervention [68]. This last strategy of subsidizing demand was used in Sweden to stimulate the utilization of the laparoscopic technology in cholecystectomy compared with the traditional open procedure by offering a higher level of reimbursement for the new technology [69]. But, how can the knowledge about the process of innovation of health technology presented in this chapter then contribute to a system for early warning of emerging health technology and the decisions made on behalf of it?

In the sustained release case early information about possible strategic market conditions might perhaps have resulted in decisions made by the public authorities with respect to new and modified rules and regulation. This could be in the form of changes in the patent rules with respect to when a *slightly* changed product (the application of the SR-technology on an existing drug) can obtain a new patent and thereby a prolonged protection in the market.

In the laparoscopy case the early learning from science, the later learning by using (decrease in the rate of complications) and the incremental development of equipment for application have significantly reduced the uncertainty in the process of innovation for laparoscopes. An early refusal in the end of the 1980s of laparoscopic cholecystectomy as result of an early warning information may have turned out to be wrong, because of the improved learning curve and the further development in equipment - a Type II decision error. However, because of the lack of larger prospective clinical trials and documentation of cost-effectiveness at least compared with mini-laparotomy, one could on the other hand argue that an early accept, on the basis of an early warning information, would later appear as a Type I decision error. This means an accept of a technology which later with more information turns out to be inefficacious and inefficient.

This illustrates the dilemma for an early warning system for emerging health technology to be able exactly to judge when the data are reliable and a decision can be made. This is the trade-off between the costs for society by delaying an introduction, the value of better information and the consequences of doing nothing, as discussed and modelled previously by Paltiel et al. (1993) [4]. However, knowledge about the process of innovation and diffusion of emerging and new health technology, and the conduct of health technology assessment at different stages of diffusion, especially the early stages, improve the reliability of the information from an early warning system.

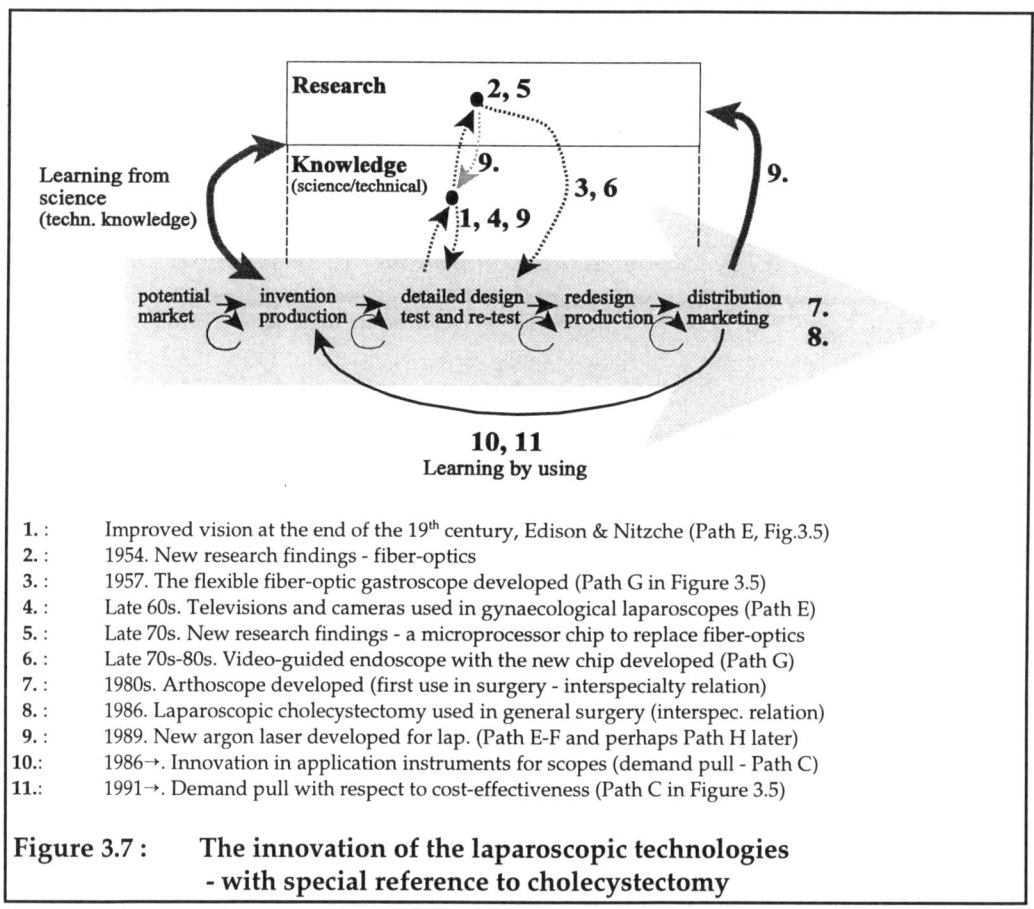

1.: Improved vision at the end of the 19th century, Edison & Nitzche (Path E, Fig.3.5)
2.: 1954. New research findings - fiber-optics
3.: 1957. The flexible fiber-optic gastroscope developed (Path G in Figure 3.5)
4.: Late 60s. Televisions and cameras used in gynaecological laparoscopes (Path E)
5.: Late 70s. New research findings - a microprocessor chip to replace fiber-optics
6.: Late 70s-80s. Video-guided endoscope with the new chip developed (Path G)
7.: 1980s. Arthoscope developed (first use in surgery - interspecialty relation)
8.: 1986. Laparoscopic cholecystectomy used in general surgery (interspec. relation)
9.: 1989. New argon laser developed for lap. (Path E-F and perhaps Path H later)
10.: 1986→. Innovation in application instruments for scopes (demand pull - Path C)
11.: 1991→. Demand pull with respect to cost-effectiveness (Path C in Figure 3.5)

Figure 3.7 : The innovation of the laparoscopic technologies
- with special reference to cholecystectomy

References

1. Walsh V. Invention and innovation in the chemical industry: Demand-pull or discovery-push? Research Policy 1984;13:211-234.

2. Poulsen PB, Hørder M, Jørgensen T. Fremtidens medicinske metoder - tidlig varsling i internationalt og dansk perspektiv. Rapport udgivet af Sundhedsstyrelsens Udvalg for Medicinsk Teknologivurdering. Sundhedsstyrelsen, København, 1996.

3. Jørgensen T, Larsen LG, Poulsen PB. Tidlig varsling af kommende medicinske teknologier - et dansk forstudie. DSI - Institut for Sundhedsvæsen. DSI - rapport. København, 1997.

4. Paltiel AD, Kaplan EH. The Epidemiological and Economic Consequences of AIDS Clinical Trials. Journal of Acquired Immune Deficiency Syndromes 1993;6:179-190.

5. Banta HD, Vondeling H. Strategies for successful evaluation and policy-making toward health care technology on the move: The case of medical lasers. Social Science and Medicine 1994;38(12):1633-1674.

6. Finkelstein SN, Homer JB, Sondic EJ. Modeling the dynamics of decision-making for emerging medical technologies. R&D Management 1984;14(3):175-191.

7. Langkilde LK, Poulsen PB. The Learning Approach to Early Economic Evaluation. CHS Working Paper 1996:2. Centre for Health and Social Policy, Odense University, 1996.

8. Jackson T, Street A, Costello A, Crowe H. Cost-effectiveness of laser ablation of the prostate. Premature evaluation. International Journal of Technology Assessment in Health Care 1995;11(3):595-610.

9. Kline SJ, Rosenberg N. An Overview of Innovation. In Landau & Rosenberg N (eds.). The Positive Sum Strategy: Harnessing Technology for Economic Growth, Washington DC: National Academy Press, 1986.

10. Mowery DC, Rosenberg N. The influence of market demand upon innovation: a critical review of some recent empirical studies. Research Policy 1979;8:103-153.

11. Yin RK. Case Study Research. Design and Methods. Second Edition. Applied Social Research Methods Series Volume 5. SAGE Publications. London, 1994.

12. Hall P. Innovation, Economics and Evolution. Theoretical Perspectives on Changing Technology in Economic Systems. Harvester Wheatsheaf. New York, 1994.

13. Usher AP. Technical Change and Capital Formation. Chapter 2 in Rosenberg N (ed.). The economics of technological change. Penguin Modern Economics Readings. Penguin Books, 1971.

14. Stoneman P. Introduction. Chapter 1 in Stoneman P (ed.). Handbook of the Economics of Innovation and Technological Change. Basil Blackwell, Oxford, 1995.

15. Elster J. Explaining Technical Change. Studies in Rationality and Social Change. Cambridge University Press, Cambridge, 1983.

16. Mansfield E. The Economics of Technological Change. NY:W.W.Norton & Company, 1968.

17. Rosenberg N. Inside the Black Box: Technology and Economics. Cambridge University Press, Cambridge, 1982.

18. Warner KE. The Need for Some Innovative Concepts of Innovation: An Examination of Research on the Diffusion of Innovations. Policy Sciences 1974;5:433-451.

19. Layton E. Conditions of Technological Development. Chapter 6 in Spiegel-Rösing I & Solla Price D (ed.). Science, Technology and Society. Sage Publication. London, 1977.

20. Gelijns AC. Comparing the Development of Drugs, Devices and Clinical Procedures. Appendix A in Gelijns AC. Modern Methods of Clinical Investigation. Medical Innovation at the Crossroad. Volume I. Committee on Technological Innovation in Medicine. Institute of Medicine. National Academy Press, Washington, D.C., 1990.

21. Maxwell RA. The state of the art of the science of drug discovery - an opinion. Drug Development Research 1984;4:375-389.

22. Spilker B. Multinational Drug Companies: Issues in Drug Discovery and Development. Raven Press, New York, 1989.

23. MEFA. Facts 1994. Medicine and health care. Denmark, 1994.

24. Schwabe U, Paffrath D (ed.). Arzneiverordnungsreport' 94. Gustav Fishers Verlag. Stuttgart, 1994.

25. Pavitt K. Sectoral patterns of technical change: Towards a taxonomy and a theory, 1984. Chapter 12 in Freeman C. The Economics of Innovation. An Elgar Reference Collection. Edward Elgar Publishing Company, Vermont, 1990.

26. Grabowski HG, Vernon JM. Returns to R&D on new drug introductions in the 1980s. Journal of Health Economics 1994;13:383-406.

27. Littell CL. Innovation in Medical Technology : Reading the Indicators : Datawatch. Health Affairs Millwood 1994;13(3):226-235.

28. Council Directive. 93/42/EEC, of 14 June 1993. Medical Devices.

29. Sundhedsstyrelsen. Specialeplanlægning og lands- og landsdelsfunktioner i sygehusvæsenet. Vejledning. København 1996.

30. Christiansen T, Enemark U, Clausen J, Poulsen PB. Cost Containment in Denmark. Chapter 5 in Mossialos E & Le Grand J (eds.). Health Care and Cost Containment in the European Union. Ashgate: Aldershot, 1999.

31. Indenrigsministeriet. Amtskommunalt udgiftspres og styringsmuligheder. Betænkning fra det af Indenrigsministeren nedsatte udvalg om amtskommunalt udgiftspres og styringsmuligheder. Betænkning nr. 1123. København, December 1987.

32. Dosi G. Technical Change and Industrial Transformation. St. Martin's Press, New York, 1984.

33. Langrish J, Gibbons M, Evans WG, Jevons, FR. Wealth From Knowledge. Studies of Innovation in Industry. The MacMillan Press. London, 1972.

34. Lotz P. Demand-Side Effects on Product Innovation. Ph.D.serie 9.92. Handelshøjskolen i København. Det Økonomiske Fakultet. Samfundslitteratur, 1992.

35. Andreasen PB, Lotz P. The Research Laboratory "DENMARK". Innovation in Danish Health Care Industry. Prepared for the Danish Ministry of Foreign Affairs, May 1990.

36. Dosi G. Technological paradigms and technological trajectories. A suggested interpretation of the determinants and directions of technical change. Research Policy 1982;11:147-162.

37. Gelijns AC, Rosenberg N. The Changing Nature of Medical Technology Development. Chapter 1 in Rosenberg N, Gelijns AC, Dawkins H (ed.). Sources of Medical Technology: Universities and Industry. Medical Innovation at the Crossroad. Volume V. Committee on Technological Innovation in Medicine. Institute of Medicine. National Academy Press. Washington, D.C. 1995.

38. Gelijns AC, Rosenberg N. From the Scalpel to the Scope: Endoscopic Innovations in Gastroenterology, Gynecology, and Surgery. Chapter 4 in Rosenberg N, Gelijns AC, Dawkins H (ed.). Sources of Medical Technology: Universities and Industry. Medical Innovation at the Crossroad. Volume V. Committee on Technological Innovation in Medicine. Institute of Medicine. National Academy Press. Washington, D.C. 1995.

39. Metcalfe S. The Economic Foundation of Technology Policy: Equilibrium and Evolutionary Perspectives. Chapter 12 in Stoneman P (ed.). Handbook of the Economics of Innovation and Technological Change. Basil Blackwell, Oxford, 1995.

40. Arrow K. The Economic Implications of Learning by Doing. Review of Economic Studies 1962;29:155-173.

41. Wickham JEA. An Introduction to Minimally Invasive Therapy. Health Policy 1993;23:7-15.

42. Dansk Lægemiddelstatistik. Lægemiddelforbruget i Danmark. København, 1991.

43. Lægeforeningens Medicinfortegnelse, 1993.

44. Lossius WW. Selo-Zok - dyrt fremskridt. Tidsskrift for Norsk Lægeforening 1991;1:111.

45. Kirchberger S. Health care technology in Germany. Health Policy 1994;30:163-205.

46. Mühe E. Die erste Cholecystektomie durch das Laparoskop. Langenbecks Archiv für Chirurgie 1986;369:804.

47. Weill C. Minimally Invasive Therapy: The French case study. Health Policy 1993;23:31-47.

48. Hansen OH, Bardram L, Haakonsen TU, Lauritsen K. Laparoskopisk kolecystektomi - minimal invasiv kirurgi. Ugeskrift for Læger 1991;153:3222-3224. [Laparoscopic Cholecystectomy - minimal invasive surgery (English abstract and legends)].

49. Jensen SL, Jensen PMF, Wara P, Rokkjær M. Laparoskopisk kolecystektomi. De første 45 operationer. Ugeskrift for Læger 1991;153:3225-3228. [Laparoscopic Cholecystectomy. Report of the first 45 operations (English abstract and legends)].

50. Adamsen S, Hansen OH, Jensen PMF, Schulze S, Stage JG, Wara P, Jensen LP. Laparoskopisk kolecystektomi i Danmark. En prospektiv registrering. Ugeskrift for Læger 1995;157 (32), 4449-4454. [Laparoscopic Cholecystectomy in Denmark. A nationwide prospective case registration (English abstract and legends)].

51. Danneskiold-Samsøe B (ed.). Abdominal Laparoscopic Surgery. Report from a medical consensus conference 3-5 March 1997. Copenhagen: Danish Medical Research Council and Danish Institute for Health Services Research and Development. Consensus Report, 1997.

52. Banta HD. The cost-effectiveness of 10 selected applications in Minimally Invasive Therapy. Health Policy 1993;23:135-151.

53. Gelijns AC, Pannenborg CO. The development of contraceptive technology. Case studies of incentives and disincentives to innovation. International Journal of Technology Assessment in Health Care 1993;9(2):210-232.

54. White JV. Laparoscopic Cholecystectomy: The Evolution of General Surgery. Annals of Internal Medicine 1991;115(8):651-653.

55. Wickham JEA. The new surgery. British Medical Journal 1987;295(6613):1581-1582.

56. Legoretta AP, Silber JH, Constantino GN, Kobylinski RW, Zatz SL. Increased Cholecystectomy Rate After the Introduction of Laparoscopic Cholecystectomy. Journal of American Medical Association 1993;270(12):1429-1432.

57. Schou I.. Minimally Invasive Therapy in Denmark. Health Policy 1993;23:17-30.

58. Banta HD. Introduction. Minimally invasive therapy in five European countries. Health Policy 1993;23:1-5.

59. Gelijns AC, Fendrick AM. The dynamics of innovations in Minimally Invasive Therapy. Health Policy 1993;23:153-166.

60. Fendrick M. Assessing New Treatments: The Case of Gallstone Disease. In Szczepura A & Kankaanpää J (eds.). Assessment of Health Care Technologies. John Wiley & Sons, Chichester, 1996. pp. 105-122.

61. Ure BM, Lefering R, Troidl H. Costs of laparoscopic cholecystectomy. Analysis of potential savings. Surgical Endoscopy 1995;9(4):401-406.

62. Vandenbergh HC, Wilson T, Adams SE, Inglis M J. Laparoscopic cholecystectomy: its impact on national health economics. The Medical Journal of Australia 1995;162:587-590.

63. Wenner J, Graffner H, Lindell G. Laparoskopisk kolecystektomi. Kostnadseffektiv gallstenskirurgi. Läkartidningen 1995;92(8):763-765.

64. Southern Surgeons Club. A prospective analysis of 1518 laparoscopic cholecystectomies. The New England Journal of Medicine 1991;324(16):1073-1078.

65. Adamsen S, Hansen OH, Funch-Jensen P, Schulze S, Stage JG, Wara P. Bile duct injury during laparoscopic cholecystectomy: A prospective nationwide series. Journal of the American College of Surgeons 1997;184:571-578.

66. Spiby J. Health care technology in United Kingdom. Health Policy 1994;30:295-334.

67. Poulsen PB, Adamsen S, Vondeling H, Jørgensen T. Diffusion of Laparoscopic Technologies in Denmark. Health Policy 1998:45(2):149-167.

68. Cummings RG, Schulze W. Economic Analysis of a Technology in the Early Stages of Its Development. In Tolley GS, Hodge JH, Oehmke JF (eds.). The Economics of R&D Policy. Praeger Publishers, New York, 1985, pp. 138-148.

69. Jonsson E, Banta HD. Health care technology in Sweden. Health Policy 1994;30:257-294.

Chapter 4

Models of Diffusion in Economics and Sociology

Table of contents

Abstract 121

1.0 Introduction 122

2.0 Models of diffusion based on economic theory 123

3.0 Models of diffusion based on sociological theory 128

4.0 Discussion 132

References 135

Abstract

Studies of diffusion have been undertaken in different fields of science such as sociology, economics, organisation theory and political science. This chapter describes and discusses similarities and differences between the models of diffusion presented in economics and sociology with the special attention to their use on health innovations and health technology. In the models based upon economic theory diffusion is separated from the process of innovation, whereas the models based upon sociological theory include diffusion as part of the process of innovation. Economic and sociological models differ as well in their focus upon the factors explaining diffusion. In the economic models, diffusion is regarded as a phenomenon guided by supply and demand in the market, e.g. profitability as an important factor. In the sociological models communication channels is the central element and the focus of diffusion factors have been on adopter-specific attributes, e.g. age, social status and interpersonal relations.

1.0 Introduction

Diffusion is the process by which an innovation enters and becomes part of the health care system [1]. In this process the technology will be incorporated into standard practice by dissemination to its potential users [2,3]. The process of diffusion of health technology is, however, complex and still not well understood. The knowledge and findings with respect to the process of diffusion depend on circumstances like *the type of health technology* studied[127], *the type of adopter or adopting unit*[128] as well as *the structure, organisation and payment system* [129] adapted in the specific health care sector, in which the health technology is introduced. Furthermore, studies of diffusion have been undertaken in different fields of science, such as sociology, economics, organisation theory and political science, with their specific perspectives and theories to understand the phenomenon of diffusion [5]. Finally, the methods used for analysing cases of diffusion and their data differ quite a lot. These methods range from applications of econometric methodology, such as multiple regression analysis, used to study the international diffusion of pharmaceuticals [6,7], to more qualitative-oriented studies using interviews to explain the diffusion of new health technology into local practice [8]. Each of these issues influences in different degree the knowledge base concerning the diffusion process of health technology.

Among these issues, the present chapter[130] focusses upon the models of diffusion in economics and sociology as presented in the literature. As a brief review, the purpose is to describe some of the models of diffusion with special attention to their use on health innovation and health technology. In general, models of diffusion based on economic and sociological theory differ with respect to the integration of diffusion within the process of innovation, as described in chapter 3.

The process of diffusion can be said to contain two phases. The initial decision made within an organisation by the potential users to *adopt* the technology and on the other hand a certain *use* of the technology within the same organisation at a given point in time [1]. Both phases have been investigated empirically in diffusion studies, which usually have been concerned with describing three phenomena of diffusion: the speed

---

[127] Divided in pharmaceuticals, medical devices and medical procedures, or alternatively distinguished in high-ticket technologies, medium-ticket technologies and low-ticket technologies based on the resources that they mobilize, as done in Battista et al. (1989) [4].

[128] E.g. studying the hospital as the adopting unit instead of the individual physicians, or at the individual level studying hospital physicians adoption instead of adoption by general practitioners.

[129] E.g. studying diffusion of technologies in hospitals with prospective reimbursement payment systems opposed to retrospective reimbursement payment systems, or studying the adoption of technology at the hospital level compared to the level of the primary care sector.

[130] Prior to the empirical studies of diffusion presented in chapter 5 and chapter 6.

of diffusion[131], the extent of use and the patterns of diffusion [5]. These patterns are often described by graphical presentation of the time path of diffusion, the geographical variation, and the differences between adopters. Another more explanatory part of diffusion studies has been to identify the factors and characteristics, which have influenced the diffusion in terms of earlier or later adoption of the specific technology or groups of technologies. Several factors and characteristics, e.g. the size of the adopting hospital, have, based upon the different theoretical approaches, been identified to explain the diffusion of health technology. The models of diffusion seem to have been used especially for this part of the studies.

However, why do we have to be interested in diffusion theory and models of diffusion and to study diffusion of health technology? An understanding of the diffusion process of health technology provides a higher insight into the characteristics, factors and structures which determine the degree of technological innovation and technological change in the health care sector. This knowledge improves the ability to suggest policy mechanisms and instruments to control and regulate the adoption of new health technology, which can be necessary to increase the effectiveness and efficiency of the diffusion and use of health technology. This is important as Newhouse (1992) recently concluded that the use of technologies made the highest contribution to the growth in health care costs [9]. On the other hand, to be able to evaluate the effects of existing regulation on technology diffusion, knowledge is needed on how the industry and the users of technology *ought* to behave and on how they *do* behave in the absence of regulation. Diffusion studies can help in answering this. Finally, to be able to conduct technology assessments early in the life cycle and iteratively during diffusion, as advocated for in chapter 7, an understanding of the process of diffusion and technological change is needed as well.

The structure of the chapter is as follows. Section 2.0 describes the models of diffusion in economics, in which the primary focus has been on economic characteristics. In Section 3.0 the models of diffusion in sociology, primarily the *classical theory*, and the factors found are described. Finally, the similarities and differences between economic and sociological models are discussed in section 4.0.

2.0 Models of diffusion based on economic theory

Although, diffusion forms the last stage of technological change, the process of innovation and the process of diffusion are regarded as separate activities in the economic models [2]. Apart from the innovation process[132], the process of diffusion in the economic models deals with the application of new products. When an innovation is put on the market for the first time at the end of the process of innovation potential

---

[131] Or rate of adoption - the relative speed by which an innovation is adopted.

[132] The production of technological goods. This includes all the necessary activities for bringing a new product onto the market leading to technological change.

users will then respond by adoption, if successful, and the process of diffusion begins in the economic models.

The economic models focus upon economic variables as central driving forces and explanations for diffusion of innovations. In microeconomic theory, diffusion is primarily considered in terms of demand and supply, in which the individual firms adjust the supply to the demand until a market equilibrium is obtained (demand pull effects[133]), eventually by undertaking new innovative activities. The speed by which inventions are transformed into innovations, and consequently diffused, will depend upon the actual and expected trajectory of performance improvement and cost reduction [10]. Mansfield (1986) argues on behalf of empirical evidence that the rate of diffusion of an innovation depends on the average profitability of the innovation, the size of the investment needed for introduction, the number and average size of firms in the industry, and the amount spend on R&D [11]. The firm will innovate if the present value of the stream of profits expected from the innovation is positive [12]. Firms, in which the expected returns from innovation are highest, tend to be the quickest to introduce an innovation. These models have primarily been applied to study the diffusion in a variety of for-profit industries, usually on an aggregated level. However, they have also been applied to the, basically *not-for-profit*, hospital sector to explain diffusion of health technology. An example is Sloan et al. (1986), who used an economic model in a study of the diffusion of surgical procedures[134] in American hospitals [12]. For surgical procedures, higher prospective profit was expected as a result of higher anticipated product prices, lower investment outlays and lower wage rates for non-physician personnel. Studying 521 hospitals in the period 1971-1981, Sloan et al. (1986) found that the mix of payment sources as a measure of price level, and thereby profit, affected the diffusion of surgical technology. This means that a high share of commercially-insured patients[135] will be conducive for diffusion, whereas high shares of public and self-payers predict a slow diffusion [12]. Another study by Romeo et al. (1984) using the profit approach to adoption, found that prospective reimbursement slowed the rate of adoption of new low-ticket technologies in American hospitals [13].

Forces which may delay the introduction and widespread adoption of a new substitute technology may be if a production cost differential still persists between the old and the new technology, if entrepreneurs have certain unmet expectational patterns regarding the improvements, or if high costs are associated with shaping and replacing the supporting infrastructure [10]. However, the economic models do also recognize that diffusion may be impeded if the innovation requires new kinds of knowledge on the part of the users, new types of behaviour, and the coordinated effects of a number of organisations [11]. Special interest has been attached to learning effects, especially

---

[133] As presented in chapter 3.

[134] Procedures of hip arthroplasty, coronary bypass surgery, morbid obesity surgery, retina repair and cataract surgery [12].

[135] Who pays the highest proportion of hospital charges on average [12].

learning by doing introduced by Arrow (1962) [14], but also effects from learning from the R&D process and learning by using.[136] Innovations and investment decisions are future-oriented for which reason they inevitably involve a high degree of uncertainty. The adopter has to consider the trade-off between the early potential profits of an early introduction and the possible gain of waiting upon expected profit later due to additional scientific advances and increased experience.

According to Warner (1974), learning by doing can result both from intrafirm and interfirm diffusion [15]. Intrafirm diffusion will be in the form of learning, which comes from the experience of the use of the new technology within the firm, as illustrated with internal feedback in the central chain in the chain-linked model in chapter 3. The efficiency in the use is expected to increase with experience. Interfirm diffusion will be in situations, in which the first firm's learning is expected to have spin-offs for other firms [15]. Rosenberg calls this last type for *learning by using*, which is generated as a result of the utilization of the new technology by its final users [16].[137] However, the economic literature has only focussed on one aspect of learning, and its influence upon diffusion, the effect of experience upon efficiency - learning by doing or learning by using - whereas other factors have been left out [15].

The human capital theory has also been applied to the study of diffusion in the form of innovation cycle models [3]. Investment in the skills and abilities of human beings, through more experience (learning) and training, improves the stock of human capital. The idea of the model is that the producer with the highest skills and lowest learning costs is the first to adopt innovations, due to a greater ability to recognize opportunities and solve adaption problems [3].[138] In the second part of the innovation cycle in which the information about the innovation is accumulated through increased experience and learning, the less skilled producers are expected to adopt. The increased experience, and reduced uncertainty, in the second part of the model may come from impersonal sources like journals, meetings, conferences, etc., discussion with colleagues or transfer of personal experiences, especially from opinion leaders - an informational externality.[139] Using this kind of economic model including human capital investments and externalities, Escarce (1996) examined the surgeons' access to information and human capital attributes (*skills*) on their adoption of laparoscopic cholecystectomy [17]. Besides

---

[136] For a more elaborate description of learning effects the reader is referred to chapter 3.

[137] The iterative user feedback alongside the central chain in the chain-linked model.

[138] Assuming a utility maximizing decision-maker.

[139] There is another externality involved in the adoption decision - a cost externality. Adoption by some physicians in a hospital reduces non-adopters costs of adoption, because they by waiting have local access to experts, logistics and organisation may be changed, supporting staff may be trained in the new procedure, other equipment are already available, etc. [17].

factors as higher profit[140] and decreasing costs of adoption, it was hypothesized that adoption by some surgeons in a hospital would provide valuable information to (risk-averse) non-adopters about the consequences of adopting. This would reduce adoption costs for non-adopters, and thereby result in an earlier adoption. The findings in the study support this model of externalities, as well as the innovation cycle model is supported because surgeons' access to information and their human capital attributes (*skills*) had a significant influence on surgeons' adoption behaviour [17]. On the hospital level the typical findings in accordance with this model have been that hospitals with teaching status, a high degree of specialization and research-intensity are earlier adopters, as they are expected to employ the physicians with the highest skills.

Between rates of improvement in a new product and rates of adoption there may be a highly non-linear relationship [10]. Due to the initial uncertainty and potential learning effects resting in the innovation, the economic models usually put forward, based upon empirical evidence, that the process of diffusion for health technology, as well as other technologies, have a sigmoidal shape [5,15]. This is illustrated below in Figure 4.1.

Figure 4.1 : The process of diffusion (Warner (1975) [15])

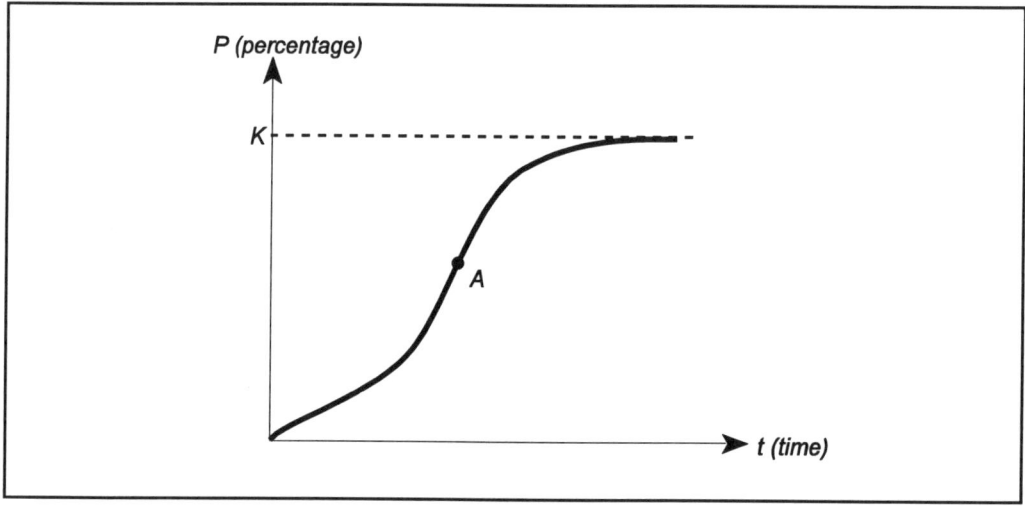

The following formula - reflecting the percentage of potential adopters P at time t - can describe this logistic curve [15];

$$P = \frac{K}{1+e^{-(a+bt)}}$$

Initially the spread of technology will be slow due to the uncertainty and risks of using the new technology in the early stages [5,18].[141] However, when the uncertainty diminishes as experience and learning thereby increases, the diffusion will increase at

---

[140] As in Mansfield (1986).

[141] In the formula a defines the starting point of the diffusion process.

an acceleration rate b (the speed of diffusion) throughout the first half of the process, until the inflection point A is reached. Afterwards diffusion still increases, although at a lower acceleration rate, until a maximum rate of diffusion K is reached due to fulfilled market demands. The logistic pattern is consistent with imitative behaviour, where the propensity for an individual's probability of adoption rises with increasing adoption by others [5]. The same as suggested in the innovation cycle model. Empirically, this sigmoidal shape of diffusion has been found for health technologies, such as *intensive care units* in the United States (1955-1974) [1], and *laparoscopic cholecystectomy* in most countries.[142]

However, diffusion of a number of health technologies has not experienced a sigmoidal pattern. Based upon empirical evidence from two case studies, Homer found that *a rise and decline pattern* can describe the diffusion of health technology in some situations [23]. The rise follows the same expectations of a sigmoidal shaped diffusion, whereas the decline happens as a result of discouraging new evaluative evidence, e.g. because the initial assessment providing expectations of a high effectiveness was biased due to lack of data and experience at the early stage in development.[143] The two cases with *rise and decline* patterns of diffusion were in *implantable cardiac pacemakers* and the antibiotic drug *clindamycin* [23].

Another important factor to guide the rate and speed of diffusion is the perceived need for an innovation [5]. When the need is high, the diffusion may be fast, despite uncertainty, and will then not reflect the gradual sigmoidal pattern of diffusion. In studying the diffusion of leukemia chemotherapy, Warner (1975) showed that chemotherapy had a very fast diffusion [5]. New drugs made drug therapy in leukemia inexpensive and easy to adopt. Furthermore, leukemia involves a high degree of *desperation* as a rapidly fatal illness in childhood. On behalf of modelling treatment decisions, Warner (1975) proposed a three-stage *desperation-reaction diffusion model* to explain diffusion of *easy to adopt* technologies aimed at serious (*desperate*) medical problems [5]. In stage 1 a rather high pre-experimental diffusion can take place depending upon the initial expectations of efficacy and the degree of desperation. If desperation is high, the physicians tend to be risk-seeking with an early adoption of the yet unproven technology. In stage 2 the arriving evidence - both scientific and in practice - will adjust the level of diffusion. If the expectations made in stage 1 cannot be supported by the new evidence a negative diffusion will then appear, as happened in the leukemia case. The final stage is characterized by informed decision making, where diffusion is a function of learning. Depending upon the information from stage 2, this stage can result in a continuation of diffusion, a renewed diffusion, or in no diffusion at all [5].

---

[142] Although sigmoidal in shape, the diffusion curves found for laparoscopic cholecystectomy have, however, been rather steep [19-22].

[143] This illustrates the importance of considering technology assessment as an iterative process during diffusion of health technology - see chapter 7.

Warner (1975) has, furthermore, made an important contribution by enlarging the usual microeconomic thought of factors influencing the decision to adopt and thereby the speed of diffusion, e.g. the potential profit, with a number of other factors - some of them having an origin in sociology [5]. These factors can be divided into three groups. The *innovation-specific characteristics* represent factors about the relative advantage, the amount and nature of the monetary costs, compatibility, complexity and testability of technology. The *adopter-specific characteristics* deal with factors about the single adopter and factors characterizing the adopting organisation. Finally, the *situation-specific characteristics* contain contextual and environmental factors, e.g. hospital reimbursement systems as studied in Romeo et al. (1984) [13].

The three groups can be used in the case of laparoscopic cholecystectomy to categorize the potential factors found likely to influence the adoption and diffusion in a number of countries.[144] In the group of *innovation-specific characteristics* potential diffusion factors found were *the nature of technology, state-of-the-art, surgical technique, planning and logistics, extra benefit, budget, investment, fee-for-service, convincing evidence* and *possibilities for organizing studies* [20,21,24-28]. In the group of *adopter-specific characteristics* the studies found factors related to the individual adopter - *age, sex, certification, uncertainty, conservatism* and *medical innovators*, as well as factors related to the adopting organisation - *type of practice, hospital size, location* and *training residency* [17,20-22,24-26,29-31]. Finally, the group of *situation-specific characteristics* consisted of factors such as *competition, prestige, patient preferences, patient demand, media, commercial pressure, service from the industry, policy measures, reimbursement, financial incentives*, and *regulation* [17,20,24-26,28-30,32-34].

Another grouping of factors on diffusion may be to categorize into factors affecting the diffusion and adoption of new health technology at the macro level, at the meso level and at the micro level. At the macro level factors will be on the overall level related to the organisation and financing of the health care sector, e.g. regulation in the sector or budgetary and reimbursement policies. At the meso level factors will specifically be related to the adopting organisation - the hospital, e.g. size and type of adopting hospitals. Finally, factors at the micro level focus upon the individual adopter and the innovation itself, e.g. human capital factors such as education or the extra benefit of the innovation (relative advantage).

3.0 Models of diffusion based on sociological theory

Contrary to the economic models of diffusion, the sociological models of diffusion look at diffusion as being part of the *innovation-development* process. The innovation-development process consists of all the decisions and activities, and their impact

---

[144] A literature review was carried out prior to the conduct of the empirical study presented in chapter 5, *Diffusion of laparoscopic technologies in Denmark*, with the aim to reveal the factors investigated internationally in the case of laparoscopic cholecystectomy. This information was used in the construction of questionnaires (See Appendix 5.1).

occurring from recognition of a need or of a problem, through research, development, and commercialization of an innovation, through diffusion and adoption of the innovation by users, to its consequences [35]. Diffusion then constitutes one of the last stages of the innovation process and is thus considered part of the same [2].

In *the classical theory of diffusion*, diffusion is defined as *the process by which an innovation*[145] *is communicated through certain channels over time among members of a social system* [35,36]. Communication is regarded as a process in which participants - the potential adopters - create and share information with one another in order to reach mutual understanding [35]. These channels of communication may be the mass media, scientific journals, meetings, networks, conferences or interpersonal channels. The potential adopter is expected to make his decision regarding adoption or rejection of the innovation through a process of five stages - the *innovation-decision* process [35]. First the potential adopter needs to have knowledge about the new idea (knowledge), where after he forms his attitude towards the innovation (persuasion) and makes the decision leading to adoption or rejection (decision). This decision is then implemented by starting to use the innovation (implementation) and finally seeking further information about the innovation confirming the use of the innovation (confirmation). In this decision making process, the innovation carries with it much uncertainty for the potential adopter [36]. Information about the innovation through communication in the social system is a mean of reducing the uncertainty, e.g. information about the expected efficacy and safety of the innovation. Diffusion will then imply some kind of social change, because alterations will most likely occur in the structure and function of a social system, if an innovation is developed and diffused [35]. On the other hand, the norms of the system will affect the diffusion and the potential adopters. It is assumed that an innovation should be diffused to all members of a social system - the more rapidly, the better. This is referred to as *pro-innovation bias* [37].

Consistent with the uncertainty in the early stages of diffusion and the later communication of the value of the innovation to the members of a social system resulting in a gradual adoption, the sociological models also assume that the rate of adoption over time usually follows a pattern of a sigmoidal shaped curve of diffusion (S-shaped), as presented previously in Figure 4.1. According to Rogers (1995), most innovations have an S-shaped rate of adoption, although there can be variations in the slope [35]. However, Coleman et al. (1966) investigating the adoption and diffusion of a new drug among doctors in the United States, showed that the pattern of diffusion differed for different groups of adopters [38]. The cumulative curve of the new drug adoptions by doctors, which were integrated into three social networks of advice, discussion and friendship among professionals, was S-shaped with an increasing rate of adoption, whereas among the more isolated doctors adoption proceeded at a nearly constant rate.

---

[145] An idea perceived as new by an individual or an organisation [36].

Opposed to the economic models, who have focussed on the aggregate of individual adopters' decisions, the sociological models have concentrated on studying characteristics related to the degree of innovativeness of individual adopters [15]. A primary focus for research in the process of diffusion by the sociological models has, therefore, been upon characteristics of the individual adopter - *the adopter-specific attributes*. These attributes can be divided into *socioeconomic characteristics, personality variables,* and *communication behaviour* [35].[146] The *socioeconomic characteristics* include factors such as age, educational level, social status, social mobility, and size of unit in which the individual adopts. Coleman et al. (1966) found in their study that an early prescriber of the new drug studied was most likely to be middle aged, but not old [38].

With respect to *personality variables*, early adopters are expected to have greater empathy, be less dogmatic, have a greater rationality and intelligence, have a more favourable attitude towards change, be able to cope better with uncertainty and risk, be more favourable towards science compared with later adopters [35]. As an example, the early drug prescriber in Coleman et al. (1966) was more likely to be highly interested in medicine as a science and to orient his work to others within the profession than towards the patients [38].

In the sociological definition of diffusion communication is seen as a central act for diffusion to occur. A third group of adopter-specific attributes - *communication behaviour* - therefore focusses on how the individual adopter and the rate of adoption are affected by the channels of communication - interpersonal and mass media [35,37]. Early adopters are expected to have a greater exposure to mass media and involvement in interpersonal communication networks and to be more cosmopolitic. These early adopters will also be the ones, who seek the information, for which reason they are expected to have more knowledge about the innovation. As a result they possess a higher degree of opinion leadership than later adopters. Again Coleman et al. (1966) confirmed some of these factors [38]. They found that the early prescriber was often attending meetings of specialty societies, subscribed a large number of medical journals, had a high social participation rate and was involved in different kinds of interpersonal networks [38]. However, Greer (1985) criticises that the literature in explaining the diffusion of health technology has been preoccupied with the communication flows of information at national and international levels, and the role of opinion leaders at these levels, having the consequence that more local subcultures and norms have been ignored [8]. Studying the receipt and use of medical information by practising physicians in local community hospitals, she concludes that doctors foremost rely on local consensus and local clinical experience, as opposed to knowledge emanating from external sources. The reduction of uncertainty in a local medical community with respect to a dynamic health technology happens through a process initiated by local

---

[146] Opposed to the adopter-specific characteristics formulated by Warner (1975) [5], the adopter-specific attributes in the sociological models focus solely upon the individual.

individual innovators, promoted by idea champions, and assessed by local opinion leaders [8].[147]

Other characteristics explaining the degree of innovativeness and rate of adoption have been put forward as well. Attributes related to the innovation are also expected to influence the rate of adoption.[148] *The relative advantage* deals with how the innovation is perceived as superior to the existing practice [36]. It can both be understood objectively, e.g. the profit of innovation as used in the economic models, or it can be understood subjectively, e.g. the status and prestige following the adoption [15,35]. Another attribute is *compatibility*, which is the degree to which an innovation is perceived as consistent with the existing values, norms, past experiences, and needs of potential adopters [15,35,36]. *Complexity* is the degree to which an innovation is perceived as relatively difficult to understand in the social system [36]. The ability to test the innovation on a limited basis - *trialability* - will influence the rate of adoption as well [35]. Finally, an attribute is the *observability* of the innovation, which is the degree to which the results of an innovation are visible to others [35]. Dynamic technologies which are still evolving remain longer in the observation stage than formed technologies[149] [8]. In general, diffusion is expedited by greater relative advantage, simplicity, ready trialability, and higher observability [15]. The CT scanner exemplifies a technology with attributes expected to have speeded the adoption [1]. However, the perceived attributes depend upon the adopter's perspective and judgement of the innovation rather than on the objective attributes of an innovation obtained from the conduct of clinical trials.

Rogers (1995) defines different ideal types of adopters during diffusion by their degree of innovativeness and rate of adoption [35,36]. The *innovators* are the first group adopting the innovation, as they are characterized by having a risk seeking nature and a high interest in innovations and their transfer to the local system. They are marginal to mainstream and are not the local opinion leaders [8]. The next type adopting is the *early adopters*, who exhibit a large degree of opinion leadership, because others in the system respect them. Their adoption of innovation reduces the uncertainty and the rate of adoption will usually take off. Coleman et al. (1966) found that the more deeply integrated a physician was in the local medical community the more likely he was to be an early user of the new drug [38]. A large group of adopters will be in the *early majority* group, who adopts the innovation just before the average member of the system, when it is still not totally accepted. Another large group is the group of *late majority*, who, from

---

[147] For formed technology (complete products) involving an expected low degree of uncertainty, such as the laparoscopic technology, diffusion at local levels may, however, be guided by information from external sources, e.g. journals and opinion leaders at national or international levels.

[148] Some of these attributes correspond to the group of innovation-specific characteristics presented in Warner (1975) [5].

[149] As complete products, they move quickly through the stage of consensus and a potential "take-off" in local adoption.

being more sceptical and following the system norms, adopts the innovation just after the average member of a system. As the last group to adopt in a social system, the *laggards* are as traditionalists in general resistant against innovations, locally oriented and isolated in the social networks.

However, Greer (1985) [39] claims that the relevance of the literature, based on the classical theory of diffusion describing individuals adoption of health innovations to adoption by organisations, is problematic. Similarly, Mohr (1969) argues that, even though *size* of organisations is a powerful predictor of innovation as found in the classical theory, *size* should only be expected to predict innovativeness insofar as it implies the presence of motivation, obstacles and resources [40].[150] The subject of study, using organisational theory, should instead be the health care organisation, e.g. a hospital [2]. Studying twenty-five hospitals' decisions of potential technology adoptions Greer proposes three hospital decision systems. The *medical-individualistic decision system* is dominant in evaluations of new clinical tools, e.g. endoscopes, requested by the individual physician when treating patients [39].[151] This decision making context, representing the classical diffusion of innovations, focuses on maximizing patient benefit with the assessment of clinical effects and to reduce risk. Decisions to adopt rely on personal experience, professional media and short courses. The *fiscal-managerial decision system* applies to the replacement and accretion of technologies used in hospital departments, e.g. in ancillary service departments [39]. Decision making, involving chief executives, department heads, etc., is driven by rationality with quantitative assessments of costs and benefits, thinking in terms of organisational concerns and patient aggregates, instead of individual patients. However, when decisions to adopt innovations are made, that imply substantial changes in the nature or future of a hospital, the *strategic-institutional decision system* has to be examined [39].[152] With the focus of decision making on long-range strategic planning and policy making using forecasts, the primary participants are the governing boards of the hospitals, although others can participate as well. Greer's conclusion is that attempt to influence diffusion will only be successful if they are directed to the relevant decision system responsible for the hospital adoption of the technology [39].

4.0 Discussion

This chapter has shown that there are differences between the economic models and the sociological models in the interpretation and understanding of the process of diffusion. The models in the two fields differ with respect to their definition of diffusion and perspectives, as well as the factors or characteristics studied and verified as explaining

---

[150] Found as important determinants for innovation in a study of 93 health organisations [40].

[151] *Optional innovation-decision* in Rogers (1995) [35].

[152] Corresponds to what Rogers (1995) calls an *authority innovation-decision* made by few individuals in the system, who possess power, status, or technical expertise [35].

the adoption and diffusion of health technology. A central difference between the economic models and the sociological models is the separation of the process of innovation from the process of diffusion. In the models based on economic theory the process of diffusion is regarded as separated from the process of innovation by the marketing of a product. Then the process of innovation ends and the process of diffusion starts. In sociological models, however, diffusion is considered as part of the innovation-development process, as one of the last stages.

Whereas diffusion is regarded as a phenomenon guided by supply and demand in the market by the economic models, *communication channels* are the central element in the sociological definition of diffusion defined as the communication of the innovation through certain channels over time among the members of a social system [35]. However, the way the concept of diffusion is handled empirically is usually the same in both fields. Diffusion will then either be defined as *the decision to adopt* a technology made by an individual or an organisation, or diffusion will be defined by a *certain extent of use* of the technology by an individual or within an organisation [1]. The first of these empirical definitions is, however, criticized by Warner (1975), who argues that the full picture is not provided by defining diffusion as *the aggregate of adopters making the initial decision to adopt* [5]. Making a decision to adopt at one point in time does not necessarily imply that the technology will be used later. This dilemma will especially be present, if diffusion experiences a *desperation-reaction* pattern or a *rise and decline* pattern as described previously. A solution to this empirical problem is, however, to define diffusion by the actual use of the technology at different points in time [5].

Due to the recognition of the uncertainty in the early stages of the life cycle of an innovation, a gradual increasing spread of the technology, to either the market or the members of the social system, is expected both in the economic and the sociological models. The economic and sociological models therefore both describe diffusion as following a sigmoidal curve, although a number of empirical studies of diffusion have shown that this is not always the case.

The perspective of the economic models is on the aggregate of individual adopters' decision - *the diffusion*, whereas the perspective of the sociological models is on the degree of innovativeness of the individual adopter - *the adoption*. This difference in perspective is also reflected in the factors or characteristics explaining diffusion upon which the two fields of models focus. In the sociological models, the main focus has been on *adopter-specific attributes*, divided in socioeconomic characteristics, personality variables and communication behaviour[153] of the individual adopter, to explain diffusion of health technology. By considering learning effects and human capital investments in skills and abilities of human beings, the economic models have also recognized the importance of the individual on adoption. However, the economic models have only investigated the effects of learning and stock of human capital upon efficiency. Traditionally, the models of diffusion based on economic theory have been

---

[153] Through interpersonal channels or networks and mass media.

far more interested in a higher level of decision making regarding diffusion - the level of the firm.[154] The economic incentives of the firm to adopt in terms of *firm-specific economic characteristics*, especially the *profitability* by adoption, have been a central factor of explanation. The sociological models have also studied the effect of factors related to the innovation upon the rate of adoption, e.g. its relative advantage. Finally, it is worth mentioning the three groups of characteristics presented by Warner (1975) to explain diffusion - *the innovation-specific characteristics, the adopter-specific characteristics*, and *the situation-specific characteristics*, due to the fact that they are based on a mix of variables studied, both economic and sociological [5].

Many empirical studies on diffusion of health technology presented in the literature have not been carried out to *test a specific theory*. Instead these studies are more exploratory with a typical aim to identify potential factors or characteristics which explain the diffusion of a specific health technology or group of health technologies in a predefined area, e.g. a country. This has especially been the case in recent international comparative projects investigating the diffusion in a number of countries with respect to expensive health technologies in fast-changing areas [26,41,42].[155] Naturally explorative-oriented studies use elements from different theoretical frameworks and previous empirical findings in order to formulate the expectations of the area studied. In a way the explorative diffusion studies can then be regarded as a type of testing-out existing research knowledge on diffusion in the specific area. The empirical studies of the diffusion of laparoscopic surgery presented in the next chapters had an exploratory purpose as well. Besides a literature review of the empirical findings of factors explaining diffusion, the theoretical basis for example in the study in chapter 5 was primarily found in Warner's *mix of variables* explaining diffusion [5].

This understanding of the diffusion process of health technology still warrants further investigation by researchers both theoretically and empirically. As illustrated in this brief review of theoretical models and empirical findings concerning diffusion, it can be concluded that diffusion neither is an economic phenomenon exclusively, nor purely sociological, nor political [15]. Each of these fields of science contributes partially with their theories and empirical findings to understand the phenomenon of diffusion. The complexity of the diffusion phenomenon should then ideally be reflected in the mix of variables from different fields which are studied, regardless of the principal orientation of the researcher.

---

[154] Using this model in the health care sector, the firm can be set equal to the hospital or another producer of health services.

[155] Presented as case-studies.

References

1. Banta HD, Behney CJ, Willems JS. Towards Rational Technology in Medicine. Considerations for Health Policy. Springer series on health care and society, Volume 5. Springer Publishing Company, New York, 1981.

2. Bonair A, Persson J. Innovation and Diffusion of Health Care Technologies. In Szczepura A & Kankaanpää J (eds.). Assessment of Health Care Technologies. Case Studies, Key Concepts and Strategic Issues. John Wiley & Sons, Chichester, 1996, pp. 17-28.

3. Feeny D. Neglected issues in the diffusion of health care technologies. The role of skills and learning. International Journal of Technology Assessment in Health Care 1985;1:681-692.

4. Battista RN. Innovation and diffusion of health-related technologies. International Journal of Technology Assessment in Health Care 1989;5:227-248.

5. Warner KE. A "Desparation-Reaction" Model of Medical Diffusion. Health Services Research 1975;Winter:369-383.

6. Parker JES. The international diffusion of pharmaceuticals. St. Martin's Press, New York, 1984.

7. Andersson F. The international diffusion of new chemical entities. A cross-national study of the determinants of difference in drug lag. PhD Dissertation. Linköping Studies in Arts and Science. Linköping, 1990.

8. Greer AL. The state of the art versus the state of the science. The diffusion of new medical technologies into practice. International Journal of Technology Assessment in Health Care 1988;4:5-26.

9. Newhouse JP. Medical care costs: how much welfare loss? Journal of Economic Perspectives 1992;6(3):3-21.

10. Rosenberg N. Exploring the black box. Technology, economics, and history. Cambridge University Press, Cambridge, 1994.

11. Mansfield E. Microeconomics of Technological Innovation. In: Landau R, Rosenberg N (eds.). The Positive Sum Strategy. Harnessing Technology for Economic Growth. National Academy Press, Washington, D.C., 1986. pp. 307-325.

12. Sloan FA, Valvona J, Perrin JM, Adamache KW. Diffusion of surgical technology. An exploratory study. Journal of Health Economics 1986;5:31-61.

13. Romeo AA, Wagner JL, Lee RH. Prospective reimbursement and the diffusion of new technologies in hospitals. Journal of Health Economics 1984;3:1-24.

14. Arrow K. The Economic Implications of Learning by Doing. Review of Economic Studies 1962;29:155-173.

15. Warner KE. The need for some innovative concepts of innovation: an examination of research on the diffusion of innovations. Policy Sciences 1974;5:433-451.

16. Rosenberg N. Inside the black box: Technology and Economics. Cambridge University Press, Cambridge, 1982.

17. Escarce JJ. Externalities in hospitals and physician adoption of a new surgical technology: An explorative analysis. Journal of Health Economics 1996;15:715-34.

18. Carlsson P, Garpenby P, Bonair A. Kan sjukvården styras? En rapport om spridning och kontrol av medicinsk teknologi. CMT Rapport 1991:5. Center for Medical Technology Assessment, Universitetet i Linköping, 1991.

19. Poulsen PB, Adamsen S, Vondeling H, Jørgensen T. Diffusion of laparoscopic technologies in Denmark. Health Policy 1998;45(2):149-167.

20. Dirksen CD, Ament AJH, Go PMN. Diffusion of six surgical endoscopic procedures in the Netherlands. Stimulating and restraining factors. Health Policy 1996;37:91-104.

21. Menon D, Marshall D. Diffusion of laparoscopic cholecystectomy in Canada. International Journal of Technology Assessment in Health Care 1994;10(2):287-292.

22. Fendrick M, Escarce JJ, McLane C, Shea JA, Schwartz JS. Hospital adoption of laparoscopic cholecystectomy. Medical Care 1994;32(10):1058-1063.

23. Homer JB. A diffusion model with application to evolving medical technologies. Technological Forecasting and Social Change 1987;31:197-218.

24. Vondeling H, Haerkens E, de Wit A, Bos M, Banta HD. Diffusion of minimally invasive technologies in the Netherlands. Health Policy 1993;23:67-81.

25. Escarce JJ, Bloom BS, Hillman AL, Shea JA, Schwartz JS. Diffusion of laparoscopic cholecystectomy among general surgeons in the United States. Medical Care 1995;33(3):256-271.

26. Banta HD (ed.). Minimally invasive therapy in five European countries: diffusion, effectiveness and cost-effectiveness [special issue]. Health Policy 1993;23:1-177.

27. Hailey D. Health care technologies in Australia. Health Policy 1994;30:23-72.

28. Tunis SR, Gelband H. Health care technology in the United States. Health Policy 1994;30:335-396.

29. Bos M. Health care technologies in the Netherlands. Health Policy 1994;30:207-255.

30. Weill C. Health care technology in France. Health Policy 1994;30:123-162.

31. Marshall D, Hailey D, Hirsch N, Clark E, Menon D. The introduction of laparoscopic cholecystectomy in Canada and Australia. Australian Institute of Health & Welfare (AIHW) and Canadian Coordinating Office for Health Technology Assessment (CCOHTA), May 1994.

32. Jonsson E, Banta D. Health care technology in Sweden. Health Policy 1994;30:257-294.

33. Kirchberger S. Health care technology in the Federal Republic of Germany. Health Policy 1994;30:163-205.

34. Spiby J. Health care technology in the United Kingdom. Health Policy 1994;30:295-334.

35. Rogers EM. Diffusion of Innovations. 4th edn. New York: Free Press, 1995.

36. Rogers EM. Lessons for guidelines from the diffusion of innovations. The challenge. Joint Commission Journal on Quality Improvement 1995;21:324-328.

37. Bonair A. Conceptual and empirical issues of technological change in the health care sector. Innovation and diffusion of hemodialysis and renal transplantation. PhD Dissertation. Linköping University, 1990.

38. Coleman JS, Katz E, Menzel H. Medical Innovation. A Diffusion Study. The Bobbs-Merrill Company, Inc., Indianapolis, 1966.

39. Greer AL. Adoption of medical technology. The hospital's three decision system. International Journal of Technology Assessment in Health Care 1985;1:669-680.

40. Mohr LB. Determinants of innovations in organisations. The American Political Science Review 1969;63:111-126.

41. Stocking B. (ed.). Expensive health technologies. Regulatory and administrative mechanisms in Europe. Oxford Medical Publications, Oxford University Press, Oxford, 1988.

42. US Congress, Office of Technology Assessment, Health Care Technology and its Assessment in Eight Countries, OTA-BP-H-140, Washington, DC: US Government Printing Office, February 1995.

Chapter 5

Diffusion of Laparoscopic Technologies in Denmark[156]

Peter Bo Poulsen[a], Sven Adamsen[b], Hindrik Vondeling[c] &Torben Jørgensen[d]

[a] Institute of Public Health, University of Southern Denmark, Odense University, Denmark
[b] Department of Surgery A, Section for Gastrointestinal Surgery, Hillerød Hospital; and The Danish National Registry for Laparoscopic Cholecystectomy, Laparoscopic Surgery Committee, Danish Surgical Society, Hillerød Hospital, Denmark
[c] Department of Epidemiology and Biostatistics, Vrije Universiteit Amsterdam, The Netherlands
[d] DSI - Danish Institute for Health Services Research and Development, Denmark

---

[156] Chapter 5 is published as an article in *Health Policy 1998;45(2):149-167* as well as the results of the study were presented at *the 14th Annual Meeting in The International Society of Technology Assessment in Health Care*, Ottawa, Canada, June 9, 1998.

Table of contents

Abstract 141

1. Introduction 142
    1.1. Regulation of health technologies in Denmark 142
    1.2. Laparoscopic surgery 142

2. Material and methods 144
    2.1 Definitions and data sources 144
    2.2 Predefined factors of diffusion 145
    2.3 Statistical analysis 148

3. Results 148
    3.1 Descriptive statistics - the pattern of diffusion 148
    3.2 The type of adopters 150
    3.3 Actual use 150
    3.4 Factor assessment - univariate analysis 151
    3.5 Factor assessment - bivariate analysis 153
    3.6 Factor analysis - multivariate analysis 154

4. Discussion 154

5. Conclusion 157

Acknowledgement 158

References 158

APPENDIX 5.1: Factor analysis (elaborates Section 3.6) 162

Abstract

It has been predicted that minimally invasive therapy will have dramatic consequences for the specialty of general surgery, as demonstrated by the diffusion of laparoscopic cholecystectomy. To investigate the determinants of the diffusion in Denmark of five laparoscopic technologies (cholecystectomy, appendectomy, surgery for colon cancer, surgery for inguinal hernia and fundoplication), questionnaires on seventeen factors' influence on the adoption (*stimulating* or *impeding*) were sent to fifty-nine hospitals. Fifty hospitals (85%) responded. Overall, 98% adopted laparoscopic cholecystectomy in Denmark between 1991 and 1995, whereas the remainder of the technologies were adopted by 7 to 65 per cent of hospitals performing these operations. Large and specialized hospitals were the earliest adopters. The factors, *nature of technology* (minimally invasive versus conventional), *training* (appropriate training courses), *competition* (between specialties and between hospitals) and *media attention* have stimulated the diffusion, whereas three budget factors - *budget for investment*, *budget for operation* and *public regulation* - usually had an impeding effect. Stimulating factors prevail for all laparoscopic technologies indicating that some guidance of the adoption and use of new health technologies might be necessary. In Denmark, one of the suggested health policies to secure timely guidance is the establishment of an early warning system.

1. Introduction

1.1. Regulation of health technologies in Denmark

The Danish hospital service is decentralized, both politically, administratively and financially. These services are public responsibilities with equal and free access for the patients [1]. The task of the State in health care is primarily to initiate, coordinate and advise the regional and local levels [2]. At the regional level, the hospital service is the responsibility of the fourteen counties and one hospital authority - Copenhagen Hospital Corporation. Hospitals are primarily financed through taxation levied by the counties, although a minor share is due to state block grants. Total health expenditures were 6.5 per cent of the GNP in 1995 [3] after having been decreasing for the past decade [4].

Except for the obligatory market approval of new pharmaceuticals, there is limited regulation of new health technologies in Denmark. Medical devices are regulated by the gradual implementation of European Commission Directives focusing upon safety only [5]. However, an indirect control occurs at the national level in some instances by the National Board of Health's issuing of guidelines for the planning of specialties among the Danish hospitals [6]. These guidelines only deal with expensive high-skill and/or low volume treatments or technologies. Medium-ticket technologies, as laparoscopic surgery, escape such regulation in Denmark.

1.2. Laparoscopic surgery

Minimally invasive therapy (MIT) is a relatively new and growing area of medical treatment modalities (i.e. endoscopes, vascular catheters and shock wave lithotripters) that causes substantially reduced trauma to the patient [7]. It has been recognized that MIT has a potential to offer great advantages for the patient and to improve cost-effectiveness of health care [8]. Furthermore, it has been predicted that MIT may have dramatic consequences for the specialty of general surgery [7].

Therefore, the objective of this study was to elucidate the determinants of the diffusion of five selected laparoscopic technologies in general surgery in Denmark. The intention was to identify and analyse factors that have *stimulated* or *impeded* the decision to adopt and use the laparoscopic technologies. Simultaneously, the study served as a focused update of a previous study on the diffusion of MIT in Denmark [9] and in five other European countries in 1993 [10]. This study, among other technologies, included laparoscopic cholecystectomy and laparoscopic appendectomy. Based on the results, the authors expected that the diffusion of minimally invasive surgery would, both in Denmark and elsewhere, be hampered due to factors such as limited budgets and lack of fees for these technologies [10]. Laparoscopic cholecystectomy was regarded as an exception to this rule, due to dominance of diffusion stimulating factors, e.g. patient demand and media attention.

The laparoscopic technologies selected for this study include: *laparoscopic cholecystectomy, laparoscopic appendectomy, laparoscopic fundoplication (surgery for gastroesophageal reflux), laparoscopic surgery for inguinal hernia* and *laparoscopic surgery for colon cancer*. Besides that these technologies are not regulated in Denmark, they represent the mainstream of minimally invasive therapies in general surgery. In addition, these technologies are interesting from a Danish perspective because they constituted the object of a consensus conference on abdominal laparoscopic surgery held recently in Copenhagen [11]. Of the technologies, laparoscopic surgery for colon cancer is considered experimental, while the other four technologies are considered more or less established in clinical practice. Associated with this, the quality of the evidence documenting safety, effectiveness and cost-effectiveness differs for the five technologies. The information generated in this study could be used to guide further evaluation and diffusion of these and similar technologies both at the national and regional levels. The Danish Surgical Society could play a role in this analysis and diffusion process as well.

Of the laparoscopic technologies in this study, *cholecystectomy* was the first that quickly gained widespread use [12]. In Denmark, laparoscopic cholecystectomy was introduced at two hospitals - Hillerød Hospital and Århus University Hospital in January 1991 [13,14]. Since then a fast and uncontrolled diffusion has taken place, replacing the open surgery as the standard treatment procedure [15]. In many countries, the graph of the diffusion of laparoscopic cholecystectomy has had a steep sigmoidal shape [10,16], which is basically following sociological and economic diffusion theory [17-20]. The idea of a sigmoidal shaped curve, reflecting a gradually increasing spread of health technology, is closely connected with the initial uncertainty resting in an innovation and the communication of its value. Uncertainty then diminishes as experience increases. This is a highly generalized scheme, which of course does not apply to every health technology [17,21,22].

In the case of cholecystectomy, the advantages of the laparoscopic technology are very small scars, short hospital stay, and quick return to daily routine. However, 10 per cent of the laparoscopic cholecystectomies require conversion to an open procedure because of technical difficulties, as documented prospectively in The Danish National Registry of Laparoscopic Cholecystectomy administered by the Laparoscopic Committee of the Danish Surgical Society [12], and other larger series. Concerns have been raised as to possible risks of injury to the bile ducts with the laparoscopic technology [23], but there are not sufficiently large controlled studies or large prospective case series from the era of open cholecystectomy to confirm these concerns. A newer small-incision open surgical technology (mini-laparotomy) may have advantages similar to the laparoscopic technology, but has not gained popularity in Denmark. In total, 75 cholecystectomies per 100,000 inhabitants were performed in Denmark in 1995 [24].

Laparoscopic appendectomy has been compared with the open procedure in several, usually not blinded, randomized studies, giving no sound evidence to justify substituting laparoscopic for the open procedure [25]. However, the possibility of using laparoscopes for diagnosing other conditions with symptoms similar to appendicitis decreases the number of unnecessary appendicectomies, and increases the probability of a correct diagnosis. In total, 151 appendicectomies per 100,000 inhabitants were carried out in Denmark in 1995 [24].

Laparoscopic fundoplication is an attractive alternative to the open procedure mainly because of the significantly reduced surgical trauma, and good views via the video-laparoscope. The same advantages as mentioned for cholecystectomy have been documented [25]. Because the vast majority of patients with gastroesophageal reflux receive medical treatment in Denmark, the rarity of patients relevant for surgical treatment warrants centralization to relatively few centres. Annually, less than 3 operations are performed per 100,000 inhabitants in Denmark [11].

Surgery for inguinal hernia with the conventional technology is a short procedure using local anaesthesia. The laparoscopic technology does not seem to have particular advantages over the open procedure, except in special situations, such as re-operative surgery for recurrent hernia, where the laparoscopic approach in tissue that has been subjected to previous surgery may provide a better technical result [25,26]. Large randomized studies are necessary to assess the laparoscopic technology. Another source of information will be the Danish Hernia database, which is in the process of establishment [26]. About 230 hernia operations are performed in Denmark annually per 100,000 inhabitants [26].

Laparoscopic surgery for colon cancer is considered in its investigative stage in Denmark, and is only performed in a few centres within controlled studies. Possible advantages of a laparoscopic technology may be a reduced surgical stress response, small scars, short hospital stay and quick return to daily routine. A possible risk of implantation of malignant cells in the laparoscopic wounds has been debated and is also investigated in ongoing trials [27].

2. Material and methods

2.1 Definitions and data sources

Diffusion is the process by which an innovation is communicated through certain channels over time among members of a social system [17]. *Diffusion* could be defined either by the initial decision made within an organisation to *adopt* an innovation [21] or by a certain *extent of use* of a technology [18,21]. In the present study data is collected both on adoption and use. The *rate of adoption* is the relative speed with which an innovation is adopted by members of a social system within the time period studied (1991-1997) [19]. The *mean time of adoption* was defined as the average time of adoption for the accumulated diffusion, whereas the *median time of adoption* was the time of adoption measured, when 50 per cent of the hospitals had adopted.

Two factors that characterize a hospital and known to influence the timing of adoption markedly are: the *specialization* and the *size* of the hospital [28,29]. The size of the hospital was defined by the *number of somatic beds* in the hospital, and obtained from an official statistics [30]. The hospitals were divided into three categories of size: less than 250 beds, between 250 - 400 beds, and more than 400 beds. In the study, specialization of the hospital was defined with respect to the specialty of surgery. Nine hospitals with *departments specifically for surgical gastroenterology, most with university affiliation*, were defined as *specialized hospitals*, whereas fifty hospitals only containing *departments of general surgery* were defined as *non-specialized hospitals*. The specialty of surgical gastroenterology focuses specifically on the investigation and treatment of diseases in the gastrointestinal tract, liver and pancreas [6]. Departments of surgical gastroenterology are thereby more specialized than departments of general surgery, and are, e.g. responsible for a significant part of the education of the future specialists - the gastrointestinal surgeons. Information about specialization was also obtained from an official statistics [31].

The actual year chosen for these data was 1991, since the first of the five laparoscopic technologies (laparoscopic cholecystectomy) was adopted this year.

In July 1997, a questionnaire was mailed to surgeons representing the fifty-nine hospitals in Denmark, including the Faroe Islands and Greenland, with surgical departments, which are performing at least one of the five operations. These surgeons were selected as the *historical adopter* of the laparoscopic technology in the surgical departments. Most of the adopters were identified through The Danish National Registry of Laparoscopic Cholecystectomy. However, in a few cases other sources were necessary, due to the surgeons' shifts in position since the time of adoption. The hospital was regarded as the adopting unit in the study.

The questionnaire requested information about the *time of adoption* of each of the laparoscopic technologies (month and year) and their present use. For laparoscopic cholecystectomy, however, data about the time of adoption from the above registry were used instead, due to a presumed higher reliability of data. Furthermore, the respondents were asked to assess the influence of seventeen predefined factors on the decision to adopt. If the laparoscopic technology was not adopted, the surgeons (non-adopters) were asked about their expectations of an eventual future adoption.

2.2 Predefined factors of diffusion

Identification of relevant factors determining the diffusion of health technology was based upon a literature review, predominantly focusing on laparoscopic surgery. Since the first adoption of laparoscopic cholecystectomy in Germany in 1986 [16] a number of diffusion studies have been published in this field [10,28,29,32-36]. Some of these focus exclusively on laparoscopic cholecystectomy [28,29,34-36], while others take a broader perspective [10,32,33]. Based on these studies, seventeen factors influencing the diffusion of laparoscopic surgery were identified, which were deemed of relevance to the Danish context. For example, in our study a factor like *reimbursement* (fee-for-service) was not included due to the public running and financing of the Danish hospital sector. In this publicly integrated model, the hospital departments operate under global budgets, and those providing health services, such as the surgeons, are civil servants receiving a fixed salary [2], thus inquiring about a factor like reimbursement would not make sense.

The definitions of the seventeen factors are presented in Table 5.1 below.

Table 5.1 : Definition of diffusion factors

FACTORS	DEFINITIONS
1. Budget for investment	The budget available at the department for the capital investment in laparoscopes and other associated equipment.
2. Budget for operation	The budget available for the running costs to cover the use of personnel, equipment (minus the laparoscope), drugs and anaesthesia, expenditures for hospitalization, etc. in connection with preexaminations, operations and postoperative hospitalization using a laparoscopic technology compared with an open procedure.
3. Financial incentives	The financial incentives at the hospital, which make short stays either advantageous, neutral or disadvantageous, as well as the specific payment systems to the surgeons or the department using the laparoscopic technology.
4. Nature of technology	The need to acquire new surgical skills to use the technology safely, using for example trocars, cameras, video-monitoring, two/three dimensionality and/or miniaturized equipment, as well as the ability to catch up with the technical development of the laparoscopic technology.
5. Planning and logistics	The necessary planning and logistics to use the laparoscopic technology compared with that of an open procedure, e.g. the preparation of the operation, the composition of the personnel, the availability of instruments, the length of the operation, etc.
6. Expected extra benefit	The initial expected value of the laparoscopic technology with respect to effectiveness, cost-effectiveness, cost-advantages, safety, morbidity, convalescence.
7. Scientific evidence	The availability and quality of the published scientific evidence with respect to the safety, effectiveness and cost-effectiveness of the laparoscopic technology.
8. Organizing studies	The possibility of organizing studies to document the effectiveness of the laparoscopic technology, which is affected by problems like the presence of logistical problems, the availability of funding, the professionals' interest in the study, the patients' attitude towards participating in a study, the ethical dilemma of a study.
9. Training	The appropriate education/training courses with respect to the laparoscopic technology at the time of adoption, for example organized by the Surgical Society or the medical device industry.
10. Traditions and culture	The culture and traditions among surgeons (conservatism) with respect to the use of equipment in operations, the lack of tradition for minimally invasive openings in surgery, the surgeons' changing understanding of trauma.
11. Opinion leaders	Innovative persons in the surgical field, who advocate for the laparoscopic technology, and most often themselves are the first to adopt the technology.
12. Competition	The competition between surgeons and gastroenterologists in performing the treatment, the competition between hospitals in offering the laparoscopic technology.
13. Conferences and related activities	Experience and information about the laparoscopic technology from scientific conferences, and/or related activities, as for example meetings held by the Danish Surgical Society, the establishment of a laparoscopic cholecystectomy database organized by the Surgical Society.
14. Role of the industry	The commercial pressure by the industry and the response to this pressure from the surgeons. In addition the support by the device industry with respect to the delivery, maintenance and repair of (reusable) laparoscopes.
15. Attention from the media	What is published in the media (e.g. newspapers, weekly magazines, television, etc.) about the laparoscopic technology.
16. Patient demand	The epidemiological knowledge of the disease (prevalence), as well as the expressed demand from the patients, e.g. patient organisations, for the laparoscopic technology.
17. Public regulation	The public regulation that has affected the decision to adopt the laparoscopic technology. This could be a regulation of the number of instruments, a limitation in the number of procedures to be carried out, etc.

For each laparoscopic technology the assessment of each factor's influence on the decision to adopt the laparoscopic technology was made on a seven-point ordinal scale ranging from *very stimulating* to *neutral* to *very impeding* effect.

2.3 Statistical analysis

The results were divided into univariate, bivariate and multivariate parts. Explicit decision weights that took both median values and range of the assessments into account were used in the univariate analysis of the factor assessments. The parametric Fisher's exact and Chi-square tests, and the non-parametric Mann-Whitney U and Kruskall Wallis tests were used to analyse the rate and mean time of adoption with respect to the groups of subpopulations, as well as the differences in factor assessments for the different groups of subpopulations in the bivariate analyses. Finally, a factor analysis was carried out to summarize the characteristics of the adoption. A P-value of 5 per cent was chosen as statistically significant.

3. Results

After two mailed reminders and one telephone reminder, 85 per cent (N=50) of the fifty-nine hospitals returned the questionnaire. Two hospitals refused to answer. Among the respondents, seven were specialized hospitals (response rate 78 per cent) and forty-three were non-specialized hospitals (response rate 86 per cent).

3.1 Descriptive statistics - the pattern of diffusion

In Denmark, the first adoption of laparoscopic cholecystectomy took place at two hospitals - Hillerød Hospital and Århus University Hospital - in January 1991, see Table 5.2 below. Except for Greenland, every surgical department in Denmark and the Faroe Islands performing cholecystectomy has adopted the laparoscopic technology between January 1991 and August 1995. The median time of adoption for laparoscopic cholecystectomy in Denmark was fourteen months. The level of adoption was lower for the other laparoscopic technologies. Among the hospitals performing appendectomy, surgery for inguinal hernia, and fundoplication, between 57 and 65 per cent of the departments have adopted the laparoscopic technology between 1991 and 1997. However, as to surgery for colon cancer only four departments adopted the laparoscopic technology. This is probably due to the general consensus in the Danish surgical community that laparoscopic surgery for colon cancer is to be considered at the investigative stage at the present time. The typical department has adopted the laparoscopic technology in cholecystectomy and for surgery for inguinal hernia (56 per cent). The aggregated diffusion profiles for each of the five laparoscopic technologies are shown in Figure 5.1.

Figure 5.1 : The diffusion of laparoscopic surgery in Denmark
- figures corrected for type of operation actually made

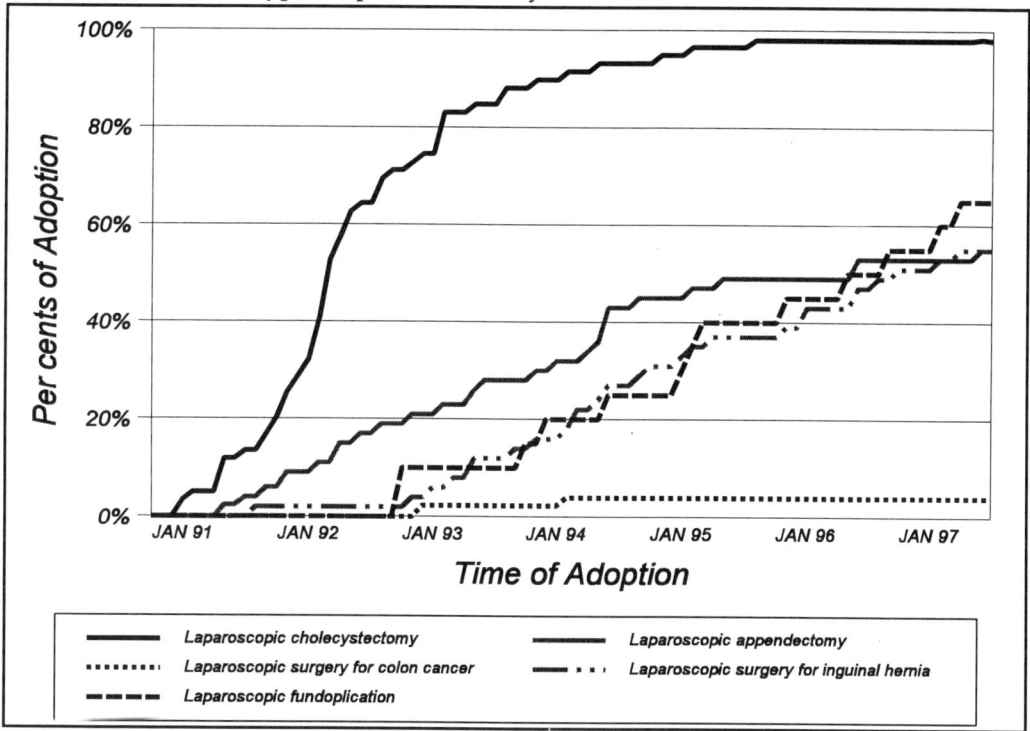

The diffusion profile for laparoscopic cholecystectomy seems to follow the typical sigmoidal pattern of diffusion with a high growth rate around the median. For laparoscopic fundoplication and laparoscopic surgery for inguinal hernia a linear growth in the diffusion profiles appear, although the median time of adoption is markedly higher for these technologies. The diffusion of laparoscopic appendectomy has also been almost linearly increasing until 1994; since then, the growth rate has been close to zero. In surgery for colon cancer, the laparoscopic technology is hardly adopted in Danish hospitals. Table 5.2 shows the time of adoption for the five laparoscopic technologies.

Table 5.2 : The total pattern of adoption of laparoscopic technologies in Denmark

Laparoscopic technologies (N= responded sample)	No.of adopting hospitals (%)	First time of adoption	Median time of adoption	Mean time of adoption
Cholecystectomy (N=59)	58 (98%)	Jan 1991	14 months	17 months
Appendectomy (N=50)	27 (46%)	May 1991	27 months	28 months
Surgery for colon cancer (N=50)	4 (7%)	Dec 1992	7 months	7 months
Surgery for inguinal hernia (N=50)	28 (47%)	Aug 1991	38 months	37 months
Fundoplication (N=50)	13 (22%)	Oct 1992	27 months	26 months

3.2 The type of adopters

The diffusion of laparoscopic technologies in hospitals of different degree of specialization and of different size were analysed.

No significant differences were found between specialized and non-specialized hospitals in Denmark with respect to the rate of adoption. A significantly earlier adoption by specialized hospitals compared with non-specialized hospitals was, however, found in laparoscopic cholecystectomy (6 months), laparoscopic appendectomy (27 months) and laparoscopic fundoplication (23 months) (Mann Whitney U test, $P<0.05$).

Another characteristic of the type of adopter was the *size of the hospital* measured by number of somatic beds. A significant difference was found in the distributions of the rate of adoption of laparoscopic fundoplication and laparoscopic surgery for inguinal hernia indicating that larger hospitals (>400 beds) had adopted the laparoscopic technology more frequently compared with smaller hospitals (<250 beds) (Chi-square test, $P<0.05$). In cholecystectomy and appendectomy, the time of adoption of the laparoscopic technology was significantly earlier for larger hospitals (at least 13 months) than for smaller hospitals (Kruskall Wallis test, $P<0.04$). The number of laparoscopic technologies adopted by the three groups of hospitals was significantly different (Kruskall Wallis test, $P<0.05$). Larger hospitals have on average adopted three technologies, whereas small hospitals have only adopted two.

3.3 Actual use

As reported by the respondents, laparoscopic fundoplication (99 per cent use on average) has almost completely replaced the traditional open procedure. For laparoscopic cholecystectomy, the average level of use reported by the respondents was 88 per cent. In contrast to this, the actual use of the laparoscopic technology in the other indications was much lower, which illustrates the limited advantage or investigational stage of the laparoscope in these cases.

3.4 Factor assessment - univariate analysis

To make an overall judgement in the univariate analysis of the effect of the seventeen factors on the decision to adopt the laparoscopic technology, five decision weights were put forward, see Table 5.3. These decision weights took both the median values and the range of the assessments into account.

Table 5.3 : Decision weights for the univariate analysis
- based on median values and the range of the assessments

Very stimulating (+ +) :
- when median > 4 and a right-sided range of values (4-7)

Stimulating (+) :
- when median > 4 and values were in the whole range (1-7), or
- when median = 4 and a right-sided range of values (4-7)

Neutral:
- when median = 4 and values were in the whole range (1-7)

Impeding (-):
- when median = 4 and a left-sided range of values (1-4), or
- when median < 4 and values were in the whole range (1-7)

Very Impeding (- -):
- when median < 4 and a left-sided range of values (1-4)

Applied to the assessment of factors by the respondents for each of the five laparoscopic technologies, these decision weights provided the results presented in Table 5.4.

Table 5.4 : Univariate analysis of the five technologies (neutral are "shown" as blank spaces)

Diffusion factors	Laparoscopic technologies				
	1	2	3	4	5
1. Budget for investment	−		−	−	
2. Budget for operation			−	−	−
3. Financial incentives					
4. Nature of technology	+	+	+	+	+
5. Planning and logistics					
6. Expected extra benefit	+ +		+	+	+
7. Scientific evidence	+			+	+ +
8. Organizing studies	+			+	
9. Training	+	+	+	+	+
10. Traditions and culture					
11. Opinion leaders	+ +			+	
12. Competition	+ +	+	+	+ +	+ +
13. Conferences & rel. activities	+ +			+	+ +
14. Role of the industry					
15. Media attention	+ +	+	+	+	+ +
16. Patient demand	+ +		+	+	
17. Public regulation					−

Laparoscopic technologies:
1. Laparoscopic cholecystectomy (N=49)
2. Laparoscopic appendectomy (N=40)
3. Laparoscopic surgery for colon cancer (N=33)
4. Laparoscopic surgery for inguinal hernia (N=41)
5. Laparoscopic fundoplication (N=33)

As seen from Table 5.4, laparoscopic cholecystectomy and laparoscopic surgery for inguinal hernia had the largest number of stimulating factors. Among these ten stimulating factors, six were judged as *very stimulating* for the diffusion of laparoscopic cholecystectomy - *expected extra benefit, opinion leaders, competition, conferences and related activities, media attention,* and *patient demand*. Only one factor was assessed as negative - *budget for investment*. The result, as the most stimulating technology, corresponded with the fast and wide diffusion of laparoscopic cholecystectomy shown in Figure 5.1. The lowest number of stimulating factors and the most neutral cases were found for laparoscopic appendectomy and laparoscopic surgery for colon cancer. This neutral picture seems to fit with the pattern of diffusion that both laparoscopic technologies have exhibited until now with a slow gradual diffusion and nearly without any growth in the number of adopting departments since 1994. When looking at laparoscopic fundoplication, the impression is that here is the highest potential for additional diffusion, as the empirical findings show that laparoscopic fundoplication was the third most stimulating technology. At the consensus conference on abdominal laparoscopic surgery in Denmark in 1997, laparoscopic surgery for inguinal hernia was recommended in very few and special situations [11]. Therefore, the positive empirical findings with respect to diffusion of this technology were a bit surprising.

Finally, an overall result of the seventeen diffusion factors could be summarized with respect to the five laparoscopic technologies. Four factors - *nature of the technology, training, competition* and *media attention* - had for all five technologies a positive effect on the diffusion as factors that stimulated the decision to adopt the laparoscopic technology. Another six factors were, depending on technology, in the positive range of the scale - *expected extra benefit, scientific evidence, organizing studies, opinion leaders, conferences* and *patient demand*. Only three factors had sometimes an impeding effect on the decision to adopt, and these factors were all related to economic restraints and regulation by public authorities. Three of the seventeen factors - *financial incentives, planning and logistics,* and *traditions and culture* - were neutral to the diffusion of all five laparoscopic technologies.

3.5 Factor assessment - bivariate analysis

Comparing the assessments of adopters and non-adopters, except cholecystectomy, non-adopters seemed to judge the laparoscopic technology more negative than adopters. A more positive assessment by the adopters compared with non-adopters was significant with respect to *budget for investment, budget for operation, expected extra benefit, scientific evidence, training* and *opinion leaders* in laparoscopic fundoplication, and *planning and logistics, training* and *scientific evidence* in laparoscopic appendectomy (Mann Whitney U test, $P<0.04$). The last factor also in laparoscopic surgery for inguinal hernia. Overall, it seems that adopters assessed factors relating to evidence, benefits and training significantly more positive than non-adopters.

Another division in groups of subpopulations was between *specialized* and *non-specialized hospitals*. For both appendectomy and fundoplication, the factor *financial incentives* significantly impeded adoption in specialized hospitals (Mann Whitney U test, $P<0.05$). This result could reflect the lack of financial incentives and increased budgetary pressure (cost containment) early in the process of diffusion when most of the specialized hospitals adopted the technology. In fundoplication, *budget for operation* was assessed as significantly impeding by non-specialized hospitals compared with specialized hospitals (Mann Whitney U test, $P<0.05$). Specialized hospitals assessed both *nature of technology* in appendectomy and *expected extra benefit* in surgery for colon cancer as more stimulating (Mann Whitney U test, $P<0.04$). Overall, however, it seems that the factors influencing the decision to adopt were not that different between the two types of hospitals.

Finally, bivariate analyses of different *hospital sizes* were made. In cholecystectomy, the only factor assessed significantly different between small and large hospitals was *traditions and culture* (Kruskall Wallis test, $P<0.02$). Small hospitals assessed the factor as stimulating, while it was impeding for the largest hospitals (Mann Whitney U test, P<0.01). The factor *nature of technology* was, in fundoplication, assessed significantly more stimulating for medium and small hospitals than for large hospitals, whereas the reverse was true for the factors *expected extra benefit* and *scientific evidence* (Kruskall Wallis test, P<0.05). In appendectomy and inguinal hernia, the factor *public regulation* was assessed as significantly impeding for large hospitals compared with a neutral effect for small hospitals, while *opinion leaders* have been more stimulating in large hospitals (Kruskall Wallis test, P<0.05). Again, not many differences in assessments appeared with respect to hospital size.

3.6 Factor analysis - multivariate analysis

By assuming cardinal properties of the scale used, a factor analysis was made to reveal a key number of interpretable and independent *general factors* through reducing the original seventeen factors of diffusion. In this section, the results are briefly reported for laparoscopic cholecystectomy. The factor analysis resulted in six general factors that described the decision to adopt laparoscopic cholecystectomy. Most important was a *communication factor* that contained original factors related to communication and information channels, such as conferences, and the industry's advertising. The second factor - a *technology factor* - included original factors about the technology, e.g. its nature and benefits. The third factor was an *economic factor*, whereas the fourth factor was characterized as an *environmental factor* according to the original factors that it captured, e.g. competition and patient demand. The two last factors - *planning* and *investment* - were identical with the original diffusion factors. A more detailed description of the results of the factor analysis are presented in Appendix 5.1.

4. Discussion

As expected in the earlier Danish diffusion study [9], the present study shows that since the introduction in Denmark in 1991 the diffusion of laparoscopic cholecystectomy has been wide and fast. Despite a short delay in the introduction, the diffusion of laparoscopic cholecystectomy in Denmark has exhibited the same pattern of a fast and wide diffusion as in countries like the Netherlands, the United States, Canada, and Australia [28,29,32-36]. The adoption phase of laparoscopic cholecystectomy in those countries, and in Denmark, took place before the technology had been proven safe and effective in large randomized controlled trials, as the first trials were only based upon few patients during the introductory years [37]. The decision to adopt laparoscopic cholecystectomy in Denmark and abroad was not postponed until scientific evidence became available.

Compared with cholecystectomy, the same fast and wide diffusion did not occur for the other laparoscopic technologies in Denmark. Laparoscopic fundoplication demonstrated a more modest diffusion process than laparoscopic cholecystectomy, with a potential for additional diffusion. Contrary to expectations [9], laparoscopic appendectomy has not had the same fast and wide diffusion. The technology was also used infrequently by the adopting departments. Reasons might be that appendicitis is an emergency condition, that the open procedure is not as invasive compared with the laparoscopic technology, and that young surgeons under training, and often without any laparoscopic experience, typically make these operations. Furthermore, there is no sound controlled evidence to justify substituting laparoscopic for the standard appendectomy [25]. These reasons, as well as factors such as budgetary pressure and financial incentives, to a low rate of adoption in appendectomy were also found in a study of diffusion in the Netherlands [32]. However, the diagnostic capabilities of the laparoscopic technology for acute abdominal pain must not be overlooked. The diffusion of the laparoscopic technology in inguinal hernia has been slow in Denmark with only little use. Reasons to this could be a lack of particular advantages with the laparoscopic technology, due to complications and the need for general anaesthesia, together with the fact that newer tension-free open procedures performed under local anaesthesia are gaining popularity [26]. In surgery for colon cancer, the low adoption and use corresponded with the fact that the use of the laparoscopic technology is in its investigational stage within controlled studies, because of the risk of possible tumour implantations in the laparoscopic wounds [25,27].

However, what were the explanations of a fast diffusion of some technologies compared with a slow diffusion of other?

First, the pattern of diffusion showed that status as a *specialized hospital* was associated with an earlier adoption of laparoscopic cholecystectomy. By characterizing the specialized hospitals as *specialist training hospitals*, due to their training of gastrointestinal surgeons, the results found in our study corresponded with results found for other countries [28,29,33]. This means that new applications are expected to be found first in specialized hospitals, because of their innovative behaviour. However, it is worth noticing that the first adopter in Denmark was not a specialized hospital at the time of adoption.

Secondly, *the size of the hospital* showed to be another characteristic associated with an earlier adoption. The same results were found in Canada [28] and in the United States [29]. It was concluded that hospital size had a positive influence upon adoption.

Thirdly, in the multivariate analysis the study found, according to the theories of Rogers [17,19], *communication* as the foremost important general factor for the adoption of laparoscopic cholecystectomy in Denmark.

Fourthly, among all seventeen factors of diffusion the survey revealed four factors with a stimulating effect for the decision to adopt all of the laparoscopic technologies. Technical advantages, such as the video-monitored 3-D facility, makes it no surprise that the factor *nature of the technology* was stimulating. The factor *training* stimulated also the adoption of all laparoscopic technologies, which reflects the importance of training activities along with the adoption of a new technology, as stated at the consensus conference [11]. Training has primarily been provided by the Danish Surgical Society, and the manufacturers. In the future, however, this responsibility ought to be shared by the National Board of Health, the counties and the Surgical Society [15]. The third stimulating factor was *competition*. This factor covers both the competition between hospitals and the historical competition between the medical gastroenterological field and the surgical field. The development of pharmacological and lithotripsy alternatives to conventional surgery induced surgeons, at least internationally, to develop laparoscopic cholecystectomy [38]. The last of the factors that showed to be stimulating for all the laparoscopic technologies was *media attention*. All four factors were found stimulating in the Netherlands as well [32,33]. Only three budget factors - *budget for investment, budget for operation* and *public regulation* - especially for the four laparoscopic technologies with low or moderate diffusion, showed to have an impeding effect upon the decision to adopt. This is consistent with an international study that concluded that the diffusion of laparoscopic technologies, besides cholecystectomy, has been constrained by limited budgets and lack of fees in Europe [10].

To explain the fast diffusion in cholecystectomy with the laparoscopic technology substituting the existing open procedure only with a moderate capital outlay, the factor *expected extra benefit* has to be considered. Expectation of reduced hospital length of stay from laparoscopic surgery is of interest for all health systems. However, Battista et al. (1995) [39] doubts whether these bed-days are actually freed, and they conclude that the use of laparoscopic cholecystectomy in several countries has had a growth greater than the rate of the natural increase of the open procedure it replaces. Denmark has also experienced this growth in cholecystectomies with the introduction of laparoscopes. The marginal effect from a reduction in bed-days seems furthermore to be limited by a changing tradition in open surgery towards shorter length of stay. The result of the introduction of the laparoscopic technology may then well be that the overall expenditures on surgery are increased.

The source of information used in our study was questionnaire responses from surgeons representing the hospital as the adopting unit. The reliability of this source of information and the time perspective of the data could, however, be criticized. Greer (1985) [40] found three salient decision making systems for adoption of new technologies in hospitals; *medical-individualistic, fiscal-managerial* and *strategic-institutional*. The *medical-individualistic* decision system was found dominant in evaluations of new clinical tools, e.g. fiberoptic endoscopes. This supports our choice of surgeons as source of information. Furthermore, to increase the reliability of the study, the surgeons asked were selected as the historical adopter in the surgical department. However, asking other decision-makers, e.g. county politicians or hospital technicians, could have revealed different perspectives. Another point to criticize, is the retrospective design that makes the conclusions concerning the factors uncertain. The results found are, nevertheless, relevant for future policy-making, because diffusion is not yet complete for four of the laparoscopic technologies. Furthermore, to carry out prospective studies of diffusion is problematic as it is difficult to predict, which technologies then actually will diffuse.

Besides studies at the hospital level, a study on the individual level regarding each surgeon as the adopting unit could have found other important explanations. Escarce et al. (1995) [34] found surgeon characteristics as *age, sex* and *board certification status* significantly associated with earlier adoption of laparoscopic cholecystectomy. A tendency with respect to age appeared also in our study, because *surgeons with few years of graduation age from medical school* showed to be earlier adopters than surgeons with a higher *age of graduation*. Surgeons research activity, the clustering of adopters in certain counties, the role of fiery souls or entrepreneurs, etc., are other determinants that could have had some impact on the timing of the adoption in Denmark. A more thorough investigation of these characteristics could be of interest for quantitative and qualitative research projects in the future.

5. Conclusion

Since the introduction in 1991, laparoscopic cholecystectomy has had an immense impact on the surgical field with its uncontrolled and fast diffusion in Denmark. In contrast to this, the study showed that the other laparoscopic technologies have not had the same fast and wide diffusion in Denmark. However, due to the lack of regulation in a Danish health care system, this limited diffusion is not a result of any control exercised on the process of diffusion.

For future and existing minimally invasive technologies, some control and guidance of the diffusion process, even before a 100 per cent adoption is attained, will be necessary to secure the adoption and use of effective and cost-effective technologies [9,15]. Which tools and interventions do the findings then suggest for health policy-makers to obtain a higher degree of control of the diffusion in a decentralized Danish health care system with limited regulation of technologies?

Battista et al. (1995) [39] concluded that the case of laparoscopic cholecystectomy showed that despite the growth in technology assessment activities, such activities still may be unsuccessful in identifying technological innovations early enough to influence their diffusion. However, the establishment of an early warning system, the aim of which is to identify and monitor emerging health technologies with an expected impact for the health care sector, might be one policy mechanism [41]. Although, it can be argued that early warning would not have avoided the fast diffusion of laparoscopic cholecystectomy, early warning can still act timely with respect to the other laparoscopic technologies. The establishment of an early warning system also coincides with a recommendation of the consensus conference, emphasizing the need for a complete overview of the future use of the laparoscopic technologies [11]. In Denmark, the contribution to the development and establishment of an early warning system is part of the Danish National Strategy for Health Technology Assessment [42], and suggestions for an early warning system were made recently [41]. Today, the Danish Institute for Health Technology Assessment (DIHTA) is responsible for the establishment of such a system.

Besides early warning other tools need to be used in health policy to encourage appropriate technological change. Health technology assessment, despite its time lag as a policy mechanism, is useful to document issues like safety, effectiveness and cost-effectiveness, even of established, but not yet assessed, technologies. DIHTA could, in cooperation with the Danish Surgical Society, the counties and the Medical Research Council, in the future initiate these assessments, as has happened with the ongoing *health technology assessment of the treatment of patients with cholelithiasis in Denmark* [43]. In addition, quality assurance and support of training programmes are important. Furthermore, policies like *specific funds for capital investments in cost-effective technologies* and *certification of institutions* have been suggested for the case of MIT [8]. A combination of these policy instruments could result in appropriate technological change in the health care sector. However, appropriate evaluation and diffusion of laparoscopic surgery still offer a challenge for both health poliy-makers and health service researchers in Denmark.

Acknowledgement

The authors acknowledge Ph.D. Carmen Dirksen and Dr. Peter Go for their helpful comments in the preparation phase of this work. Dr. Ole Hart Hansen and Professor Terkel Christiansen are also acknowledged for their helpful comments to earlier versions of this manuscript.

References

1. Grønvald LF, Alban A. Health Care in Denmark. In: Alban A, Christiansen T (eds.). The Nordic Light. New Initiatives in Health Care Systems. Odense: Odense University Press, 1995: 57-67.

2. Ministry of Health. Health care in Denmark 1.ed. Copenhagen, 1997.

3. The Association of Danish Pharmaceutical Industry (Mefa). Facts 1997, Medicine and health care - Denmark. Copenhagen: MEFA, 1997.

4. Pedersen KM. Reformitis? -Sceptical Remarks on the Dismal Science of Reforms. In: Alban A, Christiansen T. (eds.). The Nordic Light. New Initiatives in Health Care Systems. Odense: Odense University Press, 1995:46-57.

5. Council Directive. 93/42/EEC, of 14 June1993. Medical Devices.

6. Sundhedsstyrelsen. Specialeplanlægning og lands- og landsdelsfunktioner i sygehusvæsenet. Vejledning. København, 1996.

7. Banta HD. Introduction. Minimally invasive therapy in five European countries. Health Policy 1993;23:1-5.

8. Banta HD, Schersten T, Jonsson E. Implications of Minimally Invasive Therapy. Health Policy 1993;23:167-178.

9. Schou I. Minimally Invasive Therapy in Denmark. Health Policy 1993;23:17-30.

10. Banta HD (ed). Minimally Invasive Therapy in Five European Countries: Diffusion, Effectiveness and Cost-Effectiveness. Health Policy 1993;23(Special Issue):1-177.

11. Danneskiold-Samsøe B (ed). Abdominal Laparoscopic Surgery. Report from a medical consensus conference 3-5 March 1997. Copenhagen: Danish Medical Research Council and and Danish Institute for Health Services Research and Development. Consensus Report, 1997.

12. Adamsen S, Hansen OH, Jensen PMF, Schulze S, Stage JG, Wara P, Jensen LP. Laparoscopisk kolecystektomi i Danmark. En prospektiv registrering. Ugeskrift for Læger 1995;157:4449-4454. [Laparoscopic cholecystectomy in Denmark. A nationwide prospective case registration (english abstract and legends)].

13. Hansen OH, Bardram L, Haakonsen TU, Lauritsen K. Laparoskopisk kolecystektomi - minimal invasiv kirurgi. Ugeskrift for Læger 1991;153:3222-3224. [Laparoscopic Cholecystectomy - minimal invasive surgery (english abstract and legends)].

14. Jensen SL, Jensen PMF, Wara P, Rokkjær M. Laparoskopisk kolecystektomi. De første 45 operationer Ugeskrift for Læger 1991;153:3225-3228. [Laparoscopic Cholecystectomy. Report of the first 45 operations. (english abstract and legends)].

15. Hansen OH. Kikkertkirurgi og dens udbredelse. I: DSI-Institut for Sundhedsvæsen og Statens Sundhedsvidenskabelige Forskningsråd. Kikkertkirurgi i bughulen. Rapport fra en konsensus-konference, København, 3.-5. Marts 1997. Copenhagen: DSI, 1997:27-33.

16. Banta HD, Gelband E, Jonsson E, Battista R(eds.). Health Care Technology and its Assessment in Eight Countries: Australia, Canada, France, Germany, the Netherlands, Sweden, United Kingdom, Unites States. Health Policy 1994;30(1-3):1-421.

17. Rogers EM. Lessons for Guidelines from the Diffusion of Innovations. The Challenge. Joint Commission Journal on Quality Improvement 1995;21:324-328.

18. Warner KE. A "Desparation-Reaction" Model of Medical Diffusion. Health Services Research 1975;Winter:369-383.

19. Rogers EM. Diffusion of Innovations. 4th edition. New York: Free Press, 1995.

20. Warner KE. The Need for Some Innovative Concepts of Innovation: An Examination of Research on the Diffusion of Innovations. Policy Sciences 1974;5:433-451.

21. Banta HD, Behney CJ, Willems JS. Towards Rational Technology in Medicine. Considerations for Health Policy. New York: Springer Publishing Company, 1982. (Springer Series on Health Care and Society, volume 5).

22. Homer JB. A Diffusion Model with Application to Evolving Medical Technologies. Technological Forecasting and Social Change 1987;31:197-218.

23. Adamsen S, Hansen OH, Funch-Jensen P, Schulze S, Stage JG, Wara P. Bile duct injury during laparoscopic cholecystectomy: A prospective nationwide series. Journal of the American College of Surgeons 1997;184:571-578.

24. Nordic Medico Statistical Committee. Health Statistics in the Nordic Countries 1995. Copenhagen: NOMESCO, 1997. (Nordic Medico Statistical Committee 1997:49).

25. Johnson A. Laparoscopic surgery. The Lancet 1997;349:631-635.

26. Stage JG. Kikkertkirurgi ved blindtarmsbetændelse og brok. I: DSI-Institut for Sundhedsvæsen og Statens Sundhedsvidenskabelige Forskningsråd. Kikkertkirurgi i bughulen. Rapport fra en konsensus-konference København 3.-5. Marts 1997. Copenhagen: DSI, 1997:69-72.

27. Schulze S. Kikkertkirurgi ved mave-tarm cancer. I: DSI-Institut for Sundhedsvæsen og Statens Sundhedsvidenskabelige Forskningsråd. Kikkertkirurgi i bughulen. Rapport fra en konsensus-konference København 3.-5. Marts 1997. Copenhagen: DSI, 1997:73-75.

28. Menon D, Marshall D. Diffusion of Laparoscopic Cholecystectomy in Canada. International Journal of Technology Assessment in Health Care 1994;10:287-292.

29. Fendrick M, Escarce JJ, McLane C, Shea JA, Schwartz JS. Hospital Adoption of Laparoscopic Cholecystectomy. Medical Care 1994;32:1058-1063.

30. Sundhedsstyrelsen. Virksomhed ved sygehuse 1991. (Sygehusstatistik II:56:1993). København, 1993.

31. Sundhedsstyrelsen. Sygehusklassifikation og kommunekoder pr. 1. januar 1991. København, 1990.

32. Vondeling H, Haerkens E, de Wit A, Bos M, Banta HD. Diffusion of Minimally Invasive Technologies in the Netherlands. Health Policy 1993;23:67-81.

33. Dirksen CD, Ament AJH, Go PMN. Diffusion of six surgical endoscopic procedures in the Netherlands. Stimulating and restraining factors. Health Policy 1996;37:91-104.

34. Escarce JJ, Bloom BS, Hillman AL, Shea JA, Schwartz JS. Diffusion of Laparoscopic Cholecystectomy Among General Surgeons in the United States. Medical Care 1995;33:256-271.

35. Escarce JJ. Externalities in hospitals and physician adoption of a new surgical technology: an exploratory analysis. Journal of Health Economics 1996;15:715-734.

36. Marshall D, Hailey D, Hirsch N, Clark E, Menon D. The introduction of laparoscopic cholecystectomy in Canada and Australia. Ontario: Australian Institute of Health & Welfare and Canadian Coordinating Office for Health Technology Assessment, 1994.

37. Adamsen, S. Kikkertkirurgi ved galdestensoperationer. I: DSI-Institut for Sundhedsvæsen og Statens Sundhedsvidenskabelige Forskningsråd. Kikkertkirurgi i bughulen. Rapport fra en konsensus-konference København 3.-5. Marts 1997. Copenhagen: DSI, 1997:57-60.

38. Gelijns AC, Fendrick AM. The dynamics of innovations in Minimally Invasive Therapy. Health Policy 1993;23:153-166.

39. Battista R, Banta HD, Jonsson E, Hodge M, Gelband H. Lessons from the eight countries. In: US Congress, Office of Technology Assessment, Health care technology and its assessment in eight countries, OTA-BP-H-140, Washington, DC: U.S. Government Printing Office, February 1995, p. 335-354.

40. Greer AL. Adoption of Medical Technology. The Hospital's Three Decision Systems. International Journal of Technology Assessment in Health Care 1985;1:669-679.

41. Poulsen PB, Hørder M, Jørgensen T. Fremtidens medicinske metoder - tidlig varsling i international og dansk perspektiv. København: Sundhedsstyrelsen, 1996.

42. The Danish National Board of Health, the Health Technology Assessment Committee. National Strategy for Health Technology Assessment. Copenhagen, 1996.

43. Personal Communication with Assistant Professor Jørgen Clausen, Ph.D., Centre for Health and Social Policy (today: Institute of Public Health), Odense University, Denmark, 1997.

APPENDIX 5.1 : Factor analysis (elaborates section 3.6)

A factor analysis is a multivariate method intended to explain relationships among several correlated variables in terms of a few conceptually meaningful, relatively independent factors. In order to explain as much of the total variation in the data as possible with as few factors as possible the *principal-components analysis* was chosen as the model. Due to the exploratory aim no limitations were made with respect to the total number of factors. By rotation (orthogonal[157]) the initial factors found in the principal-component analysis were rotated to get a simple and interpretable structure of the factors. The factor analysis, presented in section 3.6, resulted in a total the six factors that described 67 per cent of the variation in the original model. The result of the factor analysis and full rotation component matrix are shown in Table A1 and A2.

Table A1 : Results of factor analysis - orthogonal rotation

New factors	1. Communication	2. Technology	3. Economy	4. Environment	5. Planning	6. Investment
	Opinion-leaders (0.631)	Nature of the technology (0.535)	Budget for operation (0.828)	Traditions & cultulture (0.653)	Planning & logistics (0.848)	Budget for investment (0.756)
	Conferences & rel.activity (0.794)	Expected extra benefit (0.754)	Finanvial incentives (0.850)	Competition (0.658)		
	Role of the industry (0.788)	Scientific evidence (0.652)	Public regulation (0.619)	Patient demand (0.768)		
	Attention from media (0.606)	Organizing studies (0.639)				
		Training (0.734)				
	\multicolumn{6}{c}{Rotation sums of squared loadings}					
Total (eigenvalue)	2.424	2.356	2.195	1.685	1.446	1.443
%of variance	14.259	13.861	12.913	9.913	8.506	8.486
Cumulative %	14.259	28.128	41.032	50.945	59.451	67.937

---

[157] Extraction method: Principal component analysis. Orthogonal rotation method: Varimax with Kaiser Normalization (7 iterations). Other orthogonal methods and the oblique rotation method resulted in the same factors.

Table A2 : Full Rotation Component Matrix

Components → / Original variables	1. Communication	2. Technology	3. Economy	4. Environment	5. Planning	6. Investment
Budget for investment	-0.047	0.094	0.12	-0.17	0.18	**0.756***
Budget for operation	0.103	0.049	**0.828***	0.004	0.161	0.196
Financial incentives	-0.156	0.061	**0.850***	-0.065	-0.063	-0.11
Nature of technology	-0.266	**0.535***	-0.275	0.168	-0.223	0.474
Planning and logistics	0.0562	0.167	0.153	0.072	**0.848***	0.084
Expected extra benefit	-0.035	**0.754***	0.101	0.108	0.181	-0.053
Scientific evidence	0.23	**0.652***	0.152	0.018	0.119	0.178
Organizing studies	-0.041	**0.639***	-0.212	-0.116	0.085	-0.5
Training	0.31	**0.734***	0.029	0.074	-0.079	0.066
Traditions and culture	-0.106	0.14	0.108	**0.653***	0.337	-0.307
Opinion leaders	**0.631***	0.191	0.079	0.12	0.056	-0.26
Competition	0.279	0.052	-0.047	**0.658***	-0.362	-0.285
Conferences and related activities	**0.794***	0.161	0.07	0.139	-0.024	0.116
Role of the industry	**0.788***	-0.003	-0.035	-0.029	-0.031	-0.029
Attention from media	**0.606***	-0.007	-0.38	0.301	0.315	0.043
Patient demand	0.216	0.047	-0.2	**0.768***	0.038	0.176
Public regulation	0.095	0.005	**0.619***	-0.117	0.452	0.105

* Highest factor loading between an original variable and a factor component.
Extraction method: *Principal Component Analysis*.
Rotation method: Varimax with Kaiser Normalization. Rotation converged in 7 iterations.

Chapter 6

Timing of Adoption of Laparoscopic Cholecystectomy in Denmark and in the Netherlands

A comparative study[158]

Peter Bo Poulsen[1], Hindrik Vondeling[2], Carmen D. Dirksen[3], Sven Adamsen[4], Peter M.N.Y.H. Go[5] & André J.H. Ament[6]

---

[1] Institute of Public Health, University of Southern Denmark, Odense University, Odense, Denmark.
[2] Department of Epidemiology and Biostatistics, Vrije Universiteit Amsterdam, Amsterdam, the Netherlands.
[3] Research Unit Patient Care, University Hospital Maastricht, Maastricht, the Netherlands.
[4] Department of Gastrointestinal Surgery K, Bispebjerg Hospital, University Hospital Copenhagen, Copenhagen, Denmark, and The Danish National Registry for Laparoscopic Cholecystectomy, Laparoscopic Surgery Committee, Danish Surgical Society, Denmark.
[5] Department of Surgery, St.Antonius Hospital, Nieuwegein, the Netherlands.
[6] Department of Health Organisation, Policy and Economics, Maastricht University, Maastricht, the Netherlands.

---

[158] The results of the study were presented at *the 14th Annual Meeting in The International Society of Technology Assessment in Health Care*, Ottawa, Canada, June 9, 1998

Table of contents

Abstract 167

1.0 Introduction 168

2.0 Methods 169
    2.1 Definition 169
    2.2 Data Sources 169
    2.3 Statistical Analysis 170

3.0 Results 170
    3.1 Adoption of laparoscopic cholecystectomy 170
    3.2 Hospital characteristics 172
    3.3 Proportional hazard regression 173

4.0 Conclusions 177

References 179

Abstract

Background: Laparoscopic cholecystectomy was introduced in the Netherlands in February 1990 and in Denmark in January 1991. Today laparoscopic cholecystectomy is used routinely in both countries.

Objectives: To describe the diffusion of laparoscopic cholecystectomy in Denmark and in the Netherlands, and to analyse the influence of three factors; size, teaching status and location of the hospital on the timing of adoption.

Data and design: As for Denmark, data about the time of adoption in 59 hospitals were extracted from a database, whereas for the Netherlands data of 109 hospitals were obtained from questionnaires and data on hospital characteristics were obtained from various official statistics. To analyse the data, bivariate and multivariate methods (proportional hazard regression) were used.

Results: All Dutch hospitals adopted laparoscopic cholecystectomy compared with 98 per cent of the Danish hospitals. The sigmoidal patterns of diffusion were similar in both countries. Using the proportional hazard regression method, increased hospital size was associated with an earlier adoption in Denmark, whereas size did not influence the timing of adoption in the Netherlands. Teaching status and location of the hospital were no determinants for the timing of adoption in any of the two countries.

Conclusion: Proportional hazard regression is helpful in elucidating differences between countries of the impact of hospital characteristics on the adoption of medium-ticket technologies. Only in Denmark, hospital size explained an earlier adoption. In a similar study in the United States, residency training facility was associated with earlier adoption.

1.0 Introduction

The first laparoscopic cholecystectomy reported in the literature was carried out in France in 1987 by a general surgeon with a gynecological background [1]. However, later evidence suggests that the first laparoscopic cholecystectomy was performed in 1986 by a practitioner in Böblingen in Germany [2]. Since then laparoscopic cholecystectomy has diffused quickly and widely in most industrialized countries. Laparoscopic cholecystectomy was for example introduced in the United States in 1989 [3]. The method was introduced in the Netherlands in February 1990, and adopted by the first Danish hospitals in January 1991 [4-6]. The conventional open surgical procedure has been almost fully replaced by the laparoscopic technology, which is preferred in around 80 per cent of the surgical treatments of symptomatic cholelithiasis in countries like the United States, the Netherlands and Denmark [7-9]. Replacement of conventional open cholecystectomy by laparoscopic cholecystectomy was based upon expectations of effectiveness and cost-effectiveness of laparoscopic cholecystectomy due to advantages such as small scars, short hospital stay and quick recovery [10]. Today, laparoscopic cholecystectomy is considered routine.

Diffusion of health technology is complex and not well understood. Both factors within and outside the health care system have been identified to determine the process. Restricted to the health care sector the impact on adoption of new technology can be distinguished in three levels. The *macro* level focuses on factors related to the organisation and financing of the sector, the *meso* level considers hospital characteristics, whereas the *micro* level focuses on characteristics of the surgeons and factors such as patient demand. A number of descriptive and analytical studies of diffusion have been carried out in the United States, Canada, Australia, the Netherlands and Denmark to describe and explain the diffusion of laparoscopic cholecystectomy [3,8,9,11-13]. The descriptive findings in all studies were a rapid diffusion of laparoscopic cholecystectomy. However, at the explanatory level many issues are still unaddressed, fragmented or only addressed at the level of one country. In fact, only one study compared diffusion in more than one country [13]. In addition, the data analysis in many of the studies did not take the interaction between characteristics of the process of diffusion into account by undertaking multivariate analyses. However, using a multivariate method to analyse factors at the meso level Fendrick et al. (1994) demonstrated that hospital status as a residency training facility was associated with earlier adoption of laparoscopic cholecystectomy in the United States [3]. A Canadian study investigated the meso level as well (size and teaching status), although without undertaking multivariate analysis [12]. Based on bivariate analyses, two studies in Denmark and in the Netherlands found factors of diffusion mostly related to the micro level, e.g. *nature of the technology, opinion leaders, extra benefit, conferences, patient demand* and *media attention*, although hospital characteristics, e.g. *teaching status*, at the meso level were identified as well [8,9].

Considering the fragmented knowledge of the role of hospital characteristics in the diffusion of medium-ticket technology in general and for laparoscopic cholecystectomy in Denmark and in the Netherlands in particular, as well as the lack of studies on a comparative level, the objectives of this study were threefold. Firstly, to describe the diffusion of laparoscopic cholecystectomy among surgical departments in hospitals in both countries. Secondly, to analyse and compare three hospital characteristics with respect to their influence upon the timing of adoption of laparoscopic cholecystectomy: size, teaching status and location of the hospitals, using multivariate methods. Thirdly, to analyse differences in the relative role of these factors between the two countries. As a spin off, the results of this study could guide policy-making regarding the adoption and evaluation of medium-ticket technologies in the future.

The two countries, Denmark and the Netherlands, were selected for this European comparative study for several reasons. The countries are fairly homogeneous at the macro level, due to a lack of regulation and control upon the introduction of medium-ticket technologies, besides the gradual implementation of European Commission Directives focussing upon safety of devices [14-16]. As a result, decisions whether or not to introduce medium-ticket surgical technologies in the health care sector are primarily made by surgeons and hospital boards at the department and hospital levels. Furthermore, previous studies, which were updated recently, have documented the role of the individual surgeon (*the micro level*) in both countries, to which the present study is complementary [8,9,15,17].

2.0 Methods

2.1 Definition

Diffusion was defined as the decision made within each surgical department in the two countries to adopt the laparoscopic technology for cholecystectomy.

2.2 Data Sources

In Denmark, including the Faroe Islands and Greenland, 59 surgical departments were identified as performing cholecystectomy [9]. Data about the time of adoption by the surgical departments of the laparoscopic technology in cholecystectomy was found in the Danish National Register for Laparoscopic Cholecystectomy administered by the Laparoscopic Committee of the Danish Surgical Society [6,18]. In the Netherlands, 135 surgical departments perform cholecystectomy [4,8]. The adoption of laparoscopic cholecystectomy has been identified by questionnaires in two Dutch studies [4,8]. The data on adoption used in the present study originates from the study by Dirksen et al. (1996) [8].

The *size of the hospital* was measured in number of somatic beds and categorized in three independent groups (< 250, 250-500, > 500). Information was obtained from the Danish National Board of Health and from the Dutch Ministry of Health [19,20]. *Teaching status* describes whether hospitals provided teaching in the laparoscopic procedure as a facility. Information came from the Danish National Board of Health and Dirksen et al. (1996), respectively [8,21]. Finally, the variable *location* was divided into hospitals located in *areas with more than 100,000 inhabitants* and hospitals located in *areas with less than 100,000 inhabitants.* This is consistent with grouping made by the national statistic bureaus in the two countries. In Denmark, the Copenhagen metropolitan area and three cities fulfilled this criterion, compared with 21 cities in the Netherlands [22,23].

The relevant year chosen for these data corresponded with the first adoption in each country, which for the Netherlands was in 1990 and for Denmark in 1991.

2.3 Statistical Analysis

Shapiro-Wilk W tests and plots revealed that none of the hospital characteristics were normally distributed [24]. Non-parametric tests (Mann-Whitney U and Kruskal Wallis tests) were therefore used to elucidate possible differences between the two countries, as well as to test for associations between time of adoption and hospital characteristics for both countries. As a multivariate method, proportional hazard regressions were carried out to give information on the timing of adoption of laparoscopic cholecystectomy and the association with hospital characteristics in the two countries. Proportional hazard regression was chosen due to censored data and a left-skewed distribution of adoption data. The method is a semi-parametric procedure (non-parametric in time and parametric between groups) which provides simultaneous estimates of hazard ratios in the presence of multiple explanatory variables [25]. It uses the hazard function to estimate the relative risk of failure, and is based upon a sequence of conditional probabilities - adoption at date t given non-adoption at previous dates [26]. A higher hazard implies then earlier arrival of adoption. In this study, censoring was made at the end of data collection - June 1994 in the Netherlands and August 1997 in Denmark [8,9]. The level of significance chosen was 5 per cent.

3.0 Results

3.1 Adoption of laparoscopic cholecystectomy

Among the 59 surgical departments at Danish hospitals performing cholecystectomy, 58 hospitals (98 per cent), except for Greenland, had adopted the laparoscopic technology between January 1991 and August 1995. A hundred and nine of the 135 surgical departments in the Netherlands responded to the questionnaire in the study made by Dirksen et al. (1996) [8]. However, hospital characteristics were not significantly different between respondents and non-respondents in the Netherlands. The 109 surgical departments had adopted laparoscopic cholecystectomy between February 1990 and December 1993. Times of adoption are summarized in Table 6.1.

Table 6.1: Adoption of laparoscopic cholecystectomy in Denmark and the Netherlands

	Total adoption (in per cent of hospitals)	First adoption	Median time of adoption	Mean time of adoption
Denmark	58 (98 %)	January 1991	14 months	17 months
The Netherlands	109 (100 %)	February 1990[a]	16 months	17 months

[a] Based on 98 responses concerning *time of adoption* in Dirksen et al. (1996), and University Hospital Maastricht.

The median time of adoption was 14 months for Denmark and 16 months for the Netherlands. The mean time of adoption was, however, equal. The distribution of the time of adoption was not significantly different between the two countries. Figure 6.1 shows the aggregated pattern of diffusion of laparoscopic cholecystectomy in the two countries.

Figure 6.1 : Aggregate Diffusion of Laparoscopic Cholecystectomy in Denmark and in the Netherlands

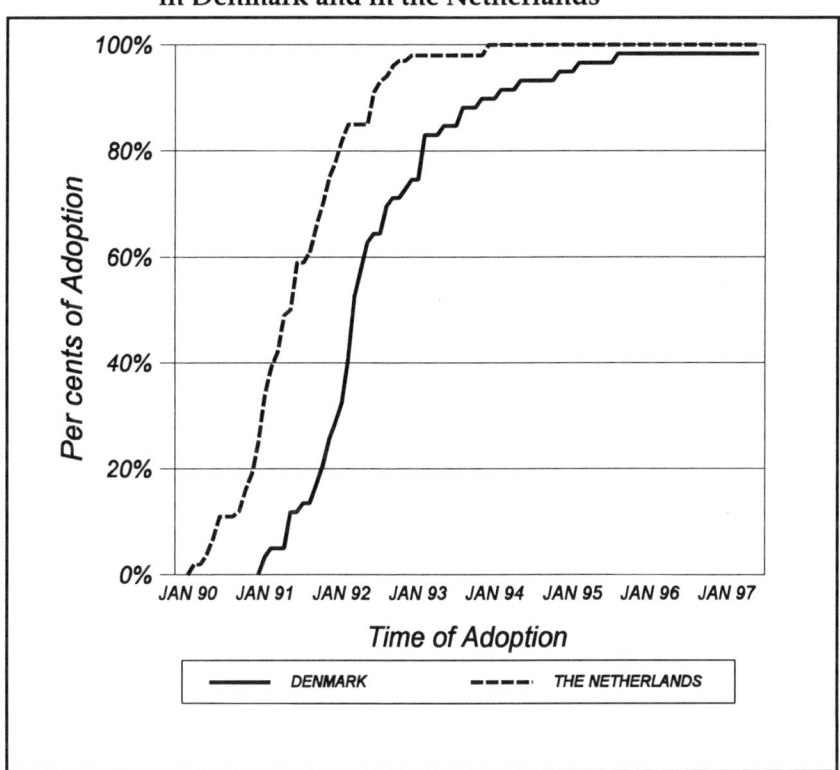

The Dutch diffusion curve is a bit steeper than the Danish curve and is characterised by a higher overall growth rate. The explanation for this is that it took around 3 years to obtain a complete diffusion of laparoscopic cholecystectomy in the Netherlands compared with 4½ years in Denmark.

3.2 Hospital characteristics

To investigate initially for differences in hospital characteristics between Denmark and the Netherlands, country-specific data about the size, teaching status, and location of the hospitals are summarized in Table 6.2.

Table 6.2 : Hospital Characteristics for Denmark and the Netherlands

	Denmark		The Netherlands		Significance
	No.	%	No.	%	P-value
Hospitals with surgical departments	59	100	135	100	N.A.
Size :					
≥ 500 beds	12	20 %	40	30 %	
250-500 beds	17	29 %	56	41 %	
< 250 beds	30	51 %	39	29 %	0.009**
Teaching status :					
Teaching hospital	9	15 %	39	29 %	
Non-teaching hospital	50	85 %	96	71 %	0.043*
Location of hospitals:					
Areas with more than 100,000 inhabitants	13	22 %	68	50 %	
Areas with less than 100,000 inhabitants	46	78 %	67	50 %	0.0002*

* Mann-Whithey U Test ** Kruskall Wallis Test

Hospitals with surgical departments in the two countries were not similar with respect to any of the three hospital characteristics studied. Compared with Danish hospitals, Dutch hospitals are larger, more frequently located in areas with more than 100,000 inhabitants and are more likely to have a status as teaching hospitals (Mann-Whitney U test and Kruskall Wallis test, P<0.05). The consequence is then that comparability between the two countries will be restricted in some way.

Table 6.3 presents the bivariate associations of the time of adoption and the hospital characteristics.

Table 6.3 : Adoption of laparoscopic cholecystectomy and hospitals characteristics

	Denmark N=59		The Netherlands N=99°	
	Median time of adoption	P-value*	Median time of adoption	P-value*
Size:				
≥ 500 beds	9 months		12 months	
250 - 500 beds	14 months		14 months	
< 250 beds	19 months	0.005**	18 months	0.11**
Teaching status:				
Teaching hospital	9 months		11 months	
Non-teaching hospital	15 months	0.017*	16 months	0.009*
Location of hospitals:				
Areas with more than 100,000 inhabitants	14 months		14 months	
Areas with less than 100,000 inhabitants	14 months	0.275*	16 months	0.10*

*Mann Whitney U test **Kruskall Wallis test
° Based on 98 responses concerning *time of adoption* in Dirksen et al. (1996), and University Hospital Maastricht

The bivariate analyses show quite similar patterns of time of adoption and hospital characteristics in the two countries. In Denmark, earlier adoption of laparoscopic cholecystectomy was significantly associated with increasing size of the hospitals, as large hospitals (>500 beds) adopted the procedure ten months earlier than small hospitals (< 250 beds) (Kruskall Wallis test, P<0.005). Adoption was significantly earlier in Danish hospitals with teaching status. However, the location of the hospital was not associated with the time of adoption in Denmark. As for the Netherlands, only teaching status was significantly associated with a five-month earlier adoption of laparoscopic cholecystectomy (Mann Whitney U test, P<0.01). Size and location were not related to the time of adoption in the Netherlands.

3.3 Proportional hazard regression

In the multivariate analysis, two country-specific models (a model including the Danish sample and a model including the Dutch sample) and a pooled model including data from both countries were put forward. In the country-specific models the influence of three covariates - *size*, *teaching status* and *location* - on the timing of adoption was analysed. Size was treated as a continuous variable (in beds per 100), whereas the two other variables were dichotomous (yes or no). The Danish model included 59 cases, with one case censored due to non-adoption (2 per cent). The Dutch model included 109 cases, with 10 surgical departments censored (9 per cent) due to incomplete or missing information about time of adoption.

The pooled model included 168 surgical departments in Denmark and in the Netherlands, with a total of 11 cases censored (7 per cent). A fourth covariate, *country*, and three interaction effects, *country by size, country by training* and *country by location*, were entered in the pooled model. The aim of determining the interaction effects was to describe how each of the hospital characteristics interacts with the covariate *country* to affect the dependent variable, *timing of adoption*. The coefficients of the interaction effects measure the differences in hospital characteristics between Denmark and the Netherlands.

Checking for the existence of proportional hazards of the covariates, independent plots of baseline hazard functions and log minus log plots were produced. These plots showed that the levels of each of the covariates remained fairly proportional over time, which supports the assumption of proportional hazards in the empirical models. Location could be one exception. Therefore proportional hazard regressions were both carried out with and without the inclusion of location.

To reveal an added value of the inclusion of covariates, tests of the overall models with covariates compared with the baseline models without covariates were carried out. The Danish model and the pooled model were both significant on a 1 per cent level, showing a clear added value of the inclusion of covariates. The Dutch model was, however, not significant on a 5 per cent level. The results of the proportional hazard regression models are shown in Table 6.4.

Table 6.4 : Proportional hazard regression models of the timing of adoption - two country-specific and a pooled model

Dependent variable: *Timing of adoption*

Covariates	Denmark* (Events = 58; Censored = 1)			The Netherlands** (Events = 99; Censored = 10)			Pooled Model* Difference NHL & DK; [β_{NHL} - β_{DK}] (Events = 157; Censored =11)		
	$\hat{\beta}_{DK}$	Hazard ratio $e^{\hat{\beta}_{DK}}$	CI$_{95\%}$	$\hat{\beta}_{NHL}$	Hazard ratio $e^{\hat{\beta}_{NHL}}$	CI$_{95\%}$	$\hat{\beta}_{Pooled}$	Hazard ratio $e^{\hat{\beta}_{POOLED}}$	CI$_{95\%}$
Country [a]	-	-	-	-	-	-	0.382	1.465	0.75 - 2.86
Size (in beds per 100)	0.299	1.348+	1.12 - 1.63	-0.0096	0.991	0.88 - 1.12	0.272	1.312+	1.10 - 1.57
CountryBYsize [d] (IE)	-	-	-	-	-	-	-0.282[d]	0.755+	0.61 - 0.94
Teaching hospital [b]	-0.652	0.521	0.09 - 3.14	0.395	1.485	0.80 - 2.75	-0.54	0.583	0.10 - 3.38
CountryBYteaching [e] (IE)	-	-	-	-	-	-	0.943	2.568	0.40 - 16.5
Urban location [c]	-0.514	0.598	0.21 - 1.72	0.139	1.15	0.74 - 1.79	-0.471	0.624	0.22 - 1.78
CountryBYlocation [f] (IE)	-	-	-	-	-	-	0.612[f]	1.845	0.59 - 5.75

1) A hazard ratio higher than 1.0 signifies that the hospital characteristic is associated with an earlier adoption of laparoscopic cholecystectomy.
+ P<0.05

* Model significant
** Model not significant

Reference groups:
a) Denmark
b) Non-teaching hospitals
c) Areas with less than 100,000 inhabitants

Interaction Effects (IE):
d) Difference w.r.t. size of hospitals between Denmark and the Netherlands; δ_{size}=[β_{NHL} - β_{DK}]
e) Difference w.r.t. teaching hospitals between Denmark and the Netherlands; $\delta_{teaching}$=[β_{NHL} - β_{DK}]
f) Difference w.r.t. location of the hospitals between Denmark and the Netherlands; $\delta_{location}$=[β_{NHL} - β_{DK}]

Table 6.4 shows that increased size of the Danish hospitals, as the only significant covariate, was associated with earlier adoption of laparoscopic cholecystectomy. The relative probability of adoption was significantly increased by 35 per cent when size was increased by 100 beds ($e^{\hat{\beta}_{DK}}=1.348$; $P<0.05$). In the Dutch model, hospital size was not significant, and did not influence the timing of adoption.

The coefficients of the interaction effects δ in the pooled model explain the difference in slope of a covariate between Denmark and the Netherlands ($\delta = \beta_{NHL} - \beta_{DK}$). Controlling for interaction, the three original covariates - size, teaching status and location - are now in the pooled model interpreted as the covariates' effect upon the timing of adoption in Denmark β_{DK}. Knowing δ and β_{DK} from Table 6.4, hazard ratios for the Netherlands ($e^{\hat{\beta}_{NHL}}$) can be calculated for the three hospital characteristics (Equation 6.1).

$$e^{\beta_{NHL}} = e^{(\beta_{DK} + \delta)} \qquad (6.1)$$

The pooled model still shows that the probability of adoption increases significantly (31 per cent), when hospital size in Denmark was increased by 100 beds ($e^{\hat{\beta}_{Pooled}} = 1.312$; $P<0.01$). Opposed to this, hospital size did not have any effect upon the timing of adoption in the Netherlands with a hazard ratio around one ($e^{(\hat{\beta}_{DK} + \hat{\delta})} = e^{(0.272 + (-0.282))} = 0.990$). This difference between the two countries with respect to the importance of hospital size in explaining the timing of adoption was significant (countryBYsize - see Table 6.4).

With a negative coefficient and a hazard ratio lower than one, teaching status of Danish hospitals was shown, although insignificant, to decrease the relative probability of adoption ($e^{\hat{\beta}_{Pooled}} = 0.583$; NS). In the Netherlands, a reverse effect was found, as the relative probability of adoption increased by a factor 1½, when hospitals had teaching status ($e^{(\hat{\beta}_{DK} + \hat{\delta})} = 1.496$). The same pattern appeared for location of the hospitals. In Denmark, the probability of adoption decreased, insignificantly, for hospitals located in areas with more than 100,000 inhabitants, whereas a sligthly reverse effect appeared for the Netherlands ($e^{(\hat{\beta}_{DK} + \hat{\delta})} = 1.151$). Difference in number of iterations in the proportional hazard regressions performed might explain the small variations in estimates obtained by country-specific and pooled models, respectively.

In general, hospitals in areas with less than 100,000 inhabitants will be smaller than hospitals in areas with more than 100,000 inhabitants. Therefore, due to suspicion of collinearity with size in the regression, location of the hospital was omitted in the regression models. However, omitting this covariate did not change the results presented in Table 6.4.

4.0 Conclusions

As in countries like the United States, Canada and Australia laparoscopic cholecystectomy has diffused rapidly in both Denmark and the Netherlands [3,11-13]. The patterns of diffusion are remarkably similar in both countries showing a steep sigmoidal shape, following the theories of diffusion, although the process of adoption in Denmark occurred with a time lag of 11 months relative to the Netherlands [27-29]. Opinion leaders and their activities may explain the time lag of the introduction of laparoscopic cholecystectomy in the two countries, since two Dutch innovators introduced laparoscopic cholecystectomy to most of their colleagues throughout the country in a short period by providing training courses. In addition, as patient demand and competition both have shown to be important for the diffusion in Denmark and in the Netherlands [8,9], there may have been a strong pressure on all hospitals, irrespective of other factors, to adopt the laparoscopic technology in cholecystectomy.

The multivariate analyses showed that the *size of the hospitals* had a positive influence upon the timing of adoption of laparoscopic cholecystectomy in Denmark. Increasing hospital size resulted in an earlier adoption. In the Netherlands, this characteristic did not influence the timing of adoption. Different organisation and financing of health care in the two countries may be reasons for this difference.

Location of the hospitals did not influence the timing of adoption of laparoscopic cholecystectomy in Denmark and in the Netherlands. A reason could be that both countries are small and have a reasonably high number of hospitals with surgical departments.

The multivariate analyses did not confirm *teaching status* to be a significant determinant for the timing of adoption. Teaching hospitals might have been expected to be more innovative, as found in bivariate analyses, with a higher hazard of adoption. However, the results were not significant and are in opposite directions for the two countries. The decreasing, although insignificant, hazard in Denmark may be explained by the fact that some of the earliest adopters were not teaching hospitals at that time.

The data representing the two countries in the models came from different sources. As for Denmark, data of the time of adoption were from a database covering all adopters, while the Dutch data came from questionnaires. Although the response rate was fairly high in the Dutch sample, questionnaires always include a risk of selection bias with missing answers from the least innovative adopters. However, investigating for differences in hospital characteristics of responding and non-responding hospitals did not confirm any selection bias in the Dutch sample.

In the United States, Fendrick et al. (1994), using the same multivariate method, demonstrated that hospital status as a residency training facility was associated with an earlier adoption of laparoscopic cholecystectomy [3]. In addition, this study found neither location (divided in urban and rural areas) nor size to predict the timing of adoption of this procedure [3].

Comparing the results of these studies shows that different characteristics of the hospitals seem to explain the diffusion of laparoscopic cholecystectomy in the United States, Denmark and in the Netherlands, due to the fact that no common characteristics were found for any of the countries. In drawing this conclusion one has, nevertheless, to be aware of the limitations of the multivariate models presented in the present study and the study made by Fendrick et al. (1994) [3]. Both these studies were based on models that exclusively used hospital characteristics, which are available in the public domain. However, literature suggests that for a more comprehensive and predictive model of the diffusion of medium-ticket technologies, data of the hospitals (*the meso level*) need to be complemented with data about the health care system (*the macro level*), and data on the level of the individual adopter (*the micro level*). Researchers of both studies of one country and multinational studies could try to conduct more comprehensive and multivariate analyses, considering factors at all three levels.

Proportional hazard regression seems to be helpful in elucidating differences between countries of the impact of hospital characteristics on the adoption of medium-ticket technologies. However, so far only few examples exist in the literature of the use of hazard models in diffusion research of health technology. Hazard models have been used to explain hospitals' or surgeons' adoption of laparoscopic cholecystectomy [3,10,30] and physicians' adoption of antibiotic therapy to eradicate Helicobacter Pylori infection [31]. Hazard models are relevant, when duration data are considered. Proportional hazard regressions are especially relevant, when the variables entered are proportional, the distribution is skewed and censoring appears (e.g. non-adoption). The application of hazard models in diffusion research needs to be further tested.

In conclusion, this study shows that in Denmark, in the absence of regulation, increased hospital size is associated with earlier adoption of laparoscopic cholecystectomy. The policy implications of this finding are that the national government and the counties responsible for the provision of the hospital services [15] in cooperation with the Danish Surgical Society [32] could stimulate in particularly larger hospitals to develop protocols for the evaluation of new technologies during adoption. In the case of the Netherlands, in the absence of a clear pattern of diffusion, no specific policy measures can be formulated based on this study. In general, coordinated introduction and concurrent evaluation, stimulated by the government, and organized and supported by the Society of Surgeons, may be a way to avoid haphazard uncontrolled diffusion of new surgical procedures.

References

1. Weill C. Minimally Invasive Therapy: The French case study. Health Policy 1993;23:31-47.

2. Kirchberger S. Health care technology in the Federal Republic of Germany. Health Policy 1994;30:163-205.

3. Fendrick M, Escarce JJ, McLane C, Shea JA, Schwartz JS. Hospital Adoption of Laparoscopic Cholecystectomy. Medical Care 1994;32:1058-1063.

4. Go PMNYH, Schol F, Gouma DJ. Laparoscopic cholecystectomy in the Netherlands. British Journal of Surgery 1993;80:1180-1183.

5. Go PMNYH, Dirksen CD. Five years of Laparoscopic Cholecystectomy in The Netherlands. International Journal of Surgery 1995;80:304-306.

6. Adamsen S, Hansen OH, Jensen PMF, Schulze S, Stage JG, Wara P, Jensen LP. Laparoskopisk kolecystektomi i Danmark. En prospektiv registrering. Ugeskrift for Læger 1995;157:4449-4454. [Laparoscopic cholecystectomy in Denmark. A nationwide prospective case registration (English abstract and legends)].

7. NIH Consensus Development Panel on Gallstones and Laparoscopic cholecystectomy. Journal of American Medical Association 1993;269:1018.

8. Dirksen CD, Ament AJH, Go PMN. Diffusion of six surgical endoscopic procedures in the Netherlands. Stimulating and restraining factors. Health Policy 1996;37:91-104.

9. Poulsen PB, Adamsen S, Vondeling H, Jørgensen T. Diffusion of laparoscopic technologies in Denmark. Health Policy 1998;45(2):149-167.

10. Banta HD, Scherstén T, Jonsson E. Implications of minimally invasive therapy. Health Policy 1993;23:167-178.

11. Escarce JJ, Bloom BS, Hillman AL, Shea JA, Schwartz JS. Diffusion of Laparoscopic Cholecystectomy Among General Surgeons in the United States. Medical Care 1995;33:256-271.

12. Menon D, Marshall D. Diffusion of Laparoscopic Cholecystectomy in Canada. International Journal of Technology Assessment in Health Care 1994;10:287-292.

13. Marshall D, Hailey D, Hirsch N, Clark E, Menon D. The introduction of laparoscopic cholecystectomy in Canada and Australia. Australian Institute of Health & Welfare (AIHW) and Canadian Coordinating Office for Health Technology Assessment (CCOHTA); May 1994.

14. European Council Directive. 93/42/EEC, of 14 June 1993. Medical Devices.

15. Vondeling H, Haerkens E, de Wit A, Bos M, Banta D. Diffusion of Minimally Invasive Therapy in the Netherlands. Health Policy 1993;23:67-81.

16. Christiansen T, Enemark U, Clausen J, Poulsen PB. Cost Containment in Denmark. Chapter 5 in Le Grand, J. & Mossialos, E. (eds). Health expenditure in the European Union - Cost and control. Ashgate: Aldershot, 1999.

17. Schou I. Minimally Invasive Therapy in Denmark. Health Policy 1993;23:17-30.

18. Adamsen S, Hansen OH, Funch-Jensen P, Schulze S, Stage JG, Wara P. Bile duct injury during laparoscopic cholecystectomy: A prospective nationwide series. Journal of American College of Surgeons 1997;184:571-578.

19. The Danish National Board of Health. Hospital activities 1991. Statistics on Hospitals II:56:1993. The Danish National Board of Health. Copenhagen; 1993.

20. Ministry of Health. Financial Oversight on Care 1992. Dutch Parliament, Second Chamber, Meeting Year 1991-1992, 22 311 nrs. 1-2. Sdu Publishers, the Hague, 1992, p. 211-213.

21. The Danish National Board of Health. Classification of doctors positions at hospitals per January 1st 1995. The Danish National Board of Health. Copenhagen; 1994.

22. Statistics Denmark. Statistical Yearbook 1993. Statistics Denmark. Copenhagen; 1994.

23. Central Statistics Agency (CBS). Statistical Year Book 1991. Sdu Publishers, the Hague, 1991.

24. Altman DG. Practical Statistics for Medical Research. 1th ed. London: Chapman & Hall; 1991.

25. Bull K, Spiegelhalter D. Tutorial in biostatistics. Survival analysis in observational studies. Statistics in Medicine 1997;16:1041-1074.

26. Kiefer NM. Economic Duration Data and Hazard Functions. Journal of Economic Literature 1988;26:646-679.

27. Rogers EM. Diffusion of Innovations. 4th ed. New York: Free Press, 1995.

28. Warner KE. A "Desperation-Reaction" Model of Medical Diffusion. Health Services Research 1975;Winter:369-383.

29. Warner KE. The Need for Some Innovative Concepts of Innovation: An Examination of Research on the Diffusion of Innovation. Policy Sciences 1974;5:433-451.

30. Escarce JJ. Externalities in hospitals and physician adoption of a new surgical technology: An exploratory analysis. Journal of Health Economics 1996;15:715-734.

31. Hirth RA, Fendrick AM, Chernew ME. Specialist and generalist physicians' adoption of antibiotic therapy to eradicate Helicobacter pylori infection. Medical Care 1996;34:1199-1204.

32. Danneskiold-Samsøe B (ed). Abdominal Laparoscopic Surgery. Report from a medical consensus conference 3-5 March 1997. Copenhagen: Danish Medical Research Council and and Danish Institute for Health Services Research and Development. Consensus Report, 1997.

Chapter 7

Economic Evaluation and the Diffusion of Health Technology

- objectives of economic evaluation and methodological issues

Table of contents

Abstract 185

1.0 Introduction 186

2.0 Purpose 188

3.0 The Process of Diffusion 189

4.0 Phase I-II: Early Economic Evaluation 191
    4.1 Decisions about further R&D and HTA 191
    4.2 Decisions about early adoption 193
    4.3 Uncertainty in the early economic evaluation 195
        4.3.1 A decision analytic model 197
        4.3.2 A learning model 198

5.0 Phase III: Economic Evaluation and Randomised Controlled Trials 199
    5.1 Efficacy versus effectiveness 201
    5.2 Design Issues 202
        5.2.1 Which comparator? 202
        5.2.2 Location of the trial 203
        5.2.3 Sample size 203
    5.3 Resource use 204
        5.3.1 Collection of data on resource use 204
        5.3.2 Collection and estimation of unit costs 206
    5.4 Choice of outcome measures 207

6.0 Phase IV: Economic Evaluation of Routine Practice Settings 209

7.0 Discussion 211

References 215

Abstract

Among the types of health technologies the assessment of safety and efficacy prior to widespread diffusion is only required for pharmaceuticals. The conduct of economic evaluation is not required for any health technology, although the assessment of cost-effectiveness can provide important input to decision making during diffusion. This chapter describes and discusses the objectives of economic evaluation in the life cycle of health technology and methodological issues are highlighted. In this chapter an iterative and ongoing approach to economic evaluation during diffusion is advocated for. In the early stages in the life cycle an early economic evaluation has in general two objectives; to inform decision making about further R&D and technology assessment and to inform decision making about early adoption of health technology. Later economic evaluations prior to widespread diffusion, typically based upon randomized clinical trials (phase III) and informed by earlier assessments, can be used by the regulatory authorities with respect to decision making about reimbursement (of pharmaceuticals). Finally, an important objective of economic evaluation late in the life cycle, especially of interest for system and hospital managers, is the assessment of health technology in routine practice settings. However, conducted in an iterative approach the timing of assessment warrants special attention.

1.0 Introduction

The amount of resources available in every society is limited. This is true for the health care sector as well, making the need to prioritize alternative uses of resources evident. More so because an increasing number of health technologies[159] are developed and adopted in Denmark and internationally with important implications for the health care sector, as shown with laparoscopic cholecystectomy and Beta-interferon. New health technologies are generally more expensive, than the existing technologies which they replace. Finally, increasing awareness of topics like evidence-based medicine and health technology assessment have put a higher demand upon the need to document the effectiveness and cost-effectiveness of existing health technologies.

Especially, the group of medical devices seems to be put on the market early with the possibility of an uncontrolled and fast diffusion in the health care sector. In Denmark as in other European countries, the efficacy of medical devices, unlike pharmaceuticals[160], does not require documentation through the conduct of clinical trials prior to market introduction. The only requirement with respect to medical devices is the gradual implementation of European Commission Directives focusing upon safety of the product [1]. There is no demand for documentation about efficacy (and effectiveness) as in the FDA premarket approval or premarket notification system of devices in the United States [2]. With respect to existing health technologies already in use, there are no control and regulation, even though an existing technology finds a new application as happened with the laparoscopic technology, when it was transferred from the gynaecological field to the field of general surgery to be used in areas as appendectomy and cholecystectomy. Finally, there is no formal requirement in Denmark to document the efficiency and cost-effectiveness of the health technologies developed, adopted and used.

This shows the problem the decision-maker is facing today, confronted with prioritization, not knowing with certainty, whether the new health technologies introduced, as well as many existing health technologies, are effective, safe and cost-effective. According to Grimes (1993) some new technologies have clearly improved health and reduced costs, but others have not [3]. Using the terminology of Finkelstein et al. (1984), the decision-maker can due to uncertainty make two errors when deciding whether to advocate the adoption of a new technology or not [4]. A Type I decision error is to recommend an unfavourable technology, which corresponds to a situation in which actions taken to facilitate the rapid diffusion of a technology resulted in its (later) overuse. A Type II decision error is to reject a favourable technology, which corresponds to situations in which actions are taken to prevent or slow down the diffusion of a favourable technology, effectively deny access or inhibit the development of a potentially beneficial package. As both decision errors can have severe health and

---

[159] Understood as pharmaceuticals, medical devices and medical procedures.

[160] Obligatory FDA-like market approval (FDA - Food and Drug Administration).

economic consequences, a major objective for decision-makers should be to minimize them.

Focusing upon policy making the aim of health technology assessment[161] (HTA) and economic evaluation are to provide input to decision making and policy making about the adoption and use of new health technologies and to improve the evidence regarding existing technologies [5,6]. HTA and economic evaluation can be seen as corner stones in decision making to inform decision-makers about the evidence and consequences of the adoption of new technologies before a widespread diffusion occurs. Early assessments could be integrated into the activities of an early warning system for emerging health technologies [7]. Reassessment of existing technologies may also be necessary because of the availability of new data, innovation in the technology itself or changing epidemiology, leading to changes in patient management, resource consumption or treatment options [8]. The conduct of HTA and economic evaluation may then be a key tool to improve the management of scarce health care resources as well as scarce R&D[162] resources [5].

However, as technologies diffuse in the health care sector, the timing of HTA and economic evaluation becomes important. Ideally, HTA and economic evaluation should be done as continuous assessments in phase with the life cycle of a particular technology [5,8,9]. Sculpher et al. (1997) and Mowatt et al. (1998) both advocate for an iterative approach to economic evaluation incorporated into the process of clinical research and HTA [10,11]. The success of this approach rests of course upon whether the decisions made in the health care sector are reversible. Difficulties in convincing providers to discard an intervention once it has been adopted into clinical practice illustrate this dilemma [8]. Therefore, the earlier a technology is assessed, the more likely its diffusion is to be rationalized [12]. However, the problem at an early stage in the life cycle is information about the health technology and the uncertainty of this early information with the risk for decision-makers of making the decision errors as presented above. At later stages of diffusion the knowledge and learning with respect to the technology are expected to increase and the uncertainty decreases, although, e.g. changes in practice patterns in the real world clinical setting can result in decision errors post-adoption as well. The complexity of assessment reflects both the difficulties in selecting health care technologies for evaluation and increasing pressures to reduce the length of time it takes for evaluation, so the results can have value in decision making in which clinical practice and health policy are concerned [9]. Therefore when deciding upon a proper timing for assessment, a trade-off exists between decision-makers' wish for early assessments prior to widespread diffusion of health technologies and the problem of reliability and uncertainty of the information available early in the life cycle. This dilemma in decision making has been formulated by Martin Buxton (1997) as *Buxton's law* stating that "it's always too early to evaluate until, unfortunately, it's suddenly too late" [13].

---

[161] The reader is reffered to chapter 2 for a definition of health technology assessment.

[162] Research and development.

Since the early 1990s guidelines or recommendations to standardize the methodology and conduct of economic evaluation have been or will be presented in a number of countries, e.g. Australia, Canada, Denmark, the United Kingdom, Spain and Norway [14-18]. Furthermore, cooperation among experts both in Europe[163] and the United States[164] have resulted in the development of recommendations for the practice of economic evaluation. As a benefit, standardization of methodology may increase the comparability, transparency, replicability, credibility and usefulness of economic evaluation studies in policy making [17,19]. However, except for the Canadian *Guidelines for economic evaluation of pharmaceuticals* issued by CCOHTA[165] [15], none of these guidelines or recommendations deal with the timing of the economic evaluation during the life cycle of the health technology. Most of the guidelines focus on issues of methodology in the conduct and use of economic evaluation for reimbursement decisions in phase III prior to marketing of pharmaceuticals.

2.0 Purpose

The focus of the present chapter is on economic evaluation and not on HTA in general. The aim is first to describe and discuss the different objectives of economic evaluation during the process of diffusion of health technology. The focus of the use of economic evaluation is from the perspective of the society, i.e. decision making and policy making in the health care sector. The use of economic evaluation from the perspective of the producers of technology, such as the industry's strategic decision making in the R&D process or pricing and marketing considerations, will not be addressed. The need for assessment vary over time depending on the life cycle of the technology and the target group requesting information at different stages during diffusion. Secondly, the chapter discusses the form and the methodological issues relevant for the economic evaluation at different stages of diffusion.

In the chapter, section 4.0 considers the conduct of early economic evaluation in the early life cycle of the health technology. Section 5.0 describes the objective of economic evaluation and methodological issues related to its conduct in phase III of the life cycle, where information from randomized controlled clinical trials (RCT) are available. Section 6.0 deals with economic evaluation after a widespread diffusion of the health technology has taken place, also known as the stage of reassessment. Finally, the iterative use of economic evaluation during diffusion is discussed in section 7.0. However, before going into detail with the objective of economic evaluation during diffusion, it may be appropriate to describe this process of diffusion.

---

[163] HARMET - the European Project for Methodological Harmonization financed by the European Union [17].

[164] The US Panel on Cost-Effectiveness in Health and Medicine [20].

[165] The Canadian Coordinating Office for Health Technology Assessment.

3.0 The Process of Diffusion

The early stages of diffusion are defined, as the final stages of technological change [21]. Especially for pharmaceuticals due to legal requirements, the early diffusion process is formalized in a clinical development programme of testing efficacy and safety before widespread diffusion is allowed [22]. The clinical development programme is often classified in four main phases of experimentation [23]. These phases control the initial diffusion of pharmaceuticals in the health care sector. For the other types of health technologies this is, however, not so. A fast and widespread diffusion can occur prior to any attainment of documentation of the technology's effect, as had happened with *high-ticket technologies* such as CT-scanners [24], *medium-ticket technologies* such as laparoscopic cholecystectomy [25] and a large number of *low-ticket technologies* [26]. However, a description of the process of diffusion and the target groups for information during diffusion can be given within the stages in the clinical development programme. Figure 7.1 shows the logistic process of diffusion.

Figure 7.1 : The process of diffusion, clinical trials and economic evaluation

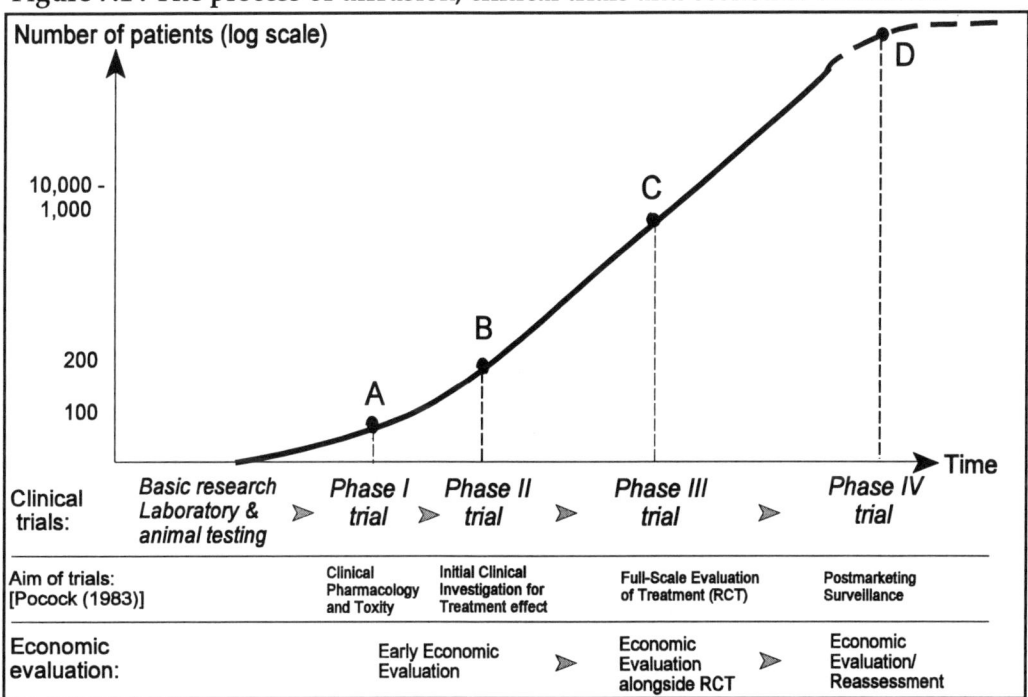

In *phase I*, which is early developmental, diffusion is limited as illustrated by *A* in Figure 7.1. The health technology will only be used by a small number of innovators in the country from which the technology originates [10]. The clinical trial conducted will be a small pilot or case study involving only around 20-80 patients [23]. The focus of a phase I clinical study is the safety of the health technology with the evaluation of the maximum tolerated dose and toxicity [27,28]. The target group for the early clinical information are foremost the developing firm and the clinicians, especially the innovators.

The next stage in a clinical development programme is to undertake *phase II* trials. Besides safety issues, the uncontrolled case series performed in phase II focuses upon investigations of the efficacy of the technology (pharmaceutical) and requires close monitoring of each patient [23,27]. This is an assessment of drug activity (efficacy), in addition to an assessment of toxicity [28]. The company's *go-or-no-go decision*, whether to continue development and testing of the pharmaceutical, is made in phase II. The trials are typically carried out at few key specialist centres selected as the opinion leaders to facilitate additional diffusion and include around 100-200 patients. The industry and clinicians are still target groups, although regulatory authorities are interested too in information about safety.

After showing some efficacy in phase II, it is essential to compare the efficacy of the new health technology (pharmaceutical) with the current standard treatment in *phase III* [23]. This comparison is for pharmaceuticals made in full-scaled RCTs including a large number of patients. To include as many patients as necessary, a multi-center or even multinational approach including the main clinical centres in one or more countries will often be used in the conduct of RCTs in phase III. The health technology will then be close to a more widespread diffusion as shown by C on the diffusion curve in Figure 7.1 [10]. For pharmaceuticals, phase III trials are considered as the pivotal trials for the generation of this information for registration, reimbursement and marketing [22]. This is the reason, why the regulatory authorities and the developing company, who wants to market their product, as well as the health care providers are the main target groups for the clinical information [8].

The last stage of experimentation is *phase IV* trials, which eventually will be undertaken after marketing approval has been obtained and most clinical centres have adopted the health technology in routine clinical practice, as illustrated by the dotted line in Figure 7.1. In phase IV, the technology is used under average conditions facilitating the (re-) assessment of the real world effectiveness. Monitoring of complications, adverse effects of the technology and additional large-scale, long-term studies of morbidity and mortality are furthermore in focus with regard to post marketing trials [23]. The types of decision-makers requesting effectiveness information in this late stage of the life cycle are system and hospital managers, rather than the regulatory authorities [8].

The four phases in the clinical development programme are used as the framework to describe and discuss the different purposes and types of economic evaluation during diffusion of health technology in general. As an iterative process in the life cycle, the stages of economic evaluation are *early economic evaluation* (phase I and II), *economic evaluation alongside RCT* (phase III) and *late economic evaluation of routine practice settings* (phase IV), as seen in Figure 7.1. The following sections will go through these three stages of economic evaluation.

4.0 Phase I-II: Early Economic Evaluation

The early life cycle of a health technology is considered as the earliest clinical trials conducted in phase I and II.[166] In these phases, as described above, diffusion of the new technology will approximately be limited to less than 200 patients at a few clinical centres. The clinical trials - pilot studies and uncontrolled case series - carried out provide some indications of the safety and efficacy of the new technology. The uncertainty inherent in the parameters of safety and efficacy is of course high, for which reason the results should only be considered as preliminary in a clinical development programme approach. However, in the literature it has been stated that the HTA process can be thought of in terms of the life cycle of a technology [9,29]. Ideally, HTA and economic evaluations should be done as continuous assessments following this life cycle [5]. Subsequent changes of diffusion over time and the expected clinical utilization and cost of the health technology can then be predicted [8]. The first stage in this continuous assessment process are to undertake an early economic evaluation of the emerging technology in phase I-II.

Early economic evaluations are basically carried out with the aim both to increase knowledge, and thereby reduce the uncertainty, and to produce timely information at an early phase in the life cycle of a technology. Due to limitations in the initial clinical trial setup and uncertainty of information in the early life cycle of a health technology, the results of an early economic evaluation will, however, be more indicative than definite. This is especially the case in phase I, where the small clinical studies primarily focus upon safety issues. In phase II, initial information about efficacy of the new health technology will be collected, although the early analyses based upon this information still are indicative. Conducted in the iterative approach suggested by Sculpher et al. (1997) each stage of early economic evaluation will then ideally update and inform later stages of analyses [10]. Langkilde (1997) presents two cases related to early economic evaluation and HTA, in which decisions are made sequentially and the decision-maker's knowledge increases between decisions (updating) [30]. The first case is the situation where *decisions on information acquisition* are integrated into the early economic evaluation, e.g. deciding to carry out additional clinical trials of a new health technology. The second case is the situation where early, preliminary assessments of new health technologies are performed solely with the aim of producing timely information for *decisions about early adoption* and diffusion of health technologies, e.g. as part of an early warning activity. These two cases of decision making are interdependent and both represent important objectives of early economic evaluation.

4.1 Decisions about further R&D and HTA

The acquisition of additional information about health innovations cannot be made without incurring costs. Furthermore, the resources available for the health services

---

[166] At least for pharmaceuticals.

produced and the resources available for research and HTA are scarce. Some kind of priority setting of research and HTA activities will then inevitable be needed to maximize the value of collecting additional information within a given budget for research and HTA - a problem of optimization. A number of approaches to priority setting for HTA based upon different societal (and scientific) criteria have been presented [31-34].[167]

However, using an efficiency criteria early economic evaluation can also guide decision making and set priorities regarding additional research and HTA of emerging health technologies. A major objective for early economic evaluation is therefore to assist in the planning of the next stages in the HTA process with respect to decisions about future research [10,13]. The early economic evaluation can show the scope for improvements in cost-effectiveness and highlight variables to which the cost-effectiveness of the new health technology is likely to be sensitive [10]. Further clinical trials and economic evaluation can then be planned specifically for the investigation of these sensitive variables. If, however, the improvement in cost-effectiveness of the new health technology seems to be limited or a certain threshold value cannot be obtained, then a decision should be made not to undertake further investments in R&D and HTA of the new technology [13]. This will be a situation, where the marginal benefit of information acquisition equals the marginal costs. In situations where the evidence provided is unlikely to change behaviour or the new technology is adopted anyway, despite the lack of evidence, further studies and gathering of information for decision making have no value either [30,35].

To maximize the benefit of information acquisition, within a specified budget, will be important for both public and private investments in R&D and HTA. For the pharmaceutical manufacturer early information, prior large investments in information acquisition, is essential to decide whether there is a reasonable expectation that a new chemical entity or formulation will have significant clinical and economic benefits, resulting in profit for the company [36]. Early assessments may be strategic tools to guide future R&D decisions and marketing planning [15,36]. However, the focus here will be upon the public investments in R&D and HTA.

The public investments in R&D and HTA comes from a number of sources, e.g. by National Research Councils and national funds for HTA. As with the private investments, the benefit of the public investment in information from the conduct of R&D and HTA should be optimized, due to scarcity of resources [37]. To maximize the value for money of the NHS R&D in the United Kingdom, the iterative use of economic evaluation has been suggested in order to provide guidance on the most appropriate

---

[167] E.g. the Committee on Priorities for Assessment and Reassessment of Health Care Technologies in the United States proposed in a model-based approach three objective societal criteria (prevalence, unit costs and variation in use) and four subjective societal criteria (burden of illness, the likelihood that assessments affected patient outcomes, costs, and ethical, legal and social issues) [31].

design of further HTA studies [10]. Technology assessment and major clinical trials, e.g. RCTs, are expensive to perform and an opportunity cost of funding a specific research project will be involved.[168]

Several authors have argued that (simple) prospective economic evaluations can be used in decision making a priori to identify the most efficient research solution, before large-scale, expensive trials and further HTA are funded [35,37,38]. As an example of this, Togerson et al. (1996) - focussing on research in prevention of osteoporosis - used modelling of five years treatment of a cohort of 100,000 women to estimate the potential cost-effectiveness of different therapies for the prevention of osteoporotic hip fracture [38]. From an economic viewpoint they concluded on behalf of efficiency information from the economic evaluation and literature review of the quality of the clinical evidence that *annually vitamin D injections* was the intervention which should receive research priority in a randomized trial, because it only required to be slightly effective to justify its costs.

Using the Diabetic Retinopathy Study (DR-study) retrospectively, Drummond et al. (1992) have earlier presented a methodology based upon principles of economic evaluation to analyse the benefits of initiating an RCT compared with its costs [37]. They concluded, due to large net savings to society by the adoption of photocoagulation therapy for patients with proliferative diabetic retinopathy, that the DR-study showed to be cost reducing and that the methodology could be applied prospectively to assess the potential net social benefit from clinical trials in prioritizing medical research [37]. However, there seem to be some unresolved problems in using this method prospectively. E.g. how should reliable data of the costs of a new intervention be obtained a priori, when the use of it is very limited. Although, the authors are aware of this problem and suggest some tentative solutions, their success is not tested using the methodology prospectively.

Reliability of data was not an essential problem in the ex ante evaluation (scenario analysis) of a potential clinical trial in hormone replacement therapy by Townsend & Buxton (1997) [35]. The reason was that the potential trial was planned late in the life cycle of the drug (phase III), where detailed cost-effectiveness analyses of its use (not its evaluation) had already been made, why existing evidence could inform the assumptions made.

4.2 Decisions about early adoption

As stressed previously with *Buxton's law*, a problem with respect to relating evaluation of health technology to policy measures is the timing of assessment [9]. For decision-makers (and researchers) a too early assessment may be of little benefit, because of the lack of information as discussed above, whereas a too late assessment may be of little

---

[168] The other research projects which are left unfunded.

use to decision-makers due to irreversibility of decisions. In this context of decision making, the timing of the information generated by assessment is as important as the information itself [8]. Therefore, a second objective for early economic evaluation, although related to the role of decision making regarding information acquisition, is to perform an assessment early in the life cycle of an emerging health technology to provide timely information for decision making before an early adoption is decided. Especially with respect to the less regulated health technologies belonging to the groups of medical devices and medical procedures, which are adopted early in the life cycle and often before any assessment, there is a need for early assessment. An early (preliminary) assessment can then assist in the decision making, whether the emerging health technology should be adopted or not, or whether resources should be devoted to initiate additional research and assessments prior to allow a more complete diffusion. Opposed to the first aim of early assessment this means that an early economic evaluation can suggest that existing evidence, although imperfect, is already sufficiently robust to provide confidence in order to justify the use of technology [35]. Opponents to this strategy will argue that there is a risk that the early assessment may be done at a time where the technology is not fully developed, which then leaves limited space for additional innovation. However, this fear underlines what was previously mentioned that early economic evaluations are only indicative and that economic evaluation and HTA should be conducted iteratively within the progress of a technology's life cycle.

Because of the lack of efficacy or effectiveness information about the new technology in phase I, the early economic evaluation conducted will primarily consider the cost-effectiveness of the routine practice which the new technology is supposed to replace [10]. Using expert judgement and eventually a few existing patient data in the analysis of the new technology, a tentative comparison of existing and new technology can be made. The highest potential for adoption of a new technology will be, where the existing routine practice is (clearly) ineffective. Developing a Markov model Sharples et al. (1996) used probabilities for key events, patient management patterns as well as unit costing from one English hospital to characterize a cardiac transplant service and to estimate the relevant costs and survival over a period of 5 years [39]. The aim of their model, presenting a number of scenarios based upon existing practice, was then that the potential cost-effectiveness of recent advances in immunosuppression therapy could be assessed using the model. With the more reliable phase II clinical data including efficacy information, the early economic evaluation can then identify threshold values of variables which the new technology needs in order to be below or above to be able to represent good value for money [10,13]. Parameters to which cost-effectiveness results are sensitive, but to which the values are simply unknown at this early stage, will be highlighted as well.

With scarce resources for health services and many new technologies introduced, a potential area for the use of early economic evaluations could be in early warning systems for emerging health technologies. Today early warning systems are established in the Netherlands, Sweden and the United Kingdom.[169] Besides early identification an important task in these systems is early assessment prior to the introduction of the technology [7]. With a time horizon between zero and five years before marketing (phase III for pharmaceuticals), depending upon system, it is possible to perform the early assessments described above within an early warning activity. Among the three systems mentioned, the Swedish early warning system is the only system, in which the conduct of early assessment actually is planned to be part of the activity, although no collection of primary data will take place [40]. There seems to be less focus upon early assessment in the two other systems. The early warning system, nevertheless, benefits from early assessments both with respect to decision making about early adoption and decisions about additional research and HTA. In general, this will add to the faith in the outcome from these systems and reduce the risk of decision errors.

However, although conducting early economic evaluations, the risk of decision errors cannot be ignored, because of the huge uncertainty present at this stage of analysis. Uncertainty therefore represents a central methodological issue in early economic evaluation.

4.3 Uncertainty in the early economic evaluation

A fundamental problem with early economic evaluation of new health technologies is uncertainty and how to handle it.[170] According to Johansson (1993) [41] uncertainty can be divided into *project uncertainty* and *evaluation uncertainty*. Project uncertainty refers to stochastic incomes, prices, quality, etc. and is understood as the uncertain outcome, when using a health technology [41]. Evaluation uncertainty is the uncertainty caused by the perception of the expected outcomes at the time of evaluation. This is due to the restricted knowledge available about parameters at the early stage in the life cycle and the little experience about the distribution of the expected costs and outcome of the health technology. An example could be an early economic evaluation of a new health technology which often depends upon small clinical studies. The efficacy of the innovation is here tested upon small and selected target groups isolated from a routine

---

[169] Early warning systems are further described in chapter 8.

[170] Although uncertainty is expected to decrease, as the technology develops and learning increases, there are still some uncertainty involved in economic evaluations carried out later in the life cycle. This could be the uncertainty due to the measurement of efficacy instead of effectiveness in phase III economic evaluations (see section 5.0) or the uncertainty due to widening of indications for treatment in phase IV (see section 6.0).

practice setting. The *internal validity*[171] may be high, whereas the *external validity*[172] of this early clinical information most likely is very low. An extrapolation of this study upon a larger population is therefore with the risk of imposing a bias in the result of the economic analysis. Other sources of *evaluation uncertainty* are the information used in assessments based upon expert opinions, guesses and assumptions.

The implication is that the data upon which the early economic evaluation are based are very uncertain and the distribution of costs and outcomes is therefore unknown, because of incomplete knowledge at the time of evaluation. The predicted costs and effects will hardly ever reflect the use of the new technology in daily routine clinical practice setting. Hence, corresponding with the two general objectives of early economic evaluation, a prominent role will then be to highlight possible pivotal estimates, which need to be assessed and observed further to reach an increased knowledge [30].

As economic evaluations are usually not conducted within an iterative and ongoing approach updated by new information arriving during diffusion, one traditional answer to evaluation uncertainty has been to perform sensitivity analysis. The aim of sensitivity analysis is to demonstrate how sensitive the relevant quantities are to variations in inputs. The simplest form of a sensitivity analysis is a non-stochastic analysis, in which the expected uncertain parameters are varied either individually (one-way) or in groups simultaneously (multi-way) to see how the result of the evaluation is affected [43]. In a recent review of journal articles one-way sensitivity analysis was found to be the most frequently used method to handle uncertainty in the economic evaluations [44]. However, the one-way or multi-way methods result in many possible results for the parameters varied, for which reason more advanced methods could be used. Threshold analysis solves the problem of multiple results by identifying break-even values for parameters [43]. In the method called analysis of extremes (scenarios) a base-case analysis including the best estimates of inputs is compared with alternative analysis, which looks at extreme estimates.

Another solution to evaluation uncertainty is to adopt statistical analyses to assess the probabilistic uncertainty inherent in the data and thus in the conclusions of an economic evaluation [45]. In this probabilistic sensitivity analysis, the uncertain parameters are assigned likely ranges and distributions, which allows probabilistic inference on relevant measures. A way to handle this will be to obtain confidence intervals for cost-effectiveness ratios. Wakker et al. (1995) have shown a method for constructing confidence intervals for cost-effectiveness ratios [45]. Barrager & Gildersleeve (1984) use this method to handle uncertainty inherent in evaluation of R&D projects [46]. A deterministic phase (simple sensitivity analysis) is combined with a probabilistic phase based on the identified sensitive parameters. From a specification of subjective probabilistic distributions for each single parameter and the cost model a probabilistic distribution of the cost difference between technologies is derived.

---

[171] Whether we can confidently make statements about treatment cause and effect in the sample of patients studied [42].

[172] The attribute of generalizability to populations not represented in the study [42].

In Sculpher et al. (1997) the uncertainty rested in early-stage economic evaluation is identified [10]. They propose an iterative evaluation strategy, in which the information generated early is used to update the knowledge available for later analysis, which has been suggested by others as well [8,9,29]. The aim of this kind of sequential approach is to help in the planning of the next stage of the R&D process. However, none of these authors present a model or methodology that indicates how the knowledge should be updated in the iterative approach, nor how the perceived effect on observation should be used in the decision made ex ante. Decision analytical modelling techniques are nevertheless, as seen with the examples presented previously, e.g. Sharples et al. (1996) [39], often employed in early economic evaluation to provide an intuitive framework and a means of synthesising data from various sources [10]. These models could be decision analytic models, extrapolation models, epidemiological models and Markov models [47]. The next sections briefly describe two models which take the sequential nature of decision making regarding emerging health technologies and thereby uncertainty into consideration. These models are *a decision analytic model* presented by Phelps & Mushlin (1988) [48] and *a learning model* presented by Langkilde (1997) [30].

4.3.1 A decision analytic model

Using medical decision theory and epidemiologic information Phelps & Mushlin (1988) have shown that early assessment can help the decision-maker to estimate the value of an emerging diagnostic technology and to decide whether further trials and HTA are needed. They propose a two-step process designed to eliminate the most expensive evaluation steps, when it can be shown that they are not needed to reach a decision about a technology's desirability [48]. The first preliminary evaluation (Hurdle I) uses the expected value of perfect information[173] (EVPI), conditional of the fallback action[174], as a first test of a technology relying on published data, but not new clinical trials. The decision rule is that the technology's use should be recommended whenever the population's EVPI associated with the use exceeds the costs to operate the technology (in the *challenge region of cost-effectiveness*) [48]. Then we can continue to Hurdle II. However, if EVPI does not exceed the costs to operate, the technology fails Hurdle I and should not be used at all. Hurdle II, the second step, focuses upon the expected value of imperfect information. In this stage, new clinical studies are initiated, e.g. to measure diagnostic accuracy, and used to adjust the cost-effectiveness result obtained in the preliminary evaluation. An *imperfect* diagnostic technology has expected value of clinical information (EVCI) lower than the corresponding EVPI. The decision rules are that the technology will fail Hurdle II if costs to operate are higher than EVCI and pass if costs are lower than EVCI. Phelps & Mushlin (1988) argues that the benefit of this strategy

---

[173] The value of perfect information, conditional of a treatment strategy, depends upon the probability that a person is healthy multiplied by the difference in the utility gain of not treating a healthy person and the cost of this avoided treatment (the reverse with a non-treatment strategy).

[174] The action undertaken without this information (EVPI).

using the techniques of decision analysis is, at least for many diagnostic technologies, that it will not require the conduct of RCTs [48].

4.3.2 A learning model

In a forward-looking approach of evaluating the value of information related to new technology, as an important issue in early economic evaluation, Langkilde (1997) shows in a *learning model*, based upon the Bayesian sequential decision theory, how knowledge can be updated and how the perceived effect on observation can be used [30]. Making a decision to adopt a new technology a forward-looking decision-maker must consider that his knowledge about the technology may change due to emerging knowledge and that the technology itself may change due to an emerging technology. The learning model considers the analysis of emerging knowledge. Learning is concerned with the possible reduction of evaluation uncertainty and the connected decision errors (type I and II) which arise if decisions are made sequentially and the outcome of actual use of a technology between decisions is observed. This will not be obtained using a myopic strategy performing only one initial evaluation. Considering a two-stage decision process in the forward-looking strategy, the first decision made to adopt the new technology early in its life cycle is based upon available *a priori* information (the prior distribution) with a number of uncertain parameters [30]. If adopted, the use of the technology is observed. In this period of observation additional evidence and experience, e.g. from day-to-day use of the technology, which reduces the uncertainty may then arrive - the learning effect. The second decision is then made on behalf of the updated initial parameter estimates (the posterior distribution), in which the minimum expected present value costs can be calculated for each posterior distribution in order to find the action which yields the smallest expected costs. Assuming that decisions are reversible, the decision-maker can then compare different technologies and alter the initial decision of adoption if necessary. In this approach learning becomes the process of adjusting the parameter estimates to observed outcomes, where the value of learning feeds back into the initial decision [30]. The choice of current action then affects the information basis for the next period.[175]

The learning model for early economic evaluation has been applied in a case study of the analysis of a new diagnostic procedure for patients with symptoms of colorectal cancer, the Calprotect Phical-Elisa test compared with conventional procedures such as colonoscopy and x-ray [49]. The problems of performing an early economic evaluation of this test were that the clinical study available prior to adoption did only include a very small and selected target group and that the test could be used differently than expected in the early clinical trial. Using the learning methodology, a formal decision problem (cost minimization) was constructed to aid the decision-maker in the choice between adopting the test or continuing with the conventional practice [49]. Assuming

---

[175] For technical description about learning models the reader is referred to Langkilde (1997) [30].

500 patients per year and a 10-year planning horizon the result showed, comparing the minimal expected cost of the two programmes[176] given a shadow price, that the net present value without learning (myopic evaluation) amounted to 16.0 mill. DKK, while it was 15.6 mill. DKK with learning from a period of observation (forward-looking evaluation) [49]. This means that the expected gain from learning is 410,000 DKK, which is comparable with a 2.6 per cent reduction in costs with learning. In a similar way, the learning model has been applied to an economic evaluation of Interferon-2b in the treatment of chronic active hepatitis C [30].

However, the practical usefulness of the learning model needs to be tested and investigated further, before its practical value for decision making can be decided. Unknown factors are the computational limits with respect to number of parameters, the problems and cost of establishing prior distributions for parameters, as well as the complexity of the calculations which increases exponentially as the number of uncertain parameters increases [49]. Finally, the reversibility of decisions is questionable, although a sequential decision making strategy is assumed.

5.0 Phase III: Economic Evaluation and Randomised Controlled Trials

In phase III of the life cycle, the new health technology will be close to a more widespread diffusion in the health care sector. For pharmaceuticals, phase III will consider both approval and reimbursement decisions. The difference between the two decisions is that a pharmaceutical still can reach the market for adoption, although reimbursement was denied, whereas the opposite cannot happen. With a FDA-like market approval system of pharmaceuticals used in Denmark and the rest of the OECD countries, information is required at this late stage of the clinical development process to document issues like clinical efficacy and safety of the product before any product licensing and marketing are allowed. The typical full-scale trial carried out, as a golden standard, is the randomized controlled trial. These phase III trials are *comparative*, where the experience of a group of patients on the new drug treatment is compared with a *control* group of similar patients receiving a standard treatment or placebo [23]. Requirements for the documentation of efficacy and safety of other types of health technologies do not exist in Denmark, besides the gradual implementation of European Commission Directives regarding safety of devices [1]. Budgetary pressure (cost containment) and greater awareness of evidence-based medicine and health technology assessment may have an indirect effect upon the wish to document clinical effect, as RCTs of selected devices and procedures are made. However, several cases, e.g. laparoscopic cholecystectomy, show that these RCTs are conducted rather late in the life cycle, when a widespread diffusion has already occurred.

---

[176] The Calprotect test strategy versus the conventional diagnostic strategy.

The objective of economic evaluation in phase III is to investigate and document the technical efficiency[177], e.g. cost-effectiveness, of a new technology compared with a relevant (existing) alternative, before any widespread diffusion takes place. Ideally, the phase III evaluation should be part of the iterative approach suggested by Sculpher et al. (1997) in which the knowledge is updated by learning from earlier evaluations [10]. The use of economic evaluation has received most attention with respect to reimbursement decisions, although it can be used for approval decisions as well. In some countries, e.g. Australia and Canada, documentation of efficiency through the conduct of economic evaluation is encouraged in the decision making regarding reimbursement of new pharmaceuticals [14,15].[178] In Denmark, the usefulness of economic evaluations in reimbursement decisions is investigated by the authorities in a trial period of 3-5 years, where the pharmaceutical companies can submit economic analyses on a voluntary basis when applying for subsidisation of their product [16]. A problem with the use of economic evaluations in phase III is the problem of which treatment group to focus upon. The cost-effectiveness of a new pharmaceutical depends on the patient group in which it is used, why decisions about approval versus no approval and reimbursement versus no reimbursement can be inefficient ways to achieve cost-effective use of a pharmaceutical [50]. Ensuring that the pharmaceutical is used afterwards only on this group of patients may be problematic. If the decision on the other hand should be based on overall cost-effectiveness of the pharmaceutical in all patient groups, then it will probably imply that the pharmaceutical cannot be used for the specific group of patients, due to a risk of a general non-approval (or non-reimbursement) decision, although it could have shown to be cost-effective for the specific group. For life-threatening diseases such as AIDS, where there are few alternatives available, the approval time can in itself be an issue for economic evaluation [50]. If the approval system allows it, the potential gain in health from a shorter approval time has to be weighted against the increased risk of side-effects and the expected costs of a pharmaceutical.

The main source of clinical information for the economic evaluation in phase III will be information from RCTs. More economic evaluation studies are being made within the context of RCTs [51]. The economic evaluation is conducted alongside the clinical trial or even integrated into the clinical trial protocol. There are several advantages of the integration of economic studies in clinical trials. The first advantage of the integration is that RCTs are seen as the golden standard (best source of information) and have thereby increasingly been considered as a natural vehicle for economic evaluation, depending on the quality of the underlying medical evidence [51,52]. The second advantage is that the prospective collection of economic data as part of a clinical trial results in patient-specific data on both cost and outcomes with a high internal validity [47]. A prospective collection of economic data carried out properly can be closer to the real marginal resource use, whereas a retrospective collection often is less detailed and

---

[177] Opposed to allocative efficiency.

[178] In Australia, the conduct of economic evaluation - cost-effectiveness analysis - is mandatory for listing of pharmaceuticals under the Pharmaceutical Benefit Scheme (PBS) [14].

more inexact. A third advantage is that the extra resources needed to collect economic data incorporated into a clinical protocol are limited, because most of the costs for data collection are already incurred in the clinical part [47]. However, it is still very important only to identify significant cost and resource use drivers.

Another approach in phase III economic evaluation is to model the economic analysis, as in the early phases of assessment, based on information of the clinical effectiveness from a systematic review, a synthesis or a meta-analysis of a number of published RCTs.[179] Data on resource use and unit costs will then typically have to be added to the model from other sources. Economic analyses based upon models are a frequent used method in HTA, where a review of the clinical evidence provides the baseline information for the economic modelling. An example is the NHS R&D programme in England, which emphasises the importance of RCTs and economic evaluation as part of HTA [10]. In this HTA strategy, the economic evaluation will typically be based upon systematic reviews of RCTs, if available. Otherwise, an RCT will have to be initiated and the economic evaluation attached to it. The initiation of new RCTs happened in one third of the English HTA projects reviewed in *the international comparative study* presented in chapter 2.

However, a number of methodological issues and pitfalls need to be considered, when an economic evaluation, either conducted alongside or integrated into the trial, is based upon clinical information from an RCT. Some of these issues are furthermore relevant, when a phase III economic evaluation is modelled, based on information from existing RCTs. These issues and pitfalls are discussed in the rest of section 5.

5.1 Efficacy versus effectiveness

The aim of RCT is to test the efficacy of a technology. Efficacy deals with *how well the intended objectives are realized in ideal settings* [20]. These ideal settings are controlled by the clinical protocol, extra follow-up and monitoring in order to reduce the number of patients lost and to maximize the compliance. This yields a high internal validity of the RCT, whereas the external validity is generally low [47]. The efficacy result will most likely be an overestimate of the *true* effectiveness of the technology *used in average settings*. Extrapolation to routine practice settings with all types of patients may then be problematic. Design issues like *choice of comparator* and *trial location* do also contribute to the differences between efficacy and effectiveness.

The focus of economic evaluation is to provide guidance for health care decision-makers about resource allocations (efficiency) in routine practice. Therefore efficacy data with a high internal validity is not highly useful in an economic evaluation [42,47]. External

---

[179] In situations where RCT-information is missing, a modelled retrospective economic analysis can rely on clinical data from historical controls and databases (retrospective cohort design) reflecting the actual use of the technologies in question, as well as uncontrolled clinical studies.

validity and effectiveness information are due to the decision making context of higher interest in an economic evaluation and in an HTA [42,53]. If this problem with regard to trade-off between efficacy and effectiveness data (internal versus external validity) is significant, there are generally two ways to handle it.

One, rather radical, solution for the collection of effectiveness data and data with economic end points is to design a *pragmatic* economic trial (prospective cost-effectiveness clinical trial) based on less exclusion and follow-up which thereby increases the external validity [47,54]. However, this strategy can be problematic. First, it will increase the costs needed for data collection as these trials are lenghty. Secondly, this strategy is impossible to follow for a pharmaceutical in phase III, because it has not yet been used in a routine practice setting, for which reason these trials usually cannot begin until close to or after the launch of the pharmaceutical [54]. Thirdly, it may be unethical to perform the *effectiveness RCT* in routine practice settings, once an RCT has demonstrated efficacy, although it is necessary for the conduct of the pragmatic economic evaluation [20]. Therefore the most frequently used solution to deal with this trade-off problem is to add a decision analytic model to the economic evaluation integrated into the RCT. To reflect the use of the technology in routine practice, a number of significant parameters can then be varied in a model, e.g. effectiveness data, prolongation of the follow-up time and adjustment of data on resource use to a routine practice setting. The assessment of the technology is, furthermore, the interest of phase IV economic evaluation as described in section 6.0. The US Panel on Cost-Effectiveness in Health and Medicine (1996) recommends that models should be used as complements to, not substitutes for, direct primary or secondary empirical evaluation of effectiveness [55]. The Canadian *Guidelines for economic evaluation of pharmaceuticals* state as well that *if effectiveness data are not available appropriate modelling techniques based on sound pharmacoepidemiology are permissible* [15]. A review of economic evaluations financially supported by CCOHTA showed, however, that effectiveness information only supplemented efficacy information in four out of twelve studies [56].

5.2 Design Issues

5.2.1 Which comparator?

Another important methodological issue to consider, when an economic evaluation is planned to be conducted alongside an RCT in phase III, and in other phases, is the choice of comparator. Which alternative should the technology in question be compared to? For pharmaceuticals, the comparator to test efficacy and safety in an RCT is very often a placebo therapy [42]. A placebo comparator will, however, threaten the external validity of the economic evaluation which is interested in answering the question of optimal resource allocations in routine practice given a specified budget. In a routine practice setting every patient in need will get some kind of treatment, for which reason the placebo option is only realistic in very few situations, e.g. where a pharmaceutical will be a new adjunctive therapy instead of a substitute [47].

If a placebo therapy, not reflecting routine practice, is used as a comparator, the economic evaluation will be biased, because the real incremental costs and benefits of the new technology cannot be shown. Therefore, the comparator used in the economic evaluation needs to be as close as possible to the actual choices facing health care decision-makers - the technology used in current practice, if the new technology was not available [52]. This was also recommended in the Canadian guidelines [15]. If the comparator used in the RCT is a placebo therapy, the most frequently used existing technology will have to be identified and the effectiveness result modelled, before comparing it with the new *trial-proven* technology in an economic evaluation. This is done to increase the external validity, but will at the same time decrease the internal validity.

5.2.2 Location of the trial

The different aims of RCT and economic evaluation could also imply different locations preferred in the studies. RCTs are often undertaken in atypical settings like specialist centers (academic or teaching) with highly committed investigators, using state of the art equipment on a selected group of patients who tend to comply with therapy [57,58]. This yields a high internal validity. However, with the focus upon external validity, it will also be of interest in economic studies to include average and non-specialized hospitals in the analysis of effectiveness and resource implications. This is, however, very seldom done in economic evaluations.

The increasing use of multi-center and multinational studies can, besides the advantages of having a larger sample of patients included and significant clinical differences found, make the issue of trial location even more problematic [52]. The problem of a multinational approach can be that only a few highly specialized centres are included for each participating country implying a limited external validity in the countries. However, on the other hand, it can be argued that a multi-center study by incorporating data from a diverse range of settings within a country may increase the external validity of both clinical and economic results, if pooling can be made [59].

5.2.3 Sample size

In the clinical trial, the calculation of sample size is based on the minimum number of observations required to detect a given (predetermined) *clinically important difference*, with a given power, at the conventional levels of statistical significance [52,60]. The greater the variation in patients responses to identical therapeutic interventions, the larger size of study sample needed [61]. When gathered alongside clinical trials, the economic data can be viewed as being *stochastic* with a mean and variance [58]. However, to test economic hypotheses of expected differences in the economic data, the power analysis carried out has to focus upon the economic end points instead. This is the case both with respect to significantly obtain differences in resource consumption, in incremental cost-effectiveness ratios and in the effectiveness measure relevant to the economic evaluation, where the primary clinical (intermediate) end point is not always relevant [59]. To demonstrate these significant differences the size of the sample in the economic evaluation may then very well have to be larger than in the clinical trial. To be able to calculate the sample size it has to be decided, what an important economic difference is, although this is more difficult with economic evaluations, since the main outcome is a ratio of two variables (costs and effects) with two variances [59]. To determine this important difference a priori information is required from earlier analyses. An additional problem related to the size of the sample and the ability to demonstrate significant differences is random variation of certain high cost items [52,60]. The variance in total costs may be quite large, because of variability in resource use and unit costs [58]. A few patients' high resource consumption can result in high mean costs and large variances, which can make it difficult to show significant differences between alternatives.

Sample size is not a problem for economic studies integrated into large clinical studies like *the GUSTO IIb study* which involves 12.000 patients suffering from acute manifestation of coronary heart disease, although the study has a multinational approach involving 14 countries [62]. However, on many occasions the RCTs are much smaller, especially for surgical procedures, where clinical studies often only involve about 50 patients due to ethical considerations. The consequence of adding an economic evaluation to this kind of RCT without enlarging the sample is that significant economic differences probably cannot be found.

5.3 Resource use

The economic costs of a programme can be calculated by using the knowledge of two components - data about *resource use* measured in physical quantities and estimates of *unit costs*. The overall cost of an intervention is the sum of the quantities of resources used multiplied by their unit costs [57]. Physical quantities of resource use can be collected prospectively, when the economic evaluation is integrated into the clinical trial, whereas it is recommended that unit costs should be collected in a parallel study rather than as an integral part of the prospective data collection [59]. Especially, if the clinical trial is conducted on a multinational basis. Issues with respect to the collection and measurement of these two components are discussed in the following sections.

5.3.1 Collection of data on resource use

The identification and prospective collection of data on resource use in physical quantities is an important argument for the integration of an economic evaluation into a clinical trial. The prospective collection with patient-specific data warrants to a higher degree that the real marginal resource use will be identified. An exhaustive list of resources to be collected prospectively should be evaluated [60]. However, ideally only resource use which are believed to vary between patients, or which are costly or difficult to collect retrospectively, e.g. from patient records, needs to be collected prospectively.

Resource use that is equal between the alternatives can be collected retrospectively without any loss of detail. On the other hand, parameters like length of stay and intensity of care will be parameters with some variability justifying a prospective collection. Detailed examination should be undertaken only as it becomes clear that it will be required for subsequent economic analysis, as the aim is to reduce the cost of data collection [52]. Using the iterative approach, sensitive parameters relevant for prospective collection can be identified in earlier phases (I-II) [10]. For purposes of randomization and blinding in the RCT a number of tests and examinations are usually made. In routine practice - the focus of the economic evaluation - these tests and examination will not be used. A problem then with basing cost estimates on data gathered as part of a trial is the extent to which one is capturing resource use associated with the trial per se (protocol-driven costs) rather than the costs of providing the therapy [42,47].

The prospective collection of the data can be made by the direct integration of items on resource use in the clinical protocol and/or by the use of different case report forms, e.g. about hospital length of stay, nursing home length of stay and outpatient resource use, alongside the clinical trial [47,63]. In the outpatient situation the case report forms can be either questionnaires on resource use fulfilled retrospectively on behalf of patient recall or cost diaries fulfilled prospectively by patients at home. An alternative to the use of case report forms in the hospital is to use the hospital's information systems, although these are rarely optimal for this kind of information. Finally, expert panels are a solution, although the method is less accurate and the prospective advantage is lost [57]. Collection of resource data outside the trial is justified, when a large difference between efficacy and effectiveness appears and when the trial is conducted in an atypical setting.

In the economic evaluation it can be decided to limit the collection of data on resource use generated at later stages as a result of the patients' treatment (e.g. new diseases in the prolonged lifetime). However, the time horizon of the clinical trial can also limit the data collected. In many diseases, the relevant time horizon for the economic evaluation may be longer so as to capture the recurrence of a disease or a problem associated with therapy, e.g. patient dropouts [42]. It can then be necessary to prolong the data collection for these patients or to use statistical models, e.g. Markov modelling, to estimate recurrence rate and associated resource use. An example of an RCT with a too short follow-up is a study of different kinds of antithrombotic therapy with heparin in patients with unstable coronary artery disease to reduce the rate of ischemic events [64]. The time horizon of the clinical trial was only 30 days, although the risk of acute myocardial infaction and death is present after 30 days. The consequence of the economic analysis integrated in this trial is that it probably underestimate the resource use associated with heparin therapy due to the short follow-up perspective [65]. However, a trade-off exists between an ideal length of prospective follow-up and the costs long-term data capture [58]. At the very least, it is necessary to establish that the patients do not incur significant costs during relevant follow-up periods [58].

In the multinational or multi-center trials the collection of data on resource use is further complicated by two ways of handling the data collection. The prospective collection can either be specific to each centre or country (country-specific data) or it can be limited to one representative centre and afterwards extrapolated to all the participating centres, if geographical transferability exists (pooled data) [51]. Which strategy to choose will depend upon the difference between the settings. Are there substantial organisational or historical differences between the centres, e.g. differences in experience and practice, which are important determinants of service provision, utilization and opportunity costs, then one may consider using data specific to each centre and not pooled data [59]. On the other hand, the multinational trial might be underpowered for the analysis of resource data at the individual country level, which could be an argument for the use of pooled data to have sufficient statistical power [47,52]. Obviously, there is a trade-off with respect to the choice of strategy for collection of data on resource use in a multinational study.

5.3.2 Collection and estimation of unit costs

As previously stated, the other component needed to calculate the overall cost of a programme, besides resource use, is *unit costs*. Ideally, these unit costs (or prices) of resources can be collected either as part of the trial or in a parallel exercise [57]. However, the most frequent advice given is to assess the cost of these resources outside the clinical trial through a separate data collection exercise [22,52,59]. One reason for this, at least in public organized and financed health care systems as in Denmark, is that market prices for health care activities only rarely exist and that the charges used do not reflect the marginal opportunity costs associated with these activities. The unit costs will therefore have to be estimated. Another reason for the estimation of unit costs in a parallel study, is not to burden the clinical investigators with collecting cost data within the clinical trial [22]. Finally, possibilities for changes in prices, salaries, etc. and thereby changes in the cost-effectiveness ratio exist during a long clinical trial period. However, an estimation of unit costs as a separate activity as late as possible in the trial period will secure a relevant and updated cost-effectiveness result, when the study is finished.

Furthermore, price levels may differ from one setting to another and thereby limiting extrapolation and generalizability of the result [52,60,61,66]. In economic evaluations integrated into clinical trials this problem is present, when the trials are conducted at atypical settings, e.g. in highly specialized hospitals, as discussed previously. Price levels in these settings will hardly reflect price levels in average local settings. However, estimation of unit costs as a separate activity allows the costs to be recalculated for settings, where the price levels differ [52]. In practice a *hybrid* approach is often used to gather unit cost data, taking some from the trial centre(s) and some from national statistics [57].

Multinational or multi-center trials are associated with additional methodological issues related to variations in costs (price levels) between centres or between countries [60]. Country- or centre-specific unit costs for each site may need to be derived independently, if the countries' health care systems, practice and salaries differ too much, instead of using an average unit cost and then applying this to the country-specific or pooled data on resource use [59]. In the multinational *GUSTO IIb study* involving 525 centres, country-specific baseline costs are estimated for the 14 countries involved and then applied to a calculated pooled proportional difference in resource utilization across countries [62]. However, if limited differences appear among the centres participating, pooled unit costs can be used as the best approximation instead of unit costs specific to each centre. The cost structure of the site chosen for this estimation has then to demonstrate that the structure is typical for all other sites included in the study [59]. In a multinational trial this strategy is more problematic, because of cross-country differences in health care systems and an eventual lack of transferability between countries. Unit costs, resource use and thereby pharmacoeconomic evidence gathered in one country do not always extrapolate well to other countries [42,66]. A solution in the economic evaluation based upon pooled multinational cost data could therefore be to use purchasing power parities for each country to adjust the pooled price [52].

In summary, there are three possible combinations of handling the issues of resource use and unit cost data in multinational or multi-center trials [52]. 1) Data on resource use could be country-specific with pooled unit cost data applied. 2) Data on resource use could be pooled and multiplied by country-specific unit costs. 3) Both data on resource use and unit costs could be specific to each centre or country participating. Although, the final strategy is advocated for [59], the choice of strategy will depend upon a number of factors, e.g. the *size of the country-specific samples* if the purpose is to find significant economic differences within the trial, *cross-country differences in health care systems, differences in price levels and settings (location)*, etc.

5.4 Choice of outcome measures

To be able to calculate cost-effectiveness ratios for a new health technology compared with an existing alternative in an economic evaluation, the economists are interested in knowledge about the outcome of a treatment, besides information about its costs. When conducting a clinical trial, the clinical researchers are also interested in information about the outcome of a treatment involving a new technology. However, a difference in opinion, caused by different objectives, seems to appear between clinical researchers and economists about the relative importance of different kinds of outcome measures [52,60].

With the aim of phase III clinical trials to establish the efficacy of new technologies most of these trials fail to capture all of the end points relevant to the economic evaluation [58]. In clinical trials, it has been customary to study and report intermediate physiological or biochemical makers as outcomes, e.g. venous thromboembolism, total blood cholesterol, instead of final health outcomes as mortality and morbidity [42,47,52,53,58]. The focus is on how particular patients should be treated, for which reason measures must be clinically meaningful. Furthermore, testing for differences in final outcomes is often prohibited by the sample size in clinical trials which explains the use of intermediate outcomes [42,47]. Short time horizon in many RCTs does also limit the possibility to deal properly with final health outcomes, although this is sometimes done anyway [65].

As the objective of economic evaluation is to inform the health care decision-makers about resource allocation, knowledge about the impact of health programmes and technologies on final health outcomes and utility measures is of interest [42,47,52]. Furthermore, an advantage is that the measures have meaning for the patient, e.g. life years gained, compared to intermediate measures like venous thromboembolism [58]. Especially, utility measurement in quality adjusted life years (QALY) with the valuation of improvements in health per se is attractive from the economist's perspective of resource allocation [60,67]. The outcome measure must be generalizable to enable comparisons (prioritization) to be made across a number of health care programmes [52]. However, a number of limitations and unresolved theoretical and methodological problems exist with respect to QALYs, although going deeper into this matter will be beyond the scope of this book.[180]

Intermediate outcomes are often considered a reliable predictor of final outcomes, e.g. control of blood pressure as a predictor of avoidance of fatal and non-fatal stroke [58]. A solution in economic evaluations conducted alongside clinical trials is to use existing epidemiological data to construct models which can predict changes in final outcomes from changes in risk factors [42,47]. However, in both cases the overall validity will be very dependent upon the causality of the relationship between intermediate and final outcomes [42,53]. Lack of empirical evidence, complicated biological relations[181] and use of technologies under average conditions can dilute this relationship. An example of an economic evaluation modelling life years as final end points is a recent cost-effectiveness analysis by Gyrd-Hansen et al. (1998) of colorectal cancer screening both based upon data from an RCT and epidemiological data on the incidence of colorectal cancer by age and gender [70]. Finally, a solution could be to fully integrate the collection of final outcomes and quality of life measures relevant for the economic evaluation into the prospective clinical trial. However, with ethical considerations of overloading the patients, the complexity and costs of the trial due to the need for a longer time horizon and an increased sample size to find significant associations focussing upon final outcomes instead, some resistance from clinical researchers should be expected [52,60]. Therefore, if a prospective collection of outcomes relevant for an economic evaluation is chosen, this will normally be conducted as an additional activity alongside the clinical trial, eventually on a smaller part of the total sample and not at the expense of the original collection of intermediate outcomes. E.g. in the GUSTO IIb study data about health related quality of life (generic measures, general health profiles (SF-36) and QALYs) are prospectively collected only from a random subsample of patients participating and only in one country (the United States), as well as the measurement

---

[180] Theoretical and methodological limitations and problems in QALYs and other utility measures have been discussed previously in Poulsen (1994) [68].

[181] E.g. between an intermediate outcome measure like venous thromboembolism and final outcomes such as death rate and life-years gained [69].

is added to the clinical trial as an extra activity, because the clinical trial focuses upon deaths and nonfatal myocardial infarctions as primary outcomes [62].

6.0 Phase IV: Economic Evaluation of Routine Practice Settings

In phase IV, the health technology will be adopted in routine practice settings by most clinical centres and thereby widely diffused in the health care sector. For pharmaceuticals, this happens after the marketing approval has been obtained by the RCT's carried out in phase III to document the efficacy and safety. For medical devices and procedures, e.g. surgical techniques, this wider diffusion can occur earlier in the life cycle due to the limited regulation and control of these types of health technology. However, it is common to all health technologies in phase IV is that the technology is used under *average conditions of use* in routine practice settings to treat all types of patients entering the hospital. This means that there will be no possibility of controlling and monitoring the patients closely as it was done within the clinical trial protocols in phase III.

Because of the use of the technology in routine practice settings the focus of phase IV (post-marketing) clinical trials are therefore measurement of *effectiveness*, rather than efficacy. At this stage the aim will therefore be to generalize the results found in the controlled settings in phase III to monitor the complications and adverse effects of the use of the technology. Furthermore, large-scaled and long-term clinical trials of the health technology will typically be undertaken in phase IV to strengthen the epidemiological knowledge about the morbidity and mortality within a specified population [23].

In this late stage of the life cycle, the economic evaluations carried out in phase IV, similar to the post-marketing clinical trials, are comparative validation studies in which the preliminary economic analysis from phase III can be reassessed to study the health technology in a real world clinical setting [22]. Besides updating previous studies on the basis of the new effectiveness data, these phase IV economic studies will provide better evidence regarding utilization and adverse events of the health technology in question [15]. Due to the limitation of the follow-up period in phase III trials resulting in intermediate outcome measures only, the aim in phase IV may furthermore be to undertake a thorough economic analysis to determine the relationship between the intermediate outcomes and long-term substantive health benefits (i.e. morbidity and mortality) and changes in costs [10]. Extrapolation and generalization of the results found in phase III in earlier analyses can then be possible. This process may rely on careful observational studies of the technology in use or will ideally be informed by large pragmatic economic trials, as previously mentioned in section 5.1 [13]. Opposed to the exploratory RCTs in phase III, the aim of pragmatic trials in phase IV is to evaluate the effectiveness or cost-effectiveness of an intervention under real conditions that would prevail from the technology in routine use [47]. This will increase the external validity. In this type of trial, designed for economic purposes, there are fewer restrictions for recruitment of patients, who are followed during routine practice and a wide range of end points will be measured, e.g. long-term end points such as quality of life. However, if this large and long-term trial cannot be initiated, as it is expensive, a modelled economic evaluation of the use of the technology in routine practice use can still be conducted instead, as it was done in evaluations in the earlier phases of the life cycle. Besides the possibilities of having a higher external validity, larger sample sizes and availability of final end points, if a pragmatic trial is carried out, the methodological issues to consider, when conducting an economic evaluation in phase IV, are identical to the issues discussed previously in section 5.0.

The target group for the information about the health technology in routine clinical practice produced by economic evaluation and HTA activities in phase IV are the system and hospital managers, who are responsible for the provision and financing of the health care services [8]. Their needs increase throughout the diffusion cycle, depending upon the amount and speed of diffusion of the technology in the health care sector. Physicians and patients are other groups who will have an interest in phase IV evaluations. As the decision about marketing approval has been made at this stage of the life cycle, this phase is on the other hand not of primary interest for the regulatory authorities. The industry has less interest in phase IV clinical trials and economic evaluation compared to their interest in phase III trials and assessments which were made to obtain marketing approval and reimbursement of the product. However, the industry will still have an incentive to prove that their marketed products are effective and cost-effective in routine practice as well, although this need is less important if the adoption decisions in the health care sector to some extent are characterized as irreversible [8,9].

Due to the late stage in the life cycle of the technology and the assumed high data quality at this stage, phase IV is regarded as the ideal time to undertake an economic study [22]. With the technology used in routine practice settings learning about the technology increases, whereas the uncertainty decreases. Then the population of patients who can benefit clinically from the technology as well as the appropriate indication for the use of technology can best be identified. Due to the gathering of this effectiveness information, the result will be that the external validity of the economic evaluation will be extremely high [22]. The economic evaluation in phase IV can be incorporated into the development of (local) clinical treatment guidelines, which can lead to a more efficient use of resources [50]. However, the drawback with this *late* economic evaluation is that the decisions about adoption and reimbursement have been made, which means that phase IV economic evaluation at least in the perspective of the regulatory authorities not necessarily represents a situation of optimal timing for the decision-maker. This dilemma highlights the trade-off in the assessment of a technology between a timely assessment and the best data available as described in the previous sections. Many economic evaluations, at least in the past, were usually carried out as retrospective assessments at this late stage in the life cycle of health technologies, when the clinical documentation had been achieved, e.g. from RCTs, and the technology was (fully) adopted in the health care sector. The usefulness of this late information for decision making was of course limited due to a likely reversibility of adoption decisions already made. This illustrates, however, to perform a good phase IV economic evaluation late in the life cycle of a health technology, this evaluation needs to be informed by economic evaluations conducted in earlier phases.

As suggested in the Canadian guidelines, the conduct of an economic evaluation of routine clinical practice (post-marketing) should be scheduled on the basis of time, which means three to five years after the product is marketed[182] or on the basis of "trigger" events [15]. These "trigger" events could be changes in epidemiology, medical practice, costs, comparators or the emergence of new adverse or beneficial events.

This shows that there will be situations, even at this late stage in the life cycle of the health technologies, where evaluation uncertainty is present, for which reason phase IV not necessarily need to be characterised by the best data available for the economic evaluation. Evaluation uncertainty may be caused by a change in the indications for use of the technology or because new uses of the (obsolete) technology have been found [29]. The transfer and application of the laparoscopic technology few years ago from surgical fields as appendectomy and cholecystectomy to be used in areas such as colon cancer and gastroesophageal reflux represent the last example of uncertainty. Evaluation of a technology for applications previously not assessed would be a form of reassessment [29]. If "trigger" events have major implications for the use of the health technology and evaluation uncertainty is present, then a reassessment of the technology will be necessary [9]. These reassessments could be carried out to evaluate use and to determine whether replacement or abandonment should take place [29]. The importance of reassessment is similar to the importance of early and timely assessments confirming that HTA and economic evaluation are iterative and ongoing activities throughout the life cycle of a health technology. However, with some exceptions, assessments of existing technologies have failed to stimulate interest comparable to that shown for the assessment of new technologies.

7.0 Discussion

An overall goal of HTA, and thereby economic evaluation, is to provide input to decision making in policy and practice, e.g. to obtain an efficient diffusion and use of health technology [71]. This means that there should be a close connection between the field of science, where the HTA information, i.e. economic evaluation, is normally produced and the field of decision making, where decisions about the health care sector are made. As a bridge between the *pure scientific paradigm* and the *policy paradigm* [72]. However, apart from problems of developing appropriate methods and obtaining the necessary data as discussed in section 5.0, the main problem, according to Johannesson (1995), is the link between economic evaluation and decision making [50]. Drummond (1987) claims too that the main deficiency is the lack of a clear link between those

---

[182] This recommendation is specifically for pharmaceuticals. However, for devices and procedures a time schedule for a phase IV economic evaluation will likewise be three to five years after the technology was first adopted in the health care sector and a wide diffusion has occurred.

undertaking the evaluations and those making the decisions [26]. Two parallel decision making processes exist within health care - one for planning decisions and one for clinical decisions. As a mechanism to secure the link more clearly and to encourage a rational diffusion and use of health technology, regulation has been suggested [26]. Either as regulation by directives[183] or regulation by incentives.[184] These are important mechanisms, even in a decentralized Danish health care system, and should be developed and tested further to obtain a more obvious and direct role for HTA and economic evaluation in health care decision making than what may be the case today.

In a different approach the present chapter has investigated the link between economic evaluation (and HTA) and decision making from the perspective of the life cycle of health technologies. The different objectives of economic evaluation throughout the process of diffusion of health technologies have been described and discussed. Like the iterative (sequential) and ongoing activity suggested in the literature [8,9,29,30], economic evaluation has in general two main objectives during diffusion of health technologies which are interdependent and related to scarcity of resources. The importance of these objectives depends off course upon the different stages of diffusion and the different types of technologies considered.

The main objective of conducting economic evaluation during the initial phases of the diffusion of health technologies is to secure that the resources devoted to the HTA-process and the conduct of R&D are used efficiently, because an opportunity cost is involved in information acquisition. Deciding to spend resources upon an additional clinical trial in the HTA-process due to uncertainty about the information available a priori could implicate that other trials cannot be initiated as the scarce resources are gone. This is both the case with respect to public and private investments in additional R&D and HTA. Opportunity costs and scarce resources were experiences in Denmark in the field of HTA, where the Danish Institute for Health Technology Assessment (DIHTA) allotted a state grant of DKK 10 millions and called for proposals for HTA projects [73]. However, DIHTA received 113 applications applying for DKK 138 millions in total, which means that the financial wishes of only 7 per cent of the total sum applied for could be fulfilled.[185] In the early phases of the life cycle of the technology (phases I and II), the uncertainty of the information about the emerging health technologies is significant and their diffusion still limited. Before a widespread diffusion occurs, an early economic evaluation can then inform the decision-maker, whether it is efficient to undertake further HTA-activities about a new health technology with the aim of information acquisition to reduce the uncertainty. The early assessment can also

---

[183] Examples are the planning of specialties in Denmark and the exclusion of specific pharmaceuticals from reimbursement.

[184] Examples are the introduction of management by contracts in hospitals and competition between hospitals (in Denmark, especially between hospitals in different counties).

[185] Among the 113 applications, twenty-six HTA-projects received financial support [73]. The opportunity cost was that the other projects did not receive the 7 per cent funding instead.

highlight possible pivotal estimates to be investigated further in new trials and HTA, which then can be used to update the economic evaluation, if an iterative approach is planned. Efficiency of the process of HTA and R&D is furthermore an important criteria in later phases of the life cycle depending on the uncertainty resting in the technology, e.g. from changes in clinical practice which warrant a reassessment of the technology.

The main objective of conducting economic evaluation during later phases of diffusion is to obtain an efficient diffusion and use of the health technology. As is the case with information acquisition, the decision to adopt new health technologies and new applications of exiting technologies involves an opportunity cost, because the resources available for health services are scarce. To secure an efficient provision of health services in an ideal world, the health technologies adopted and used - both new and existing technologies - should prove cost-effectiveness. This need for assessment exists throughout the life cycle of a health technology. Early economic evaluation provides important information with respect to decisions about adoption of the less regulated types of health technologies - medical devices and medical procedures - which in general are adopted earlier in the routine clinical practice compared with pharmaceuticals. However, advocating for economic evaluation as an iterative activity early economic evaluation is furthermore important with respect to inform and update later economic evaluations. So far the largest focus and use of economic evaluation of health technologies have been in phase III of the clinical development programme. The regulatory approval system for pharmaceuticals at this stage of diffusion with potential roles for economic evaluation to document cost-effectiveness in both the decisions regarding approval and decisions regarding reimbursement is the reason to this focus [50]. Finally, when a widespread diffusion has occurred in phase IV economic evaluations or reassessments are performed to document efficiency of routine practice, e.g. decisions about treatment guidelines, although irreversibility of decision could be a problem especially at this stage of diffusion.

As discussed in the present chapter, a dilemma of having a clear link between the conduct of HTA or economic evaluation and the context of decision making is the timing of the assessment. Due to early adoption and diffusion of health technology[186] in the health care sector the decision-maker requests the efficiency information timely to be able to rationalize diffusion [12]. Opposed to this the data and information available about the technology early in its life cycle, and before a widespread diffusion has taken place, are limited and associated with a high degree of uncertainty. The consequence is that the HTA and economic evaluation based upon these data are more indicative than definitive. To make a final decision on behalf of this information will entail a significant risk of making the decision errors described in the introduction (type I and II). For rapidly evolving health technologies, such as surgical procedures, which are improving continuously, this is even more problematic. In later stages of diffusion, when information improves through the conduct of additional trials and learning about the technology in routine practice increases, the data become more valid and reliable. With

---

[186] Eventually besides pharmaceuticals in which the formal regulation system exist.

irreversibility this may, however, be too late for decision-makers to change decisions, if necessary. This illustrates that there is a trade-off inherent in the timing of assessment - on one side to provide timely information for decision making and on the other side to provide reliable information. The iterative and continuous conduct of economic evaluation during the development and diffusion of a health technology provides some guidance in this trade-off dilemma, if the early assessments are used to inform and update later assessments, and the results of these early assessments, depending on the situation, are only considered as preliminary and indicative by decision-makers.

However, different technologies warrant different timing of assessment, since the speed of diffusion varies among the three types of health technology. Surgical procedures are fast diffusing and constantly being improved, for which reason long-term clinical trials and economic evaluation may not reflect the current status of surgery [28]. Therefore, surgical procedures illustrate a type of technology with a need for an early assessment to judge initial cost-effectiveness prior to adoption and the HTA-process ought to be ongoing during diffusion, while improvements are made.

The method used for the economic evaluation differs throughout the life cycle of health technologies. In the early phases, in which knowledge is limited and uncertainty high, the economic evaluation will often be modelled. When the clinical information improves in the later phases, the economic evaluation can be adapted prospectively into the clinical study based upon the data gathered. However, models are also used in the later phases, e.g. in reassessments of existing technology, and modelled economic evaluation are a typical approach used within an HTA.

Advocating for an iterative approach to economic evaluation during diffusion of health technologies, how to handle uncertainty, updating of knowledge, as well as the perceived effect of information of additional trials and observation become important. In this chapter, two models dealing with sequential (iterative) decision making were briefly described and where especially the learning model by Langkilde (1997) [30] presented a framework for integration of updating and the perceived effect of information in the early assessment. In general, however, there seems to be a need for further research into methods to handle uncertainty and sequential decision making in order to avoid the introduction of an iterative economic evaluation process just resulting in a number of myopic assessments conducted instead. Furthermore, the number of methodological issues discussed in section 5.0 is important, if economic evaluation should accomplish its overall goal to be relevant for policy making. These methodological issues will in different degree be relevant for all phases in the life cycle of a health technology.

To standardize the economic evaluations carried out guidelines have recently been presented in many countries, as described in section 1.0. However, the primary focus of these guidelines for economic evaluation seems to be on methodology and use in decision making with respect to decisions about reimbursement of pharmaceuticals in phase III. Besides the Canadian guidelines [15], they do not consider the timing issue at all, i.e. different objectives and methodological issues during development and diffusion of a health technology. This chapter has, nevertheless, shown that economic evaluation has other objectives and target groups throughout the process of diffusion, than those oriented towards phase III in the life cycle.

References

1. Council Directives. 93/42/EEC, of 14 June 1993. Medical Devices.

2. Littell CL. Innovation in Medical Technology: Reading the Indicators: Datawatch. Health Affairs Millwood 1994;13(3):226-235.

3. Grimes DA. Technology Follies. The Uncritical Acceptance of Medical Innovation. Journal of American Medical Association 1993;269:3030-3033.

4. Finkelstein SN, Homer JB, Sondic EJ. Modelling the dynamics of decision-making for emerging medical technologies. R&D Management 1984;14(3):175-191.

5. Banta HD, Luce BR. Health Care Technology and its Assessment. An International Perspective. First edition. Oxford University Press. Oxford. 1993.

6. Sassi F. Health Technology Assessment. An Introduction. Eurohealth 1996;2(4):9-10.

7. Poulsen PB, Hørder M, Jørgensen T. Fremtidens medicinske metoder - tidlig varsling i internationalt og dansk perspektiv. Rapport udgivet af Sundhedsstyrelsens Udvalg for Medicinsk Teknologivurdering. Sundhedsstyrelsen, København, 1996.

8. Bloom BS, Fendrick AM. Timig and Timeliness in Medical Care Evaluation. PharmacoEconomics 1996;9(3):183-187.

9. Banta HD, Vondeling H. Strategies for successful evaluation and policy-making toward health care technology on the move: the case of medical lasers. Social Science & Medicine 1994;38(12):1663-1674.

10. Sculpher M, Drummond M, Buxton M. The iterative use of economic evaluation as part of the process of health technology assessment. Journal of Health Service Research and Policy 1997;1:26-30.

11. Mowatt G, Bower DJ, Brebner JA, Cairns JA, Grant AM, McKee L. When is the 'right' time ti initiate an assessment of a health technology. International Journal of Technology Assessment in Health Care 1998;14(2):372-386.

12. Goodman C. A Basic Methodology Toolkit, pp. 29-65. In Szczepura A & Kankaanpää J (Ed.). Assessment of Health Care Technologies. Case Studies, Key Concepts amd Strategic Issues. John Wiley & Sons. Chichester. 1996.

13. Buxton M. Economic evaluation early in the life cycle of a medical technology. Abstract. European Workshop: Scanning the Horizon for Emerging Health Technologies. Copenhagen, September 12-13, 1997.

14. Hailey D. Australian economic evaluation and government decisions on pharmaceuticals compared to the assessment of other health technologies. Social Science & Medicine 1997;45(4):563-581.

15. Canadian Coordinating Office for Health Technology Assessment. Guidelines for economic evaluation of pharmaceuticals. 2nd ed. Ottawa: Canadian Coordinating Office for Health Technology Assessment (CCOHTA); 1997.

16. Alban A, Keiding H, Søgaard J. Rapport om Retningslinier for Samfundsøkonomisk analyse af lægemidler. Bilag 1 i Sundhedsministeriet. Udfordringer på lægemiddelområdet. Betænkning afgivet af Sundhedsministeriets Medicinudvalg. Sundhedsministeriet, København, juni 1998.

17. Rovira J. Standardization of the economic evaluation of health technologies. European developments. Medical Care 1996;34(12):DS182-DS188.

18. Statens Legemiddel kontroll. Utkast til norske retningslinjer for legemiddeløkonomiske analyser. Upubliceret.

19. Rovira J. Standardizing economic appraisal of health technology in the European Community. Social Science & Medicine 1994;38(12):1675-1678.

20. Gold MR, Siegel JE, Russell LB, Weinstein MC (eds.). Cost-Effectiveness in Health and Medicine. Oxford University Press, New York, 1996.

21. Warner KE. The Need for Some Innovative Concepts of Innovation: An Examination of Research on the Diffusion of Innovations. Policy Sciences 1974;5:433-451.

22. Towse A, Drummond M (eds.). From efficacy to cost-effectiveness. OHE briefing. Office of Health Economics, London, May 1998;37:1-12.

23. Pocock SJ. Clinical Trials. A Practical Approach. John Wiley & Sons, Chichester, 1983.

24. Banta HD, Behney C, Willems JS. Toward Rational Technology in Medicine. Springer and Co., New York, 1981.

25. Poulsen PB, Adamsen S, Vondeling H, Jørgensen T. Diffusion of laparoscopic technologies in Denmark. Health Policy 1998;45(2):149-167.

26. Drummond MF. Economic evaluation and the rational diffusion and use of health technology. Health Policy 1987;7:309-324.

27. Spilker B. Multinational Drug Companies: Issues in Drug Discovery and Development. Raven Press, New York, 1989.

28. Friedman LM, Furberg CD, DeMets DL. Fundamentals of clinical trials. Second efition. PSG Publishing Company, Inc., Massachusetts, 1985.

29. Banta HD, Thacker SB. The Case for Reassessment of Health Care Technology. Once Is Not Enough. Special Communication. Journal of American Medical Association 1990;264(2):235-240.

30. Langkilde LK. Uncertainty, Information and Health Technology Assessment. Ph.D. Afhandling fra det samfundsvidenskabelige fakultet på Odense Universitet, Odense, 1997.

31. Donaldson MS, Sox HC. Setting priorities for health technology assessment. A model process. Committee on Priorities for Assessment and Reassessment of Health Care Technologies. Institute of Medicine. National Academy Press, Washington, D.C., 1992.

32. Eddy DM. Selecting technologies for assessment. International Journal of Technology Assessment in Health Care 1989;5:485-501.

33. Oortwijn WJ, Vondeling H, Bouter L. The use of societal criteria in priority setting for health technology assessment in the Netherlands. Initial experiences and future challenges. International Journal of Technology Assessment in Health Care 1998;14(2):226-236.

34. Henshall C, Oortwijn W, Stevens A, Granados A, Banta D. Priority setting for health technology assessment. Theoretical considerations and practical approaches. A paper produced by the Priority Setting Subgroup of the EUR-ASSESS Project. International Journal of Technology Assessment in Health Care 1997;13(2):144-185.

35. Townsend J, Buxton M. Cost effectiveness scenario analysis for a proposed trial of hormone replacement therapy. Health Policy 1997;39:181-194.

36. Clemens K, Garrison LP, Jones A, Macdonald F. Strategic Use of Pharmacoeconomic Research in Early Drug Development and Global Pricing. PharmacoEconomics 1993; 4(5):315-322.

37. Drummond MF, Davies LM, Ferris FL. Assessing the costs and benefits of medical research: The Diabetic Retinopathy Study. Social Science & Medicine 1992;34(9):973-981.

38. Togerson D, Donaldson C, Reid D. Using economics to prioritize research: a case study of randomized trials for the prevention of hip fractures due to osteoporosis. Journal of Health Services Research and Policy 1996;1(3):141-146.

39. Sharples LD, Briggs A, Caine N, McKenna M, Buxton M. A model for analyzing the cost of main clinical events after cardiac transplantation. Transplantation 1996;62(5):615-621.

40. Carlsson P. ALERT. Et nationellt system för identifiering, information och tidig bedömning av nya medicinska metoder. Projektplan SBU. På uppdrag av Styrgruppen för Hälso- och sjukvärdsfrågor för redovisning den 19 februari 1997.

41. Johansson PO. Cost-benefit Analysis of Environmental Change. Cambridge University Press, Cambridge, 1993.

42. Rittenhouse BE, O'Brien BJ. Threats to the Validity of Pharmacoeconomics Analyses Based on Clinical Trial Data. Chapter 126 in in Spilker B. (ed.). Quality of Life and Pharmacoeconomics in Clinical Trials. Second Edition. Lippincott-Raven Publishers, Philadelphia, 1996.

43. Briggs AH, Sculpher MJ, Buxton MJ, Uncertainty in the economic evaluation of health care technologies: The role of sensitivity analysis. Health Economics 1994;3:95-104.

44. Briggs A, Sculpher M. Sensitivity analysis in economic evaluation: A review of published studies. Health Economics 1995;4:355-371.

45. Wakker P, Klaasen MP. Confidence intervals for cost/effectiveness ratios. Health Economics 1995;4:373-381.

46. Barrager S, Gildersleeve O. A Methodology to Incorporate Uncertainty into R&D Cost and Performance Data. In Tolley GS, Hodge JH, Oehmke JF (eds.). The Economic of R&D Policy. Prager Scientific, New York, 1985. pp. 149-169.

47. Drummond MF, O'Brien B, Stoddart GL, Torrance GW. Methods for the Economic Evaluation of Health Care Programmes. Second Edition. Oxford Medical Publications, Oxford University Press, Oxford, 1997.

48. Phelps CE, Mushlin AI. Focusing Technology Assessment Using Medical Decision Theory. Medical Decision Making 1988;8:279-289.

49. Langkilde L, Poulsen PB. The Learning Approach to Early Economic Evaluation. CHS Working Paper 1996:2. Centre for Health and Social Policy, Odense University, 1996.

50. Johannesson M. Economic evaluation of health care and policymaking. Health Policy 1995;33:179-190.

51. De Graeve D, Nonneman W. Pharmacoeconomic studies. Pitfalls and Problems. International Journal of Technology Assessment in Health Care 1996;12:1:22-30.

52. Drummond MF, Davies L. Economic Analysis Alongside Clinical Trials. Revisiting the Methodological Issues. International Journal of Technology Assessment in Health Care 1991;7(4):561-573.

53. Liberati A, Sheldon TA, Banta HD. EUR-ASSESS Project Subgroup Report on Methodology. Methodological Guidance for the Conduct of Health Technology Assessment. International Journal of Technology Assessment in Health Care 1997;13(2):186-219.

54. Drummond MF, Luce B. Socioeconomic Evaluation of Pharmaceuticals. Chapter ten in Szcezepura A, Kankaanpää J (eds.). Assessments of health care technologies : case studies, key concepts and strategic issues. John Wiley & Sons, Chichester, 1996.

55. Weinstein MC, Siegel JE, Gold MR, Kamlet MS, Russell LB. Recommendations of the Panel on Cost-Effectiveness in Health and Medicine. Consensus Statement. Journal of American Medical Association 1996;276(16):1253-1258.

56. Baladi J-F, Menon D, Otten N. Use of economic evaluation guidelines: 2 years' experience in Canada. Health Economics,1998;7:221-227.

57. Drummond M. Economic Analysis Alongside Clinical Trials: Problems and Potential. Journal of Rheumatology 1995;22:1403-1407.

58. Drummond MF, Menzin J, Oster G. Problems in Undertaking Pharmacoeconomic Assessment in Phase III Clinical Trials: The Case of Colony-Stimulating Factors. Chapter 122 in in Spilker B. (ed.). Quality of Life and Pharmacoeconomics in Clinical Trials. Second Edition. Lippincott-Raven Publishers, Philadelphia, 1996.

59. Coyle D, Davies L, Drummond MF. Trial and tribulations. Emerging Issues in Designing Economic Evaluation Alongside Clinical Trials. International Journal of Technology Assessment in Health Care, 1998;14:1:135-144.

60. Bennett CL, Armitage JL, Buchner D, Gulati S. Economic Analysis in Phase III Clinical Trials. Cancer Investigation, 1994; 12:3:336-342.

61. Ellwein LB, Drummond MF. Economic analysis alongside clinical trials. Bias in the Assessment of Economic Outcomes. International Journal of Technology Assessment in Health Care, 1996;12:4:691-697.

62. Jönsson B, Weinstein MC. Economic evaluation alongside multinational clinical trials. Study Considerations for GUSTO IIb. International Journal of Technology Assessment in Health Care, 1997;13(1):49-58.

63. Mauskopf J, Schulman K, Bell L, Glick H. A Strategy for Collecting Pharmacoeconomic Data During Phase II/III Clinical Trials. Special Article. Pharmacoeconomics 1996;9:3:264-277.

64. Cohen M, Demers C, Gurfinkel EP, Turpie AGG, Fromell GJ, Goodman S, Langer A, Califf RM, Fox K, Premmereur J, Bigonzi F. A comparison of low-molecular-weight heparin with unfractionated heparin for unstable coronary artery disease. The New England Journal of Medicine 1997;337:7:447-452.

65. Fox KAA, Bosanquet N. Assessing the UK cost implications of the use of low molecular weight heparin in coronary artery disease. The British Journal of Cardiology 1998;5:2:95-105.

66. Bonsel GF, Rutten FFH, Uyl-de Groot CA. Economic Evaluation Alongside Cancer Trials: Methodological and Practical Aspects. European Journal of Cancer 1993;29A(7):S10-S14.

67. Drummond MF, Stoddart GL. Economic Analysis and Clinical Trials. Controlled Clinical Trials 1984;5:115-128.

68. Poulsen PB. Hvem skal behandles - for hvad? - Økonomiske prioriteringsmål i sundhedssektoren. CHS Arbejdsnotat 1994:2. Center for Helsetjenesteforskning og Socialpolitik, Odense Universitet.

69. Detournay B, Planes A, Vochelle N, Fagnani F. Cost-Effectiveness of a Low-Molecular-Weight Heparin in Prolonged Prophylaxis Against Deep Vein Thrombosis After Total Hip Replacement. Pharmacoeconomics 1998;13:81-89.

70. Gyrd-Hansen D, Søgaard J, Kronborg O. Colorectal cancer screening: efficiency and effectiveness. Health Economics 1998;7:9-20.

71. Banta HD, Werkö L, Cranovsky R, Granados A, Henshall C, Jonsson E, Liberati A, Matillion Y, Sheldon T. Introduction to the EUR-ASSESS Report, pp.133-143. In the Special Section *Report from the EUR-ASSESS Project* in the International Journal of Technology Assessment in Health Care 1997;13(2):133-340.

72. Battista RN, Hodge MJ. The Development of Health Care Technology Assessment. An International Perspective. International Journal of Technology Assessment in Health Care 1995;11(2):287-300.

73. Lange M, Jørgensen T, Kristensen FB. Analysis of the national need for information, training and standards in HTA. Danish Institute for Health Technology Assessment. Poster presented at the 14th Annual Meeting in the International Society of Technology Assessment in Health Care, Ottawa, Ontario, Canada, June 7-10, 1998.

Chapter 8

Systems for Early Warning of Emerging Health Technology[187]

---

[187] Earlier versions of section 1-4 have previously been published in: *Poulsen PB, Hørder M, Jørgensen T. Fremtidens Medicinske Metoder - tidlig varsling i international og dansk perspektiv. Sundhedsstyrelsens Udvalg for Medicinsk Teknologivurdering. Sundhedsstyrelsen, København, 1996.* [Health technologies of the future - early warning in an international and Danish perspective].
An earlier version of section 4 have as well been published in II. *Jørgensen T, Larsen LG, Poulsen PB. Tidlig varsling af kommende medicinske teknologier - et dansk forstudie. DSI - Institut for Sundhedsvæsen. DSI - rapport, 1997.* [Early warning of emerging health technologies - a Danish feasibility study].

Table of contents

Abstract 223

1.0 Introduction 224

2.0 The Concept of Early Warning 225

3.0 Early Warning Systems in Health Care 227
    3.1 The major functions of a system 227
    3.2 The sources of information 229
    3.3 The target groups 230
    3.4 The time horizon 231

4.0 International Experiences with Early Warning 232
    4.1 Early Warning in Sweden 232
    4.2 Early Warning in the Netherlands 234
    4.3 Early Warning in the United Kingdom 237
    4.4 Other countries and international collaboration 239

5.0 Models of Early Warning in Denmark 240
    5.1 An independent system for early warning 240
    5.2 Early warning as part of a technology assessment programme 242

6.0 Discussion 243

References: 246

Abstract

With a rapid technological change and an increasing number of health technologies emerging in contrast to scarcity of the resources, the decision-makers in the health care sector face a dilemma. To be able to provide better planning and priority-setting in the health care sector the decision-makers need information about new and emerging health technologies to be expected. Systems for early warning may be a way of improving this information. In this chapter systems for early warning are described. Its major functions are early identification, early assessment and early dissemination of information about emerging technologies. Today, systems are established in countries like Sweden, the Netherlands, the United Kingdom and Canada. Their organisation and experiences are described. However, there is no system in Denmark yet. In the chapter, two potential systems are presented and discussed; *an independent system for early warning* and *early warning activities as part of a technology assessment programme.* The last type of system is integrated into a technology assessment programme with the aim of performing the early identification task and has a short time horizon (zero to two years prior to marketing). The system has the time horizon that was revealed as important in a Danish feasibility study covering the potential target group of the system - decision-makers at the regional levels. They found this period most important for decision making and health care planning. For this reason the system is recommended. Furthermore, a high reliability and usefulness of the information produced are expected to result from the system.

1.0 Introduction

There is a rapid growth in the technological density and change in the health care sector. The sector faces an increasing number of possibilities from science (technology push) and the industry as well as a higher community demand for health and health care services (demand pull), as described in chapter 3. New health technologies are developed in complex and multi-disciplinary innovation processes with contributions from diverse scientific areas such as molecular biology, computer science and telecommunication [1]. Examples of emerging health technologies have been technologies for diagnostic purposes (e.g. computed tomography and magnetic resonance imaging scanners (MRI)), surgical technologies (e.g. the laparoscopic technologies transferred to the field of general surgery [2] and an expected future use of virtual reality technologies in surgery [3]) and secondary prevention (e.g. genetic screening for hereditary diseases [4]). This process of development has been characterised as a *biological revolution* in the field of health care [1].

However, the introduction of new technology has economic and social consequences. Newhouse (1992) showed that the most significant factor explaining health care costs was the use of technology [5]. The resources available in the health care sector, as in other sectors, are scarce, for which reason the need to set priorities among alternative activities is always present. Furthermore, health technologies, other than pharmaceuticals, are often introduced early without any documentation about their safety and effectiveness. Due to scarce resources and the rapid technological change a need appear to improve the information available for the decision-makers about emerging health technologies.

How should this be attained in society then? In the process of prospective health technology assessment (HTA) the initial step is the *stage of identification* of the potential health technologies for priority-setting with respect to an eventual future technology assessment. For emerging[188] and new[189] health technology, as well as existing health technology with new applications, this task of identification is the objective of *systems for early identification and early assessment* - also known as *early warning systems*. It is expected that these systems improve the possibility to identify, assess[190] and systematically monitor the development of potential emerging health technology early in the life cycle. In planning and setting priorities among activities in the health care sector, the policy- and decision-makers can then benefit from this early information.

The purpose of the present chapter is to describe and discuss the idea behind systems for early warning in the life cycle of health technology and the process of health technology assessment, because systems for early warning are seen as an integral part

---

[188] Defined as a technology prior to adoption [6].

[189] Defined as a technology in the phase of adoption [6].

[190] By conducting an early and preliminary HTA.

of a broader systematic approach to health technology assessment [1]. Systems and experiences from other countries with early warning systems are described as well. Finally, two models for early warning in Denmark are presented briefly and the practicality of the models is discussed.

2.0 The Concept of Early Warning

The interest in early warning seems to have the historical origin in the military field. The classical examples are the development of radar systems during the Second World War to warn about bombing raids and the superpower nations' launch of satellites with the purpose of spying in the Cold War period. Today systems for early warning are established within many different areas. One area is the United Nations' role as a peace-keeping and conflict resolving actor, why the United Nations in 1992 agreed upon a resolution about the development of a *UN Early Warning System of potential catastrophes*, e.g. wars, famines, epidemics and refugees [7]. A related example with respect to international cooperation, in which the concept and idea of early warning has been used, is the G-7 countries, who in 1996 considered the establishment of a strategic warning system for the worlds' economies and currencies - an economic *turn out* force in the form of an emergency fund under the International Monetary Foundation. The use of early warning has also been advocated for in industries and business sectors, in which competition and fast changing market structures make the firms to demand knowledge about the future. The establishment of early warning systems by a firm in a sector of industry has the objective to secure the monitoring of competing firms' attempt to act prospectively [8]. To strengthen the firms' strategical abilities, the warning activity focuses upon other firms radical changes in activities, the consequences of these changes for the monitoring firm and prediction of the likely possibilities within this evolution.

However, in defining early warning we have to differentiate between the concepts of *early warning* and *technology forecasting*. The idea of both is the possibility of identifying future actions and activities at an early time. The focus is therefore proactive rather than reactive. Technology forecasting and early warning differ, however, in the time horizon considered and thereby the activities identified, the methodology used as well as their use in general.

Technology forecasting - or technology foresight - is oriented towards the future and has therefore a long time perspective, e.g. ten to twenty years. One aim of technology forecasting may be to identify scientific findings which can potentially result in future technologies[191] to be developed [9]. The methods used in technology forecasting such

---

[191] Defined as a technology not yet (fully) developed [6].

as scenario analysis[192] and Delphi technique[193] are known from research having the future as the principal subject. However, technology forecasts are often conducted as a one-off exercise as part of a strategic future planning and not as a permanent and continuos activity. This was the case with scenarios of the future health care sector made in the county of Funen in Denmark in 1995 [11]. Furthermore, the focus of technology forecasts will typically be on overall levels such as trends in sectors and developments in areas of disease and not on the detailed level of a specific technology. This was the case in another one-off exercise of technology forecasting, the *Steering Committee on Future Health Scenarios* in the Netherlands (1985-1987), where the focus was on areas like home care technologies and developments in the regeneration, repair and reorganisation of nervous tissue [9]. Having a ten-years perspective the aim of this project was to develop sufficient information on future technological development (innovation) in health care to assist in long-range health planning efforts. However, due to the long time perspective there will most likely be a limited success by using technology forecasting as a system to identify technologies with an impact in the next ten years. In Norway, a re-evaluation in 1993 of results forecasted by experts in 1986 confirmed this lack of success [12]. Furthermore, a Danish feasibility study showed that decision-makers only found limited relevance of the provision of information five to ten years before the future health policy and planning activities [13].

Opposed to the technology forecast activity, the time period monitored in providing *early warning information* is shorter and the activity is more likely to be carried out as a continuos activity in a permanent system. An early warning system can be defined as the systematic and concrete collection of information in a number of predetermined areas, e.g. emerging health technologies, considered to have a significant influence upon the near future. The focus of the early warning system will, in contrast to technology forecasting, be on specific emerging technologies in the period zero to five years prior to their adoption in the health care sector. This corresponds to the later stages in the innovation process. The consequence is that the early warning system considers *probable futures*, whereas technology forecasting activities due to the longer time perspective focus upon the more uncertain *possible futures* made in scenarios. The data and thereby the methods used in early warning can be characterized by being more reliable and can be collected in sources like literature, conferences, media, etc. Because of the narrower perspective, the continuos activity and the higher reliability of information, a system for early warning may also more naturally be integrated into a health technology assessment programme. In the rest of the chapter the systems in the health care sector described will belong to the group of early warning systems. In the next section early warning systems in the health care sector are presented.

---

[192] Defined as hypothetical sequences of events constructed for the purpose of focussing attention on causal processes and decision-points [9].

[193] Delphi technique is a formal and a systematic method of tapping expert knowledge about the present and judgement about the future. General characteristics are; anonymity through the use of questionnaires, iteration of rounds, controlled feedback between rounds, and a final statistical group response where a consensus is sought [10].

3.0 Early Warning Systems in Health Care

Opposed to some of the uses of early warning referred to above, e.g. the military use, early warning in health care does not only focus upon threats from outside and has only a limited use as a strategic tool between competing providers, as in the industry.[194] In the health care sector, systems for early warning focus both upon the likely future *threats*[195] and upon the *opportunities* of the development and adoption of new health technology.[196]

3.1 The major functions of a system

In the health care sector, a system for early warning of emerging health technologies performs three major functions [14]. The first major function is early identification of emerging health technologies and new applications of existing health technologies. This identification and monitoring task should focus upon health technologies expected to have a significant impact on the health care sector as it is stated in the National Strategy for Health Technology Assessment in Denmark [15]. In systems for early warning the criteria for a significant impact of the emerging health technology could be based on some of the same criteria used in the stage of priority-setting in HTA, e.g. the criteria presented by Donaldson et al. (1992) [16]. However, a critic to these criteria is that they partly rest upon a cost-of-illness approach, because parameters like total costs and burden of illness are included. A high cost-of-illness ratio does, nevertheless, not provide a good foundation for priority-setting. What instead will be of interest are the expected incremental costs related to the expected incremental effects (health gains) of the emerging technology.

With the early warning information the decision-makers can prospectively monitor the innovation and diffusion of the technology and in the later stage of priority-setting obtain further possibilities for action and get additional time in the early phase of the life cycle. If the early warning information suggests that an emerging technology is likely to be a *threat*, if introduced, then a policy response may be to try to hinder the introduction or the widespread diffusion of the emerging technology, perhaps until more evidence will be available, or only allow limited use of the technology when introduced. If, on the other hand, the early warning information concludes that the emerging technology may provide positive future consequences for the sector, then a policy response can be to support further development financially and thereby

---

[194] At least in publicly-run health care sectors.

[195] E.g. an emerging drug which may have dramatic economic consequences for the third-party payer if complete diffusion is allowed, as was the fear in Denmark with Beta-interferon, before an HTA was carried out in 1996.

[196] This may be new medicine which is able to prolong the life of chronically ill patients or new health technology with potential of being cost-effective or even cost-saving.

accelerate the time for introduction, or even to decide to introduce the technology immediately, if the evidence is judged to be enough. Early information does also raise the possibilities to present alternatives to the emerging technology, if necessary. Finally, early information improves the ability to secure favourable conditions for planning purposes and that the health care sector and the society is prepared for the emerging health technology.[197]

The aim of an early warning system is not only to identify potential emerging health technologies as timely as possible for decision making. A second major function might be prospectively to assess a number of high-priority technologies or areas of technological change [1].[198] As described in chapter 7, with respect to early economic evaluation only limited evidence is available in the early stages of the life cycle of the health technology, e.g. small pilot studies in phase I in the clinical development programme. The early assessment of the emerging technology can be based upon these small studies or other evidence from the literature. If there is no or only limited evidence and information about the emerging technology, then an approach to assessment may be to assess the routine practice which the emerging technology is expected to replace [18]. This early assessment can then for example show how cost-effective an emerging health technology has to be to warrant adoption. The early assessment can also focus on the potential intended and unintended consequences of the technology [11]. Depending upon the system, its time horizon and purpose, the early assessment will in some situations be more like an *early judgement* than an actual assessment, in which the technology is judged in relation to a number of predefined parameters and assumptions.

During the early stage in the life cycle the information from the early assessment is uncertain, why the assessments are only preliminary and more indicative than definite. The uncertainty will decrease as the technology develops and diffuses in the health care sector and new (re-) assessments will then have to be carried out, as the early assessment should also be part of the iterative assessment approach to HTA advocated for in chapter 7. However, new applications of existing technologies, which are also of interest for an early warning system, may increase uncertainty again. For the policy-maker using the early warning system, this preliminary information from the early assessment can then assist in decision making regarding the emerging technology, e.g. decisions about the need for further R&D and HTA and decisions about early adoption of the technology.

---

[197] This may be an early discussion about ethical considerations of the emerging technology prior to introduction, which e.g. seems to be relevant in fast growing areas as genetic technology.

[198] However, there are situations where information of the identified emerging health technology is directed towards the decision-makers without the conduct of an early assessment. The study by Warner (1975) of the diffusion of leukemia chemotherapy in childhood, as described in chapter 4, was such an example, because the physician, due to desperation, will be risk-seeking with an early adoption of the emerging, unproven, technology [13].

Finally, a third major function of an early warning system is to disseminate the early knowledge and results, if the information should be used by decision-makers [14]. As with HTA information, early warning information is useless unless it is disseminated to the potential target group. The dissemination of early warning information can be closely connected to rules and regulations in the health care sector. This is the case in the Netherlands, as described in section 4. Alternatively, the early warning information can just be aimed at informing the users, the providers and the payers of health care and through the provision of this information aim at changing practice, when necessary. This seemed for example to be the solution chosen in the decentralised Swedish health care system with the first early warning system - *New Methods in Medicine*.

3.2 The sources of information

To fulfill the three major functions presented above, especially the role of identification and assessment, a system for early warning of emerging health technology needs information. Although the time schedule may be early in the life cycle, there are many sources of information available. These sources vary depending upon the type of health technology. However, overall major sources of information include medical journals, medical expert groups, standing committees, Internet, scientific meetings, research proposals and industry [14]. Other sources are medical societies, press releases, the media, existing databases, informal documents and the health care professionals. Surveys and expert methods[199] asking health care professionals and other experts of their expectations about the emerging health technologies to be expected within a number of medical specialties have been carried out in some countries. However, only a survey in the United Kingdom had a time horizon within five years to be useful in early warning [19]. The rest tended more to be technology forecasting [9,12,20]. Finally, the patient group in expressing their needs has been recognized as a source of information on emerging technologies [14].

For the group of pharmaceuticals, regulated by the FDA-like approval, the existing documentation about approval and reimbursement will be a reliable and important source of information which ought to be obtainable for a national early warning system. Other sources specifically for pharmaceuticals may be commercial databases on innovations, patents and licenses [1]. Some of these depend of course upon, whether they will be available for an early warning system. Sources like databases on innovations and patents are furthermore likely to be biased, because these data overestimate the reality with respect to the future innovations and potential technologies likely to emerge in the health care sector. In the process of development of new pharmaceuticals only 1,000 of roughly each 10,000 compounds synthesized will go into animal research [22]. Ten of these will initiate human testing and finally one will reach the health care market as a final product.

---

[199] E.g. the Delphi technique.

As for pharmaceuticals, a registration of the market introduction can also be used as a source of information about the group of medical devices. However, this is only done in a few countries as, e.g. the United States.[200] Commercial databases on innovations, patents and licenses are also relevant sources for devices, although with the same limitations as presented above. Ideas used for the development of medical devices are often transferred from other applications in other sectors and from learning from science and available scientific knowledge.[201] An example of technologies transferred to the health care sector from other sectors are the laser and the extra-corporeal shockwave lithotripter. Therefore a final source of information may be to look at the technological innovation and trends in other sectors, e.g. the military sector.

With respect to medical and surgical procedures the sources of information for an early warning system about emerging innovations seem to be more problematic, because there is no registration made at the time of introduction and procedures are not patented. Unless the medical or surgical procedure is closely connected to a device or pharmaceutical there will be no other sources of information available than medical societies, expert judgements, conferences, databases of ethics committees, informal documents and literature.

Finally, it is worthwhile mentioning that the costs of collecting information from various sources must be weighed against the value of the additional information for the specific users [1].

3.3 The target groups

As with HTA information, early warning information is primarily produced for policy purposes and decision making. A system for early warning is essentially a mechanism to allow communication between policy-makers and experts (professionals) [9]. The primary target group for the early warning system may therefore be the policy-makers and health service planners at the national level and, in countries with decentralised health care systems, at the regional level as well. In the health care sector the group of policy-makers is usually isolated from the scientific community, in which the future and emerging technologies are developed and identified. The early information will therefore improve the policy- and decision-makers' knowledge about emerging innovations and their alternatives and provide a more informed position when scarce resources are going to be prioritized. A Danish feasibility study showed that those requesting early warning information mostly were decision-makers at the regional levels, e.g. hospital managers and staff in the hospital administrations in the counties [13]. Policy-makers' interest was limited, although the sample was too small to make any final conclusion. Another interested target group for early warning information may

---

[200] The FDA *premarket approval* and *premarket notification* system for medical devices [21].

[201] The last source of innovation was called the Inter-intra science path in the chain-linked model presented in chapter 3.

be the health care professionals themselves [14]. However, it should be noticed that professionals, as the potential informants for the system, are rather well-informed and may already know which innovations and developments are to be expected in the health care sector, before the system itself does. Some of their sources of information will be their colleagues and the medical societies. Professionals may therefore not be regarded as a primary target group for early warning information. The industry might also be a potential target group [14]. The information could also be considered relevant for the patients and the population, although it is unlikely that the system and its information specifically will be produced for these broader groups.

3.4 The time horizon

To be able to use the early warning information the decision-makers need the information timely for decision purposes, which means before the emerging technology is adopted. However, the information about the technology is limited at the early stages of development and the available information will be uncertain, especially the effectiveness and cost-effectiveness of the technology in routine practice, as discussed in chapter 7. The implication is then, when deciding upon an optimal time horizon for an early warning system, that a trade-off will be inherent. This is a trade-off between the value of early, although uncertain, information and on the other hand the value of too late, but certain, information.[202] Early uncertain information increases the risk of decision making errors, whereas late and certain information may have limited relevance for decision-makers due to the likely irreversibility of earlier decisions made. Depending upon the system and its purpose, the timing of the early warning can differ. Following the clinical development programme, the focus of the early warning information may be on the early stages of R&D (phase I), which corresponds to at least five years before introduction. Having more definite information, later stages in the clinical development programme (phase II-III) with a time horizon for the system of zero to five years prior to market introduction can also be the focus for an early warning system. Finally, the timing of the information can be even closer to the time of market introduction with a time horizon of zero to two years before introduction. The choice of time horizon for identification, data collection and monitoring will depend on the aim of the system and the type of technology to be identified. A system for early warning which is closely integrated into the HTA activities and used as the initial stage of identification in the HTA process may have a time horizon of zero to two-three years before market introduction.

---

[202] This dilemma of decision making is refered to as Buxton's law, see chapter 7.

4.0 International Experiences with Early Warning

In this section the international experiences with early warning information and early warning systems for emerging health technologies are presented. Special attention is given to existing systems for early warning in the three most experienced countries; Sweden, the Netherlands and the United Kingdom. For each of these systems the purpose, organisation and functioning, sources of information, potential target groups, information disseminated will be described. In addition, early warning activities in other countries and international collaboration on early warning are briefly addressed.

4.1 Early Warning in Sweden

In 1990 a statement underlined the value of early identification of new methods capable of replacing ineffective and expensive clinical routine [23]. This led the Federation of the Swedish County Councils and the National Board of Health and Welfare to an agreement on further investigation of the idea of early warning. A 1991 report, discussing the need for a system, target groups, channels of information, etc., recommended the creation of a national early warning system for emerging health technologies - *New Methods in Medicine* (NMM) - to be tested in a two-year trial period [23]. A few years delayed, this project was started in 1995 with the two organisations mentioned above carrying the overall responsibility [24].

The purpose was to test the utility of an early warning system and its usefulness in early decision making in health care. The elements in the system were *early identification* of emerging technologies[203], *early assessment* about extent and consequences for the quality, economy and structure in the sector, and *early information* to the health care decision-makers [24]. The sources of information used in the system were the special sections of the Swedish Society of Medicine, scientific boards of the National Board of Health and Welfare, the Swedish Council on Technology Assessment in Health Care's (SBU) group of experts, the HTA Committee of the Swedish Medical Research Council and the planning chiefs of the county councils liaison committees and these organisations' national and international contacts.

The target group for the information was the political decision-makers at the highest levels, i.e. health care politicians, directors of the counties, chiefs of the hospital regions' liaison committees, hospital directors, chief medical officers, chiefs of the National Board of Health and Welfare's regional units, and the medical deans [25]. In total 500 decision-makers in Sweden were identified as recipients. The target group received one or two pages information sheets about selected technologies. These sheets included information about: *the method and its knowledge basis, the status for the practical/clinical testing, advantages, safety/risk, costs, sources for additional information,* and contact persons were mentioned. The technical and medical descriptions of the method were dealt with to a

---

[203] Pharmaceuticals were not included in the system.

less extent compared with the assessment part (prognosis), e.g. judgement by experts of the costs and advantages of a new technology. The description of the technology was, however, often enlarged by the later issuing of scientific review articles.

After a dissemination of information sheets about 22 emerging health technologies[204], the project was evaluated externally in 1996 [25]. Overall, the conclusion of the evaluation was positive. Among the types of information in the material issued, the target group regarded information about safety and effectiveness as particularly important. The conclusion of the evaluation of NMM was that the dissemination of information should continue after the testing period and that SBU ought to have the main responsibility of a future system [25]. The implication would then be that the early warning activity was integrated into a formal HTA process. Advisory recommendations in the early warning information were furthermore recommended. In June 1996 the organisations responsible for the trial project advocated for a continuation of the system at SBU.

SBU has therefore in 1997, as a continuation of the NMM project, been charged with developing a national early warning system - *Alert*. As a national warning system the aim of Alert is to improve forecasting and make early assessments of the knowledge base underlying new medical methods [26]. Alert contains the same three elements as in NMM - *early identification, early assessment* and *dissemination of information*.

In the phase of identification, the difficult tasks are the selection of suitable technologies for warning and to make the early assessment timely due to a high number of emerging technologies. A basis for priority-setting must therefore be established [26]. The basic principle in Alert is that the technologies, which are expected to have a major impact upon health services and generate definite changes, should receive priority [27]. This impact concerns both medical, economic, ethical, structural and organisational aspects [28]. However, the interest of the system is not only on large medical breakthroughs, as breakthroughs or controversial methods affecting smaller groups of patients are considered as well. An SBU Alert Advisory Board participates in the selection and priority-setting of methods to be assessed [27]. The technologies selected for Alert should be in the process from clinical research to daily routine practice, used on patients in treatment situations or in research projects.

Due to limitation of data, judging all consequences of emerging technology at an early stage is difficult, especially with regard to economic and organisational consequences. The main principle of Alert is, however, that no collection of primary data for the assessment should take place, for which reason existing, secondary data, documented experiences and general considerations will be used instead [28]. The researchers should not be the only sources of information, because of the risk of *pro-innovation bias*. An important task in the early assessments is to identify potential gaps which can be

---

[204] With *percutaneous transluminal coronary angioplasty in myocardial infarction, teleradiology* and *MRI in small hospitals* as the most popular information sheets.

addressed in future studies [26]. The system and its assessments serve mainly as a complement to the extensive literature review which SBU already conducts.[205]

The major change in Alert compared with NMM happened in the phase of dissemination. In Alert, choosing an Internet database as the method of dissemination, the information is made easily accessible and easy to update when new data arrive [26,27]. The consequence is that the target group for Alert has been widened from decision-makers only, to everyone with an interest in the development, innovation and diffusion of new technologies. Although demanded by the target group in NMM, no concrete recommendations will be provided by Alert about specific technologies to adopt. The fear of transferring the responsibility for technology adoption towards the central authorities in a decentralised Swedish health care sector is a reason [28].

As in NMM, the *target group* for Alert are decision-makers and executives. However, dissemination through the Internet can make the information available to a wider group. Besides Swedish networks, the *sources of information* in Alert are international network of early warning systems, Swedish and international scientific literature and conferences, newspapers and magazines, databases about ongoing trials and meta-analyses, the board of SBU and the Alert Advisory Board, SBU experts and project groups, State-of-the-art documents, drug registrations, and drug and research ethic committees [28].

At present, three methods of treatment have been assessed by Alert; *the ketogenic diet for epilepsy, therapeutic drug monitoring in epilepsy treatment, and thrombolytic therapy in stroke* [27]. The information provided by Alert (4-5 pages) follows the model of a broad and comprehensive HTA. In general, the early assessments include information about the methods and epidemiology (target groups), findings concerning effectiveness, risks, side-effects, cost and cost-effectiveness, consequences for structure and organisation, ethical aspects, diffusion, ongoing research and names of medical experts in the new technology. Another twenty-five methods are now being assessed. In a period of five years Alert is expected to identify 150-200 emerging technologies [28].

4.2 Early Warning in the Netherlands

In the Netherlands, early identification has been a topic from the mid-eighties with the *Steering Group on Future Scenarios for Health Care* (STG) [1]. As a technology forecasting project, the aim of STG was to develop sufficient information on potential future technologies in the health care sector as early as possible having a twenty-year perspective [9]. Simultaneously, the State Secretary of Health of the Netherlands asked in 1984 the central authority *the Health Council* to advise on how to identify relevant developments in health care with the shorter early warning perspective [29]. This led to the recommendation of the establishment of a permanent structure of early

---

[205] A description of SBU and its HTA activities are provided in chapter 2, Appendix 2.2.

identification of emerging health technology at the Health Council [30]. The reasons for the establishment of a permanent early warning system were the increasing technological intensity in the health care sector, as a result of pressure from the industry[206], increased demand from the patients[207], and the lack of data about effectiveness, practice variations and use of certain health technologies. Associated with economic implications in the sector.

The early warning task was integrated within another important activity of the Health Council: to serve as a national advisory board with respect to HTA (see Appendix 2.2). Additional resources by the government to the Health Council intensified this warning system - *system for early identification of emerging health technologies* - in 1992. The purposes of the early warning activity by the Health Council are scanning the sources of information, identification and priority setting of emerging health technologies, as well as dissemination of information about the appearance of selected new technologies in the Dutch health care sector. As an early warning system the time horizon is three to five years before marketing. The *early warnings* made, should contain information on a number of parameters of each identified technology. With this activity incorporated into the Health Council's HTA-activity, the parameters follow, as in Sweden, an HTA model. This means that information about the technology's quality (safety and effectiveness), epidemiological aspects (morbidity and mortality), and health economic, social and ethical aspects are described and judged [31].

One objective of the identification of emerging health technology by the Health Council focuses upon priority-setting of research. The Health Council can suggest new or old technologies to be studied within an HTA research programme, e.g. the Investigational Medicine Fund, or to be addressed in a quality assurance programme [29]. Likewise early warning information plays an important role in policy making, e.g. with respect to Article 18 of the Hospital Provision Act of 1971 and the Population Screening Act. Article 18 enables the Dutch government to regulate the planning of supra-regional, high-technology services in terms of introduction and use in the health care sector [32]. In their Annual Reports the Health Council advises about new technologies possibly qualifying for or removing from Article 18 [33]. Prospective technology assessments, to be undertaken before additional diffusion is allowed, may be recommended under this article. In this context, the early warning information has central importance. However, whether the strategy is timely enough, before widespread diffusion appears, is questionable. A reason is that the Council, after *warning* about an emerging technology, needs to have a request from the Minister to undertake a formal HTA. The success depends also on whether the health service is actually regulated as part of Article 18, which is not the case for many medium-ticket technologies.

The sources of information and methods of data collection for the early warning system are first of all scanning of scientific literature (e.g. Medline). Furthermore, informal

---

[206] Technology push.

[207] Demand pull.

documentation (e.g. conferences), network cooperation in both the Netherlands and internationally, as well as expert judgement from the Health Council's staff or the appointed *Core Group for Early Identification* are used [29]. Previously this task of identification and signalizing was the responsibility of the Council's eight technology assessment advisory boards who consisted of medical specialists from the Dutch health care sector. However, because of lack of success, e.g. due to the specialists' insufficient interest in providing information to the Health Council's early warning activity, the central Core Group was appointed in 1994.[208]

With the location at a central authority the target group for the Dutch early warning activity are primarily policy-makers at the government level, and specifically *the Minister of Health* and Parliament. Other interested parties, when deciding whether new technologies should be introduced and financed in the Dutch health care sector or not, are *the Standing Committee on Investigational Medicine* [32], and *the Sick Fund Council*. Finally, actors on the supply side such as the provinces, the hospitals and the health care professionals, the insurance companies (third party payers), and the industry producing the health technologies have an interest in the information.

The early warning information is disseminated together with the HTA-information through a monthly newsletter issued by the Health Council[209], and through advisory letters, advisory committee reports (HTA reports), Annual Advisory Report on Health Care and arrangement of workshops and symposia. Most of these advisory reports are made on behalf of a request from the Minister of Health.

Among the emerging technologies identified by the Health Council are; *population screening* (1983,1991); *liver, pancreas and lung transplantation* (1984,1985,1990); *laparoscopic cholecystectomy* (1990), *artificial reproduction* (IVF[210] and ICSI[211] (1986,1991,1994,1996)); *surgery in the unborn patient* (1990); and *laser corneal sculpting* (1993) [29].

A recent example of an early warning and monitoring activity made by the Health Council is the case of xenotransplantation.[212] In 1995 xenotransplantation was predicted to become an emerging health technology in the nearest future [31]. In December 1996 an early warning was signalized through the Health Council's newsletter *Network* [34]. A status for the international experiences and trials of this technology and its future perspective was included. In the Netherlands it was, however, recommended that the life-cycle of this technology still was too early and experimental to initiate clinical trials

---

[208] Personal communication with Dr. ten Velden, the Health Council.

[209] Graadmeter or Network (English version).

[210] In vitro fertilization.

[211] Intracytoplasmic sperm injection.

[212] The use of animals as organ donors.

of xenotransplantation including humans. The discussion of ethical and social issues in the use of animals for human transplantation purposes has not started yet either. Nevertheless, the Netherlands, and the United States and Sweden, are interested in further clinical research about xenotransplantation with respect to determining the specific effects of transplantation of bone marrow cells from monkeys to patients with AIDS.

4.3 Early Warning in the United Kingdom

A specific early warning system first arose in the context of the United Kingdom's Health Technology Assessment Programme with the establishment of the Standing Group on Health Technologies (SGHT) in 1993 [35].[213] The purpose of this system was to identify emerging technologies predicted to have an impact on the National Health Service (NHS). In 1995, the Department of Health delegated this task to *the Wessex Institute of Public Health Medicine* at the University of Southampton [36]. As part of the National Co-ordinating Centre for Health Technology Assessment (NCCHTA), the responsibility to establish and run a *Forecasting Secretariat* on behalf of the Department of Health and the SGHT and its panels was commissioned to the Wessex Institute.

The Secretariat should, as a model for an English system for early warning, develop and operate a *horizon scanning activity* for identifying new and emerging technologies as well as existing technologies expanding in use [37]. Furthermore, an approach to select technologies with a significant impact for the NHS in the next five years should be developed. As policy-makers at different levels in the NHS require early warning information of new technologies for different purposes, the aim was to develop and prioritize an HTA research programme, to issue guidance to purchasers and to anticipate change in clinical practice, as well as to estimate future cost and planning implications of health care, e.g. potential diffusion [19,38].

The target group for the early warning information produced by the Forecasting Secretariat were therefore policy- and decision-makers in the NHS, e.g. planners and clinical decision-makers, although the primary recipient was SGHT and its panels. One further task for the Secretariat was to develop an effective method for dissemination.

For a 1995 baseline, the Forecasting Secretariat chose three main strategies to identify new and emerging health technology (horizon scanning) [19]. With these strategies, a number of different sources of information have been used in the identification. The first strategy consisted of a search in written materials such as selected medical, pharmaceutical, and scientific journals, conference abstracts, and formal reporting of phase I-III drug trials [19,35]. In the second strategy experiences and work both in the United Kingdom, e.g. *the Changing Medical Practice Group*, and in international

---

[213] See Appendix 2.2 in chapter 2 for a description of HTA in England.

cooperation, such as *the EUR-ASSESS project, MEMT*[214] and *the Health Council* in the Netherlands, were utilized [19]. Finally, the third strategy for identification of emerging health technology in the United Kingdom was a nationwide postal survey. In 1995, this was sent to all clinical directors representing the clinical specialties and selected individuals in specialized areas identified as particular fast-moving fields [19]. In total 3,500 respondents were invited to participate. The survey requested information about a maximum of five emerging technologies, which the respondents expected could have an impact on the NHS in the next five years. For each technology identified, information about *time frame of impact of the technology* (1996-2001), *size of impact, reason for its impact* (e.g. benefits, costs, rapid diffusion), *extent of research in the technology*, and a name of an expert on each particular technology was collected and included in the database [19].

In total, the three strategies resulted in a database consisting of 1,099 identified technologies, in which 41 per cent were pharmaceuticals, 12 per cent were medical devices and 38 per cent were medical procedures [19]. Among the technologies the survey identified 705, whereas the two other search strategies found the rest.

The five most frequently mentioned emerging health technologies in this horizon scanning activity were magnetic resonance imaging (*major impact in 1996*), minimal invasive surgery (*major impact in 1996*), drugs for the treatment of refractory schizophrenia (*moderate impact in 1996*), implantable vascular stents (*moderate impact in 1996-97*) and peripheral blood stem cells (*major impact in 1996*) [17]. However, as the most frequently mentioned technologies may not necessarily be the technologies with the highest impact for the NHS, the technologies with the highest impact were predicted among all the identified technologies. Three of the identified emerging health technologies expected to have the highest impact for the NHS in the next years were *repair of abdominal aortic aneurysm with transfemoral endovasculate graft, ICSI* and *CT scan advances*. The majority of the technologies identified was expected to have an impact for the NHS in 1996-1997, which means that the focus of the identified material had a *medium term* time perspective (one to three years) [38].

One important addition in 1998 to the NCCHTA's task of identification and priority-setting on behalf of SGHT and the Department of Health is that the horizon scanning, and its database of 1,099 emerging technologies, will be included into the NHS Health Technology Assessment programme [39]. This should allow useful research to be carried out prior to a widespread diffusion of the emerging technology in the NHS. As a further development in 1998 the users of technology can now make suggestions directly for possible assessments to the Internet site of the NCCHTA [40].

The work in the early warning project still considers and evaluates the primary sources of information which are available to identify and predict the impact of emerging health technologies, and to establish an international Delphi-panel. The purpose of this Delphi-panel is to obtain a consensus about the best strategy for identification and forecasting

---

[214] *Monitoring Emerging Health Technologies* - a former European project.

of emerging health technologies. The temporary conclusion from this part of the project indicates that a key word is *flexibility* of the sources of information and the strategy of identification [36]. The best sources vary depending on both the type of technology and the stage in its life cycle, and the different sources often need to be combined.

The early warning system in the United Kingdom is primarily focussed on identification and monitoring of emerging health technologies, and dissemination of information to different users of the system. Due to its close integration into the NHS Health technology Assessment Programme, the early assessment has been limited to initial judgements of the technologies' future impact for the NHS, e.g. the economic burden.

4.4 Other countries and international collaboration

In Canada, CCOHTA has initiated an early warning system (CETAP[215]) in 1997. The purpose is to identify key sources for scanning, prepare information on emerging health technologies and to test different formats of dissemination to a target audience of policy-makers in the provinces in Canada [41]. The key sources for scanning are the Internet and existing sources at CCOHTA [42]. Examples are Internet news sites, e.g. *Reuters Medical News*, newsletters, government & regulatory agency sites and industry association sites. The information prepared contains information on four topics; disease background, current therapy, new technique (effectiveness & adverse effects) and costs (cost of illness & drug costs). So far information (2-4 pages) on three emerging technologies has been disseminated through CCOHTA's *Issues in emerging health technologies*. The first technology identified was the drug therapy *Troglitazone* for type II diabetes, approved by Health Canada for limited use [43]. The second technology, a device, was *endovascular grafts* in abdominal aortic aneurysm [44]. The third technology was antileukotriene agents used as a drug therapy in asthma [45]. The two warnings of drugs have a rather late time horizon. The evaluation of the project was expected in 1998.

In the United States different organisations, e.g. ECRI, the American Hospital Association, the Blue Cross Shield Association and Clinical Practice Alert, are involved in some early identification activities issuing different kinds of newsletters [13,42].

Due to the fact that innovation and technological change are universal, early warning can be regarded as an international task. The possibilities of creating a European system for early warning were investigated in 1995 in the *MEMT* project. A European workshop was held in Copenhagen in 1997 to explore the feasibility of international collaboration [14]. The outcome of the workshop was the establishment of a European expert group on emerging health technology identification - *Euro-Scan* - in 1998 with participants from six European countries and Canada. The aim is to develop links between national systems for early warning in order to share intelligence and experience.

---

[215] CCOHTA Emerging Technologies Program (as a pilot project).

5.0 Models of Early Warning in Denmark

The Danish National Strategy for Health Technology Assessment stated in 1996 that *one of the roles and responsibilities of the central government health organisations is to contribute to the development and establishment of a Danish early warning system for new health technologies and to co-operate with international centres for continued development and operation of such a system* [15]. A system has, however, not yet been established, although Denmark participates in Euro-Scan and a specific proposal for an early warning system has been put forward [46]. The Danish feasibility study revealed that most of the potential users, especially hospital managers and regional authorities, and the potential informants found a system for early warning relevant and desirable in a Danish context [13]. In the National Strategy it is furthermore assumed that the counties and Copenhagen Hospital Corporation, responsible for the Danish hospitals, will participate in a Danish and international early warning system [15]. In the county of Funen thoughts about a regional early warning activity were made in 1995 [11]. No system was established then, but in 1997 a permanent committee for HTA and early warning was appointed in the county of Funen. Considerations about early warning have also taken place in other regions, e.g. at Århus University Hospital.

This section will briefly present and discuss two models for potential systems for early warning in Denmark. Looking at the limited Danish activity, the previously proposed systems and the feasibility study, the primary target group for early warning information in Denmark seems foremost to be the decision- and policy-makers at the regional levels. The proposed systems differ in organisation, aim and focus, e.g. the time horizon of the systems and their relation to the process of HTA.

5.1 An independent system for early warning

The first model for the provision of early warning information is the establishment of an independent system for early warning of emerging health technologies having a time horizon of zero to four years prior to market adoption. This corresponds to previous suggestions for a Danish system and the NMM system in Sweden [24,46].

The tasks of the system will be early identification, early assessment (judgement) and dissemination of information on potential emerging technologies. Due to a time frame of four years the system searching for emerging technologies at the stage of development corresponds to phase II-III of the clinical development programme for pharmaceuticals. However, this may differ for medical devices and procedures, because of a limited regulation with the possibility of earlier adoption. The system should only focus on emerging technologies expected to have an impact on the health care sector. It could be considered to use some of the criteria normally used for the stage of priority-setting in HTA to judge whether an emerging technology has an impact.

The sources of information to be used for identification and judgement may be scientific journals, conferences, networks of specialists, medical societies, different databases (e.g.

registration of the safety of medical devices, patent databases, and databases of ethics committees), press releases and the media [46]. These sources are also quite similar to the sources used in NMM [24]. Advisory boards of specialists can be appointed for the identification part. Their role and incentives need, however, to be evaluated initially considering both the experiences of the Dutch Health Council and the limited interest of potential Danish informants to provide information for an early warning system as demonstrated in the feasibility study [13]. Due to the status as an independent system for identification and signalizing, the early assessments carried out will provide judgements about the emerging technology on a number of parameters such as relevant population, safety and effectiveness, and investment needed. With the provided information, the dissemination from the system will be in the form of short data sheets distributed to the main target group; decision-makers at the national and regional levels.

The information disseminated from the system could follow an HTA model with information of the emerging technology based on preliminary data about safety, its use, efficacy or effectiveness, costs, potential cost-effectiveness, potential time frame for introduction and diffusion, as well as ethical, legal and social implications. Information on these issues ought to be considered in relation to an existing alternative if present. Most frequently it is expected that clinical and economic information about the emerging technology will be disseminated. However, the choice of parameters to inform about will depend on the technology in question. For some technologies information on other parameters instead of clinical effect and costs will be very important as is the case with the report from the Health Council concerning genetic screening for hereditary disorders focusing on psychological, legal, ethical and social considerations [47].

The development and transfer of technologies are international. A system for early warning ought therefore to be established at the national level, although the regional nature of the Danish health care sector should be kept in mind. In the feasibility study, the potential users of the information showed only interest in a national system [13]. Regional activities are, nevertheless, expected to support a system. In addition, the involvement of the medical societies might stimulate the system.

With this organisation of the system, no formal HTA is expected to be initiated because the system is not directly part of an HTA programme. Other actors can initiate technology assessments. However, the risk of an independent early warning activity is that a systematic and ongoing HTA process does not automatically follow the provision of information about the identified emerging technologies. In Sweden the evaluation of the effect of the independent Swedish system (NMM) showed likewise a great wish for an integration and close connection between the early warning activity and the national HTA programme with SBU as the responsible organisation of a future system [25]. This resulted in the creation of Alert within SBU, as described in section 4.1.

5.2 Early warning as part of a technology assessment programme

The highest rate of success and use of early warning information are expected in a model where the system for early warning is integrated into an existing technology assessment programme. Having early warning as an integrated part of a systematic approach to a prospective technology assessment programme will identify emerging technologies needing assessment and set priorities among these candidates for assessment, enhance primary data collection and synthesis efforts and disseminate the results of the technology assessment [1]. This is the way the most experienced countries have organised their early warning systems today. Furthermore, the time horizon suggested for this system is narrower than in the first model. The early warnings ought to focus on emerging technologies expected to be adopted in the market within two years. A primary reason for this choice is the results from the feasibility study. The study revealed that the potential users of early warning information, i.e. decision-makers, had the highest need for knowledge about emerging health technologies within two years before they had to make a decision related to health policy or planning [13]. The reliability and usefulness of the information obtained having this time frame are also expected to be higher.

The focus of this model for early warning will then constitute part of the first step in an HTA - the phase of identification. The aim of this phase is the identification of technologies possible for assessment [48]. As a proactive HTA activity the focus using the early warning information will be on identification of emerging health technologies - early identification.[216] The next phase, when the early warning information has been used for identification, will be the phase of priority setting, where the technologies, both emerging and existing, with the expected highest impact will be selected for assessment. The phase of priority-setting is important because further monitoring and assessment of technologies showing not to be important will be a waste of scarce resources available for assessment. The aim of identifying priorities is therefore to maximize the benefit from HTA [48]. If prioritized, an early assessment of emerging technology can then be undertaken within the prospective and iterative assessment approach described in chapter 7.

The sources of information will be the same as in the last model, although less uncertain due to the later stage in the life cycle of the emerging technology. For the same reason, initial clinical trials might now be ongoing and will provide important information for early warning. If available, the early identification and the early assessment, e.g. assessing economic parameters, could use the primary data from these early trials. Significant or pivotal parameters where information is missing or uncertain should be highlighted and investigated further in additional trials. Information on whether a trial involving human beings is ongoing may be registered by databases of the ethics committees. Expert opinions will still be needed in this *late* model, especially to judge

---

[216] Existing technologies showing reactively a potential for assessment will, however, not be covered by a system for early warning in the phase of identification. These technologies must be identified by other means and sources, such as programmes for quality assurance.

the consequences of the use of technology in routine practice setting, which is not addressed in the early clinical trials, focusing upon efficacy.

This model of early warning integrated into a prospective process of HTA reminds of the organisation of early identification (early warning) by the Health Council in the Netherlands. The objectives of the early identification activities by the Health Council are to conduct early warning, to control the introduction of new technologies, promote prospective technology assessment (and eventually reassessment), and for the technologies selected not allow wider diffusion before the merits of the technology has been proven [31]. Then early warning will become an integrated part of the HTA process. Keeping these Dutch experiences in mind as well as the decentralised structure of health services in Denmark, the highest impact of early warning upon policy making may be expected from a future system for early warning organized within an existing HTA programme with the specific aim of conducting early identification. The drawback of the integrated system for early warning might be that its focus primarily will be on emerging technologies identified for assessment, and not just on technologies identified with the purpose of signalizing the information concerning their future arrival to the decision-makers and the health care sector.

6.0 Discussion

Due to a rapidly growing technological intensity and scarce resources available in the health care sector it appears that there is a need for improving the information available for the decision- and policy-makers about new and emerging health technologies to be expected in the sector. This chapter described the idea behind *systems for early warning of emerging health technologies* which integrated into a prospective process of health technology assessment might be a way of improving the information available for decision making. In Denmark, the establishment of a system for early warning is part of the National Strategy for Health Technology Assessment issued by the National Board of Health [15]. Today, this strategy is the responsibility of the Danish Institute for Health Technology Assessment. However, although suggestions for a Danish system have been put forward [46], a system for early warning is not established yet. Based upon experiences in other countries, this chapter has presented two models for a potential early warning system in Denmark.

In the chapter a distinction was made between *technology forecasting activities* and *systems for early warning* due to the fact that they differ with respect to some important aspects. Technology forecasting is an activity oriented towards the future having a long-term perspective of ten to twenty years, such as the Dutch STG-project [9]. A technology forecasting activity cannot make specific and precise answers with respect to future technologies, but will only give ideas about what may happen as well as opportunities for influencing the future. Because of the long-term perspective technology forecasts search for *possible futures*, which might happen if the scientific findings go in certain directions when entered in a development process. However, there is no guarantee that the scenarios made actually will be fulfilled. This is different with systems for early warning as they operate with a short-term perspective (zero to five years), which means that the specific technology is identified and monitored while it is developing, but still before it reaches the market. The system for early warning then searches for the *probable futures* that will happen within the short-term perspective of the system. Early warning then deals with predictions of how the future *will* be, whereas technology forecasting deals with how the future *might* be. This different time horizon between the two concepts will naturally imply different degrees of certainty from their information with early warning information as the least uncertain. The methods used by the two frameworks differ also. Technology forecast uses methods from future research such as scenario techniques, whereas early warning due to its later stage in the life cycle of technology uses more quantitative methods with information from literature, databases, etc. Finally, a difference between the two concepts appears with respect to their organisation. Technology forecasts are often *one-shot* activities carried out only once or in a short period of time opposed to early warning incorporated in a continuos system approach, e.g. in an HTA programme. These differences must be kept in mind, when designing an early warning system or discussing the success of a system. The focus in this chapter has been on systems for early warning.

In general, the tasks of a system for early warning will be to perform early identification and early assessment of emerging health technology with a potential impact for the health care sector in the short-term perspective, as well as to disseminate the information to the relevant target group. In Denmark, due to a decentralized health care sector, the target group for this kind of information seems first of all to be decision-makers at the regional level, such as regional health planners, hospital managers and staff in the hospital administrations [13]. For professionals the likely benefit of the information might be regarded as low because of their role as experts and therefore potential informants for a system.

Due to uncertainty early in the life cycle of technology the decision making dilemma described in chapter 7 may be involved in provision of early warning information. The uncertainty may also be present two years before an expected adoption because no one knows at this stage, how the technology will be used in routine practice. A trade-off exists between early and uncertain information compared to late but certain information. In the first situation the information may be too uncertain leading to decision errors, whereas the last situation may be too late for the decision-maker to react before diffusion. The time horizon of the system has to be chosen in a way that optimizes the reliability of the information as well as the ability to react timely.

Among the two models for a Danish system for early warning, the model most advocated for is the system for early warning integrated into a prospective national HTA programme focusing upon the identification of emerging health technologies from zero to two years before marketing. This time horizon is chosen, because the Danish feasibility study revealed that this is the period in which the decision-makers have the highest need for information [13]. Furthermore, information at this late stage in the development process will have a high reliability. The integration of early warning into the HTA process is identical to the organisation of the systems for early warning in the

Netherlands, Sweden and the United Kingdom. An integration which secures the continuity and use of the information. The early warning system suggested forms part of the identification phase in the prospective HTA programme focusing upon emerging and new technologies. The early technology assessments carried out among the emerging technologies prioritized for HTA can then be undertaken in the iterative and ongoing approach being updated by new clinical trial information, as presented in chapter 7.

Besides the distinction between systems for early warning and technology forecasting activities and the dilemma in decision making, other important issues are also related to early warning information and its use.

A central issue that is relevant to discuss when advocating for an early warning system is whether the development of emerging health technology follows fixed patterns like the unidirectional processes of scientific-push and demand-pull presented in chapter 3. Or is this development process a more complex process of both pushes and pulls as well as feedback and iterations as in *the chain-linked model*? If development of technology does not follow the deterministic unidirectional processes, but instead an iterative model, it will have implications for the success of an early warning system to be able to identify emerging technologies. This may differ with respect to the type of technology, where scientific-pushes mostly may characterize pharmaceuticals, opposed to devices and procedures which are expected to result from more iterative processes.

Another central issue relates to the decision making process in the health care sector with respect to technology adoption. Which actors make the decisions with regard to adoption and diffusion of technologies in the health care sector? And what are the reasons behind the decisions made? The target group for the information from a system for early warning is policy- and decision-makers. However, many technologies used in the health care sector have been introduced by the professionals themselves, e.g. the laparoscopic technologies. To investigate the roles of different actors upon the decision making process concerning technology adoption and the factors influencing this process, further research needs to be carried out. The design of a system for early warning and the task of identification, i.e. which factors to look for, will benefit from this knowledge. Some of this information can be obtained from diffusion research and empirical studies about selected health technologies.

Considering the case of laparoscopic cholecystectomy, the factors found to influence the diffusion of this technology in Denmark (see chapter 5) may be relevant for early warning activities with respect to other medium-ticket technologies with the same characteristics of an apparently promising technology. The factor analysis performed in the study found *communication* to be the foremost important factor for the adoption of laparoscopic cholecystectomy in Denmark [49]. Using this knowledge in a future early warning activity has the consequence that an early warning system, in an attempt to identify and control diffusion, should effectively use channels of communication, such as opinion leaders, the media, conferences, medical societies, etc. Other factors were, however, also identified as important - *the technology* (e.g. whether it provides extra health benefit), *the economy* (e.g. the budget for operation) and *the surrounding environment* (e.g. size of the adopting hospital and its degree of specialization) [49]. It is likely that these factors must be identified as well to make an early warning strategy of medium-ticket technologies effective. This example illustrates that prospective early warning of emerging health technologies is not an easy and simple task. Therefore, the decision making processes of technology adoption in a decentralized Danish health care sector need further investigation.

Finally, international cooperation and investigation with respect to the tasks of early warning and prospective technology assessment are warranted due to the international diffusion of most health technologies.

References

1. Banta HD, Gelijns AC. The future and health care technology: Implications of a system for early identification. World Health Statistics Quaterly 1994;47(3-4):140-9.

2. Gelijns AC, Rosenberg N. From the Scalpel to the Scope: Endoscopic Innovations in Gastroenterology, Gynecology, and Surgery. Chapter 4 in Rosenberg N, Gelijns AC, Dawkins H (ed.). Sources of Medical Technology: Universities and Industry. Medical Innovation at the Crossroad. Volume V. Committee on Technological Innovation in Medicine. Institute of Medicine. National Academy Press. Washington, D.C. 1995.

3. Schersten T. Virtual Reality in Surgery. Abstract. European Workshop: Scanning the Horizon for Emerging Health Technologies. Copenhagen. 12-13 September 1997.

4. Asch DA, Hershey JC, Pauly MV, Patton JP, Jedrziewski MK, Mennuti MT. Genetic Screening for Reproductive Planning: Methodological and Conceptual Issues in Policy Analysis. American Journal of Public Health 1996;86(5):684-690.

5. Newhouse JP. Medical care costs: how much welfare loss? Journal of Economic Perspectives 1992;6(3):3-21.

6. Banta HD, Luce BR. Health Care Technology and its Assessment. An International Perspective. Oxford University Press, Oxford, 1993.

7. Duffy G. A UN Early Warning System: What Should It Be? Prepared for The Mershon International Studies Quaterly 1995;Feb:6 pages. Http://www.ccst.uiuc.edu/people/gmk/projects/uncmcw/documents/earlywrng.

8. Schousboe K. Early Warning Systems - eller hvorfor det er væsentligt at vide, når de "andre" flytter på sig. Netværk;8-10.

9. Banta HD, Gelijns A. Aniticipating and Assessing Health Care Technology. Volume 1. General Considerations and Policy Conclusions. A report commissioned by the Steering Committee on Future Health Scenarios. Martinus Nijhoff Publishers, Dordrecht, 1987.

10. Rowe G, Wright G, Bolger F. Delphi. A Reevaluation of Research and Theory. Technological Forecasting and Social Change 1991;39:235-251.

11. Fyns Amt. Rapporter fra Varslingsudvalget. Rapport 1. SygehusProjektgruppen, Fyns Amt, Juni1995.

12. Piene H. Kan vår medisinsk-teknologiske fremtid forutsees? HMT 1994;13(5):14-16.

13. Jørgensen T, Larsen LG, Poulsen PB. Tidlig varsling af kommende medicinske teknologier - et dansk forstudie. DSI - Institut for Sundhedsvæsen. DSI - rapport, 1997.

14. Carlsson P, Jørgensen T (eds.). European Workshop: Scanning the Horizon for Emerging Health Technologies. Copenhagen. 12-13 September 1997.

15. The Danish National Board of Health, the Health Technology Assessment Committee. National Strategy for Health Technology Assessment. Copenhagen, 1996.

16. Donaldson MS, Sox HC. Setting priorities for health technology assessment. A model process. Committee on Priorities for Assessment and Reassessment of Health Care Technologies. Institute of Medicine. National Academy Press, Washington, D.C., 1992.

17. Warner KE. A "Desparation-Reaction" Model of Medical Diffusion. Health Services Research 1975;Winter:369-383.

18. Sculpher M, Drummond M, Buxton M. The iterative use of economic evaluation as part of the process of health technology assessment. Journal of Health Services Research and Policy 1997;1:26-30.

19. Steven A, Robert G, Gabbay J. Identifying new health care technologies in the United Kingdom. International Journal of Technology Assessment in Health Care 1997;13(1):59-67.

20. Spiby J. Advances in medical technology over the next 20 years. Community Medicine 1988;10(4):273-278.

21. Littell CL. Innovation in Medical Technology: Reading the Indicators: Datawatch. Health Affairs Millwood 1994;13(3):226-235.

22. Gelijns AC. Appendix A. Comparing the Development of Drugs, Devices, and Clinical Procedures. In Gelijns AC. Modern Methods of Clinical Investigation. Medical Innovation at the Crossroad. Volume I. Committee on Technological Innovation in Medicine. Institute of Medicine. National Academy Press, Washington, D.C., 1990.

23. Midunger T, Karlberg I. Förslag till system för indetifiering och bedömning av nya medicinska metoder, NMM. Socialstyrelsen. Oktober 1991.

24. NNM-info. "Startpaket". Vänersborg, april 1995 (Utvecklingsprojektet "Nya Medicinska Metoder", projektleder Henric Hultin).

25. Socialstyrelsen. Nya Medicinska Metoder (NMM). Et försök att utveckla en modell för tidig identifiering, information och bedömning av nya medicinska metoder. Projektrapport och Utvärderingsrapport. Ett projekt av Socialstyrelsen och Landstingsförbundet. Stockholm 1996.

26. SBU. SBU Alert. A New Project at SBU. A System for Identification and Early Assessment of New Technologies in Health Care. SBU Information Sheet, Stockholm, 1998.

27. SBU ALERT home page on the Internet. http://alert.sbu.se. 1998.

28. Carlsson P. ALERT. Et nationellt system för identifiering, information och tidig bedömning av nya medicinska metoder. Projektplan SBU. På uppdrag av Styrgruppen för Hälso- och sjukvärdsfrågor för redovisning den 19 februari 1997.

29. ten Velden G. Identification of new health care technologies by the Health Council of the Netherlands. Abstract. European Workshop: Scanning the horizon for emerging health technologies. Copenhagen. 12-13 September 1997.

30. Gelijns AC, Rigter H. Health care technology assessment in the Netherlands. International Journal of Technology Assessment in Health Care 1990;6:157-174.

31. ten Velden G. Early Identification by the Health Council of The Netherlands. Paper presented for the international MEMT-group, Danish Hospital Institute, Copenhagen, January 17, 1995.

32. Bos M. Health care technology in the Netherlands. Health Policy 1994;30:207-255.

33. Rigter H. Assessment of health care technology in the Netherlands. Chapter 19 in Banta HD, Luce BR. Health Care Technology and its Assessment. An International Perspective. Oxford University Press, Oxford, 1993.

34. Health Council. Network. December 1996.

35. Stevens A, Robert G. Early Warning of New Health Care Technologies in the United Kingdom. Abstract. European Workshop: Scanning the horizon for emerging health technologies. Copenhagen. 12-13 September 1997.

36. Robert G, Stevens A, Gabbay J, Milne R. Primary information sources for identifying, and predicting the impact, of new medical technologies (NMTs). Conference Abstract in the Book of Abstracts from the conference in the *International Society for Technology Assessment in Health Care*, held in Barcelona 25th-28th May 1997.

37. Forecasting Secretariat. Summary Report of the Forecasting Secretariat to the National Standing Group on Health Technology. Wessex Institute of Public Health Medicine (IPH). University of Southampton, November 1995.

38. Smee C. The Need for Early Warning in Health Policy Making and Planning. Abstract. European Workshop: Scanning the horizon for emerging health technologies. Copenhagen. 12-13 September 1997.

39. NHS Executive. The Annual Report of the NHS Health Technology Assessment Programme 1997. Identifying Questions, Finding Answers. The National Coordinating Centre for Health Technology Assessment. Department of Health. September 1997.

40. http://www.soton.ac.uk/~hta/form.htm

41. Canadian Coordinating Office for Health Technology Assessment. Update. New and emerging health technologies: an early warning system. Newsletter of CCOHTA. Issue 29, Summer/Fall 1997.

42. Canadian Coordinating Office for Health Technology Assessment. A preliminary list of information sources for emerging health technologies. Prepared for the European Workshop on Scanning the Horizon for Emerging Medical Technologies, Copenhagen, September 12-13, 1997.

43. Canadian Coordinating Office for Health Technology Assessment. Troglitazone for Type II Diabetes. Issues in emerging health technologies. Issue 1. October 1997 (revised Jan. 1998). http://www.ccohta.ca/research/ews/index.html

44. Canadian Coordinating Office for Health Technology Assessment. Abdominal Aortic Aneurysm: Endovascular grafts offer a potential alternative to surgery. Issues in emerging health technologies. Issue 2. January 1998. http://www.ccohta.ca/research/ews/index.html

45. Canadian Coordinating Office for Health Technology Assessment. Antileukotrienes: An emerging generation of drug therapies for asthma. Issues in emerging health technologies. Issue 3. April 1998. http://www.ccohta.ca/research/ews/index.html

46. Poulsen PB, Hørder M, Jørgensen T. Fremtidens Medicinske Metoder - tidlig varsling i international og dansk perspektiv. Sundhedsstyrelsens Udvalg for Medicinsk Teknologivurdering. Sundhedsstyrelsen, København, 1996.

47. Health Council of the Netherlands: Committee on Genetic Screening. Genetic Screening. The Hague: Health Council of the Netherlands, 1994; publication no. 1994/22E.

48. Henshall C, Oortwijn W, Stevens A, Granados A, Banta D. Priority setting for health technology assessment. Theoretical considerations and practical approaches. A paper produced by the Priority Setting Subgroup of the EUR-ASSESS Project. International Journal of Technology Assessment in Health Care 1997;13(2):144-185.

49. Poulsen PB, Adamsen S, Vondeling H, Jørgensen T. Diffusion of laparoscopic technologies in Denmark. Health Policy 1998;45(2):149-167.

Chapter 9

Concluding Remarks
- policy recommendations and future research

Concluding remarks

Health technology assessment takes a broad view of technology and of technological change and carries out analyses of such issues from a number of perspectives [1]. The present book has taken this broad view due to the fact that the focus in particular has been on the concept of health technology assessment and its definition as well as on the processes of innovation and diffusion of health technology. As a thesis, the original contributions to knowledge have been the conduct of new empirical studies, transfers of theory to the field of health technology, as well as literature reviews of theoretical and methodological issues. In this last chapter the main issues and conclusions from the studies presented are summarized as concluding remarks. On the basis of the research findings some policy recommendations for the field of HTA and technology diffusion are put forward. Finally, suggestions for further research topics in the areas dealt with are presented.

Although the broad and comprehensive definition of technology assessment[217] was introduced in the health care sector as early as 1975 by Office of Technology Assessment (OTA) in the United States and has been adopted in most countries, e.g. in Denmark, there still seem to be differences of opinion with respect to its definition and its practical use. In chapter 2, the *International Comparative Study of Health Technology Assessment* presented evidence on this subject. Comparing the actual use of the concept of HTA in 124 HTA projects from five national HTA-institutions showed that HTA had a more partial, and thereby less comprehensive, interpretation when used in practice. Supporting the tendency in the HTA literature, the empirical study showed that the HTA projects most often included information about clinical parameters (e.g. effectiveness and safety) and economic parameters (e.g. costs and cost-effectiveness). Less frequently information about issues such as, e.g. ethics, diffusion and training were included. The study revealed that only 14 per cent of the HTAs could be characterised as broad and comprehensive technology assessments with information related to clinical, economic, patient and organisational issues. Often the HTAs were more partial in their form, e.g. as cost-effectiveness analyses or randomized controlled trials (RCT). Among the institutions compared, SBU in Sweden produced the most comprehensive

---

[217] *As a comprehensive form of policy research that examines the short- and long-term social consequences of the application or use of technology* [2].

technology assessments. The use of existing methods in the health care sector, e.g. RCT, the involvement of different actors from different fields, as well as differences in the technologies assessed may explain a more partial approach to HTA. However, the most important explanation for the different use of technology assessment is guided by the specific decision making context and the policy purpose of HTA [1]. Finally, the study underlined that the most frequent method used in HTA was a literature review of existing scientific findings due to the fact that HTA less frequently involved the conduct of primary research.

Chapters 3-8 in the book focused on the earlier stages in the life cycle of health technology - the processes of innovation and diffusion. Economic models described the process of innovation. This is a complex and iterative process which most likely consists of a mix of pushes from science and technical abilities and demand pulls from users as well as learning effects (learning in the R&D process, learning by doing and learning by using). These elements were included in *the Chain-Linked Model of Innovation* presented in chapter 3. Next after the process of innovation is the process of diffusion, in which the potential users in the market adopt the innovation (chapter 4). Models based on economic- and sociological theories dominates. In the economic models diffusion is regarded as a phenomenon guided by supply and demand in the market with focus upon economic factors explaining diffusion, e.g. profitability. In the sociological models channels of communication and characteristics of the specific adopter, e.g. social status, have had central importance in explaining diffusion. However, many empirical studies on diffusion have not been performed in order to test a specific theory, but rather have had exploratory purposes.

This was also the purpose of presenting *the laparoscopic technologies in general surgery* as a case in the book, especially in chapters 3, 5 and 6. The development of the laparoscopic technology has emerged from fields such as gastroenterology, gynaecology and orthopaedic surgery. The technology was transferred to general surgery with an application in treating appendicitis, although it was first in 1986 with the use in cholecystectomy that the laparoscopic technology got its breakthrough in general surgery. The transfer of this minimally invasive therapy to the field of general surgery can be characterised as a *scientific push*. After the transfer to cholecystectomy the development in laparoscopes was characterised by *demand pull* effects, e.g. innovation in application instruments and a demand for cost-effective technologies due to competition from other specialties. The consequence was that adoption and rapid diffusion of laparoscopic cholecystectomy followed in most industrialized countries in the late 1980s and the early 1990s. This uncontrolled and rapid diffusion of laparoscopic cholecystectomy took place without evidence from larger trials documenting effectiveness, safety and cost-effectiveness.

Laparoscopic cholecystectomy was first adopted in Denmark in 1991 and fully adopted within 4½ years, except for Greenland (chapter 5). Some factors which showed to have stimulated the surgeons' decision to adopt the technology in Denmark were the size of the hospital, the nature of the technology (minimally invasive), the facility of training courses, the competition between specialties and between hospitals, and attention from the media. Only a few economic factors were impeding. The laparoscopic technology was applied in other areas of general surgery; 1) in appendectomy, 2) in surgery for colon cancer, 3) in surgery for inguinal hernia and 4) in fundoplication. However, in none of these cases the same rapid and uncontrolled diffusion has been experienced.

Comparing with the Netherlands the pattern of diffusion of laparoscopic cholecystectomy was quite similar in both countries, although the adoption in Denmark had a time-lag of 11 months (chapter 6). The same pattern of diffusion also appeared in the United States, Canada and Australia. It was only in Denmark that increased hospital size showed to be associated with an earlier adoption of laparoscopic cholecystectomy. In the Netherlands other factors than the three hospital characteristics considered seem to explain diffusion of laparoscopic cholecystectomy.

After a period of rapid and uncontrolled diffusion of laparoscopic cholecystectomy, increased interest towards scientific documentation of the procedures expected benefits seems to appear in the surgical field. The consensus conference held in Denmark in 1997 illustrates this [3].

As an iterative and ongoing approach during diffusion economic evaluation has different objectives at different stages in the life cycle of health technology as described in chapter 7. In the early stages, in which limited clinical evidence is available (phase I & II), the economic evaluation has two objectives; 1) to ensure that the resources devoted to additional information acquisition are used efficiently (further R&D and HTA), and 2) to inform decision-makers in early adoption decisions, e.g. as part of a system for early warning. In an iterative and prospective HTA process these early assessments are relevant to inform and highlight uncertain pivotal estimates to be investigated in later assessments. Later in the life cycle (phase III) the clinical information will typically be in the form of RCTs. The economic evaluation can then be incorporated or at least be undertaken alongside the RCT with a prospective collection of data on resource utilization and clinical efficacy. The final objective for economic evaluation during diffusion is reassessment, when widespread diffusion has appeared (phase IV). The need for reassessment appears when the previous assessment carried out in controlled settings in phase III (focusing on internal validity) differs from the use of technology in routine practice settings (focusing on external validity).

To improve planning and priority-setting of potentially emerging technologies in the early stages of the life cycle, *systems for early warning* has been suggested (chapter 8). The tasks of these systems are early identification, early assessment and early dissemination of information about potential emerging technologies with an expected impact on the health care sector. Decision-makers are the primary target group for the information. A system integrated into a prospective HTA programme with a time horizon between zero and two years is expected to have the highest reliability and usefulness of information. The role of early warning will then be to function as the stage of early identification in the HTA process. A central issue in early warning is to find the relevant factors to be able to identify emerging technology. Identifying laparoscopic cholecystectomy, learning retrospectively, would have required searching the channels of communication, due to the fact that they showed to be the most important for adoption in Denmark.

Policy recommendations

As stated in the introductory chapter research findings and experience, when relevant, ought to influence policy. Furthermore, research in the field of HTA can be characterized as applied research, where many findings may have direct implications for decision making. This book presents therefore a number of potential policy recommendations.

A modified definition of health technology assessment

Supported by the evidence from the *International Comparison of Health Technology Assessment* presented in chapter 2, a new modified definition of health technology assessment in Denmark and internationally is recommended. Because technology assessment is conducted for policy reasons[218], a definition of HTA ought to start with a purpose of policy making [4]. The policy purpose is important due to the fact that it separates technology assessment from research carried out for scientific purposes. HTA is not research for knowledge sake [1]. At the same time, the *comprehensiveness* of HTA should be recognized. The multidisciplinary nature of HTA will often result in comprehensive assessments. However, used for policy purposes the degree of comprehensiveness will be decided by the policy question stated. This means that an HTA should only be as comprehensive as the policy purpose requires it to be. Given by its intent [1]. A suggestion for a new modified definition of health technology assessment may then be;

> Defined by its **policy purpose** a health technology assessment is a **comprehensive** assessment of a number of parameters related to health technologies and their use in the health care sector.

When choosing parameters for assessment a trade-off may exists between the policy purpose and the comprehensiveness. Some potential parameters of the technology to assess could be; *effectiveness and safety; indications for use; costs and cost-effectiveness; social, legal and ethical issues; diffusion and utilization; skills and training*. Other parameters are

---

[218] Technology assessment made for clinical decision making, e.g. the establishment of clinical guidelines, is in this context also regarded as a policy purpose.

relevant as well.[219] Again, however, the number of parameters to be assessed depends upon the policy question stated.[220]

The definition will now also cover less comprehensive assessments such as cost-effectiveness analyses, if they are carried out for policy reasons and the policy question stated only requires the study of cost-effectiveness. At the same time, the broad and comprehensive HTA demanded for policy reasons as well will still be entailed. Using the modified definition, the initial considerations of which parameters to assess will also bring focus upon the step of specifying the assessment problem and the step of synthesising the evidence [4]. It is important that both the reasons for including parameters as well as the reasons for excluding parameters from the assessment are made explicit. Furthermore, by introducing a *policy purpose*, the Danish definition will be closer to the original definition stated by Office of Technology Assessment in the United States in 1975 [2]. Finally, it will probably be more efficient only to conduct broad and comprehensive assessments, when needed for policy reasons, because the production of HTA, especially broad and comprehensive, is expensive and takes a long time [5,6].[221] It must at least be remembered that opportunity costs are involved in the funding of technology assessment.

Diffusion of medium-ticket technologies

The laparoscopic technologies studied represent the group of medium-ticket technologies. Laparoscopic cholecystectomy in particular showed a rapid and widespread diffusion in Denmark. In the future some control and guidance of the diffusion of similar medium-ticket technologies may be necessary to ensure the use of effective and cost-effective technologies, before obtaining a 100 per cent adoption.

Recently it was argued that to be able to control health technologies, Denmark should learn from experiences in the Netherlands, where a centralized system for planning and regulation of the introduction of selected health technologies is based on evidence from HTA.[222] However, chapter 6 showed that diffusion of laparoscopic cholecystectomy in the Netherlands was earlier and quicker compared to Denmark. No regulation was

---

[219] See chapter 2, Table 2.2 for other parameters

[220] The four main elements assessed in HTA according to the Danish definition (technology, economy, patient and organisation) are left-out from a new modified definition for two reasons. *First*, the selection of the four main elements seems arbitrary and the elements are not mutually exclusive. *Secondly*, these elements are only used in Denmark. Abroad, e.g. at HTA-institutions, a list of potential parameters to be assessed are shown instead.

[221] In 1972, Coates found that the average costs of comprehensive technology assessment (not HTA) was US$ 381,000 with an average elapse time of 16 months [2].

[222] The National Board of Health's Annual Meeting 1998 for Health Technology Assessment and Quality Asurance. Copenhagen 27 April 1998.

present. The reason is that Article 18 of the Hospital Provision Act in the Netherlands relates specifically to the planning of supra-regional, high-technology services, e.g. cardiac surgery and computed tomography.[223] Medical devices, e.g. medium-ticket technologies such as laparoscopes, are poorly regulated in the Netherlands [7]. The problem of an uncontrolled diffusion of medium-ticket technologies in Denmark is not solved then by adopting the Dutch system with respect to Article 18.

The Investigational Medicine Fund in the Netherlands, who funds research projects with the aim of deciding whether technologies should be reimbursed under the insurance system or not, might result in some control of medium-ticket technologies. Technologies enrolled in these projects carried out at university hospitals may in an HTA approach be investigated prospectively in RCTs for efficacy, cost-effectiveness, etc. [7]. The system is, however, not a compulsory system and it only includes a minor share of the technologies in the Dutch health care sector.

The Dutch experience with the Investigational Medicine Fund and the findings in chapters 5-6 lead to a policy recommendation for Denmark with respect to the control of the diffusion of medium-ticket technologies. As a kind of top-down mechanism, the national health authorities could in cooperation with the counties stimulate[224] the larger Danish hospitals, as early adopters, to introduce new technologies similar to laparoscopic cholecystectomy in a trial phase within assessment protocols. The hospital selected for the trial period may be chosen through negotiation between the counties and the national health authorities as it happens today with respect to the planning of specialties among Danish hospitals. A system for early warning performing the early identification task may be used to identify the technologies expected to have an impact on the health care sector. Widespread diffusion in the health care sector should then only take place after presenting an evaluation with a positive result.

A complementary bottom-up mechanism for controlled diffusion is to influence professionals, e.g. surgeons, to use HTA information in their adoption decisions. The professionals represent the central decision-makers in the adoption of medium-ticket technologies. Global budgets at the hospital- and department levels have the consequence that a high degree of autonomy is involved in the decisions concerning medium-ticket technology. The medical societies are very important when convincing the professionals to use evidence from HTA in their decisions regarding adoption. At later stages of diffusion the medical societies are needed for the implementation of additional policies about clinical guidelines, training programmes and quality assurance. These policies can be necessary in surgery to maintain a high learning curve.
    Generally, the transfer of findings from diffusion research into recommendations for health care policy has to be improved.

---

[223] As well as the Population Screening Act concerns screening programmes.

[224] E.g. by financial incentives.

System for early warning

A potential source of information about emerging technologies warranting assessment in a controlled diffusion approach may be a system for early warning. Simultaneously, the asymmetry of information between professionals and policy-makers in health care decision making is recognized. To ensure that the early warning information produced will be used, it is recommended that a system for early warning is integrated into a prospective national HTA programme with a time horizon of zero to two years before marketing. This is similar to arrangements in other countries. The major role of the system will be to function as the early identification phase of emerging technologies in the HTA process. Finally, due to the fact that the market entry of pharmaceuticals is regulated, it may be considered to focus only upon medical devices and procedures.

Economic evaluation and decision making

As discussed both by Drummond (1987) and by Johannesson (1995), the lack of a clear link between economic evaluation (and HTA in general) and decision making represents an important problem [8,9]. In decision making the timing of assessment is important. Because a trade-off exists between (uncertain) early information and reliable (late) information, this book advocates for an iterative and continuous conduct of economic evaluation during diffusion. In order to avoid decision errors, the result of an early economic evaluation can inform and can be updated by economic evaluations with more reliable information in later stages of diffusion. However, this strategy relies on whether decisions in the health care sector are reversible or not. In general, the expected value of additional information from further economic evaluations has to be weighted against the risk of making decision errors.

At present, the focus of economic evaluation in decision making is, unfortunately, not on the full process of diffusion of health technologies. The major interest of economic evaluation in decision making, as illustrated by the pharmacoeconomic guidelines presented in a number of countries, e.g. recently in Denmark [10], appears to be on reimbursement decisions with respect to pharmaceuticals in phase III. However, the guidelines made for policy purposes ought to include thoughts about the issue of timing, and the early and iterative uses of economic evaluation during diffusion. Today, these issues seem only to be included in the Canadian guidelines.

Further research

Working with the research projects has identified areas in which further research may be beneficial for the broad field of HTA and diffusion. These research topics for the future are presented below.

To provide a more thorough picture of the parameters assessed in HTA the database used in the international study presented in chapter 2 should be enlarged with additional HTA institutions from other countries. This can be institutions in the United States, France and Spain, who have significant national HTA activities. Including regional institutions existing primarily in Canada and Spain may be considered too. In the present study the activities of the institutions already included need, furthermore, to be updated as the deadline for collection of data for the study was summer 1996. In a perspective of two-three years the Danish HTA-activities funded by the Danish Institute for Health Technology Assessment may be considered for inclusion in the database. This is, especially, relevant if the modified definition of health technology assessment suggested for Denmark is adopted.

When examining the HTA reports in the comparative study and the HTA literature, the author finds that research in the step of synthesising the evidence is required. First there is a need to identify the different methods available for synthesising evidence, both quantitative methods[225] and qualitative methods.[226] Secondly, investigations are needed of the use of synthesis in practice to put forward policy recommendations, i.e. when to use the different methods. A recently finished European project concerning HTA, *HTA-Europe*, did also recommend more emphasis on synthesis in HTA and development of the methods available [12].

With respect to knowledge of the process of diffusion of health technologies more evidence is needed with respect to the characteristics or factors influencing adoption and use. This is relevant for both low-ticket technologies, medium-ticket technologies and high-ticket technologies to show eventual differences in characteristics of diffusion patterns. Technologies with an expected slower speed of diffusion compared to laparoscopic cholecystectomy should be assessed as well. An example is the transfer of laparoscopic technologies to surgery for colon cancer which, due to less success, only has resulted in very limited diffusion in Denmark [13].[227] A prospective follow-up of the process of diffusion in colon cancer in the next years might be interesting. Furthermore, there is a need for *testing-out* empirically the high number of theories of diffusion in the fields of economics and sociology.

Because of the many existing sociological-oriented diffusion studies of health technology using qualitative methods, e.g. case study descriptions, the quantitative statistical analysis of diffusion data seems to deserve more attention to analyse diffusion in the future. Especially, multivariate methods are attractive because variation between factors influencing diffusion is accounted for (co-variance). In the empirical diffusion studies in chapters 5-6, factor analysis and proportional hazard regression were used. As

---

[225] Literature syntheses, meta-analysis, decision analyses, cost- and cost-effectiveness analyses [11].

[226] Non-quantitative literature reviews, group judgement (e.g. Delphi technique), consensus development conferences and individual expert opinion [11].

[227] A technology considered to be in its investigative stage in 1997 within controlled studies, because of the risks of possible tumour implantations in the laparoscopic wounds [13].

duration data characterize the process of diffusion, the proportional hazard regression method seems useful in elucidating factors explaining diffusion, even between countries, as demonstrated in chapter 6. A requirement for the use of the method is that the variables entered are proportional. Besides proportionality, the data in diffusion studies will often fulfil two other criteria for the method; 1) censoring will appear due to non-adoption and 2) a non-normal distribution, e.g. left skewed distribution of data due to a large group of early adopters, will often, but not always, appear. However, proportional hazard regression models have only been used in a few diffusion studies of health technology. The use of the method, and extensions of the model with time-dependent variables, when the hazard is non-proportional over time, needs to be investigated further. The investigation of other multivariate methods in diffusion research, e.g. time-series models [14] or logit regression models [15], may be relevant as well.

With respect to the specific case analysed in the book, laparoscopic cholecystectomy, many studies have been carried out internationally, although mostly as case studies or studies using bivariate analyses. Multinational studies to explain country-specific differences, as the study presented in chapter 6, are almost missing. Based on a multivariate approach, a large multinational study of the international diffusion of laparoscopic cholecystectomy including a nymber of countries would be interesting to provide an overall picture. Using hazard models this study could include a number of characteristics to explain the timing of diffusion in each country, especially at the macro decision level, e.g. payment system, share of surgeons in country population, and at the meso decision levels, e.g. size and ownership of the hospital.

Furthermore, the performance of a *prospective* economic evaluation of laparoscopic cholecystectomy versus small incision surgery in cholecystectomy (mini-laparotomy) based upon evidence from a randomized controlled trial is needed in Denmark to improve the evidence available for decision making to ensure effective and efficient cholecystectomy treatments in the future. This study is the natural continuation of the model-based economic evaluation of gall stone treatments presented as part of the very recent health technology assessment concerning gallstone disease in Denmark [16].

In economic evaluation investigation is needed empirically with respect both to early evaluations and to an iterative approach to economic evaluation. This is especially relevant for devices and procedures due to their often early introduction in the health care sector. The role of early economic evaluation within systems for early warning needs also to be identified further. An important area for investigation in early economic evaluation is how to handle uncertainty. Possibilities for handling uncertainty are to use the traditional sensitivity analyses, an iterative and ongoing approach, or decision analytic models, e.g. the learning model.

Finally, an important area for additional investigation is the actual use and impact of technology assessment on decision- and policy making in Denmark. A Dutch study concluded that the utilization of information from HTA in health policy decision making is limited, although HTA knowledge is extensively used in reports from the advisory councils to the Dutch government [17]. A reason might be that the four cases[228] analysed all were political issues. However, the Dutch result is in line with one main conclusion in the *HTA-Europe* project which emphasizes that "HTA must interact with health policy much more than it has in the past" [12]. The effect of HTA on policy decisions and clinical practice remains also to be documented in Denmark [18]. In a period with an intensified Danish effort and with an increasing amount of resources devoted to HTA, the evaluation of the effect of HTA on policy decisions as well as on clinical decisions will, however, be important to perform within a few years.

References

1. Banta HD. Introduction to the EUR-ASSESS Report. International Journal of Technology Assessment in Health Care 1997;13(2):133-143.

2. US Congress, Office of Technology Assessment. Development of Medical Technology: Opportunities for Assessment. Washington, DC: US Government Printing Office, 1976.

3. Danneskiold-Samsøe B (ed). Abdominal Laparoscopic Surgery. Report from a medical consensus conference 3-5 March 1997. Copenhagen: Danish Medical Research Council and and Danish Institute for Health Services Research and Development. Consensus Report, 1997.

4. Poulsen PB, Hørder M. Medicinsk teknologivurdering i praksis. Ugeskrift for Læger 1998;160(35):5041-5044. [The practice of health technology assessment (English abstract)].

5. Andersen M. En fællesnævner for lægen og økonomen. Ugeskrift for Læger 1998;160(29):4338-4340.

6. Andersen M. Sund fornuft på skemaform. Journal for Sundhedsvæsen 1998;10(2):7-8.

7. Bos M. Health care technology in the Netherlands. Health Policy 1994;30:207-255.

8. Drummond MF. Economic evaluation and the rational diffusion and use of health technology. Health Policy 1987;7:309-324.

9. Johannesson M. Economic evaluation of health care and policymaking. Health Policy 1995;33:179-190.

---

[228] Breast cancer screening, serum alphaprotein screening, in vitro fertilization and lung transplantation [17].

10. Alban A, Keiding H, Søgaard J. Rapport om Retningslinier for Samfundsøkonomisk analyse af lægemidler. Bilag 1 i Sundhedsministeriet. Udfordringer på lægemiddelområdet. Betænkning afgivet af Sundhedsministeriets Medicinudvalg. Sundhedsministeriet, København, juni 1998.

11. Goodman C. A Basic Methodology Toolkit, pp. 29-65. In Szczepura A & Kankaanpää J (Ed.). Assessment of Health Care Technologies. Case Studies, Key Concepts amd Strategic Issues. John Wiley & Sons. Chichester. 1996.

12. Banta HD, Oortwijn WJ (eds.). Health Technology Assessment in Europe: the challenge of coordination. HTA-Europe. TNO research report. (forthcomming).

13. Poulsen PB, Adamsen S, Vondeling H, Jørgensen T. Diffusion of laparoscopic technologies in Denmark. Health Policy 1998;45(2):149-167.

14. Sloan FA, Valvona J, Perrin JM, Adamache KW. Diffusion of surgical technology. An exploratory study. Journal of Health Economics 1986;5:31-61.

15. Klausen L, Olsen TE, Risa AE. Technological diffusion in primary health care. Journal of Health Economics 1992;11:439-452.

16. Jørgensen T. Behandling af patienter med galdesten. En medicinsk teknologivurdering. Statens Institut for Medicinsk Teknologivurdering og Dansk Institut for Klinisk Epidemiologi (DIKE). København, 1999.

17. Van der Heivel WJA, Wieringh R, van der Heuvel LPM. Utilisation of medical technology assessment in health policy. Health Policy 1997;42:211-222.

18. Jørgensen T, Hvenegaard A, Kristensen FB. HTA in Denmark. In Banta HD, Oortwijn WJ (eds.). Health Technology Assessment in Europe: the challenge of coordination. Leiden, TNO, 1998,. pp. 112-160.

Literature (alphabetic order)

Adamsen S, Hansen OH, Jensen PMF, Schulze S, Stage JG, Wara P, Jensen LP. Laparoskopisk kolecystektomi i Danmark. En prospektiv registrering. Ugeskrift for Læger 1995;157:4449-4454. [Laparoscopic cholecystectomy in Denmark. A nationwide prospective case registration (English abstract and legends)].

Adamsen S, Hansen OH, Funch-Jensen P, Schulze S, Stage JG, Wara P. Bile duct injury during laparoscopic cholecystectomy: A prospective nationwide series. Journal of the American College of Surgeons 1997;184:571-578.

Adamsen, S. Kikkertkirurgi ved galdestensoperationer. I: DSI-Institut for Sundhedsvæsen og Statens Sundhedsvidenskabelige Forskningsråd. Kikkertkirurgi i bughulen. Rapport fra en konsensus-konference København 3.-5. Marts 1997. Copenhagen: DSI, 1997:57-60.

Alban A, Keiding H, Søgaard J. Rapport om Retningslinier for Samfundsøkonomisk analyse af lægemidler. Bilag 1 i Sundhedsministeriet. Udfordringer på lægemiddelområdet. Betænkning afgivet af Sundhedsministeriets Medicinudvalg. Sundhedsministeriet, København, juni 1998.

Altman DG. Practical Statistics for Medical Research. 1th ed. London: Chapman & Hall; 1991.

Andersen M. Sund fornuft på skemaform. Journal for Sundhedsvæsen 1998;10(2):7-8.

Andersen M. En fællesnævner for lægen og økonomen. Ugeskrift for Læger 1998;160(29):4338-4340.

Andersson F. The international diffusion of new chemical entities. A cross-national study of the determinants of difference in drug lag. PhD Dissertation. Linköping Studies in Arts and Science. Linköping, 1990.

Andreasen PB, Lotz P. The Research Laboratory "DENMARK". Innovation in Danish Health Care Industry. Prepared for the Danish Ministry of Foreign Affairs, May 1990.

Arrow K. The Economic Implications of Learning by Doing. Review of Economic Studies 1962;29:155-173.

Asch DA, Hershey JC, Pauly MV, Patton JP, Jedrziewski MK, Mennuti MT. Genetic Screening for Reproductive Planning: Methodological and Conceptual Issues in Policy Analysis. American Journal of Public Health 1996;86(5):684-690.

Babbie E. The Practice of Social Research. Seventh Edition. Wadsworth Publishing Company, Belmont, California, 1995.

Baker TL. Doing Social Research. International Edition. Sociology Series. McGraw-Hill Book Company, 1988.

Balaban DJ, Goldfarb NI. Medical Evaluation of Health Care Technologies. Chapter 2 in Culyer AJ, Horisberger B. (ed.). Economic and Medical Evaluation of Health Care Technologies. Symposium April 1982, Wolfsberg, Switzerland. Springer-Verlag. Berlin, 1983.

Baladi J-F, Menon D, Otten N. Use of economic evaluation guidelines: 2 years' experience in Canada. Health Economics,1998;7:221-227.

Banta HD, Behney CJ, Willems JS. Towards Rational Technology in Medicine. Considerations for Health Policy. Springer series on health care and society, Volume 5. Springer Publishing Company, New York, 1981.

Banta HD. Technology Assessment and Policy Making. Chapter 3 in Banta HD. (ed.). Ressources for Health. Technology Assessment and Policy Making. Praeger Special Studies. Praeger Publishers. New York, 1982.

Banta HD, Gelijns A. Anitcipating and Assessing Health Care Technology. Volume 1. General Considerations and Policy Conclusions. A report commissioned by the Steering Committee on Future Health Scenarios. Martinus Nijhoff Publishers, Dordrecht, 1987.

Banta HD. Pushing the Limits: Technology Assessment in Health Care. Text of an Inaugural Address Given at the State University Limburg in Maastricht, The Netherlands. Elinkwijk, Utrecht, May 17, 1990.

Banta HD, Thacker SB. The Case for Reassessment of Health Care Technology. Once Is Not Enough. Special Communication. Journal of American Medical Association 1990;264(2):235-240.

Banta HD, Luce BR. Health Care Technology and its Assessment. An International Perspective. Oxford University Press, Oxford, 1993.

Banta HD (ed.). Minimally invasive therapy in five European countries: diffusion, effectiveness and cost-effectiveness [special issue]. Health Policy 1993;23:1-177.

Banta HD. Introduction. Minimally invasive therapy in five European countries. Health Policy 1993;23:1-5.

Banta HD, Scherstén T, Jonsson E. Implications of minimally invasive therapy. Health Policy
1993;23:167-178.

Banta HD. The cost-effectiveness of 10 selected applications in Minimally Invasive Therapy. Health Policy 1993;23:135-151.

Banta HD, Gelijns AC. The future and health care technology: Implications of a system for early identification. World Health Statistics Quaterly 1994;47(3-4):140-9.

Banta HD, Vondeling H. Strategies for successful evaluation and policy-making toward health care technology on the move: the case of medical lasers. Social Science & Medicine 1994;38(12):1663-1674.

Banta HD, Gelband E, Jonsson E, Battista R(eds.). Health Care Technology and its Assessment in Eight Countries: Australia, Canada, France, Germany, the Netherlands, Sweden, United Kingdom, Unites States. Health Policy 1994;30(1-3):1-421.

Banta HD, Oortwijn WJ, van Beekum WT. The Organization of Health Care Technology Assessment in the Netherlands. TNO Prevention and Health. Report produced on the behalf of the Rathenau Institute, The Hague, 1995.

Banta D. Putting Healthcare to the Test. The Science of Healthcare Technology Asessment. Odyssey 1996;2(1):18-24.

Banta HD, Werkö L, Cranovsky R, Granados A, Henshall C, Jonsson E, Liberati A, Matillion Y, Sheldon T. Introduction to the EUR-ASSESS Report, pp.133-143. In the Special Section *Report from the EUR-ASSESS Project* in the International Journal of Technology Assessment in Health Care 1997;13(2):133-340.

Banta HD. Introduction to the EUR-ASSESS Report. International Journal of Technology Assessment in Health Care 1997;13(2):133-143.

Banta HD, Oortwijn WJ (eds.). Health Technology Assessment in Europe: the challenge of coordination. Leiden, TNO, 1998.

Barrager S, Gildersleeve O. A Methodology to Incorporate Uncertainty into R&D Cost and Performance Data. In Tolley GS, Hodge JH, Oehmke JF (eds.). The Economic of R&D Policy. Prager Scientific, New York, 1985. pp. 149-169.

Battista RN. Innovation and diffusion of health-related technologies. International Journal of Technology Assessment in Health Care 1989;5:227-248.

Battista RN, Jacob R, Hodge MJ. Health care technology in Canada (with special reference to Quebec). Health Policy 1994;30:73-122.

Battista RN, Hodge MJ. The Development of Health Care Technology Assessment. An International Perspective. International Journal of Technology Assessment in Health Care 1995;11(2):287-300.

Battista R, Banta HD, Jonsson E, Hodge M, Gelband H. Lessons from the eight countries. In: US Congress, Office of Technology Assessment, Health care technology and its assessment in eight countries, OTA-BP-H-140, Washington, DC: U.S. Government Printing Office, February 1995, p. 335-354.

Battista RN, Feeny DH, Hodge MJ. Evaluation of the Canadian Coordinating Office for Health Technology Assessment. International Journal of Technology Assessment in Health Care 1995;11(1):102-116.

Bennett CL, Armitage JL, Buchner D, Gulati S. Economic Analysis in Phase III Clinical Trials. Cancer Investigation, 1994; 12:3:336-342.

Bloom BS, Fendrick AM. Timing and Timeliness in Medical Care Evaluation. PharmacoEconomics 1996;9(3):183-187.

Bonair A. Conceptual and empirical issues of technological change in the health care sector. Innovation and diffusion of hemodialysis and renal transplantation. PhD Dissertation. Linköping University, 1990.

Bonair A, Persson J. Innovation and Diffusion of Health Care Technologies. In Szczepura A & Kankaanpää J (eds.). Assessment of Health Care Technologies. Case Studies, Key Concepts and Strategic Issues. John Wiley & Sons, Chichester, 1996, pp. 17-28.

Bonsel GF, Rutten FFH, Uyl-de Groot CA. Economic Evaluation Alongside Cancer Trials: Methodological and Practical Aspects. European Journal of Cancer 1993;29A(7):S10-S14.

Bos M. Health care technologies in the Netherlands. Health Policy 1994;30:207-255.

Briggs A, Sculpher M. Sensitivity analysis in economic evaluation: A review of published studies. Health Economics 1995;4:355-371.

Briggs AH, Sculpher MJ, Buxton MJ, Uncertainty in the economic evaluation of health care technologies: The role of sensitivity analysis. Health Economics 1994;3:95-104.

Buch Andreasen P. Medicinsk Teknologivurdering. Nyttiggørelse af lægevidenskabelige forskningsresultater i sundhedsvæsenet. Rapport til Folketingets udvalg angående videnskabelig forskning. København, 1980.

Bull K, Spiegelhalter D. Tutorial in biostatistics. Survival analysis in observational studies. Statistics in Medicine 1997;16:1041-1074.

Buxton M. Economic evaluation early in the life cycle of a medical technology. Abstract. European Workshop: Scanning the Horizon for Emerging Health Technologies. Copenhagen, September 12-13, 1997.

Canadian Coordinating Office for Health Technology Assessment. Technology Assessment: National and International Perspectives on Research and Practice. Summary of Proceedings. Editors E. Clark & D. Marshall. (Revised Edition). A Satellite Symposium of the Eighth Annual Meeting of ISTAHC. CCOHTA. Ottawa, June 13, 1992.

Canadian Coordinating Office for Health Technology Assessment. Guidelines for economic evaluation of pharmaceuticals. 2nd ed. Ottawa: Canadian Coordinating Office for Health Technology Assessment (CCOHTA); 1997.

Canadian Coordinating Office for Health Technology Assessment. Update. New and emerging health technologies: an early warning system. Newsletter of CCOHTA. Issue 29, Summer/Fall 1997.

Canadian Coordinating Office for Health Technology Assessment. A preliminary list of information sources for emerging health technologies. Prepared for the European Workshop on Scanning the Horizon for Emerging Medical Technologies, Copenhagen, September 12-13, 1997.

Canadian Coordinating Office for Health Technology Assessment. Troglitazone for Type II Diabetes. Issues in emerging health technologies. Issue 1. October 1997 (revised Jan. 1998). http://www.ccohta.ca/research/ews/index.html

Canadian Coordinating Office for Health Technology Assessment. Abdominal Aortic Aneurysm: Endovascular grafts offer a potential alternative to surgery. Issues in emerging health technologies. Issue 2. January 1998. http://www.ccohta.ca/research/ews/index.html

Canadian Coordinating Office for Health Technology Assessment. Antileukotrienes: An emerging generation of drug therapies for asthma. Issues in emerging health technologies. Issue 3. April 1998. http://www.ccohta.ca/research/ews/index.html

Carlsson P, Garpenby P, Bonair A. Kan sjukvården styras? En rapport om spridning och kontroll av medicinsk teknologi. CMT Rapport 1991:5. Center for Medical Technology Assessment, Universitetet i Linköping, 1991.

Carlsson P. ALERT. Et nationellt system för identifiering, information och tidig bedömning av nya medicinska metoder. Projektplan SBU. På uppdrag av Styrgruppen för Hälso- och sjukvärdsfrågor för redovisning den 19 februari 1997.

Carlsson P, Jørgensen T (eds.). European Workshop: Scanning the Horizon for Emerging Health Technologies. Copenhagen. 12-13 September 1997.

Central Statistics Agency (CBS). Statistical Year Book 1991. Sdu Publishers, the Hague, 1991.

Christiansen T, Enemark U, Clausen J, Poulsen PB. Cost Containment in Denmark. Chapter 5 in Le Grand, J. & Mossialos, E. (eds). Health expenditure in the European Union - Cost and control. Ashgate: Aldershot, 1999.

Clemens K, Garrison LP, Jones A, Macdonald F. Strategic Use of Pharmacoeconomic Research in Early Drug Development and Global Pricing. PharmacoEconomics 1993; 4(5):315-322.

Cohen M, Demers C, Gurfinkel EP, Turpie AGG, Fromell GJ, Goodman S, Langer A, Califf RM, Fox K, Premmereur J, Bigonzi F. A comparison of low-molecular-weight heparin with unfractionated heparin for unstable coronary artery disease. The New England Journal of Medicine 1997;337:7:447-452.

Coleman JS, Katz E, Menzel H. Medical Innovation. A Diffusion Study. The Bobbs-Merrill Company, Inc., Indianapolis, 1966.

Commonwealth Department of Health and Family Services. Assessing health care technology in Australia. Diagnostics and Technology Branch. Canberra, 1996.
Council Directive. 93/42/EEC, of 14 June 1993. Medical Devices.

Coyle D, Davies L, Drummond MF. Trials and Tribulations. Emerging Issues in Designing Economic Evaluations Alongside Clinical Trials. International Journal of Technology Assessment in Health Care 1998;14(1):135-144.

Cummings RG, Schulze W. Economic Analysis of a Technology in the Early Stages of Its Development. In Tolley GS, Hodge JH, Oehmke JF (eds.). The Economics of R&D Policy. Praeger Publishers, New York, 1985, pp. 138-148.

Danmarks Statistik. Statistisk Årbog 1993. Danmark Statistik, København; 1994.

Danneskiold-Samsøe B. Technology Assessment Activities in Denmark. Technology Assessment Reports. International Journal of Technology Assessment in Health Care 1991;7(1):76-83.

Danneskiold-Samsøe B (ed). Abdominal Laparoscopic Surgery. Report from a medical consensus conference 3-5 March 1997. Copenhagen: Danish Medical Research Council and and Danish Institute for Health Services Research and Development. Consensus Report, 1997.

Dansk Lægemiddelstatistik. Lægemiddelforbruget i Danmark. København, 1991.

De Graeve D, Nonneman W. Pharmacoeconomic studies. Pitfalls and Problems. International Journal of Technology Assessment in Health Care 1996;12:1:22-30.

Department of Health. Report of the NHS Health Technology Assessment Programme 1995. Research and Development Directorate. Leeds, October 1995.

Department of Health. Assessing the Effects of Health Technologies. Paper prepared by the Advisory Group on Health Technology Assessment for the Director of R&D, 1992.

Detournay B, Planes A, Vochelle N, Fagnani F. Cost-Effectiveness of a Low-Molecular-Weight Heparin in Prolonged Prophylaxis Against Deep Vein Thrombosis After Total Hip Replacement. Pharmacoeconomics 1998;13:81-89.

Dirksen CD, Ament AJH, Go PMN. Diffusion of six surgical endoscopic procedures in the Netherlands. Stimulating and restraining factors. Health Policy 1996;37:91-104.

Donaldson MS, Sox HC. Setting priorities for health technology assessment. A model process. Committee on Priorities for Assessment and Reassessment of Health Care Technologies. Institute of Medicine. National Academy Press, Washington, D.C., 1992.

Dosi G. Technical Change and Industrial Transformation. St. Martin's Press, New York, 1984.

Dosi G. Technological paradigms and technological trajectories. A suggested interpretation of the determinants and directions of technical change. Research Policy 1982;11:147-162.

Drummond MF, Stoddart GL. Economic Analysis and Clinical Trials. Controlled Clinical Trials 1984;5:115-128.

Drummond MF. Economic evaluation and the rational diffusion and use of health technology. Health Policy 1987;7:309-324.

Drummond MF, Stoddart GL, Torrance GW. Methods for Economic Evaluation of Health Care Programmes. Oxford Medical Publication. Oxford University Press, Oxford, 1987.

Drummond MF, Davies L. Economic Analysis Alongside Clinical Trials. Revisiting the Methodological Issues. International Journal of Technology Assessment in Health Care 1991;7(4):561-573.

Drummond MF, Davies LM, Ferris FL. Assessing the costs and benefits of medical research: The Diabetic Retinopathy Study. Social Science & Medicine 1992;34(9):973-981.

Drummond M. Economic Analysis Alongside Clinical Trials: Problems and Potential. Journal of Rheumatology 1995;22:1403-1407.

Drummond MF, Luce B. Socioeconomic Evaluation of Pharmaceuticals. Chapter ten in Szczezepura A, Kankaanpää J (eds.). Assessments of health care technologies : case studies, key concepts and strategic issues. John Wiley & Sons, Chichester, 1996.

Drummond MF, Menzin J, Oster G. Problems in Undertaking Pharmacoeconomic Assessment in Phase III Clinical Trials: The Case of Colony-Stimulating Factors. Chapter 122 in in Spilker B. (ed.). Quality of Life and Pharmacoeconomics in Clinical Trials. Second Edition. Lippincott-Raven Publishers, Philadelphia, 1996.

Drummond MF, O'Brien B, Stoddart GL, Torrance GW. Methods for the Economic Evaluation of Health Care Programmes. Second Edition. Oxford Medical Publications, Oxford University Press, Oxford, 1997.

Duffy G. A UN Early Warning System: What Should It Be? Prepared for The Mershon International Studies Quaterly 1995;Feb:6 pages. Http://www.ccst.uiuc.edu/people/gmk/projects/uncmcw/documents/earlywrng.

Eddy DM. Selecting technologies for assessment. International Journal of Technology Assessment in Health Care 1989;5:485-501.

Ellwein LB, Drummond MF. Economic analysis alongside clinical trials. Bias in the Assessment of Economic Outcomes. International Journal of Technology Assessment in Health Care, 1996;12:4:691-697.

Elster J. Explaining Technical Change. Studies in Rationality and Social Change. Cambridge University Press, Cambridge, 1983.

Escarce JJ. Externalities in hospitals and physician adoption of a new surgical technology: an explorative analysis. Journal of Health Economics 1996;15:715-734.

Escarce JJ, Bloom BS, Hillman AL, Shea JA, Schwartz JS. Diffusion of Laparoscopic Cholecystectomy Among General Surgeons in the United States. Medical Care 1995;33:256-271.

Feeny D. Neglected issues in the diffusion of health care technologies. The role of skills and learning. International Journal of Technology Assessment in Health Care 1985;1:681-692.

Feeny D, Stoddart G. Towards Improved Health Technology Policy in Canada: A Proposal for the National Health Technology Assessment Council. Canadian Public Policy 1988;14(3):254-265.

Feldt K-O. Värdering av medicinska metoder och sjukvårdens ekonomi. In SBU. Värdering av medicinska metoder och sjukvårdens effektivitet. Rapport från SBU-konferens på Rosenbad den 25 november 1988. January 1989.

Fendrick M, Escarce JJ, McLane C, Shea JA, Schwartz JS. Hospital adoption of laparoscopic cholecystectomy. Medical Care 1994;32(10):1058-1063.

Fendrick M. Assessing New Treatments: The Case of Gallstone Disease. In Szczepura A & Kankaanpää J (eds.). Assessment of Health Care Technologies. John Wiley & Sons, Chichester, 1996. pp. 105-122.

Finkelstein SN, Homer JB, Sondic EJ. Modeling the dynamics of decision-making for emerging medical technologies. R&D Management 1984;14(3):175-191.

Forecasting Secretariat. Summary Report of the Forecasting Secretariat to the National Standing Group on Health Technology. Wessex Institute of Public Health Medicine (IPH). University of Southampton, November 1995.

Fox KAA, Bosanquet N. Assessing the UK cost implications of the use of low molecular weight heparin in coronary artery disease. The British Journal of Cardiology 1998;5:2:95-105.

Friedman LM, Furberg CD, DeMets DL. Fundamentals of clinical trials. Second efition. PSG Publishing Company, Inc., Massachusetts, 1985.

Fuchs VR, Garber AM. The New Technology Assessment. The New England Journal of Medicine 1990;323(10):673-677.

Fyns Amt. Rapporter fra Varslingsudvalget. Rapport 1. SygehusProjektgruppen, Fyns Amt, Juni1995.

Garber AM. Can Technology Assessment Control Health Spending? Health Affairs 1994;13(3):115-126.

Gelijns AC. Appendix A. Comparing the Development of Drugs, Devices, and Clinical Procedures. In Gelijns AC. Modern Methods of Clinical Investigation. Medical Innovation at the Crossroad. Volume I. Committee on Technological Innovation in Medicine. Institute of Medicine. National Academy Press, Washington, D.C., 1990.

Gelijns AC. Comparing the Development of Drugs, Devices and Clinical Procedures. Appendix A in Gelijns AC. Modern Methods of Clinical Investigation. Medical Innovation at the Crossroad. Volume I. Committee on Technological Innovation in Medicine. Institute of Medicine. National Academy Press, Washington, D.C., 1990.

Gelijns AC, Rigter H. Health care technology assessment in the Netherlands. International Journal of Technology Assessment in Health Care 1990;6:157-174.

Gelijns AC, Pannenborg CO. The development of contraceptive technology. Case studies of incentives and disincentives to innovation. International Journal of Technology Assessment in Health Care 1993;9(2):210-232.

Gelijns AC, Fendrick AM. The dynamics of innovations in Minimally Invasive Therapy. Health Policy 1993;23:153-166.

Gelijns AC, Rosenberg N. From the Scalpel to the Scope: Endoscopic Innovations in Gastroenterology, Gynecology, and Surgery. Chapter 4 in Rosenberg N, Gelijns AC, Dawkins H (ed.). Sources of Medical Technology: Universities and Industry. Medical Innovation at the Crossroad. Volume V. Committee on Technological Innovation in Medicine. Institute of Medicine. National Academy Press. Washington, D.C. 1995.

Gelijns AC, Rosenberg N. The Changing Nature of Medical Technology Development. Chapter 1 in Rosenberg N, Gelijns AC, Dawkins H (ed.). Sources of Medical Technology: Universities and Industry. Medical Innovation at the Crossroad. Volume V. Committee on Technological Innovation in Medicine. Institute of Medicine. National Academy Press. Washington, D.C. 1995.

Go PMNYH, Schol F, Gouma DJ. Laparoscopic cholecystectomy in the Netherlands. British Journal of Surgery 1993;80:1180-1183.

Go PMNYH, Dirksen CD. Five years of Laparoscopic Cholecystectomy in The Netherlands. International Journal of Surgery 1995;80:304-306.

Gold MR, Siegel JE, Russell LB, Weinstein MC (eds.). Cost-Effectiveness in Health and Medicine. Oxford University Press, New York, 1996.

Goodman C. It's time to rethink Health Care Technology Assessment. International Journal of Technology Assessment in Health Care 1992;8(2):335-358.

Goodman C. A Basic Methodology Toolkit, pp. 29-65. In Szczepura A & Kankaanpää J (Ed.). Assessment of Health Care Technologies. Case Studies, Key Concepts amd Strategic Issues. John Wiley & Sons. Chichester. 1996.

Grabowski HG, Vernon JM. Returns to R&D on new drug introductions in the 1980s. Journal of Health Economics 1994;13:383-406.

Greer AL. Adoption of Medical Technology. The Hospital's Three Decision Systems. International Journal of Technology Assessment in Health Care 1985;1:669-679.

Greer AL. The state of the art versus the state of the science. The diffusion of new medical technologies into practice. International Journal of Technology Assessment in Health Care 1988;4:5-26.

Grimes DA. Technology Follies. The Uncritical Acceptance of Medical Innovation. Journal of American Medical Association 1993;269:3030-3033.

Grønvald LF, Alban A. Health Care in Denmark. In: Alban A, Christiansen T (eds.). The Nordic Light. New Initiatives in Health Care Systems. Odense: Odense University Press, 1995: 57-67.

Gyrd-Hansen D, Søgaard J, Kronborg O. Colorectal cancer screening: efficiency and effectiveness. Health Economics 1998;7:9-20.

Hailey DM. The influence of technology assessements by advisory bodies on health policy and practice. Health Policy 1993;25:243-254.

Hailey DM. Health care technology in Australia. Health Policy 1994;30:23-72.

Hailey D. Australian economic evaluation and government decisions on pharmaceuticals compared to the assessment of other health technologies. Social Science & Medicine 1997;45(4):563-581.

Hall P. Innovation, Economics and Evolution. Theoretical Perspectives on Changing Technology in Economic Systems. Harvester Wheatsheaf. New York, 1994.

Hansen OH, Bardram L, Haakonsen TU, Lauritsen K. Laparoskopisk kolecystektomi - minimal invasiv kirurgi. Ugeskrift for Læger 1991;153:3222-3224. [Laparoscopic Cholecystectomy - minimal invasive surgery (English abstract and legends)].

Hansen OH. Kikkertkirurgi og dens udbredelse. I: DSI-Institut for Sundhedsvæsen og Statens Sundhedsvidenskabelige Forskningsråd. Kikkertkirurgi i bughulen. Rapport fra en konsensus-konference, København, 3.-5. Marts 1997. Copenhagen: DSI, 1997:27-33.

Health Council of the Netherlands: Committee on Genetic Screening. Genetic Screening. The Hague: Health Council of the Netherlands, 1994; publication no. 1994/22E.

Health Council. Network. December 1996.

Henshall C, Oortwijn W, Stevens A, Granados A, Banta D. Priority setting for health technology assessment. Theoretical considerations and practical approaches. A paper produced by the Priority Setting Subgroup of the EUR-ASSESS Project. International Journal of Technology Assessment in Health Care 1997;13(2):144-185.

Hirth RA, Fendrick AM, Chernew ME. Specialist and generalist physicians' adoption of antibiotic therapy to eradicate Helicobacter pylori infection. Medical Care 1996;34:1199-1204.

Homer JB. A diffusion model with application to evolving medical technologies. Technological Forecasting and Social Change 1987;31:197-218.

Hørder M. Medicinsk teknologivurdering, hvordan - hvorfor? Ugeskrift for Læger 1993;155(4):3622-3624.

INAHTA. INAHTA Newsletter. December 1996.

Indenrigsministeriet. Amtskommunalt udgiftspres og styringsmuligheder. Betænkning fra det af Indenrigsministeren nedsatte udvalg om amtskommunalt udgiftspres og styringsmuligheder. Betænkning nr. 1123. København, December 1987.

Institute of Medicine. Assessing Medical Technologies. National Academy Press. Washington, DC, 1985.

Jackson T, Street A, Costello A, Crowe H. Cost-effectiveness of laser ablation of the prostate. Premature evaluation. International Journal of Technology Assessment in Health Care 1995;11(3):595-610.

Jacob R, McGregor M. Assessing the impact of health technology assessment. International Journal of Technology Assessment in Health Care 1997;13:68-80.

Jennett B. High technology medicine. Benefits and burdens. Oxford Medical Publications. Oxford University Press, Oxford, 1986.

Jensen SL, Jensen PMF, Wara P, Rokkjær M. Laparoskopisk kolecystektomi. De første 45 operationer. Ugeskrift for Læger 1991;153:3225-3228. [Laparoscopic Cholecystectomy. Report of the first 45 operations (English abstract and legends)].

Johannesson M. Economic evaluation of health care and policymaking. Health Policy 1995;33:179-190.

Johansson PO. Cost-benefit Analysis of Environmental Change. Cambridge University Press, Cambridge, 1993.

Johnson A. Laparoscopic surgery. The Lancet 1997;349:631-635.

Jonsson E, Banta HD. Health care technology in Sweden. Health Policy 1994;30:257-294.

Jørgensen T. Teknologivurdering. Dansk Sygehus Institut. DSI-Specialrapport 80.07. København, 1980.

Jørgensen T, Danneskiold-Samsøe B. Medicinsk Teknologivurdering -hvordan? Dansk Sygehus Institut. DSI-Rapport 86.02. København, 1986.

Jørgensen T, Larsen LG, Poulsen PB. Tidlig varsling af kommende medicinske teknologier - et dansk forstudie. DSI - Institut for Sundhedsvæsen. DSI - rapport. København, 1997.

Jørgensen T, Børlum Kristensen F. Medicinsk teknologivurdering i Europa. Ugeskrift for Læger 1998;160(16):2367-2371.

Jørgensen T, Hvenegaard A, Kristensen FB. HTA in Denmark. In Banta HD, Oortwijn WJ (eds.). Health Technology Assessment in Europe: the challenge of coordination. Leiden, TNO, 1998. pp. 112-160.

Jørgensen T. Behandling af patienter med galdesten. En medicinsk teknologivurdering. Statens Institut for Medicinsk Teknologivurdering og Dansk Institut for Klinisk Epidemiologi (DIKE). København, 1999.

Jönsson B, Weinstein MC. Economic evaluation alongside multinational clinical trials. Study Considerations for GUSTO IIb. International Journal of Technology Assessment in Health Care, 1997;13(1):49-58.

Kamper-Jørgensen F. Medicinsk teknologivurdering. Månedsskrift for praktisk lægegerning 1989;67(12):957-976.

Kiefer NM. Economic Duration Data and Hazard Functions. Journal of Economic Literature 1988;26:646-679.

Kirchberger S. Health care technology in Germany. Health Policy 1994;30:163-205.

Klausen L, Olsen TE, Risa AE. Technological diffusion in primary health care. Journal of Health Economics 1992;11:439-452.

Kline SJ, Rosenberg N. An Overview of Innovation. In Landau & Rosenberg N (eds.). The Positive Sum Strategy: Harnessing Technology for Economic Growth, Washington DC: National Academy Press, 1986.

Lange M, Jørgensen T, Kristensen FB. Analysis of the national need for information, training and standards in HTA. Danish Institute for Health Technology Assessment. Poster presented at the 14th Annual Meeting in the International Society of Technology Assessment in Health Care, Ottawa, Ontario, Canada, June 7-10, 1998.

Langkilde LK, Poulsen PB. The Learning Approach to Early Economic Evaluation. CHS Working Paper 1996:2. Centre for Health and Social Policy, Odense University, 1996.

Langkilde LK. Uncertainty, Information and Health Technology Assessment. Ph.D. Afhandling fra det samfundsvidenskabelige fakultet på Odense Universitet, Odense, 1997.

Langrish J, Gibbons M, Evans WG, Jevons, FR. Wealth From Knowledge. Studies of Innovation in Industry. The MacMillan Press. London, 1972.

Layard PRG, Walters AA. Micro-Economic Theory. McGraw-Hill. New York, 1978.

Layton E. Conditions of Technological Development. Chapter 6 in Spiegel-Rösing I & Solla Price D (ed.). Science, Technology and Society. Sage Publication. London, 1977.

Legoretta AP, Silber JH, Constantino GN, Kobylinski RW, Zatz SL. Increased Cholecystectomy Rate After the Introduction of Laparoscopic Cholecystectomy. Journal of American Medical Association 1993;270(12):1429-1432.

Liberati A, Sheldon TA, Banta HD. EUR-ASSESS Project Subgroup Report on Methodology. Methodological Guidance for the Conduct of Health Technology Assessment. International Journal of Technology Assessment in Health Care 1997;13(2):186-219.

Littell CL. Innovation in Medical Technology: Reading the Indicators: Datawatch. Health Affairs Millwood 1994;13(3):226-235.

Lossius WW. Selo-Zok - dyrt fremskridt. Tidsskrift for Norsk Lægeforening 1991;1:111.

Lotz P. Demand-Side Effects on Product Innovation. Ph.D.serie 9.92. Handelshøjskolen i København. Det Økonomiske Fakultet. Samfundslitteratur, 1992.

Luce BR, Brown RE. The Use of Technology Assessments by Hospitals, Health Maintenance Organizations, and Third-Party Payers in the United States. International Journal of Technology Assessment in Health Care 1995;11(1):79-92.

Lægeforeningens Medicinfortegnelse, 1993.

Mansfield E. The Economics of Technological Change. NY:W.W.Norton & Company, 1968.

Mansfield E. Microeconomics of Technological Innovation. In: Landau R, Rosenberg N (eds.). The Positive Sum Strategy. Harnessing Technology for Economic Growth. National Academy Press, Washington, D.C., 1986. pp. 307-325.

Marshall D, Hailey D, Hirsch N, Clark E, Menon D. The introduction of laparoscopic cholecystectomy in Canada and Australia. Ontario: Australian Institute of Health & Welfare and Canadian Coordinating Office for Health Technology Assessment, 1994.

Mauskopf J, Schulman K, Bell L, Glick H. A Strategy for Collecting Pharmaco-economic Data During Phase II/III Clinical Trials. Special Article. Pharmacoeconomics 1996;9(3):264-277.

Maxwell RA. The state of the art of the science of drug discovery - an opinion. Drug Development Research 1984;4:375-389.

MEFA. Facts 1994. Medicine and health care. Denmark, 1994.

MEFA. Facts 1997. Medicine and health care. Denmark, 1997.

Menon D, Marshall D. Diffusion of Laparoscopic Cholecystectomy in Canada. International Journal of Technology Assessment in Health Care 1994;10:287-292.

Menon D, Marshall DM. The Internationalization of Health Technology Assessment. International Journal of Technology Assessment in Health Care 1996;12(1):45-51.

Metcalfe S. The Economic Foundation of Technology Policy: Equilibrium and Evolutionary Perspectives. Chapter 12 in Stoneman P (ed.). Handbook of the Economics of Innovation and Technological Change. Basil Blackwell, Oxford, 1995.

Midunger T, Karlberg I. Förslag till system för indetifiering och bedömning av nya medicinska metoder, NMM. Socialstyrelsen. Oktober 1991.

Ministry of Health. Health care in Denmark 1.ed. Copenhagen, 1997.

Ministry of Health. Financial Oversight on Care 1992. Dutch Parliament, Second Chamber, Meeting Year 1991-1992, 22 311 nrs. 1-2. Sdu Publishers, the Hague, 1992, p. 211-213.

Moatti JP, Chanut C, Benech JM. Researcher-Driven versus Policy-Driven Economic Appraisal of Health Technologies: The Case of France. Social Science and Medicine 1994;38(12):1625-1633.

Mohr LB. Determinants of innovations in organisations. The American Political Science Review 1969;63:111-126.

Mowatt G, Bower DJ, Brebner JA, Cairns JA, Grant AM, McKee L. When is the 'right' time ti initiate an assessment of a health technology. International Journal of Technology Assessment in Health Care 1998;14(2):372-386.

Mowery DC, Rosenberg N. The influence of market demand upon innovation: a critical review of some recent empirical studies. Research Policy 1979;8:103-153.

Mühe E. Die erste Cholecystektomie durch das Laparoskop. Langenbecks Archiv für Chirurgie 1986;369:804.

Neugebauer E, Ure BM, Lefering R, Eypasch EP, Troidl H. Technology Assessment of Endoscopic Surgery. Acta Neurochirogie 1994;suppl.61:13-19.

Newhouse JP. Medical care costs: how much welfare loss? Journal of Economic Perspectives 1992;6(3):3-21.

NHS Executive. Report of the NHS Health Technology Assessment Programme 1996. NHS Executive. June 1996.

NHS Executive. The Annual Report of the NHS Health Technology Assessment Programme 1997. Identifying Questions, Finding Answers. The National Coordinating Centre for Health Technology Assessment. Department of Health. September 1997.

NIH Consensus Development Panel on Gallstones and Laparoscopic cholecystectomy. Journal of American Medical Association 1993;269:1018.

NNM-info. "Startpaket". Vänersborg, april 1995 (Utvecklingsprojektet "Nya Medicinska Metoder", projektleder Henric Hultin).

Nordic Medico Statistical Committee. Health Statistics in the Nordic Countries 1995. Copenhagen: NOMESCO, 1997. (Nordic Medico Statistical Committee 1997:49).

Oortwijn WJ, Vondeling H, Bouter L. The use of societal criteria in priority setting for health technology assessment in the Netherlands. Initial experiences and future challenges. International Journal of Technology Assessment in Health Care 1998;14(2):226-236.

Paltiel AD, Kaplan EH. The Epidemiological and Economic Consequences of AIDS Clinical Trials. Journal of Acquired Immune Deficiency Syndromes 1993;6:179-190.

Parker JES. The international diffusion of pharmaceuticals. St. Martin's Press, New York, 1984.

Pavitt K. Sectoral patterns of technical change: Towards a taxonomy and a theory, 1984. Chapter 12 in Freeman C. The Economics of Innovation. An Elgar Reference Collection. Edward Elgar Publishing Company, Vermont, 1990.

Pedersen KM. Reformitis? -Sceptical Remarks on the Dismal Science of Reforms. In: Alban A, Christiansen T. (eds.). The Nordic Light. New Initiatives in Health Care Systems. Odense: Odense University Press, 1995:46-57.

Perry S, Gardner E, Thamer M. The Status of Health Technology Assessment Worlwide: Results of an International Survey. The International Journal of Technology Assessment in Health Care 1997;13(1):81-98.

Petermann Th, Sauter A. TA-Monitoring. "Stand der Technikfolgen-Abschätzung im Bereich der Medizintechnik". TAB Arbeitsbericht Nr. 39. TAB Büro für Technikfolgen-Abschätzung beim Deutschen Bundestag. April 1996.

Phelps CE, Mushlin AI. Focusing Technology Assessment Using Medical Decision Theory. Medical Decision Making 1988;8:279-289.

Piene H. Kan vår medisinsk-teknologiske fremtid forutsees? HMT 1994;13(5):14-16.

Plaisier PW, van der Hul RL, Nijs HGT, den Toom R, Terpstra OT, Bruining HA. Quality of Life After Treatment of Gallstones: Results of a Randomised Study of Lithotripsy and Open cholecystectomy. European Journal of Surgery 1994;160:613-617.

Pocock SJ. Clinical Trials. A Practical Approach. John Wiley & Sons, Chichester, 1983.

Poulsen PB. Hvem skal behandles - for hvad? - Økonomiske prioriteringsmål i sundhedssektoren. CHS Arbejdsnotat 1994:2. Center for Helsetjenesteforskning og Socialpolitik, Odense Universitet.

Poulsen PB, Hørder M, Jørgensen T. Fremtidens Medicinske Metoder - tidlig varsling i international og dansk perspektiv. Sundhedsstyrelsens Udvalg for Medicinsk Teknologivurdering. Sundhedsstyrelsen, København, 1996.

Poulsen PB, Hørder M. Medicinsk teknologivurdering i praksis. Ugeskrift for Læger 1998;160(35):5041-5044. [The practice of health technology assessment (English abstract)].

Poulsen PB, Adamsen S, Vondeling H, Jørgensen T. Diffusion of Laparoscopic Technologies in Denmark. Health Policy 1998:45(2):149-167.

Rigter H. Assessment of health care technology in the Netherlands. Chapter 19 in Banta HD, Luce BR. Health Care Technology and its Assessment. An International Perspective. Oxford University Press, Oxford, 1993.

Rittenhouse BE, O'Brien BJ. Threats to the Validity of Pharmacoeconomics Analyses Based on Clinical Trial Data. Chapter 126 in in Spilker B. (ed.). Quality of Life and Pharmacoeconomics in Clinical Trials. Second Edition. Lippincott-Raven Publishers, Philadelphia, 1996.

Robert G, Stevens A, Gabbay J, Milne R. Primary information sources for identifying, and predicting the impact, of new medical technologies (NMTs). Conference Abstract in the Book of Abstracts from the conference in the *International Society for Technology Assessment in Health Care*, held in Barcelona 25th-28th May 1997.

Rogers EM. Lessons for guidelines from the diffusion of innovations. The challenge. Joint Commission Journal on Quality Improvement 1995;21:324-328.

Rogers EM. Diffusion of Innovations. 4th ed. New York: Free Press, 1995.

Romeo AA, Wagner JL, Lee RH. Prospective reimbursement and the diffusion of new technologies in hospitals. Journal of Health Economics 1984;3:1-24.

Rosenberg N. Inside the black box: Technology and Economics. Cambridge University Press, Cambridge, 1982.

Rosenberg N. Exploring the black box. Technology, economics, and history. Cambridge University Press, Cambridge, 1994.

Rovira J. Standardizing economic appraisal of health technology in the European Community. Social Science & Medicine 1994;38(12):1675-1678.

Rovira J. Standardization of the economic evaluation of health technologies. European developments. Medical Care 1996;34(12):DS182-DS188.

Rowe G, Wright G, Bolger F. Delphi. A Reevaluation of Research and Theory. Technological Forecasting and Social Change 1991;39:235-251.

Sackett DL, Rosenberg WMC, Gray JAM, Haynes RB, Richardson WS. Evidence-Based Medicine: What it is and what it isn't. British Medical Journal 1996;312:71-72.

Sassi F. Health Technology Assessment. An Introduction. Eurohealth 1996;2(4):9-10.

SBU. SBU Alert. A New Project at SBU. A System for Identification and Early Assessment of New Technologies in Health Care. SBU Information Sheet, Stockholm, 1998.

Scherstén T. Virtual Reality in Surgery. Abstract. European Workshop: Scanning the Horizon for Emerging Health Technologies. Copenhagen. 12-13 September 1997.

Schou I. Minimally Invasive Therapy in Denmark. Health Policy 1993;23:17-30.

Schousboe K. Early Warning Systems - eller hvorfor det er væsentligt at vide, når de "andre" flytter på sig. Netværk;8-10.

Schulze S. Kikkertkirurgi ved mave-tarm cancer. I: DSI-Institut for Sundhedsvæsen og Statens Sundhedsvidenskabelige Forskningsråd. Kikkertkirurgi i bughulen. Rapport fra en konsensus-konference København 3.-5. Marts 1997. Copenhagen: DSI, 1997:73-75.

Schwabe U, Paffrath D (ed.). Arzneiverordnungsreport' 94. Gustav Fishers Verlag. Stuttgart, 1994.

Sculpher M, Drummond M, Buxton M. The iterative use of economic evaluation as part of the process of health technology assessment. Journal of Health Service Research and Policy 1997;1:26-30.

Sharples LD, Briggs A, Caine N, McKenna M, Buxton M. A model for analyzing the cost of main clinical events after cardiac transplantation. Transplantation 1996;62(5):615-621.

Sloan FA, Valvona J, Perrin JM, Adamache KW. Diffusion of surgical technology. An exploratory study. Journal of Health Economics 1986;5:31-61.

Smee C. The Need for Early Warning in Health Policy Making and Planning. Abstract. European Workshop: Scanning the horizon for emerging health technologies. Copenhagen. 12-13 September 1997.

Socialstyrelsen. Nya Medicinska Metoder (NMM). Et försök att utveckla en modell för tidig identifiering, information och bedömning av nya medicinska metoder. Projektrapport och Utvärderingsrapport. Ett projekt av Socialstyrelsen och Landstingsförbundet. Stockholm 1996.

Southern Surgeons Club. A prospective analysis of 1518 laparoscopic cholecystectomies. The New England Journal of Medicine 1991;324(16):1073-1078.

Spiby J. Advances in medical technology over the next 20 years. Community Medicine 1988;10(4):273-278.

Spiby J. Health care technology in the United Kingdom. Health Policy 1994;30:295-334.

Spilker B. Multinational Drug Companies: Issues in Drug Discovery and Development. Raven Press, New York, 1989.

Stage JG. Kikkertkirurgi ved blindtarmsbetændelse og brok. I: DSI-Institut for Sundhedsvæsen og Statens Sundhedsvidenskabelige Forskningsråd. Kikkertkirurgi i bughulen. Rapport fra en konsensus-konference København 3.-5. Marts 1997. Copenhagen: DSI, 1997:69-72.

Statens Sundhedsvidenskabelige Forskningsråd. Kikkertkirurgi i bughulen. Rapport fra en konsensus-konference København 3.-5. Marts 1997. Copenhagen: DSI, 1997:73-75.

Statens Legemiddel kontroll. Utkast til norske retningslinjer for legemiddeløkonomiske analyser. Upubliceret.

Statens Beredning för Utvärdering av Medicinsk Metodik. Preoperative Rutiner. Statens Beredning för Utvärdering av Medicinsk Metodik. Stockholm, Maj 1989.

Statens Lægevidenskabelige Forskningsråd. Rapport fra konferencen Helsetjenesteforskning og medicinsk teknologivurdering. Udvalget for helsetjenesteforskning og medicinsk teknologivurdering. København, 31. August 1982.

Steven A, Robert G, Gabbay J. Identifying new health care technologies in the United Kingdom. International Journal of Technology Assessment in Health Care 1997;13(1):59-67.

Stevens A, Robert G. Early Warning of New Health Care Technologies in the United Kingdom. Abstract. European Workshop: Scanning the horizon for emerging health technologies. Copenhagen. 12-13 September 1997.

Stocking B. (ed.). Expensive health technologies. Regulatory and administrative mechanisms in Europe. Oxford Medical Publications, Oxford University Press, Oxford, 1988.

Stoneman P. Introduction. Chapter 1 in Stoneman P (ed.). Handbook of the Economics of Innovation and Technological Change. Basil Blackwell, Oxford, 1995.

Sundhedsministeriet. Rapport fra Udvalget vedrørende Sygehusvæsenets økonomi. København, April 1994.

Sundhedsstyrelsen. Sygehusklassifikation og kommunekoder pr. 1. januar 1991. København, 1990.

Sundhedsstyrelsen. Virksomhed ved sygehuse 1991. (Sygehusstatistik II:56:1993). København, 1993.

Sundhedsstyrelsen. Medicinsk Teknologivurdering - hvad er det? København, 1994.

Sundhedsstyrelsen. Specialeplanlægning og lands- og landsdelsfunktioner i sygehusvæsenet. Vejledning. København 1996.

Sundhedsstyrelsen. β-interferon behandling af patienter med dissemineret sklerose. Sundhedsstyrelsens Udvalg for Medicinsk Teknologivurdering. København, 1996.

Sundhedsstyrelsen. Enkeltstillingsklassifikation pr. 1. januar 1997. Sundhedsstyrelsen, København; 1997.

Sundhedsstyrelsen. Ondt i ryggen. En kortlægning af problemets forekomst og oplæg til dets håndtering i et MTV-perspektiv. Sundhedsstyrelsens Udvalg for Medicinsk Teknologivurdering. København, 1997.

Swedish Council on Technology Assessment in Health Care. Literature Searching and Evidence Interpretation for Assessing Health Care Practices. Stockholm, 1993.

Swedish Council on Technology Assessment in Health Care. Health Care Technology Assessment Programs. - A review of selected programs in different countries. Stockholm, February 1993.

ten Velden G. Medical technology assessment (TA) and health policy in the Netherlands. Paper presented at the Nordic Conference on *Critical choices in the health care sector - relevant basis for decisions through Medical Technology Assessment*. Copenhagen 26-27th April 1994.

ten Velden G. Early Identification by the Health Council of The Netherlands. Paper presented for the international MEMT-group, Danish Hospital Institute, Copenhagen, January 17, 1995.

ten Velden GHM. Taxonomy of Health Technology Assessment (TA). The Health Council. The Hague, 20 September 1995.

ten Velden G. Identification of new health care technologies by the Health Council of the Netherlands. Abstract. European Workshop: Scanning the horizon for emerging health technologies. Copenhagen. 12-13 September 1997.

The Danish National Board of Health, the Health Technology Assessment Committee. National Strategy for Health Technology Assessment. Copenhagen, 1996.

The Alberta Implementation Committee for Health Technology Assessment. Report Of The Alberta Implementation Committee For Health Technology Assessment, 22 October 1993.

Togerson D, Donaldson C, Reid D. Using economics to prioritize research: a case study of randomized trials for the prevention of hip fractures due to osteoporosis. Journal of Health Services Research and Policy 1996;1(3):141-146.

Townsend J, Buxton M. Cost effectiveness scenario analysis for a proposed trial of hormone replacement therapy. Health Policy 1997;39:181-194.

Towse A, Drummond M (eds.). From efficacy to cost-effectiveness. OHE briefing. Office of Health Economics, London, May 1998;37:1-12.

Tunis SR, Gelband H. Health care technology in the United States. Health Policy 1994;30:335-396.

Ure BM, Lefering R, Troidl H. Costs of laparoscopic cholecystectomy. Analysis of potential savings. Surgical Endoscopy 1995;9(4):401-406.

US Congress, Office of Technology Assessment. Development of Medical Technology: Opportunities for Assessment. Washington, DC: US Government Printing Office, 1976.

US Congress, Office of Technology Assessment. Assessing the Efficacy and Safety of Medical Technologies. Washington, DC: US Government Printing Office, 1978.

US Congress, Office of Technology Assessment. Strategies for medical technology assessment. Washington, DC: U.S. Government Printing Office, 1982.

US Congress, Office of Technology Assessment. The Implications of Cost-Effectiveness Analysis of Medical Technology. Washington, DC: US Government Printing Office, 1980a.

US Congress, Office of Technology Assessment. The Implications of Cost-Effectiveness Analysis of Medical Technology: Methodological Issues and Literature Review. Washington, DC: US Government Printing Office, 1980b.

US Congress, Office of Technology Assessment, Health Care Technology and its Assessment in Eight Countries, OTA-BP-H-140, Washington, DC: US Government Printing Office, February 1995.

Usher AP. Technical Change and Capital Formation. Chapter 2 in Rosenberg N (ed.). The economics of technological change. Penguin Modern Economics Readings. Penguin Books, 1971.

Van der Heivel WJA, Wieringh R, van der Heuvel LPM. Utilisation of medical technology assessment in health policy. Health Policy 1997;42:211-222.

Vandenbergh HC, Wilson T, Adams SE, Inglis M J. Laparoscopic cholecystectomy: its impact on national health economics. The Medical Journal of Australia 1995;162:587-590.

Vondeling H, Haerkens E, de Wit A, Bos M, Banta HD. Diffusion of minimally invasive technologies in the Netherlands. Health Policy 1993;23:67-81.

Wakker P, Klaasen MP. Confidence intervals for cost/effectiveness ratios. Health Economics 1995;4:373-381.

Walsh V. Invention and innovation in the chemical industry: Demand-pull or discovery-push? Research Policy 1984;13:211-234.

Warner KE. The Need for Some Innovative Concepts of Innovation: An Examination of Research on the Diffusion of Innovation. Policy Sciences 1974;5:433-451.

Warner KE. A "Desparation-Reaction" Model of Medical Diffusion. Health Services Research 1975;Winter:369-383.

Weill C. Minimally Invasive Therapy: The French case study. Health Policy 1993;23:31-47.

Weill C. Health care technology in France. Health Policy 1994;30:123-162.

Weinstein MC, Siegel JE, Gold MR, Kamlet MS, Russell LB. Recommendations of the Panel on Cost-Effectiveness in Health and Medicine. Consensus Statement. Journal of American Medical Association 1996;276(16):1253-1258.

Wenner J, Graffner H, Lindell G. Laparoskopisk kolecystektomi. Kostnadseffektiv gallstenskirurgi. Läkartidningen 1995;92(8):763-765.

White JV. Laparoscopic Cholecystectomy: The Evolution of General Surgery. Annals of Internal Medicine 1991;115(8):651-653.

Wickham JEA. An Introduction to Minimally Invasive Therapy. Health Policy 1993;23:7-15.

Wickham JEA. The new surgery. British Medical Journal 1987;295(6613):1581-1582.

Yin RK. Case Study Research. Design and Methods. Second Edition. Applied Social Research Methods Series Volume 5. SAGE Publications. London, 1994.

Medicinsk teknologivurdering i praksis

ORIGINAL MEDDELELSE

Cand.oecon. Peter Bo Poulsen & Mogens Hørder

> *Resumé*
> *Baggrund og formål:* Sundhedsstyrelsen definerer MTV som en alsidig og systematisk vurdering af forudsætningerne for og konsekvenserne af at anvende medicinsk teknologi. Fokus i teknologivurderingen er på fire hovedelementer: teknologien, økonomien, patienten og organisationen. Men spørgsmålet er, om der er overensstemmelse mellem det, man i Danmark definerer som MTV, og det, der reelt udføres i praksis. Artiklen besvarer dette ved at sammenligne MTV-projekter fra udenlandske MTV-institutioner.
>
> *Materiale og metoder:* I en litteraturgennemgang er 124 MTV-projekter fra nationale MTV-institutioner i fem lande gennemgået for kriterier som anvendt metode og vurderede parametre.
>
> *Resultater:* Hovedelementerne teknologi og økonomi indgår hyppigst i MTV-projekterne, fx information om effektivitet og omkostninger. Fire typer af MTV afgrænses efter bredde og alsidighed af inkluderede hovedelementer. Resultatet viser, at kun 17 projekter kan karakteriseres som brede og alsidige totale MTV-projekter. De øvrige teknologivurderinger er mere partielle. De svenske MTV-rapporter er de mest brede og alsidige.
>
> *Diskussion:* Resultatet viser, at MTV-begrebet i praksis kun i få tilfælde har den brede og alsidige form. Langt oftere er tilgangen partiel. Læren af studiet for danske MTV-initiativer kunne derfor være, at man ud over at definere MTV som en bred og alsidig vurdering også inkluderede mere partielle fortolkninger under MTV-begrebet, fx *cost-effectiveness*-analysen, afhængigt af den beslutning der skal træffes.

I de senere år har der inden for sundhedssektoren været en stigende interesse for begrebet medicinsk teknologivurdering (MTV). I Ugeskrift for Læger er dette afspejlet, bl.a. i form af en debat om det sundhedsvidenskabelige grundlag for MTV (1-5).

I en række lande har man inden for det sidste årti oprettet nationale MTV-institutioner. Med en finanslovsbeslutning er der fra 1997 etableret et nationalt institut for MTV i Danmark – Statens Institut for Medicinsk Teknologivurdering – til afløsning af Sundhedsstyrelsens udvalg for medicinsk teknologivurdering. En række amter har ligeledes etableret amtslige MTV-udvalg og oprettet MTV-konsulentstillinger. På sygehus- og afdelingsniveau er MTV-tankegangen blevet introduceret og er i stadig større grad et kendt begreb blandt personalegrupperne.

En langvarig ressourcerestriktion i sundhedssektoren, befolkningens stigende forventninger, de hastigt øgende behandlingsmuligheder, tvivl om nye og eksisterende medicinske teknologiers virkningsfuldhed og omkostningseffektivitet, etiske aspekter af interventionen – er alt sammen forhold, der skal håndteres på såvel politisk som administrativt og professionelt niveau og sjældent kan vurderes isoleret. Ikke underligt at MTV som en bred og alsidig vurdering er kommet i fokus.

Der er derfor behov for at belyse, om der er overensstemmelse mellem det, man i Danmark definerer og opfatter som MTV, og det der reelt udføres i praksis under betegnelsen MTV. Dette gør vi ved at sammenligne gennemførte MTV-projekter fra en række udenlandske MTV-institutioner. Arbejdet bygger på et internationalt komparativt studie af MTV udført ved Center for Helsetjenesteforskning og Socialpolitik, Odense Universitet (6).

Definitioner på MTV

Begrebet teknologivurdering blev i 1975 introduceret i USA af det kongresnedsatte *Office of Technology Assessment*, der definerede en teknologivurdering som en bred og alsidig form for vurdering, der undersøger kort- og langsigtede samfundsmæssige konsekvenser af applikationen og anvendelsen af teknologi (7). Definitionen har det brede sigte ved at omfatte samfundsmæssige, økonomiske, etiske og lovgivningsmæssige implikationer. Den brede og alsidige definition blev siden overført til området for medicinske teknologier.

I Danmark blev MTV ligeledes introduceret som en bred og alsidig vurdering (8, 9). Dette er også grundlaget i den Nationale Strategi for Medicinsk Teknologivurdering fra 1996, der definerer MTV som en alsidig og systematisk vurdering af forudsætningerne for og konsekvenserne af at anvende medicinsk teknologi, der i en så fagligt bred form som muligt skal omfatte delelementer fra fire hovedelementer: teknologien, økonomien, patienten og organisationen (10).

I andre sammenhænge er mere partielle og snævre

Antaget den 20. februar 1998.
Odense Universitet, Center for Helsetjenesteforskning og Socialpolitik, og Odense Universitetshospital, afdeling KKA.

tilgange til MTV-begrebet dog anvendt, hvor en MTV sættes lig studier af teknologiers sikkerhed og virkningsfuldhed eller analyser af *cost-effectiveness* (11, 12). Spørgsmålet er derfor, om MTV i praksis altid har en bred og alsidig form med fokus på alle fire hovedelementer, eller om er der også er tale om mere partielle former for MTV?

Materiale og metoder

Ovenstående spørgsmål belyses i et komparativt studie, der består i en litteraturgennemgang af i alt 124 MTV-projekter udgået fra nationale MTV-institutioner i fem lande. Landene og deres nationale MTV-institutioner er udvalgt til studiet som væsentlige og permanente aktører på MTV-området.

Fra Sverige indgår *Statens Beredning för Medicinsk Utvärdering* (SBU) med de 19 teknologivurderinger (1989-1996), man har færdiggjort efter institutionens oprettelse i 1987. Canada er repræsenteret af 16 MTV-rapporter (1991-1996), produceret af *the Canadian Coordinating Office for Health Technology Assessment* (CCOHTA) siden etableringen i 1989 som national canadisk MTV-institution. Fra Holland er *Health Council* inkluderet, der som regeringsmyndighed har beskæftiget sig med MTV siden 1985. For den hollandske aktivitet indgår kun de 13 af *Health Council's* MTV-rapporter (1989-1996), som er oversat til engelsk. Australien er repræsenteret af *the Australian Health Technology Advisory Committee* (AHTAC) med 12 MTV-rapporter (1992-1996), der er identiske med AHTAC's MTV-aktivitet siden oprettelsen i 1990. Endelig indgår der 64 engelske MTV-projekter fra *National Health Service's* MTV-program, der siden 1993 har prioriteret og finansieret en lang række MTV-projekter udført decentralt i sundhedssektoren. Projekterne er i dag under kontrol af den engelske MTV-institution *the National Coordinating Centre for Health Technology Assessment* (NCCHTA). For de engelske MTV-projekter, der er inkluderet i det komparative studie, er der dog kun tale om projektbeskrivelser, da ingen rapporter var færdiggjort på tidspunktet for dataindsamlingen. Overordnet gælder der for alle institutioner, at der kun er medtaget projekter, hvor der er fokus på medicinske teknologier som lægemidler, udstyr, apparatur eller medicinske procedurer. Deciderede metodeorienterede projekter eller andre rapporter fra institutionerne er derimod ikke inkluderet i studiet. Yderligere beskrivelse af de fem institutioner findes i to nylige arbejder (6, 13).

Ved litteraturgennemgangen har vi set på de 124 MTV-projekter ud fra en række kriterier til metode og vurderede parametre (delelementer) fra de fire hovedelementer. Den efterfølgende analyse sigter på at vurdere, om projekterne opfylder kravene til brede og alsidige teknologivurderinger, eller om de i realiteten er mere partielle i deres udformning.

Resultater

At MTV ofte baseres på eksisterende videnskabelig viden, og derfor sjældent involverer primær dataindsamling, ses i Tabel 1. Således består hele 65% af de 124 MTV-projekter primært af litteraturgennemgange.

Tabel 2 belyser, hvilke hovedelementer og parametre der vurderes som led i MTV-projekterne, og dermed den information som teknologivurderingerne indeholder.

Tabel 1. *Metoder til indsamling af data til MTV opdelt på undersøgelsens institutioner.*

Dataindsamlingsmetoder	SBU (n=19)	Health Council (n=13)	AH-TAC (n=12)	CCOH-TA (n=16)	NCC-HTA (n=64)	Total (%) (n=124)*)
Litteraturgennemgang	19	13	7	8	33	80 (65)
Metaanalyser	1	–	–	2	1	4 (3)
Spørgeskemaundersøgelse	7	1	–	2	7	17 (14)
Randomiserede kliniske studier	–	–	–	–	20	20 (16)
Økonomisk evaluering	15	–	–	8	26	49 (40)
Andre metoder	3	1	3	1	14	22 (18)

*) Procenter refererer til en metodes anvendelse i forhold til den totale stikprøve (n=124). Procenter summerer til mere end 100, da mere end én metode var anvendt til indsamling af data i en række af teknologivurderingerne.

Tabel 2. *Vurderede parametre (del- og hovedelementer) i undersøgelsen (n=124).*

Hovedelementer	Vurderede parametre	Frekvensen	Procent af det totale antal (n=124)
Teknologien	Virkningsfuldhed	55	44
	Sikkerhed	57	46
	Effektivitet	96	77
	Resultatmål	39	32
	Indikationer	37	30
	Epidemiologi	40	32
Økonomien	Efficiens	11	9
	Omkostninger	80	65
	Cost-effectiveness	62	50
	Cost-utility	8	7
	Costbenefit	7	6
Patienten	Samfundsmæssig betydning	14	11
	Etik	10	8
	Accepterbarhed	14	11
	Psykologiske spørgsmål	16	13
	Andre patientparametre	15	12
Organisationen	Diffusion (spredning)	26	21
	Centralisering/decentralisering	14	11
	Udnyttelse	14	11
	Tilgængelighed	6	5
	Færdigheder – rutiner	20	16
	Uddannelse – træning	21	17
	Andre organisatoriske parametre	4	3

Det fremgår, at der i projekterne primært indgår information om teknologien og økonomien. Blandt disse to hovedelementer er der i teknologivurderingerne størst fokus på parametre som effektivitet, omkostninger, *cost-effectiveness*, sikkerhed og virkningsfuldhed. I langt færre tilfælde er parametre fra de to øvrige hovedelementer patient og organisation medtaget.

I praksis er ikke alle MTV-projekter således så brede og alsidige, som den oprindelige definition fordrer. For at undersøge dette yderligere afgrænsede vi fire typer af MTV ud fra antallet af inkluderede hovedelementer og dermed deres bredde og alsidighed.

Som den brede og alsidige MTV afgrænses den totale MTV som en MTV, der vurderer mindst ét parameter under hvert hovedelement og derved medtager information fra alle fire hovedelementer. Den svenske MTV-rapport fra SBU (1990): Stötvågsbehandling av njursten och gallsten (14), er et eksempel herpå. De tre øvrige typer af MTV betegnes som partielle teknologivurderinger, der vurderer og indeholder information fra parametre fra henholdsvis tre, to og ét af de fire hovedelementer. Blandt de sammenlignede teknologivurderinger er Health Council's MTV-rapport (1994): Stereotactic radiotherapy (15), et eksempel på en partiel MTV med information fra tre hovedelementer. En yderligere partiel tilgang, hvor der kun indgår information fra to hovedelementer, illustreres ved CCOHTA-rapporten (1992): Chiropractic treatment of neck and back disorders: a review of selected studies (16). Endelig er det engelske MTV-projekt Screening for stroke (upubliceret) et eksempel på den mest snævre og partielle tilgang, hvor der kun vil være indeholdt klinisk information fra teknologielementet.

Selv om der i overvejende grad er konsensus mellem de fem institutioner med hensyn til definitionen af MTV som en bred og alsidig vurdering, så viser opdelingen i studiet på de fire MTV-typer, at MTV ofte er mere partiel i praksis. Sammenligningen viser nemlig, at kun 17 af de 124 MTV-projekter (14%) kan karakteriseres som brede og alsidige totale MTV med information fra alle fire hovedelementer. 39% af projekterne kan betegnes som partielle teknologivurderinger med information fra tre af hovedelementerne. Omvendt hører næsten halvdelen af teknologivurderingerne (47%) til de mere partielle former, der kun medtager information fra et eller to af hovedelementerne, eksempelvis som *cost-effectiveness*-analyser. Blandt de nationale MTV-institutioner har de svenske teknologivurderinger fra SBU generelt den mest brede og alsidige form, idet hele 53% kan karakteriseres som totale teknologivurderinger, mens de resterende (47%) har fokus på tre hovedelementer. For de øvrige institutioner gælder det, at en stor del af projekterne tilhører de partielle MTV-typer, med de engelske projekter som de mest partielle. SBU's MTV afviger således også signifikant fra de øvrige institutioners med hensyn til bredde og alsidighed (Mann-Whitneys U-test [p<0,05]). For yderligere information om resultaterne henvises til CHS-arbejdsnotatet (6).

Diskussion

Resultaterne af det internationale komparative studie viser, at MTV i praksis kun i få tilfælde har den brede og alsidige form som en total MTV, som der ellers lægges op til i den oprindelige definition af MTV. Oftere dækker begrebet over mere partielle tilgange. Teknologivurderingerne indeholder og formidler først og fremmest information om to hovedelementer: teknologien og økonomien. Som det fremgår af Tabel 1, er det primære mål med medicinsk teknologivurdering ikke at producere ny videnskabelig viden, men at gøre informationen tilgængelig for beslutningstagerne i en brugbar form. Dette er også i overensstemmelse med konklusionerne fra en nyligt afholdt dansk konference (17).

Med baggrund i det komparative studies resultater synes der i udlandet at være konsensus om, at mere partielle former også kan indgå under betegnelsen MTV. Implikationen for danske MTV-initiativer kunne derfor være, at man ud over at definere MTV som en bred og alsidig vurdering også inkluderede mere partielle fortolkninger under MTV-begrebet, fx *cost-effectiveness*-analysen. Med en sådan *policy*-fokus for den medicinske teknologivurdering ville indholdet af teknologivurderingen herefter variere afhængigt af den information, der anses for nødvendig for den beslutning, man som beslutningstager ønsker at træffe med teknologivurderingen. En forudsætning for, at ovenstående partielle tilgange også må betragtes som MTV, ville være, at der var bevidsthed over fravalgene. Dette ville også føre til, at problemformuleringen og syntesen fik den fremtrædende plads i gennemførelsen af en MTV, som ofte savnes. Denne modificering af MTV-begrebet vil også være i overensstemmelse med en nyligt fremkommen anbefaling fra en europæisk arbejdsgruppe vedrørende MTV -- EUR-ASSESS. Her fastslås det, at definitionen på MTV ud over det oprindelige brede og alsidige sigte udvides til at rumme mere partielle tilgange til MTV, såsom randomiserede kliniske studier og *cost-effectiveness*-analyser med prospektiv indsamling af data, når disse blot er lavet med beslutningstagen for øje (18).

Omvendt skal dette dog ikke ses som en afvisning af mere brede og alsidige tilgange til MTV. Disse har deres relevans ved problemstillinger, der eksempelvis omfatter et sygdomsområde, fx Sundhedsstyrelsens nyligt udsendte MTV om ondt i ryggen (19), eller ved belysning af hele teknologiområder, fx genteknologien. Men udførelsen af MTV, specielt med en bred og alsidig tilgang, er i sig selv meget ressourcekrævende. Det begrænsede antal teknologivurderinger som den svenske SBU har produceret i en tiårsperiode, illustrerer dette. Argumentet for, at den brede og alsidige definition ikke benyttes hver gang som en generel skabelon ved udfærdigelse af MTV, er de begrænsede menneskelige og økonomiske ressourcer til MTV. Dette skal ses i sammenhæng med, at kvalitetskravene til MTV gælder, uanset om det drejer sig om en partiel eller en bred og alsidig form, og kun da kan MTV tjene som grundlag for beslutningstagen.

Summary

Peter Bo Poulsen & Mogens Hørder:
The practice of health technology assessment.

Ugeskr Læger 1998; 160: 5041-4.

With the establishment of a national institute for Health Technology Assessment (HTA), the interest in HTA is increasing in Denmark. The National Board of Health defines HTA as a comprehensive systematic evaluation of the assumptions for, and consequences of, the application of health technology. The focus is on four elements: the technology, the economy, the patient and the organisation. However, is this broad and comprehensive definition in agreement with the practical use of HTA? This article refers to an international comparison of 124 HTA-projects made by five national HTA-institutions. The article shows that only seventeen HTA-projects can be characterized as broad and comprehensive, focusing on all four elements. The rest are more restricted in their form. The future implication for Danish HTA initiatives might then be to include some partial interpretations in the HTA-definition, besides the broad and comprehensive one used today.

Reprints: *Peter Bo Poulsen*, Center for Helsetjenesteforskning og Socialpolitik, Odense Universitet, DK-5000 Odense C.

Forskningsadjunkt, ph.d. *Kristian Kidholm* og forskningsadjunkt, ph.d. *Jørgen Clausen*, Center for Helsetjenesteforskning og Socialpolitik, Odense Universitet, takkes begge for en kritisk gennemgang af tidligere manuskriptudgaver og for konstruktive ændringsforslag.

Litteratur

1. Andreasen PB. Medicinsk teknologi og fremtiden. Ugeskr Læger 1993; 154: 3801.
2. Hørder M. Medicinsk teknologivurdering, hvordan – hvorfor? Ugeskr Læger 1993; 155: 3620-2.
3. Borgwardt A. Indførelse af medicinsk teknologivurdering (MTV) i Danmark [interview af Finn Kamper-Jørgensen]. Ugeskr Læger 1996; 158: 3686-9.
4. Knudsen JL. Medicinsk teknologivurdering – hvorfor nu det? [redaktionelt]. Ugeskr Læger 1996; 159: 14.
5. Hansen NE, Karle H. Medicinsk teknologivurdering med kommandoetik [kommentar]. Ugeskr Læger 1996; 158: 5465-6.
6. Poulsen PB. An international comparative study of health technology assessment. CHS-working paper 1997:6. Centre for Health and Social Policy, Odense University, 1997.
7. Office of Technology Assessment. Development of medical technology: opportunities for assessment. Washington, DC: US Government Printing Office, 1976.
8. Andreasen PB. Medicinsk teknologivurdering. Nyttiggørelse af lægevidenskabelige forskningsresultater i sundhedsvæsenet. Rapport til Folketingets udvalg angående videnskabelig forskning. København, 1980.
9. Jørgensen T. Teknologivurdering. DSI-Specialrapport 80.07. København: Dansk Sygehus Institut, 1980.
10. Sundhedsstyrelsens udvalg for medicinsk teknologivurdering. National strategi for medicinsk teknologivurdering. København: Sundhedsstyrelsen, 1996.
11. Neugebauer E, Ure BM, Lefering R, Eypasch EP, Troidl H. Technology assessment of endoscopic surgery. Acta Neurochir 1994; [suppl] 61: 13-9.
12. Garber AM. Can technology assessment control health spending? Health Affairs 1994; 13: 115-26.
13. Poulsen PB, Hørder M, Jørgensen T for Sundhedsstyrelsens udvalg for medicinsk teknologivurdering. Fremtidens medicinske metoder – tidlig varsling i internationalt og dansk perspektiv. København: Sundhedsstyrelsen, 1996.
14. Statens Beredning för Utvärdering av medicinsk metodik. Stötvågsbehandling av njursten och gallsten. Stockholm: SBU, 1990.
15. Health Council of the Netherlands: committee on stereotactic – radiotherapy. Stereotactic radiotherapy The Hague: Health Council of the Netherlands, 1994; publication no. 1994/18E.
16. Canadian Coordinating Office for Health Technology Assessment. Chiropractic treatment of neck and back disorders: a review of selected studies. Ontario, February 1992.
17. Sundhedsstyrelsens udvalg for medicinsk teknologivurdering. Den forskningsmæssige indsats omkring medicinsk teknologivurdering – refleksioner og konklusioner fra en konference. København: Sundhedsstyrelsen, 1997.
18. Banta HD, Werkö L, Cranovsky R, Granados A, Henshall C, Jonsson E et al. Introduction to the EUR-ASSESS Report. Int J Technol Assess Health Care 1997; 13 133-43.
19. Sundhedsstyrelsens udvalg for medicinsk teknologivurdering. Ondt i ryggen. En kortlægning af problemets forekomst og oplæg til dets håndtering i et MTV-perspektiv. København: Sundhedsstyrelsen, 1997.